The Arab State

The Arab State

Edited by Giacomo Luciani

University of California Press
Berkeley — Los Angeles

University of California Press
Berkeley and Los Angeles, California

First published 1990
by Routledge
11 New Fetter Lane, London EC4P 4EE

© 1990 Istituto Affari Internazionale
Printed in Great Britain

Library of Congress Cataloging-in-Publication Data
Nation, state, and integration in the Arab world. Selections.
    The Arab state / edited by Giacomo Luciani.
        p.   cm.
    Selected essays from: Nation, state, and integration in the Arab
world.
    ISBN 0-520-06432-1 (alk. paper). — ISBN 0-520-06434-8 (pbk.)
    1. Arab countries—Politics and government—1945-   I. Luciani.
    Giacomo, 1948-   . II. Title.
    DS39.N34   1989
    909'.0974927082—dc19
88-35697
CIP

Contents

Tables

Contributors

Nazih Ayubi teaches at the Department of Politics at Exeter
University, England. Among his works are *Bureaucracy and
Politics in Contemporary Egypt*, Ithaca Press, London, 1980.
He has contributed chapters to *Rich and Poor States in the
Middle East*, (Kerr and Yassin eds.), Westview Press, Boul-
der, (Colorado), 1982; 'The Egyptian Brain Drain', *Journal
of Middle East Studies*, *15*, 1983; he is co-editor (with Tahir-
Kheli) of *The Iran-Iraq War*, New York, 1983; *The Arabian
Peninsula*, R. Stookes (ed.), Stanford, 1983; *The Middle East
in the 1980s*, P.H. Stoddard (ed.), Washington DC, 1983;
'Local government and rural development in Egypt in the
1970s', in *Cahiers Africains d'Administration Publique*, *23*,
1984; *The Mediterranean Region*, G. Luciani (ed.), Croom
Helm, London, 1984.

Hazem Beblawi is presently Chairman of the Export Development Bank of Egypt. He is the author of *The Arab Gulf
Economy in the Turbulent Age* (Croom Helm, London,
1984) and of *L'Interdépendance agriculture-industrie et le
développement économique en Égypte* (Cujas, Paris, 1968).

Michel Chatelus is Professor of Economics at the Université des
Sciences Sociales de Grenoble and head of GRESMO. He is
the author of 'Towards a new political economy of state
industrialization in the Arab Middle East' (with Yves
Schmeil, *International Journal of Middle Eastern Studies*,
1984, No. 2); 'Le monde arabe vingt ans après: les défis
économiques', *Revue Monde Arabe Maghreb-Machrek*, 1983,
p. 101; and edited *L'Industrialisation du bassin mediterran-
éen* (PUG, 1983).

Adeed Dawisha is Professor of Government and Politics at the
George Mason University, Fairfax, Virginia. Among his
books are *Egypt in the Arab World: the elements of foreign
policy*, Macmillan, London, 1976; *Saudi Arabia's Search for
Security*, IISS, London, 1979; *Syria and the Lebanese Crisis*,
Macmillan, London, 1980; *The Soviet Union in the Middle
East*, (co-ed. Karen Dawisha), Heinemann, London, 1982;
Islam in Foreign Policies, (ed.), Cambridge University Press,
London, 1983; and *The Arab Radicals*, Council on Foreign
Relations, New York, 1986.

Iliya Harik is Director of the Center for Middle Eastern Studies, Indiana University. His publications include *The Political Mobilisation of Peasants* (Indiana University Press, 1974); *The Arabs and the New International Economic Order*, (ed and co-author), (in Arabic, Beirut, 1983); co-editor and co-author, *Local Politics and Development in the Middle East*, (Westview Press, Boulder, 1984).

Fahmi Jadaane is Professor of Islamic Philosophy in the Faculty of Arts, University of Jordan, and is currently visiting professor at the University of Kuwait. He is the author of various books in Arabic.

Walid Kazziha is professor at the Department of Political Science, American University in Cairo. His main works are *Palestine in the Arab Dilemma*, London, 1979; *Revolutionary Transformation in the Arab World*, London, 1975.

Jean Leca works at the Cycle Superieur d'Etudes Politiques at the Fondation Nationale de Sciences Politiques, Paris. His books include *L'Algérie politique: institutions et régime*, (co-ed. J.C. Vatin), Fondation Nationale des Sciences Politiques, Paris, 1975; *Developpements politiques au Maghreb*, CNRS, Paris, 1979.

Giacomo Luciani is an economic consultant based in Rome. He is the author of *International Oil Companies and Arab Countries* (Croom Helm, 1984); *Egypt's Economic Potential* (with others; Croom Helm, 1985); *L'Opec nell'economia internazionale* (Einaudi, 1975); and editor and co-author of *The Mediterranean Region* (Croom Helm, 1984).

Samir Makdisi is professor of Economics at the American University of Beirut and Director of the Institute of Money and Banking. He is co-editor and co-author of a chapter in Aliboni (ed.) *Arab Industrialisation and Economic Integration*, Croom Helm, London.

Elizabeth Picard is a researcher at the Fondation Nationale de Sciences Politiques, Paris. Her works include 'Syria returns to democracy', in G. Hermet, R. Rose and A. Rouguiè (eds.) *Elections Without Choice*, Macmillan, London, 1978; 'Clans militaires et pouvoir baathiste en Syrie', *Orient*, Hamburg, 1979; 'Ouverture économique et renforcement militaire en Syrie', *Oriente Moderno, 59*, no. 7–12, 1979; 'Le rapprochement syro-iraquien', *Maghreb-Machrek*, 1979.

Sharon Stanton Russell has a PhD in Political Science from Massachusetts Institute of Technology. She specialises in manpower development issues, including migration. She is the author of 'Remittances from International Migration: A Review in Perspective', *World Development*, vol. 14, no. 6, June 1986.

Georges Sabagh is professor of Sociology and Director of the Gustav von Grunebaum Center for Near Eastern Studies at the University of California, Los Angeles. He is the author of several articles on migration and demographic developments in the Middle East.

Ghassan Salamé is a researcher at the Fondation Nationale de Sciences Politiques in Paris. His publications include *Saudi Arabia's Foreign Policy since 1945* (in Arabic), 1981; *State and Society in the Arab Levant States* (in Arabic, 1987); *Le Théâtre politique au Liban — Etude idéologique et ésthétique*, Beirut, 1975; plus numerous articles on contemporary political developments in the Arab World.

Avi Shlaim teaches at the Faculty of Letters and Social Sciences, Department of Politics, Reading University. He has written, among other works, 'Conflicting Approaches to Israel's Relations with the Arabs: Ben Gurion and Sharett, 1953–56', in *The Middle East Journal*, vol. 37, no. 2, 1981.

I. William Zartman is the Director of the Africa Programme at the School of Advanced International Studies, Johns Hopkins University in Washington DC. His main publications include *Elites in the Middle East* (ed. and co-author), Praeger, New York, 1980; *The Practical Negotiator*, 1981; *Political Elites in Arab North Africa*, (co-author), Longman, New York, 1982; *Man, State and Security in Contemporary Africa*, 1984; *The Political Economy of Morocco*, Praeger, New York, 1986.

Foreword

History moves fast, and it is the constant temptation of the expert to deny novelty and reassure the public that change is only superficial: deep down the world stays the same. This attitude is common among experts on the Middle East as well as other regions. And yet, as radical and unpredictable changes have recently taken place in the Soviet Union as well as in several developing countries; as the Soviet intervention in Afghanistan, the Iran–Iraq war and the Vietnamese intervention in Cambodia are all in the process of being settled or reversed; and, finally, as the Palestinian people's Intifada has opened an entirely new stage in the conflict over Palestine; it seems clear that change is coming fast and that social scientists must have the courage of a new departure.

The essays that are collected in this book explore several new departures: 'The Arab State' is most often characterised as illegitimate and authoritarian, as lacking roots in society, and thus at one and the same time as too strong and 'autonomous' and as too weak and vulnerable. These essays attempt to provide a different picture of the Arab state: of the interplay between state and society, between state and the economy, and of states among themselves. While the picture that is offered is far from being a coherent and all-encompassing one, it is both original in many respects and, the authors believe, closer to observed reality than several of the more widely accredited paradigms.

All of the essays have already been published in the four volumes of the series 'Nation, State and Integration in the Arab World', the product of a multi-year collective research effort. It was felt that, primarily in view of making this material accessible to the public of college students taking courses on the contemporary Middle East, it might be appropriate to offer a selection of chapters in a more compact and affordable format. As the editor of the series, I undertook the difficult task of making this further selection, and did so being fully aware that no selection could meet everybody's wishes. Several very important chapters were finally excluded by the tyranny of the maximum number of pages. I hope that this shorter volume, in combination with the original series in college libraries, will provide a reasonable compromise.

At the same time, I am confident that the growing public following developments in the contemporary Middle East will find this collection of essays interesting and challenging *per se*, even independent of the rest of the material generated under the original project.

No significant changes have been introduced in the essays that are included here, except for numbering of pages and internal references. The Introduction is based on the introductions written for the first three volumes in the series, respectively by Ghassan Salamé, myself and Hazem Beblawi, and I. William Zartman. Large sections of the original introductions have been arranged together to form a logically consistent new piece. The fact that it is not signed reflects this genesis. The introduction to the fourth volume is proposed here as Chapter 16.

The realisation of the project, of which publication of this volume is in a sense the last step, was made possible by the contribution of numerous individuals and institutions. A detailed account of these is found in the Forewords to the four original volumes, and I simply wish to renew here my sincere thanks to all of them. Special thanks go to Ghassan Salamé and William Zartman for their help and suggestions in preparing this further selection. The responsibility for it must, however, finally rest with me.

Giacomo Luciani
Rome

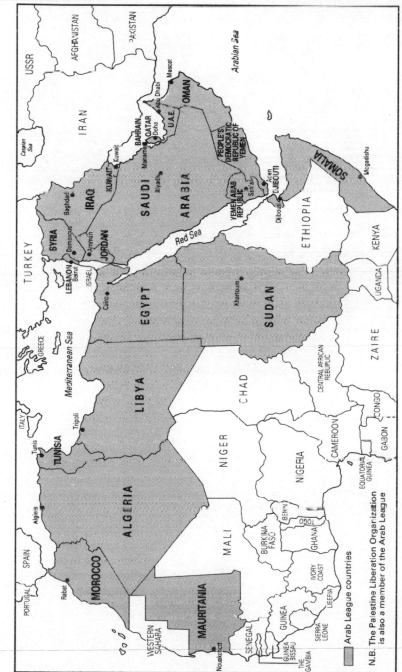

A Political Map of the Contemporary Arab World

Arab League countries

N.B. The Palestine Liberation Organization is also a member of the Arab League

Introduction

Giacomo Luciani

This collection focuses on a problem: explaining the stability and persistence of the state in the Arab World. Coming from various angles to the problem, it tries to answer the question: is the Arab state a solid creation? And why? The question is not new, but the answers today are quite different from a previous round of answers. Thirty years ago the same question was raised in many writings when analysts concluded that the state was a weak creation, an artificial part of a naturally evolving social entity called the Arab nation (Halpern, 1963; Sharabi, 1966; even Hudson, 1977). Writers judged that the state existed as a dependent artifice at the whim and tolerance of socio-political interactions across its borders, and they often completely neglected it when they turned to development sociology and away from politics. The artificial Arab states was a frequent theme and a frequent answer to questions about the nature and stability of politics and society in the Middle East.

Now it is obvious that those answers no longer apply. Today, states have at least the appearance of stability in the Arab world, and have persisted into the 1980s without fusion, secession, reconstitution, or dissolution into a larger pan-Arab entity. Despite earlier analysis to the contrary, the resilience of the post-colonial or post-imperial state should not be surprising; after all, it occurred in Latin America a century before the Arab states, and in the Balkans following World War I it is now proving true in Africa.

And as far as Arab regimes are concerned, taking 1970 as the base year, we find that for over a decade and a half they have remained solidly in power and have created a stable organisational structure around them. This runs quite contrary to what happened in the 1950s and into the 1960s.

The Arab defeat of 1967 seems to have been a turning point and partly responsible for the change (Ajami, 1981). But in a broader sense the cause is not obvious. Indeed, even the fact itself is not obvious. Many would contest the impression of stability and would claim that the state is a house of cards, its stability more apparent than real. Others would say that the Arab nation continues to be the dominant reality. These answers, however, have a difficult time explaining away the evident fact of stability even if that stability may only prove to be transient.

Our answer is 'yes, but problematically'. That is to say, this volume finds that the state — defined as the authoritative political institution that is sovereign over a recognised territory — has been stable in the last decade and a half, and the durability is not simply an artificial vision. The answer, however, does imply that there are problems inherent in that stability, problems which both limit its present extent and have implications for its future.

ON THE DEFINITION OF THE STATE

The explanation for this stability must begin with an analysis of the nature of the Arab state. State is defined as the authoritative political institution that is sovereign over a recognised territory. There are many other definitions of state, and much of the confusion over its nature can be resolved by choosing one definition and separating empirical from definitional elements (Laski, 1935; McIver, 1926; Weber, 1947; Nettl, 1968; Tilly, 1975; Evans *et al.*, 1985; Schatzenberg, 1987; Kaplan and Lasswell, 1950; Cohen and Service, 1978; Gordon, 1986; Callaghy, 1984).

This definition focuses on three elements: it considers the state to be authoritative and sovereign and hence an accepted focus of identity and arena of politics; it regards the state as an institution and therefore an organisation differentiated from other, informal practices of politics; and it sees the state as associated with a particular territory. The third element is probably the least controversial but the other two introduce some complexity.

The state as institution is both tangible organisation and

intangible symbol; and such duality is in the nature of institutions. A family, for example, is the people who compose it but also an identity which they represent. A state is not merely a large family, since state-as-organisation is not equivalent to the population of the country but only to state functionaries and politicians, it is ultimately distinguished from 'private' personnel and organisations. Yet state-as-symbol is larger than the sum of its parts (like family and other institutions). What is 'private' operates under it or within it, even if separate from it.

The implications of this definition are, first, that it suggests that some politics are outside the state. Although ultimately carried out with the aim of controlling (or abolishing) the state, some political action lies beyond officially authorised or permitted rules, and even beyond the state's recognised territoriality. Most politics, however, is carried out within the state arena, according to rules or routines established within the state.

Second, the definition of state as receptacle of legitimacy stems from the use of the word 'authority' — usually defined as legitimate or rightful power. Although this is a standard assumption, it carries certain operational problems. Operationally the state can undergo an apparent loss of legitimacy. This occurred most recently in Sudan, and some writers have suggested that the Arab state in general has a very contested legitimacy, in the eyes of many intellectuals at least (Hudson, 1977; Adam, 1985). But whatever the operational problems of the loss of legitimacy, definitionally legitimacy must be attached to state power — that is, rule carried out in the name of the state. The state must be considered the receptacle of political legitimacy, since even opposition groups seek to take it over in order to benefit from its legitimate power. What happens in the exceptional cases when this definitional assumption is challenged must be considered as it arises. Of course, the legitimacy of state power is not the same thing as the legitimacy of a particular ruling group, which has to face the test of its right to rule or actually to exercise state power. A distinction must be made between regime and state. Regimes, administrations or leaders may rise and fall, but only when the nature of the organisation and its structures change can one say a state has been altered.

Clearly, state, stability and legitimacy are core concepts whose essential or ideal nature is usually qualified in reality by empirical impurities and surrounded by large grey areas (Watkins, 1934). How much constitutional change or amendment is required to change the basic nature of the state; how many constitutional amendments and how fast, or how many new institutions (as for example in Libya) are required before one can say that the state is unstable, are all matters that are hard to set up as a quantitative test beforehand. Similarly, where is the threshold marking the degree of challenge that becomes an indicator of state instability? What degree of recovery confirms state stability? and in either case how long after the event must one wait to draw the conclusion? The change from Ben Bella to Boumedienne/Benjedid in 1965, or from Idris to Qadhafi in 1969, or from King Farouk to Nasser/Sadat/Mubarak in 1952/3 are seen as changes in the state, whereas other changes, as in Lebanon after 1975, Mauritania and Chad after 1978, or North Yemen during the civil war, are indications of chronic state instability or state collapse (Chazan, 1983).

THE HISTORICAL ROOTS OF CONTEMPORARY ARAB STATES

Partly because of the perceived weakness of the Arab states, comprehensive analyses of the pivotal relationship between states and civil societies in the Arab world have remained underdeveloped, in comparison, for example, with Western Europe or Latin America.

Many newly established countries in the region (Kuwait, Qatar, Israel) retain the word 'state' in their official name, as if their statehood was too vulnerable not to be systematically re-asserted. In fact, the debate has centred more on the viability of states as international, autonomous, 'sovereign', units than on states as actors shaping the societies they pretend to control. Notice, in this respect, the Palestinians' emotional investment in a state of their own (a flag, a passport, a national anthem) notwithstanding the lack of a detailed view of this potential state in relation to the Palestinians as a people. On the other hand, one is struck by the fact that Arab socialist trends in the 1960s and the 1970s were squeezed into a rather narrow view of what the public sector should or should not include (when this discussion was possible at all), while largely ignoring the very wide effects which the nationalisation movement had or could have on society. By the end of the 1960s, for example, one out of every four Egyptians was directly or indirectly on the government's payroll, but the discussion of this feature as a political phenomenon remained limited.

The 'oil era' has blurred the picture even more. It is indeed widely accepted that 'a state's means of raising and deploying financial resources tells us more than could any other single factor' (Evans, 1985:17) about its capabilities, autonomy, strength, and viability. But the huge amounts of external rent accruing to the oil-producing countries after 1973 and indirectly to the non-oil Arab countries (through aid and expatriates' remittances) have certainly delayed (and largely aborted) burgeoning questions about the contemporary Arab states' capabilities to continue the *dirigiste* policies adopted in the 1960s, and equally importantly, about the kind of transition that will take place towards potentially different policies.

The prevailing question was, however, posed with insistence by all kinds of local and pan-Arab nationalists. American writers tended to consider the post-World War II territorial status quo as permanent. Their attitude clearly entailed a preference for an order that was widely favourable to the expansion of American influence in the world. One could sense an almost equally strong territorial conservatism in the views of the other major beneficiary of World War II, the Soviet Union. Gradually, when it came to the Third World, the superpowers (and their social scientists) have generally shifted the discussion from the state as such to the kind of political regime (strong or weak, capitalist or socialist, authoritarian or democratic) prevalent in each of these countries. World War II seemed to have abruptly closed a lively discussion in Europe on what states to give birth to, what territories to allocate to them, and what populations to involve in this process.

This debate, concerning the original sin of state creation, was never closed in the Arab world. To what extent were the Arab states created by foreign, alien, hostile will? Today, are they perceived as foreign-made creations? To what extent have these internationally recognised units taken root, in the hearts and minds of their own inhabitants rather than merely in the present-day world state system?

In the absence of democratic practices, public opinion is very hard to assess. Several surveys give the impression that states as sovereign political units are much more readily accepted than classic integrationist Arab nationalists would want us to believe. At the same time, one is struck by the amount of dissatisfaction with the isolationist policies followed by almost all Arab regimes, whatever their public ideologies. These policies make it difficult to cross an inter-Arab border, to call another Arab city by telephone, to get a work permit here, an export licence there, and a travel visa to almost everywhere.

But the debate was never ended. Besides the old polemical diatribes against Mr Sykes and Monsieur Georges-Picot, who drew new borders for Britain and France across Greater Syria while World War I was still raging, or against that French *ministre des colonies* who reportedly gave the Sahara to France (and hence to Algeria, its successor in 1962), or against the British administrator who broke the 'natural unity' of the Nile valley, a new body of scientific research has been growing during the past two decades, offering a balanced, documented, convincing history of the moment, the ways, and the meanings of the birth of most Arab states.

Moving along this path, in the first chapter in this volume, Iliya Harik tries to capture the state-building process in the Arab world, relating the state to the type of government with which it has been associated since its inception. Harik tends to credit Arab states with old, genuine foundations. Challenging a well-established view, he thinks that Arab countries are not only old societies but also old states. With three exceptions, 'they all go back to the nineteenth century or a much earlier period'. Harik dismisses the economic factors in the emergence of the Arab state system, stating that 'the lack of change in the economy during earlier centuries rules out economic factors as an explanatory principle of the formation of the multifarious state system.' Tracing the origin of various states, he denies that the contemporary Arab state system is purely the creation of foreign powers, except for the Fertile Crescent states (but not Lebanon). Here a heterodox sect, there an alliance between a tribal leader and an Islamic reformer, or an ambitious Amir entrenched in rugged mountains, have established the nucleus of a state that will be later recognised by the foreign powers in the nineteenth century. Harik's point is clearest when he asserts that 'colonialism affected the boundaries of the Arab states, but it did not, with the exception of the Fertile Crescent cases, create them. Colonialism gave more definitive form to the indigenous states and introduced elements of modern administration to them'.

Discussing the Saudi case, Salamé's chapter on 'strong' and

'weak' states tends to demonstrate that the encounter with the West could be less of an original sin than a later inevitable and highly weakening (in terms of legitimacy) event. The Saudi case is interesting precisely for its relatively late encounter with foreign influence when its credentials as an 'authentic' Arabian power, established by genuine local forces, have been already recognised. Drawing largely from Ibn Khaldun's *Muqaddimah*, Salamé shows how the mixture of group feeling, religious call, geographic isolation, and ideological isolationism *vis-à-vis* extra-Arabian powers have led to a traditional Arabian nucleus of power which was later weakened by its expansion into a king-ship (*mulk*).

Lebanon is another example, where one *'asabiyya* (the Maronites') was gradually eroded after the creation of the state. Here the authenticity factor is real, but it is somehow weakened as a legitimising factor because of the *'asabiyya*'s early alliance with foreign forces, notably France. The erosion of the prevailing *'asabiyya* transformed Lebanon into a field in which one *'asabiyya* would trigger the emergence of another through a mimetic process that ended in civil war.

The Saudi and the Lebanese cases also show how difficult it is to transfer traditional Khaldunian ideas on states' strengths and weaknesses to the modern state units which exist today. Beside the not-so-original idea that sees strength in unity, contemporary Arab political culture does not provide us with a clear view of what the foundations of a strong state are. Indifference to the economy is matched by doubts *vis-à-vis* the military, leaving today's leaders with a rather wide margin of manoeuvre to define a state power by and for themselves, and therefore to impose their definition on their fellow countrymen.

ECONOMIC FOUNDATIONS OF THE ARAB STATES

Notwithstanding the fact that, as just mentioned, the economy plays a marginal role in Arab political preoccupations, the question of the economic foundations of state strength and weakness is inescapable. All the more so since the advent of stability has roughly coincided with the explosion in oil revenues that has radically changed the economic reality of the entire region. Which political impact is attributable to the oil rent? Which may be expected from the more recent decline in oil revenues?

From an economic point of view, the nature of a state is gauged by the quality and relative size of its revenue and expenditures. The structure of expenditure is often studied much more closely than the structure of revenue sources. Yet expenditure decisions cannot be taken independently of revenue realities, and the size and source of state revenue is a key determinant of its survival and political development.

The weakness in the taxation systems in the Arab world and the extraordinary reliance of Arab states on sources of revenue from outside their boundaries has long been noted. That this fact could not but have momentous consequences on the politics and development perspectives of the Arab countries has also been underlined by various authors. The idea that states based on external sources of income are substantially different from states based on domestic taxation has led to the proposition of the concept of rentier state. This concept was first formulated with reference to Iran by Hossein Mahdavy (1970:428-67), and is at the centre of attention in the chapters by Hazem Beblawi and Giacomo Luciani. A key hypothesis is proposed there, namely that rentier states will display little tendency to evolve towards democratic institutions, while states needing to resort to taxation of domestic incomes or facing the need to cut down on subsidies and other economic benefits extended to their population will need to look for an alternative source of legitimacy, which may come from an evolution towards democracy.

Access to oil rent thus contributes to the explanation of stability, and of the persistence in many Arab states of regimes based on a strong central figure, coupled with more or less definite tendencies towards greater political debate and participation.

Arab states, just as states elsewhere in the world, are permanently faced with expenditure obligations that exceed financial resources available to them, and must strive to expand their revenue. The need to raise revenue is the basic reason why the state has an interest in the prosperity and economic well-being of its country. Ibn Khaldun wrote in this respect: 'There also is a statement by Anosharwan to the same effect: "Royal authority exists through the army, the army through money, money through taxes, taxes through cultivation, cultivation through justice ..."' (Ibn Khaldun, 1967:40). And he goes on to suggest that a ruler must be just because this is a prerequisite for

expanding cultivation, thus increasing tax revenue, thus reinforcing the ruler himself.

It is normally assumed that economic growth per se
reinforces the state and stabilises the regime: this however
appears to be a questionable assumption in the face of the social
and cultural dislocation that economic growth often entails. Fast
economic growth may lead to an even faster growth in expectations, which may be and frequently are frustrated by later
developments, undermining the stability of the state. It is
clear, however, that economic growth reinforces the state in this
respect: that it allows the state to increase its income, therefore
in turn to increase expenditure and 'buy off' political consensus.
That political consensus may be acquired through state expenditure is a vastly safer assumption, although not a conclusion to be
taken for granted, as is done only too often.

In the context of the Arab region, opting in favour of industrialisation and economic growth has historically been closely
related with the growing role of nationalist ideologies and the
fight against foreign domination. It became clear that economic
growth and, in particular, industrial growth are a prerequisite to
the strengthening of the state and its ability to resist outside
aggression. While this is not simply a matter of public revenue,
because the strength of the state is influenced by other factors as
well, and military might is, in particular, influenced by technological capability, it is, nevertheless, clear that the state needs
access to increased revenue first and foremost.

It is clear that both the relative size of the state and the structure of income is a function of the level of development. If a
country is very poor, it cannot normally sustain a state which is
complex and diversified. Poor countries can only 'afford'
embryonic states that limit themselves to performing a few
essential functions in connection with law and order and external defence, in most cases in a highly ineffective way. The state
will absorb a small percentage of GDP; it will remain a fragile
entity, which is constantly confronted with the danger of
collapse when faced with challenges from within and/or from
without.

While financial orthodoxy is not very frequent, it is still a fact
that in numerous cases specific policies were abandoned less for
ideological motivations than for fiscal ones. The retreat from
many plans for greater socialisation of production in countries
like Egypt, Tunisia and Algeria was closely connected to the

fact that it is easier to impose taxes on a private sector than on a 'socialist' one. If this were not the case, the socialist sector would support the socialist state, and the transformation could continue through the marginalisation of the private sector. On the contrary, however, the increasing importance of the socialist sector has almost invariably led to an impoverishment of the tax base supporting the state (except when enterprises earning rent from abroad were nationalised), and this in turn has eventually led to a reversal of policies and to renewed importance of the private sector. One is reminded of Ibn Khaldun:

> You, O King, went after the farms and took them away from their owners and cultivators. They are the people who pay the land tax and from whom one gets money. You gave their farms as fiefs to your entourage and servants and to sluggards. They did not cultivate them and did not heed the consequences (they did not look for the things) that would be good for the farms. They were leniently treated with regard to the land tax (and were not asked to pay it), because they were close to the king. The remaining landowners who did pay the land tax and cultivated their farms had to carry an unjust burden. Therefore, they left their farms and abandoned their settlements. They took refuge in farms that were far away or difficult (of access), and lived on them. (The Mobedhan addressing King Bahram b. Bahram of Persia; Ibn Khaldun, 1967:239.)

The link between revenue and expenditure also works in the opposite direction: the availability of revenue causes an increase in expenditure. In the case of many oil-exporting countries it is rather clear that policies have been adopted primarily because money was available. This is especially the case for those policies which are predominantly aimed at the redistribution of oil rent, such as aid to other developing countries or land acquisition programmes. A good deal of 'development' expenditure was approved without too much concern for the need of what was being bought (especially in infrastructure) simply because money ought to be spent. Refusing to spend available revenue is not an effective way to keep power, as the colourful story of Sultan Said of Oman demonstrates. Finally, one reason for the phenomenal increase in military expenditure in the region is to be found in the ease with which large sums of money can be spend in procuring the latest military gear.

However, in more recent times the decline in oil revenues has obliged even the sparsely populated Gulf oil producers to cut down on their expenditure substantially, and the possibility of raising revenue domestically is being aired. While this is unlikely to change the fundamental rentier nature of these states anytime in the foreseeable future, it is definitely a development that faces them with new political challenges.

CHARACTERISTICS OF THE ARAB STATE

Historical and economic realities help us in the understanding of the political characteristics of a specific type of state — the Arab state of the Middle East.

The first and most important characteristic of the stable Arab states of the 1970s and 1980s is the position of a central strongman, leader and orchestrator. The Great Patron or Manipulator may adopt many different styles of leadership and may have a position that runs through many shades of centralisation and control but, in all cases of state stability, that stability is associated with one or successive single leaders. Although the Great Patron is surrounded by followers, he clearly emerges as the single manipulating and deciding leader even if he had to rise from the pack in the early years of his tenure.

Second, the political organisation of the contemporary state is associated with periodic personnel changes, when the leader from time to time introduces sweeping changes to the group around him, associated with new programmes and directions. The periodicity of the changes is neither fixed nor regular. They can be compared to the changes in elected governments imposed by electoral realignments in critical elections. Such shifts can also be related to changes in the social composition of the population and their political demands. For example, Sadat's and Benjedid's liberalised policy responded to the demands of groups which obtained new importance as a result of the policies of Nasser and Boumedienne and the softening of Sadat's liberalisation under Mubarak responded to popular reaction against the Open Door Policy. An aspect of state structure is the periodic revision of political organisation and its direction.

A third characteristic of the Arab state is the practice of

politics of limited association. The term is distinct from politics of mobilisation in which there is a direct link between mass organisations and political leadership, with the public pressing the leader and the leader playing on the demands of the public. The term is also used in distinction to the politics of control, in which there is no participation and in which politics is wrung out of the body politic by stifling political activity. The Arab states of the 1970s and 1980s are characterised by the inter-mediate stage, in which there is enough democracy to point to, but not enough to have to bow to. Therefore, as Zartman clari-fies in Chapter 9 in this volume, there is an outlet for those interested in political activity, and continual manouvring along a spectrum that runs from opposition to loyal support, but which never reaches in any significant way to the mobilised masses. The years of economic growth in the 1970s gave the Arab state the resources to meet demands of its people — satis-ficing rather than satisfying — but at least responding to the politics of association.

Fourth, the group that runs the state is based on a broad urban middle class — a theme explored by Jean Leca in Chapter 7. The class may either have been only recently urbanised or it may have been urban of longer standing, but the urban popu-lation, including both bourgeoisie and proletariat, represents a specific base for the government. This characteristic differs from a number of claims which are often made about the Arab state. Except for the Gulf oil producers, in which the rulers hand on power to members of their own family or at least people that resemble them socially, the Arab state is not run by a ruling class, which would be drawn from a much narrower social base than the one actually supporting them. Nor is an urban middle class the same as a capitalist class, since the capitalist bour-geoisie is only a part of the class base and often a very small part at that. Nor, very clearly, is the Arab state a workers' state. Urban workers may be part of the social basis of power, but they are only one among many and their role, as indicated, is one of limited association rather than mobilisation. Nor, especially, is the Arab state a peasant state. Peasants are gener-ally the neglected part of the society and are nowhere near the social basis of power. Locating the base of power in the urban middle class does not mean that the state is the organ of the middle class. It acts in relation to it, as a separate entity with which spokesmen for the urban middle class or parts of it interact.

Fifth, in all the Arab countries the state does contain a large administrative organisation, including, as Ayubi underlines in Chapter 6, in the more recently established oil exporting states of the Gulf. This organisation is important because it gives the state a means of operation and also because it constitutes a section of the population, part of whose interests are associated with the state itself. This complex relationship is rarely studied. A group of civil servants may see their interests associated with particular practices of the state in some occasions but on others may think politically as members of the urban middle class and consumers. As 'producers' of state outputs and consumers, their interests may vary widely. Nonetheless, one component of their interests is associated with the maintenance of the state, reflecting a certain professionalism, although that term must often be used extremely narrowly.

Sixth, the Arab state operates as an organisation of control or regulation. That is its role in the economy and society. Again, the distinctions here are important. The state is rarely an organisation of economic production, though it spends much of its energy controlling those who are. Even when a large part of the economy is under control of the state, the element of control is more important than the element of productivity — a point discussed by Michel Chatelus in Chapter 5. This is one of the problems of para-statal and other official organisations. The state is an organisation of political control though instruments of violence. Army, police and other regulations which control the political freedom of the citizens are all important aspects of the Arab state, as Picard confirms in Chapter 8, often to the point where the custodians actually take over or at least play as important a role as one of the leadership groups.

The orientalist tradition would add a further distinguishing characteristic of the Arab state, i.e. the influence of Islam. That Islam may have an essentially important impact on the future evolution of the Arab states hardly needs arguing, but questions remain on whether it should be understood merely as an expression of protest and dissatisfaction with the current political order, or as a full-fledged alternative political ideology. Fahmi Jedaane reviews in Chapter 10 the views of the state that are found in recent Arab-Islamic writings, and finds considerable diversity of opinion. While 'Ali 'Abd al-Raziq would not shed a tear over the collapse of the Caliphate, his 'securalist' views were condemned by Al-Azhar and a very large majority of the *ulama.* With An-Nabahani, Sayyid Qutb, and Ayatollah al-Khumayni, modern Islamic thinking, in avowedly different ways, offers radical answers to contemporary issues. These answers are, in a sense, a form of cultural nationalism, in which religion gives more substance to the rejection of Western domination. But contemporary religious fundamentalism could also be viewed as a potentially sterile reaction to the more subtle answers provided during a century of quest for a proper answer to the West's challenge, a quest opened by al-Afghani and at-Tahtawi, and represented today by Muhammad Ahmad Khalafallah or Husayn Ahmad Amin.

INTER ARAB POLITICS

Notwithstanding the progressive consolidation of the Arab state system, there still exists an arena of Arab politics, which maintains ideological undertones that go beyond the mere regional dimension. The regional dimension influences the stability of Arab states, and regimes seek legitimacy through their regional role to an extent that is uncommon elsewhere in the world, and sometimes leads to adventurism and conflict (Dawisha in Chapter 11). A debate continues on the meaning and future of the Arab nation, and of political relations between the Arab states.

This continuing debate is due, in part at least, to the fact that while nationalism has rapidly 'invaded' the Arab mind, it has not converged on a clear definition of the nation itself. Take the example of the Maronite Lebanese who is told by the historians of his community (and by modern warlords) that the Maronite nation has existed for ages. Yet those Maronites who have rallied round the 1920 French-defined 'Grand Liban' tell him that if the Maronites have ever constituted a nation, this nation has now been diluted in the wider Lebanese modern one. Then the proponents of Greater (or Natural) Syria tell him that Lebanon is a purely artificial creation of colonialist France and that his loyalty should go exclusively to a Syrian nation present since Sumer and the Akkadians. Arab nationalists will insist that the Arab nation is the only 'true' nation, either in Sati' al Husri's rather assertive way or in 'Abd al-'Aziz ad-Duri's more subtle prose. The propenents of an Islamic *umma* overshadowing all these territorially, linguistically or ethnically defined *'asabiyyas* (group feelings), tend to view these loyalties as pre-

Muhammedan and thus anti-Islamic *Jahiliyya* concepts, which should have disappeared since the emergence of the Muhammedan *Da'wa* (Call).

In the face of these conflicting conceptions, Luciani and Salamé attempt, in the final chapter of this volume, a reappraisal of the empirical content of the Arab nation and of prospects for integration among Arab states. The reappraisal is rooted in an analysis of key regional factors which is provided in the previous four chapters, touching respectively on the impact of Palestine and the Palestinians (Kazziha, Chapter 12), on economic interdependence (Makdisi, Chapter 13) and on migration (Sabagh, Chapter 14 and Stanton Russell, Chapter 15).

This dispassionate approach proves that the regional dimension certainly is very important to the future of the Arab states, but it is one that coexists with important linkages with the rest of the world outside the Arab region on the one hand, and certainly does not rule out partial subgroupings, on the other. Hence it is a dimension that, far from challenging the existing Arab states system, may contribute to its consolidation to the extent that the Arab states will be capable of engaging in meaningful, institutionalised co-operation and integration.

What distinguishes this collection is the attempt to blend together the understandings of different disciplines and come to a coherent and satisfactory view of contemporary Arab politics. Only too often, in the study of the Arab region, excessive reliance on a specific disciplinary point of view or interpretive paradigm has produced analyses that, while contributing to our understanding, remain nevertheless too unilateral. We hope to have avoided such unilateralism and oversimplification, and provided a balanced and convincing view of a very complex reality.

The complexity of it has often been used to argue in favour of a separate analysis of Arab reality, one which is based on tools that are different from those used in the rest of the world. Hence the temptation to depict the Arab world as not comparable to the rest of the developing world, and governed by separate and deviant laws of motion. Against this approach, which may sometimes offer an improved understanding of the exquisite detail but which remains nevertheless essentially unscientific, we have attempted to provide an analysis that can be readily linked to similar attempts to analyse the state in other regional realities.

In so doing, this volume fills an obvious gap. Until now, the discussion of the nature and role of the state in the developing world has almost completely ignored the Arab experience, as well as Arab political thought. It is time to remedy this lack of attention, and distil from that experience analytical tools that might be fruitfully used in other contexts.

1

The Origins of the Arab State System

Iliya Harik

THE PRE-COLONIAL ERA

Introduction

The Arab world today consists of twenty-one states, officially members of the Arab League. Three of them, Mauritania, Somalia and Djibouti, are peripheral, with the latter two more African than Arab. The remaining eighteen, to which this discussion will be limited, have gained their political independence only recently. The earliest Arab state to achieve independence was the Yemen (San'a) in 1918 and the most recent was the United Arab Emirates at the end of 1971. From the Atlantic to the Gulf, only the territory known as Najd, of what is today Saudi Arabia, has not known direct foreign rule in some form or another.

The Arab states manifest a considerable degree of diversity amongst themselves, more so than the diversity that exists amongst ethnically heterogeneous states as in Western Europe, for instance. Five of the Arab oil-producing countries enjoy a *per capita* income of over $10,000, while the poorest, such as the two Yemens, Oman, Egypt and the Sudan, all rank below $800 *per capita*. The mode of life varies from disintegrating tribalism, particularly in Arabia and the Fertile Crescent, to sophisticated urban life such as can be witnessed in the supermarkets and theatres of pre-1975 Beirut, Cairo and Tunis. Yet, despite these outstanding differences there is something important in common to these states, something of which they are strongly self-conscious. They speak the same language and

1

basically share the same religion.

Language and religion have, through the ages, generated a unified high culture which bequeaths to them a sense of collective identity. From their language present-day Arabs have drawn their sense of national identity and from Islam they have drawn a collective sense of unity that often overlaps with nationalism. Both nationalism and Islam generate a sense of identification that cuts across state boundaries and supersedes, on the ideological level, local considerations.

THE NATION-STATE PROBLEM

Herein lies the paradox in Arab politics and history. Eighteen Arab states find themselves formally independent and sovereign and yet hardly any of them unconditionally accepts the legitimacy of its own statehood. The fact of the matter is that these states have, for a good part of the twentieth century, been caught up in the pull and push of conflicting forces, some coming from domestic centrifugal sources such as ethnic and sectarian divisions and some from the universal forces of pan-Arabism and pan-Islam, both of which draw away from the legitimacy of statehood enjoyed by these countries.

Under the Wahhabis of Arabia, the idea of a state system was seriously challenged by the universal principle of pan-Islam. In the 1950s and 1960s, Arab nationalism under Nasser seriously challenged the state system from a nationalist perspective. Though no other universalist movement since the expansionist periods of Wahhabism and Nasserism has seriously threatened the state system, the growing strength of fundamentalist Islam at present is a continuous reminder of the precarious status of the state system and secularist trends.

Arab nationalism as an ideology, more so than Islam, denies legitimacy to the state system. The true and natural state is considered to be the national state whose authority is coterminous with the nation, the nation being defined as the people of one language and culture, i.e. the Arab people whose area of habitation extends from Morocco on the Atlantic to the Yemen on the Indian Ocean. Using this ideological yardstick, the eighteen states just alluded to are to be considered one nation-state. The term 'nation' (*umma*) has throughout the Islamic era referred to the universal Muslim community (Haim, 1962;

Sharabi, 1966; Hourani, 1962).

Around the end of the nineteenth century, however, the term umma started to appear in the political literature of the time in reference to the universal Arab community, thus acquiring a preponderantly secular meaning. Though Arab Christians figured prominently in pursuing this course, the new terminology was not limited to them (Antonius, 1955; Zeine, 1958). Arab nationalists, overwhelmingly Muslim, insist on this usage and stubbornly resist applying the term to the people of a single one of the Arab states. Even in the constitutions of these states, the term umma is avoided, as it is also in official usage. The name of the state, say Syria, or the term 'people' (ash-sha'b) are used instead. It is because of these conventional Arab usages of the words that the term 'nation-state' was avoided in the title of this chapter, for many would question my terminology and some would dispute it outright. It would be pointless to quibble about terms, for words have conventional or given definitions and one gains nothing by violating this understanding. I shall accept therefore the objection that these countries are not nation-states and just refer to the whole set as the 'state system' for each of them is undeniably a state in the formal sense.

The Committee on New Nations at the University of Chicago published in the 1960s a book called *Old Societies and New States* (Geertz, 1963). While this nomenclature seems reasonable, it tends to be misleading. The illusion of state novelty in the Third World among students of development may be due to the disinclination of modernisation theory to delve into historical inquiry. Social scientists have a particularly significant role in re-examining history and relating it to the present.

A quick look at the history of the eighteen Arab countries clearly shows not only that they are old societies but also old states. Except for three of them — Iraq, Syria and Jordan — they all go back to the nineteenth century or a much earlier period. The traditional state should not be overlooked or dismissed because of a modern outlook or other biases. Those who ignore it do so because of a formalistic definition of the state, and/or because of their limited historical curiosity. Indeed, very few, if any, have engaged in a study of comparative history to assess the origins and records of the state structures of the Middle East and North Africa.

An attempt will be made in this discussion to show that the states of the eighteen Arab countries under consideration are

3

not only quite old (and in some cases extremely old) but also have within themselves the sources of their own legitimacy and that this fact cannot be brushed aside by nationalists or scholars. Arab nationalists have ignored and belittled the state system as baseless and as a creation of colonialism (Haim, 1962). They have done so at their own risk and have paid a high price for their historical misperceptions.

The contempt heaped by nationalist ideologues on the state system has discouraged a detached inquiry. It is, however, to the credit of Elbaki Hermassi (1972), that he has looked at three Maghrebi states in the light of comparative history and given the state system its proper credit. Curiously enough, he received help in his endeavour from another Tunisian, that great historian of the fourteenth century, Ibn Khaldun.

I shall maintain here that fifteen of the contemporary Arab states are the product of indigenous and regional forces mostly unrelated to European colonialism, and in most cases predate it. Moreover, almost all of the fifteen states mentioned have enjoyed legitimacy in terms of the values of their peoples and times. That we may have a different set of values at present in terms of which we judge the right to rule, should not deny other people of other eras the right to their own moral judgement and its worth. However, the strength and time-honoured legitimacy of these states in the eyes of their peoples are in no way to be construed as grounds for their continued survival. States may come and go, sometimes by the will of their own people, at other times through external forces or historical accident. The traditional state of the Hijaz, for instance, did disappear (Baker, 1979). Most traditional states, however, have survived to the present day, even though with much-changed political institutions.

TYPOLOGY OF THE ARAB STATE SYSTEM

I shall try here to present a typology of the traditional Arab states according to the bases of their authority, a step which will take us to periods earlier than the nineteenth century. Then I shall discuss the impact of European influences and colonialism on these states during the nineteenth century, taking into account another dimension, namely, the emergence of new social forces that by and large reinforced the state system.

The principles which explain the emergence of the Arab state system are ideology, traditions and dominion. While the forces of ideology, traditions and dominion overlap, one can still clearly argue a predominance of one or the other of these principles in different types of Arab states. This approach may seem to ignore economic factors in explaining political formations. That is not the case. The economy of Arab states which can be traced back to the medieval period was based on subsistence and limited exchange of goods. The lack of change in the economy during earlier centuries rules out economic factors as an explanatory principle in the formation of the multifarious state system. Thus, in the first part of this discussion, economic factors will not be considered. In the second part, the money market economy will be considered as a fourth principle affecting state institutions. One can, of course, argue that the traditional economies of distant times invariably explain the authoritarian political structures that prevailed then. Nevertheless, the traditional state system of the Arab world showed considerable structural diversity, as will be made clear below.

First, let me briefly indicate here that when I use the term state I am not bound by the formal definition that would qualify the designated body for membership of the United Nations. I simply mean to refer to an established authority which enjoys jurisdiction over a core territory and people for an extended period of time, stretching over at least several generations. The jurisdiction includes powers to implement the law, impose taxation, and demand military service, loyalty and allegiance to the established authority.

The traditional Arab states, viewed from this perspective, will be found to have differed in structure, power base, legitimacy and traditions. I have been able to identify the following types, classified in accordance with these criteria and with a view to their origins.

1. *The imam-chief system.* Authority is invested in a sanctified leader. In this group of countries we find two sub-types: (a) the dissenter communities and (b) the mainstream orthodox communities. The first includes the states of Yemen, (San'a), Oman, Cyrenaica (Libya), and the second is comprised of Hijaz and Morocco.

2. *The alliance system of chiefs and imams.* In this case author-

ity is invested in a tribal chief supported and awarded a legitimate authority beyond the confines of his tribe by virtue of his identification and/or alliance with a prominent religious leader and his teachings. The main case in this category is Saudi Arabia.

In these two types, ideology plays a predominant role in state formation, while force and traditions come next in order of importance.

3. The traditional secular system. Here authority is vested in a dynasty free from religious attributes. This group includes Qatar, Bahrain, Kuwait, the United Arab Emirates, the People's Democratic Republic of the Yemen and Lebanon. The role of traditions in these cases is pre-eminent, while state hegemony is cemented further by the possession of coercive power in the hands of a cohesive group.

4. The bureaucratic-military oligarchy type. In this case, authority originates in urban-based garrison commanders, who in time develop an extensive bureaucratic apparatus. This group of countries includes Algeria, Tunisia, Tripolitania (Libya) and Egypt. Monopoly of the means of coercion in the hands of an administrative-military 'caste' is the major feature of this state type.

5. The colonially-created state system. Here we come to the modern era which will be discussed in detail in the second part of this chapter, and will only be identified briefly at this point. This category is distinctive in that it refers to states that have been carved out from the defunct Ottoman empire on the basis of foreign imperial interests and in the absence of any credible local base of authority upon which to erect new structures. The group includes Iraq, Syria, Jordan and Palestine. (To the extent that Lebanon was radically changed by the same imperial powers, it may be included in this context as well.) Colonialism left a serious impact on most Arab states, but in only the above-mentioned cases can one maintain that the state system itself was created by the colonial powers.

Since it is not possible to discuss all fifteen cases in this limited essay, I shall focus on some archetypes and touch briefly on the others.

The imam-chief type

The state of the religious chief is mainly found in a dissenter type which seeks survival in rough mountains and desert terrains on the periphery of the Arab heartland, i.e. at a considerable distance from the centre of the empire, Oman and Yemen are examples *par excellence* of this type of state.

Oman (Phillips, 1967), the forgotten backwater of the Arab world that hardly ever figures in Arab nationalist literature, enjoys one of the longest continuous statehoods in the Arab world, rivalled only by Egypt. The state started in the eighth century (its first Ibadi imam was elected in 751 A.D.) by a radical dissident Muslim group (*al-Khawarij*), which broke away from the first Arab empire of the four pious Caliphs, Al-Rashidun.

The sect found refuge in the desert- and sea-protected mountains of Oman, and there sought to live the pious life in a commonwealth based on faith. This is not, as might be thought, a state by default, but rather the product of a conscious and determined effort to design a political system consistent with the religious beliefs of the Ibadi Muslim faith. The Ibadis broke away from the body of Islam over the very issue of proper government and the legitimate election of the head of state. They believed that the right to govern Muslims lies only in a pious Muslim who is elected by the people.

The electoral process consisted of two steps. First, the learned and notables in the community would meet at Nazwa, in the hinterland of Oman, and nominate a person; then in the second stage, they would present the nominee to the people who had the right to approve or reject the nomination. Should the imam prove unworthy of his office and unjust, the people had the right to depose him, a right that was used promptly to depose the first imam of the Ibadi state soon after he was elected.

The Ibadis, without any doubt, laid down the most free principles of elections to be found in the history of the Islamic theory of state. Curiously enough, they were completely dogmatic and very narrow, even more so than the Wahhabis. Moreover, once properly elected, the imam (the chosen of God) and his acts assumed a holy character, a principle accentuated in later years by resort to a dual system based on the hereditary principle in conjunction with elections.

7

Like the others ruled by religious chiefs, with time the Ibadi state incorporated the principle of hereditary rights to power along with that of election. By the time the Bousaʻd dynasty took over in the middle of the eighteenth century, the hereditary principle had gained ascendancy over election and a separation of the imamate from the office of sultan followed. The Bousaʻd dynasty, it is worth noting, under whom Oman reached the apex of its power, is the same dynasty which is still governing Oman today under Sultan Qaboos.

Oman was not a small, isolated state, but a great one whose ships dominated the seas in the latter part of the eighteenth and first half of the nineteenth century from Kenya, Zanzibar and enclaves on the Iranian and Baluchi coasts. Its merchant fleet was the most important in the region, until it was made obsolete by British steamships in the middle of the nineteenth century.

The Yemen (Abadha, 1975) is the second important case of a state whose origins lie in the imam-chief system. The state of Yemen was founded in 900 A.D. by a descendant of ʻAli ibn Abi Talib, the fourth Caliph of Islam. The founder, Yahya ibn al-Husayn, was a believer in the doctrine of Imam Zayd ibn ʻAli, which makes the Yemen state a Shiʻi one, though, unlike the Persian Shiʻa, who believe in the twelfth imam, the Zaydis believe in a continuing line of imams. Imam Yahya began proselytising in the city of Suʻda in the northern part of the country, where he also established his state. Later the capital moved to Sanʻa.

The Zaydi doctrine is one of the more moderate versions of Shiʻi Islam and is closer to the Sunni doctrine than that of any other Shiʻi sect. Unlike extreme Shiʻa (al-ghulat), the Zaydis moderate the claim of sanctity attributed to ʻAli and his descendants. Also unlike the Ibadi doctrine of Oman where every Muslim is entitled to hold the office, authority in Yemen is vested in the descendants of ʻAli and Fatima, the daughter of the Prophet Muhammad.

The Zaydi state of Yemen is based on the principle that any one of the descendants of ʻAli and Fatima is a legitimate candidate for the throne, and furthermore, that two or more imams can legitimately rule provided there is sufficient distance between their domains, a principle that conflicts with the doctrine of the indivisibility of the community insisted upon by the pan-Islamists. The Zaydis specify a number of qualities that the candidate should posess before he is selected by the learned scholars and notables.

Two requirements for the imam had a far-reaching effect on the shape the Yemeni state took: he should be a 'warrior' and a 'just' ruler who implements the religious law. Should he fail to be one or other, his overthrow by a legitimate contender is permissable. As is to be expected, the history of the Yemen is full of unrest and infighting among the Zaydis over the office.

The Yemeni state has known periods of expansion and contraction, but its core territory remained in the mountain range, where the Zaydi doctrine was prevalent. The Yemen fell under Ottoman rule intermittently, first in the period between 1538 and 1635, and then from 1872 until 1918. The history of the Yemeni–Ottoman relations may be characterised as one in which a state of war was the normal situation. Though subjected to the Ottomans, the Yemen never fell under any other foreign rule. Oman, on the other hand, was never dominated by Ottoman rule, but suffered a short-lived Portuguese occupation of its coastal towns in the sixteenth century.

Following their normal practice, the Ottomans ruled their Arabian possessions indirectly through confirmation of the local rulers, such as the Zaydi imams in the Yemen and the sharifs of Mecca in Hijaz. The sharifian state of Hijaz, which enjoyed a longevity comparable to that of Yemen and Oman, vanished from the political map in 1925 when it was taken over by the expanding Saudi state (Baker, 1979). Though it enjoyed state features similar to the others, it was always a dependency of whoever happened to be the dominant Islamic ruler in Cairo or Istanbul. Thus, during the Ottoman era, the sharifs ruled in the name of the Ottoman sultan. Though Sunni in a Sunni state, the sharif was a descendant of the Prophet, and thus enjoyed the legitimacy of a religious chief. The Hijaz is not the only state in the region that has disappeared for political and/or military reasons.

Another country whose political system is rooted in a religious base is Morocco (Abun-Nasr, 1975; Barbour, 1965; Zartman, 1964). Morocco's early history is tied up with the Muslim empires of the West and it cannot, therefore, but fully identified as a country with a political system roughly coterminous with its present territory until the sixteenth century. However, it is reasonable to say that the Murabitun (Almoravids) of the eleventh century and the Muwahhidun (Almohads)

9

of the twelfth century were empires based in Morroco proper and originated by religious reformers. In the case of the latter, it was a reformer who later claimed to be a sharif (Ibn Tumart), i,e, a descendant of the Prophet. I shall limit this inquiry, however, to the modern history of Morocco, from the Sadian dynasty in the sixteenth century (1510-1603) to the present. The Sadian family claimed sharifian descent in addition to having been connected to a sufi order, the Jazuliyya, in much the same way as the succeeding dynasty, the 'Alawites (1668 to the present).

The founder of the 'Alawite dynasty was a sharif who was elected sultan by religious leaders of the Tafilalt oasis. It is interesting to note that the present King of Morocco, Hassan II, is a descendant of the founder of the dynasty, Moulay ash-Sharif, and refers to himself as the Prince of the Faithful, the attribute reserved to a Caliph.

Both the Sadians and the 'Alawites were of rural origin and sought additional support from the religious establishments of the urban centres. However, in no case thus far has religion been the sole base of power, but always a support of dominion established by the sword.

The alliance of chief and imam type

The second type of traditional state is that of the chief and imam alliance. Saudi Arabia is the main case in this category.

Saudi Arabia (Winder, 1965; Hopwood, 1972; Howarth, 1964; 'Abd ar-Rahim, 1975) emerged as a state in central Arabia for the first time in 1745, and its fortune lasted until 1818. It was defeated in war, then restored in 1842; it declined towards the end of the century to revive once again in full force in 1902 under 'Abd al-'Aziz II.

Central Arabia was then a region consisting of independent tribes and lacking central control. A local chief, Muhammad ibn Sa'ud of Dir'iyyah in Najd, struck up an alliance in 1745 with the fugitive reformer Muhammad ibn 'Abd al-Wahhab and expanded his domain over the other tribes in the area of Najd. By 1792, his son and successor, 'Abd al-'Aziz I, had expanded the boundaries of the Saudi state into northern Yemen, the Hasa region on the Persian Gulf and the southern borders of Ottoman lands in southern Syria and Iraq. By 1810, the Saudi state comprised all of Arabia, except for Oman, Yemen, Qatar, Kuwait, and Aden with its protectorate. The Saudis felt strong enough to try to extend their government over Syria and Iraq, thus compelling the Ottoman Sultan to check their threat through the military might of his Egyptian viceroy, Muhammad 'Ali. In a matter of seven years (1811-18), Muhammad 'Ali succeeded in destroying the Saudi state and sent its chief to be beheaded in Istanbul. It took the Saudis almost thirty years to recover from the blow.

The Saudi state was founded on the conservative Sunni doctrine of the Hanbalite school of jurisprudence. Its basic political principle is the responsibility of the ruler to implement the *Shari'ah*, and to spread and protect the orthodox faith. The Saudi princes accepted in good faith this requirement enunciated by the religious reformer Ibn 'Abd al-Wahhab, and carried it out fully. Their state spread the Saudi dominion and the revivalist doctrine at one and the same time.

As for the selection of the Muslim ruler, Ibn 'Abd al-Wahhab evidently accepted the hereditary law of succession in the established dynasty. Though this is not the best principle for selecting rulers in Islamic doctrine, the practice of hereditary rule was established early in the Muslim Arab state during the seventh century. With the decline of the first Saudi state, the sharifian state of Hijaz revived and shook off the tutelage of the Sa'uds. The Najd area fell once again into a state of tribal pluralism and independence in which the Sa'uds held partial authority.

Another Saudi state re-emerged at the beginning of the twentieth century at the hands of a Saudi prince, 'Abd al-'Aziz ibn Sa'ud (1880-1953), who in 1901 captured the former Saudi capital of Riyadh from its then ruler, Ibn Rashid, and set the course of his followers in seeking dominion and strict religious observance in Arabia. Long before his death in 1953, he had restored the first Saudi state to its former dominions in Arabia, creating this time a more centralised structure and eliminating local centres of authority.

The present Saudi state is made up of what was nominally the Ottoman territory of Najd and Hasa, and the defunct states of Hijaz and 'Asir. In so far as political unification in the Arab world is concerned, the Saudi state has been, along with the United Arab Emirates and Libya, the only successful endeavour. None of its leaders, however, professed Arab nationalist objectives.

It would be easy to leave Saudi Arabia as the only example of the chief and imam alliance type of state, but the fact is that in many ways Oman and Morocco followed the pattern in later years in which the rulers' main attribute became dominion in alliance with the religious men of their day. Invariably, however, the predominance belonged to the temporal chief, not the imam.

The traditional secular system of authority

Chronologically the emergence of the state of Saudi Arabia occurred during the middle of the eighteenth century, at the same time as many other states in the Arabian Peninsula that are still with us today, such as Kuwait, Qatar and Bahrain. These belong to the traditional secular state type and their emergence at that particular time must have had something to do with the decline of Ottoman power. In all three states, the chieftain principle was paramount and the ascendancy of the ruling dynasty has been on the increase continuously to the present. Nowhere did religious power manifest itself, nor was it associated with the ruler.

Kuwait was the first of these states to appear on the map and it could also be called the mother state of the three (Abu-Hakima 1967; Winder, 1965; Ismael, 1982). All three states come from the same clan of the 'Utub tribe which moved from Najd into the small village of Kuwait. In 1752 a certain shaykh of the clan, Sabbah, was selected by his fellow tribesmen to be chief of their city. The city flourished under the 'Utubs and became within a very short period of time a rival to the port city of Basra in southern Iraq. Kuwait was located on the border line between the Ottoman power in Iraq and the domain of the Banu Khalid rulers in al-Hasa. It was through the permission and protection of the Banu Khalid that the 'Utubs settled in Kuwait at the beginning of the eighteenth century. There seems to be no historical evidence for the claim that the Sabbah family established its government by seeking authorisation from the Ottoman Mutasallim of Basra. Rather, it pursued the independent line of its former masters, the Banu Khalid. Later, it is true that the shaykhs of Kuwait sought Ottoman confirmation, which became particularly significant under the reformer *wali* of Baghdad, Midhat Pasha (1869-72). This measure cost the

Sabbah dynasty nothing in terms of power, since Ottoman suzerainty was purely nominal. They did not pay the Ottomans
tribute nor did they have to seek Ottoman instruction regarding
the succession. In fact, it was the Ottomans who paid the
shaykhs a subsidy, which started as protection money given in
recognition of the sea power of Kuwait in order to protect Basra
from pirate and other attacks. Moreover, the shaykhs received
generous gifts from the Ottomans in the form of palm groves in
the Basra and al-Fao areas (Dabbagh, 1962; Hopwood, 1972).

A branch of the 'Utub, known for their financial power and
skills, left Kuwait to establish a city state in al-Zubara in the
area of Qatar, apparently with the permission of the Sabbahs.
These were the Khalifas, who established dominion in the
second half of the eighteenth century in Qatar and Bahrain.
Later, Bahrain and Qatar became two separate states under
separate branches of the same Khalifa family.

The 'Utub governments in the three states were basically the
same in that they were based on the pre-eminence of the Arab
shaykh who ruled supreme over the rest. In the urban setting of
Kuwait, Qatar and Bahrain, the 'Utub chiefs ruled with the aid
of councils of notables.

While these chiefs were Muslims, they did not enjoy or claim
religious attributes which set them apart from the rest of society.
Moreover, they showed no particular religious zeal nor did they
mix religion with politics. Even in the case of the implementation of justice, they resorted to secular law in addition to
religious law, a practice common among the tribes. This was
also the case in the emirate of Mount Lebanon (Harik, 1968;
Spagnolo, 1977; Salibi, 1965).

The government of Mount Lebanon is the oldest in this
category of traditional secular states. While its origin can be
traced back to the Arab chiefs who settled in the south and were
there under the Mamluks, the principality of Lebanon really
begins with the ascendancy of the Ma'nid house which coincides
with the Ottoman conquest of Syria in 1516 by Sultan Salim I,
who also confirmed the Ma'nids in the rule of the Shuf district
in return for the assistance they gave him against the Mamluks.

The Ma'nids expanded their domain towards the north and
left to their direct successors, the Shihabi dynasty, a larger
domain than the one they had received in 1516. Upon the death
of the last male Ma'nid, a Shihabi Amir succeeded, being a
descendant of the Ma'nids on the maternal side. Thus Shihabi

rule may be considered a continuation of the same dynasty over the same territory.

The government of Mount Lebanon was more complex than the secular traditional governments of eastern Arabia. It was a pluralist political system based on hereditary title among a group of aristocratic families, who were bound to the Amir of the Mountain by loyalty, though enjoying prerogatives of direct government over their subjects and by interposition between the Amir and his subjects. The government of the Lebanon was under Ottoman sovereignty, but the Ottomans left the local leaders in charge. Thus, the Amirs of Lebanon enjoyed autonomy in their internal affairs and paid tribute to the Sultan through his walis in Sidon, Tripoli and/or Damascus. During the rule of a strong wali, some interference took place in the political struggles among the rival lords in Lebanon. On the other hand, when a strong Amir ruled in Lebanon next to a weak Ottoman wali, he interfered in the wali's affairs and gained power at his expense.

A major characteristic of the Lebanese traditional system was its pluralist and secular character. Pluralism was manifested in the autonomy enjoyed by the feudal lords from the Amir and from one another. But pluralism also extended to other aspects of society: the religious realm, for instance. Though very small, this territory comprised members of various Muslim sects, schismatic and orthodox, in addition to a plethora of Christian denominations. For instance, the Amir's religion was Sunni Muslim, but the main feudal lords and also a large majority of the population were Druze and Maronite Christians. The principality also included some Shi'a, Sunnis and Orthodox Christians. Thus, there were more religious communities concentrated there than in any other Ottoman territory.

The 'clericals' of these denominations hardly interfered at all with governmental relations before the nineteenth century. Political relation cut across sectarian lines. Druze lords had, in addition to their own subjects, non-Druze, both Christian and Muslim. Similarly, Maronite lords had non-Maronite subjects. Political coalitions were made up of lords of diverse religious affiliations.

In all these cases of secular governments, the rulers were very jealous of their prerogatives *vis-à-vis* the outside world and territorial jurisdiction was generally recognised without formal boundaries; territories coincided with jurisdiction over subjects.

There were numerous violations of these informal boundaries over the years, but they were in the form of challenges to the other's authority rather than denials of the other's traditional jurisdiction.

The bureaucratic-military oligarchy

The last type under consideration here is the bureaucratic-military oligarchy. The only claim to legitimate authority of the military oligarchic government is its representation of the Ottoman Sultan, for almost all the four states under consideration, with the exception of Egypt, originated under Ottoman rule by Ottoman officers. Appearing in the first part of the eighteenth century in Algeria, Tunisia, Tripolitania and Egypt, the bureaucratic-military oligarchic system was urban-based. Its emergence reflects the decline of the Ottoman power over the outlying districts, leading local Ottoman garrisons in the main cities to seek autonomy from the Sultan.

The bureaucratic-military oligarchy in its purest form was to be seen in Algeria, where the *dey*, the 'officer-king', and his foreign troops governed without any participation of, or ties with the native population (Abun-Nasr, 1975). Tunisia and Egypt proved to be different. The first phase of the autonomous state of Tunisia witnessed the emergence of a short-lived dynasty (the Muradists), which nevertheless managed between 1637 and 1702 to consolidate its power independently of the Sultan and to replace the local Ottoman troops with local tribes as the main source of its power (ibid.). The Husaynids, who succeeded the Muradists in 1706, followed the same pattern of government, buttressing their power with local support. Tunisia enjoyed stability and prosperity under the Husaynids for the whole of the eighteenth century. Up to the first half of the nineteenth century, the Husaynids were virtually independent of the Ottoman Sultan, even more so than Egypt. They paid no tribute, sent no soldiers to fight in the Sultan's army, and sought no investiture. Moreover, they waged war, signed treaties and received foreign deputations in their own name.

One of the interesting features of this otherwise absolutist government is the Legal Council, which consisted of local *'ulama* and whose function it was to pass judgement on the conformity of governmental legislation and decrees with the

Shari'ah. With the shift in power balance away from the military and the distancing of Tunisia from the Ottoman Sultan, the Husaynid dynasty sought new sources of legitimacy for its authority in the practice of Islam and the implementation of religious law. Territorially, Tunisia under the Husaynids was almost identical with the present-day country, as was Algeria, for that matter, except for the expansion of its boundaries into the great Sahara by the French.

It is hard to think of any time in known history when Egypt did not have a central government of some sort or another (Holt, 1966; Vatikiotis, 1980). One can go as far back as one wishes, but here we shall limit ourselves to the military oligarchy which was the immediate precursor of the modern state and goes back to the Mamluk period before the Ottomans occupied Egypt in 1517. Having defeated the Mamluks, the Ottomans, in their time-honoured practice, entrusted the government to the vanquished to rule in the name of the Ottoman Sultan. So the Mamluks were reinstated. It was not until Muhammad 'Ali came to power in Egypt in the wake of Napoleon's departure that a virtually independent state emerged.

An Ottoman officer who succeeded in securing for himself the office of Pasha of Egypt in 1803, Muhammad 'Ali rapidly moved to consolidate his power and built an army of such strength that the Ottoman Sultan, his suzerain, had to seek his help as early as 1810 to recover Arabia from the Wahhabis. But before his long rule came to an end, Muhammad 'Ali was to challenge the authority of his suzerain and seek to take over his empire by invading Syria and part of Anatolia. Before he could reach the Ottoman capital, Britain and France intervened militarily on behalf of the Sultan to push the ambitious and powerful viceroy back into the confines of Egypt where he continued to rule independently with only nominal recognition of the Sultan's suzerainty. His descendants ruled after him until 1952.

Like the rest of the military oligarchic states of Ottoman origin mentioned thus far, the power of the Egyptian oligarchy rested on the Ottoman garrison of the Pasha. But like the Tunisians, Muhammad 'Ali quickly freed himself from such dependence and involved the local population in his undertaking, primarily be recruiting Egyptian soldiers and administrators into his large army and civil service. He involved Egyptians also in the economic enterprises which he established to support his growing military power. He opened schools and sent many

Egyptians to Europe for higher education.

The 'Alawid regime reduced its dependence on Ottoman soldiers by recruiting locally, but it did not seek legitimacy by increasing its ties with the people. The Egyptians were represented, if at all, by their religious men, who were the essence of Islamic learning and the custodians of the oldest continuously operating university of al-Azhar. Muhammad 'Ali respected the Shari'ah but there is no evidence that he sought legitimation from the 'ulama or the preaching of Islam beyond the conventional observation of the Islamic religion. If anything, he was, of necessity, more of a moderniser and advocate of European learning.

His descendants ruled after him as an oligarchy, but one that established increasing links with non-military influential people in the country. The 'Alawid dynasty, however, as was the case in most other Arab states, fell into a condition of dependence on European powers even before the British occupied the country in 1882.

TRANSITION TO THE MODERN STATE ERA

It has been shown in the preceding part that the origins of the Arab states are different and can be traced back, in most cases, to a period before the nineteenth century. Two points are worth underlining here: first, that most of these states were locally rooted and enjoyed legitimacy in the eyes of their people; and second, that they had recognisable boundaries, or at least a core territory where their authority endured through the vicissitudes of time. By the beginning of the twentieth century, we find the inhabitants of these states possessed of a sense of identity as people of a country and a state, regardless of whether the term nation-state applied to them or not. I shall return to this point again later.

Up to the first half of the nineteenth century, we encounter no foreign factor in the making of these states. Some Arabs may point to the Ottomans as an imperialist agent involved in the process, but this would be an untenable position, for in these pre-nationalistic periods, Arabs under Ottoman rule did not perceive themselves as subjects of foreign rulers. They identified with the Ottomans and looked upon the Sultan as the Muslim head of a Muslim commonwealth of which they were a part.

Colonialism and the state system

If, as we have seen, the seventeenth and eighteenth centuries were credited with the formation of new Arab states, the nineteenth century marked the era of colonialism and Arab subjugation by European powers. It was the period when Europeans challenged the minds of Arabs and Muslims in general, and undermined their sense of security and confidence. However, the subject of security is much too broad to be broached in this context. What I hope to do in a brief fashion here is point out the major ways in which the advent of colonialism and of intensified contacts with Europe affected the fortunes of the state system.

By the first half of the nineteenth century we can see two major forces acting on the Arab states: European penetration, on the one hand, and the reassertion of Ottoman power, on the other. The Ottomans, who had not themselves stemmed the tide of territorial losses especially in their European domains, were able to reassert their authority in Egypt after the departure of Napoleon, albeit temporarily. They restored their actual power in Tripolitania in 1835 by abolishing the military oligarchy of the Qaramanlis dynasty, and regained their nominal claims on Tunisia which, for its own reasons, sought to be reincorporated into the fold (Abun-Nasr, 1975). They succeeded in destroying the new Saudi state in Arabia, re-entered Yemen in 1872, reasserted their claims over Kuwait (Abu-Hakima, 1967), strengthened their position with the sharifs of Hijaz (Winder, 1965; Hopwood, 1972) and regained control of the Syrian provinces (Holt, 1966). Iraqi provinces were also brought under greater central control (Longrigg, 1956). Not all these successes can be attributed to a reformed central government in Istanbul. The opening of the Suez Canal and the Damascus–Hijaz railway both contributed to the reassertion of Ottoman power in Arabia.

At the same time, the Ottomans suffered major losses, just as the Arabs did, from the expansion of the European powers. Before the century was over, the Ottomans witnessed the French occupation of Algeria in 1830 and Tunisia in 1881. The British occupied Aden in 1839 and Egypt in 1882. Italy occupied Tripolitania in 1911. Earlier, seven European powers intervened in Lebanon in 1861 and served as the guarantors of its autonomy and constitution.

Other Arab states were also affected by this imperialism. Moroccan territory was whittled away by the Spanish and French and the whole country was brought under foreign rule by 1912. Oman started to come under British influence in the middle of the nineteenth century and virtually became a protectorate by the end of that century. Again before 1900, Qatar, Bahrain and Kuwait became tied to Britain by treaties which for all practical purposes reduced them to dependencies of the British Crown.

The colonial mandate system

The zenith of colonial power was reached with the conclusion of the First World War. Britain and France emerged as the superpowers of that brief era, and they reasserted and expanded their control over Arab lands. This was most visible in the remaining Arab territories under Ottoman rule, namely the Fertile Crescent, an area brought under British and French rule in its entirety. Though British influence increased in the Hijaz, it lasted for only a very short period and no additional gains by imperial interests were witnessed in Arabia.

In the Fertile Crescent, the British and French created five new states, all of which were technically put under the League of Nations' mandate bestowed on the two European powers. These states were Iraq, Syria, Lebanon, Transjordan, and Palestine. Of the five, only Lebanon then constituted an autonomous polity. The rest were ruled directly by the Ottoman Government from Istanbul in much the same fashion as the military oligarchies in other places. No nuclei of autonomous states were in existence in the region before that time. The territory of the Fertile Crescent was divided into administrative units under the Ottomans, none of which corresponded to present state boundaries.

During the decline of the Ottoman power, especially in the eighteenth century, local chiefs or ambitious Pashas, such as Dhahir al-'Umar in northern Palestine and al-Jazzar Pasha of Acre, emerged as autonomous Ottoman walis over their provinces. What these chiefs failed to do was to establish hereditary power or to perpetuate a military oligarchy. Their rule vanished with them and Ottoman power was easily reasserted (Rafiq, 1974; Hold, 1966). Members of the al-'Azm family of

19

Syria managed to fill positions as walis in various provinces such as Damascus, Tripoli, Sidon and even Egypt, but only as representatives of the Sultan at the mercy of Ottoman garrisons. And they never claimed autonomy or established hereditary rule.

In effect, when the British and French occupied the Fertile Crescent, they found no local authority or state such as that of Tunisia, Morocco, Oman, Kuwait, or Qatar; only in Lebanon was there an indigenous system of government. In the rest of the area, they had no landmarks to guide their steps; they had to create new entities on the basis of traditional claims and zones of influence.

Claims by local populations were expressed by the Syrians aided by the Hashemite Sharif of Hijaz, in Jordan by a Hashemite prince who moved into Transjordan, and in Palestine by Arab nationals and the World Zionist Organisation at one and the same time (Antonius, 1955; Zeine, 1958). While the British and French fashioned the map much to their own liking, they could not escape the pressure of the rising tide of anti-imperialism and nationalism. They had to grapple with Arab nationalism in its early stages in Syria, Palestine, Lebanon and Iraq. And though not effective in its first encounter, nationalism was the main cause of the short-lived stay of the two powers in the area.

Lebanon confirmed its autonomy under the French, and expanded its boundaries to include terrorists that were previously part of Beirut province to the west and Syria province to the east. For reasons which are not entirely clear, the origin of modern Lebanon is a source of misunderstanding. It is frequently stated that Lebanon was part of Syria and was created by the French. This is not true. It was not part of Syria, since there was no such state before 1920, whereas Lebanon enjoyed a political order all of its own. Nor was it created by the French, since it predated the French mandate. The French, indeed, affected its boundaries and remodelled its government. The Constitution of 1926 which the French introduced was based on the model of the Constitution of the French Third Republic, but the net result looked very different. The document took on an entirely local character and what was in the French Third Republic a secular cabinet system turned in Lebanon into a presidential sectarian system.

The point is, however, that a fifth type of state system emerged in the Fertile Crescent at the hands of the colonial powers, which was not the product of local historical forces. These are the states which conform to Arab nationalist theory about the emergence of the state system. That the Arab nationalist view, extrapolated from these limited cases, gained credence in other states is surprising, but perhaps it can be explained by the fact that Arab nationalist ideology emerged in the Fertile Crescent and spread from there to the rest of the Arab world. Arab nationalist ideology was at that time a clear expression of the feelings, perceptions and aspirations of the politically conscious Arabs in the Fertile Crescent countries, but it was not really applicable to the rest of the Arab lands.

In general, colonialism affected the boundaries of Arab states, but it did not, with the exception of the Fertile Crescent cases, create those states. Boundaries were by and large determined during the colonial period, but a few were left for the independent Arab states to settle later on. Colonial powers affected the structures of many governments, especially by creating a modern civil service and sometimes the nucleus of a modern standing army. They also left a major mark on the local political elites, as we shall show later on.

The economic impact of imperialism

Two major features of the legacy of colonialism — administrative centralisation and economics — must be pointed out. In the first part of this chapter we specified that the Arab state system may be explained in terms of ideology, traditions and power. By the nineteenth century we see new forces emerging, partly under the influence of colonialism. Economically, the emergence of the domestic market and social stratification contributed in no mean way to the emergence of a new ideology: nationalism. The colonial powers inadvertently contributed to the emergence of the nationalism of the state system by introducing a centralised system of administration in most countries under their control. The central administration, colonial or native, became the focus of political orientation and action by the emerging modern groups and classes, and contributed to the inception of a sense of identification with the state.

Colonialism markedly weakened the powers of regions such as the Maghreb, when, at the Congress of Aix-la-Chapelle in 1819, the European powers forced the Maghrebi states to remove trade barriers and end their practice of supporting piracy. Similarly, British insistence on ending the slave trade badly hurt the Omani economy and reduced the power of the Ibadi state. The region's intensified contacts with Europe, especially after the signing of the trade convention with the Ottoman Government in 1830, sowed the seeds of an economic revolution by stimulating trade and the use of cash. The initial effect on local industries was disastrous, but agriculture was stimulated. In other respects, the increasing conversion of the medium of exchange into cash had a tremendous effect on the creation of a new social strata and caused havoc in the fiscal administration of the state. The traditional elites showed ineptitude and irresponsibility in reacting to the revolution in finance, and their floundering laid them open to rapacious creditors and foreign intrigues which proved detrimental to their independence. This was true as much of Persia and Turkey as of Ismail's Egypt and Ahmed Bey's Tunisia (Issawi, 1984; Brown, 1974.

Aside from the weakening of the traditional state structure, the economic revolution had some interesting and long-range effects on the state system. In the first place, it created a new class of landlords and merchants who later emerged as the champions of nationalism and independence. The rising tide of nationalism weakened the old guard, because of their association with colonial rule. Merchant, landlord and professional groups emerged as the major rivals to the ruling dynasties, which had to come to terms with imperialism to preserve their status at the head of their states.

Second, a domestic market was stimulated and exchanges increased to such an extent that new linkages between the countryside and the city were created. These links were the first in a chain integrating the periphery with the centre and leading to the creation of a national society. Most notable in this respect was the emergence of a number of provincial towns and domestic merchants that served as links between villages and the capital, and of port towns which served as links between the country and the outside world (Harik, 1968).

These developments had an integrative role domestically and in most cases buttressed the forces that made for a new society and state in the Arab world. The rise of nationalism in Arab countries is most often attributed to intellectuals and their increasing contacts with the West. However, the stimulation of the domestic market is just as important, if not more so, in giving rise to nationalism, especially state nationalism.

The intensified economic exchanges and communications links, however, cannot be compared in magnitude with similar integrative forces in the European states of the nineteenth century, since the economic growth of the Arab countries remained slow and in some cases declined. Interestingly enough, the forces which tied the Arab countries to the world economy in a colonial and dependent relationship also generated the seeds of the destruction of colonialism, that is, nationalism. Port towns, I stress, appeared not as an isolated phenomenon but in conjunction with provincial towns. The first linked the country with the colonial powers and the second linked the hinterland with the capital. It was in towns that nationalists emerged and agitated for national independence.

While colonialism tied the hands of the governments of the area by financial bondage, it also gave rise to a new class, the custodians of small economic enterprises whose interests and culture were antagonistic to imperialism. These groups led the fight against imperialism. That this so-called middle and upper-middle class is now so beleaguered and castigated by contemporary political ideologies should not distract from the fact that it was indeed the pioneer of nationalism.

Structurally, the colonial administration had a complex effect on the state system of the Arab world in the nineteenth century. It bolstered the authority of a number of small states in the Persian Gulf area, while it undermined the power of one of the strongest among them, Oman. In the Fertile Crescent, it created four new states and reshaped the destiny of a fifth. In Egypt, it weakened the power of the central authority, as it did in Tunisia. In Algeria, it abolished that authority altogether and created a new colonial structure made up of *colons*. In Morocco, the case has similarity to the states of the Arabian Peninsula on the Persian Gulf, where colonialism consolidated the authority of the central government of what was previously a disintegrating monarchy.

In brief, colonialism introduced some contradictory trends in the area. It generated economic forces which tied the Arab economies to the West in a dependency relationship, on the one hand, and made for the domestic integration of state and society, on the other. A new class of businessmen, landlords and professionals emerged and held high the torch of nationalist resistance to imperialism. Finally, colonialism contributed to the weakening of the dynasties of bureaucratic oligarchies in the Maghreb states and Egypt, while it buttressed many of the traditional secular dynasties in the Gulf.

CONCLUSION

Conflict between a universal and a particular outlook in the political lives of Arab peoples has raged since the appearance of Islam, the most powerful force for universal identity that the Arabs have experienced in their entire history. It may be said that two conflicting impulses, one yearning to preserve and sharpen the particular identity of a community, and the other to submerge particularistic differences in a great and uniform whole, accompanied the very early formation stage of Islam and coexisted with it for the rest of its history. Ibadi and Shi'i particularisms appeared scarcely a generation after the death of the Prophet. States in Oman and Yemen were duly formed to embody these yearnings. Yet the force of universal political identity has always been stronger and more pervasive.

The most important and durable states in the Arab world, though their rulers were not, for the most part, ethnically Arab, were Muslim and multi-ethnically oriented states. They were based on the universal principle which binds the Muslim community.

Few states like Yemen and Oman tried explicitly to assert their particularistic identity in the face of a strident universalistic empire. The emergence of particularistic state structures in other Arab lands occurred much later, mostly in the seventeenth century in the Maghrebi states and in the eighteenth century in Arabia. This tendency coincided with the decline and, to a certain extent, breaking down of the vitality of the universal Ottoman state in the east and the religious revivalist Almohad state in the west.

In response to compelling necessity, Muslims adjusted to the inevitable diversity and started to perceive the universal as embodied in the particular. In other words, the universal principles of Islam were required to be embodied in the workings of the local state. Insistence that the ruler implement the Shari'ah and the resort of pretenders to seeking legitimacy from religious leaders are clear indications of the subscription by the small-time ruler to higher and more universal ideas.

This tendency was also manifested in another fashion: the acceptance by Muslims of the religious and temporal authority of learned scholars from other lands. It may be pointed out here that the Sanusi of Libya, whose teachings and authority were accepted by the Cyrenaican tribes, was an Algerian, and the Idrisis of 'Asir were Moroccans. Al-Mirghani was a Meccan whose following developed in the Sudan and became known as the Khatimiyah movement. The Iraqis and Jordanians accepted Hashemite kings from Hijaz who, though not learned scholars, were nevertheless sharifs.

The new state structures survived the inner strains of their locality and region for centuries; what they failed to do was to face up to the larger world that was rapidly encroaching upon them. The state system succumbed in the nineteenth century to an exogenous force coming from Europe. It failed to rejuvenate itself by promoting the science of 'umran, development, as Ibn Khaldun would have put it. Consequently, a chasm appeared between society and state. The needs of society were no longer served by the extractive policies of the state, which also failed to generate positive trends and growth. Eventually, the conflict between a no-growth society and an extractive state undermined both and opened the way for foreign intervention.

Invariably, colonial powers in the Arab countries left the outer layers of the state system intact, namely its core territory and dynasty. Only in Algeria was the ruling dynasty abolished and the boundaries expanded in an extreme way. The tendency on the part of the colonial powers to accept the state system as they found it had the effect of enforcing the particular nature of the one-country, one-state idea and provided the state with a more accomplished formal character. However, before the colonial powers had exhausted their use and potency, they had weakened the ruling dynasties beyond redemption in most of the Maghrebi states, though not in eastern Arabia where they have seen them through with a protective arm up to the present. Obviously, the impact of colonial rule, though in many ways pernicious, is more diverse than we generally credit it to be.

At any rate, the confirmation of the particularistic state by colonialism later encountered the revivalist universalistic forces of religion and Arab nationalism. Colonialism was opposed for two reasons: for occupying Arab lands and for reinforcing the particularistic development of states, considered in the nationalist universalistic world-view as symptoms of decline.

25

In much the same way, in the memory of younger generations the association of the localistic states with the imperialist period earned them the contempt of nationalists and pan-Islamists alike. Nationalists who had hoped to create a universalistic state anyway found in the colonial association a good excuse to undermine and discredit the state system. They did not, however, undermine the legitimacy and staying power of that time-honoured arrangement. Not only nationalists, but also social scientists, often overlook the fact that the structure creates the myth. Once an organisation is set up, it develops forces of vested interests and generates among individuals, almost habitually, a sense of identification with the structure.

Traditional authority, Weber tells us, is the force of habitually accepting the ways of one's forbears as the right ways. It does not even take centuries to develop this habitual sense of identity with the structure. In Kuwait, for instance, where one social scientist refers to his country as a 'gas station', it was found that the inhabitants have repeatedly opted against mergers with neighbouring states and prefer the identity of a 'gas station'!

Not even in Lebanon, after years of brutal and violent civil war, has anyone sought unification with Syria or lost his/her sense of Lebanese identity, despite all the pull of centrifugal forces and early opposition by many Lebanese Muslims to becoming incorporated into the Lebanese state. Arab nationalists in particular, therefore, would be well advised seriously to consider that the state system is here to stay and for good reasons. They may also consider that the state system is not necessarily a negation of Arab nationalism but may well be the main pillar upon which a federated Arab state may develop.

Looking towards the future, it would seem clear that the state system has gained strength and endurance despite the instability of particular regimes. True, there has not been any marked effort to provide the state system with legitimacy through intellectual treatises as is the case in universalistic ideologies. What we witness, rather, is the almost involuntary inculcation in the people of a sense of identity with their own state gained through habit, vested interests, local peculiarities and sensitivities, and common experiences. These things should not be underestimated, for in some cases they have both confirmed and lent legitimacy to the existing system and also generated a new particularistic nationalism such as the Palestinian ideology which has in recent years distinguished itself clearly as a separate national-ism, complementary to, but separate from, Arab nationalism. Uniformities created by state policies which affect only the people of that state often increase their tendency to draw together and result in their having common characteristics distinct from those of their neighbours.

Power considerations have also tended to strengthen the local state system. One can observe this tendency in the emer-gence of autocratic regimes jealous of their power and willing to unite with others only on their own terms of hegemony and dominion. Such approaches have tended also to distance Arab states from one another. Growing bureaucracies and the power of governments, coupled with stringent centralisation, have strengthened the patterns set in the past. Thus, curiously enough, the principle of dominion is still effective in explaining the state system at present as at the time of its inception. Absence of democratic freedoms has discouraged the develop-ment of inter-Arab relations by private citizens outside official channels.

Similarly, one sees that social forces have also tended to favour the state system. Different Arab economic systems have been developed which often resist integration and manifest protectionist tendencies dictated by particular needs and peculi-arities. More recently, the sudden wealth of some Arab oil producers has tended to encourage the particularistic sentiments of the 'going it alone and protecting our privileges' attitude. On the other hand, the pull of the universalistic principle of Arab nationalism is not entirely dead as is sometimes claimed, and may be working in conjunction with particularistic trends towards a new order, whereby the sovereign states permit the growth of supra-national institutions leading eventually to some sort of future confederation.

Evidence of some remaining vitality in the principle of Arab nationalism is demonstrated by growing Arab co-operation in economic development activities and continued co-ordination regarding security and national issues. There is still something called mutual Arab engagements generating constant action and constant attention. Universalistic principles do not fade easily, and this is the case with Arab nationalism which has been weakened but not defeated.

Finally, I cannot, as a social science historian, let slip the temptation of drawing some academic lessons from the preceding arguments. We are all familiar with Weber's types of legitimate authority. I have strived to perceive the indigenous states which I have sketched out here through Weberian spectacles, but I could not always see a clear picture. This led me to wonder whether Weber's general category of traditional legitimate authority is not a bit too general to be useful.

Two lines of thought call for further attention in this context. Should we, for instance, consider an authority which is drawn up deliberately in the name of a higher ideal, and a divine one too, for that matter, simply as traditional, as is the case with a tribal chieftain or a medieval monarch? If we take the imam-chief type, and considering the explicit design and creativity involved in the Islamic making of that state type, it becomes difficult to accept the idea that it is a traditional system of authority in the Weberian sense. The conceptualisation of the divine in rational terms, plus the legalistic procedures for the selection of a legitimate ruler, do not allow us to consider the imam as a charismatic leader either. The imam-chief type fits neither the traditional Weberian idea nor the charismatic one. This may suggest that a comparative study of the types of Arab states may serve to enrich and help differentiate further the Weberian categories of legitimate authority.

NOTES

1. I am indebted to L. Carl Brown for suggesting the term 'bureaucratic' in place of 'military', which I had originally used.

2

'Strong' and 'Weak' States:
A Qualified Return to the
Muqaddimah

Ghassan Salamé

'The desert' (says the Hebrew Prophet), 'shall become a plough-
land', so might all this good soil, whose 'sun is gone down whilst
it was yet day', return to be full of busy human lives; there lacks
but the defence of a strong government.
(Charles M. Doughty, *Travels in Arabia Deserta*, New York,
1936: 56)

There is, in contemporary political sociology, a clear reluctance
to distinguish between 'strong' and 'weak' states. This 'habit' is
thought to be restricted to limited circles, where 'some
Weberian-minded comparativists started labelling states, especially modern national states, "stronger" or "weaker", according
to how closely they approximated the ideal type of centralized
and fully rationalized Weberian bureaucracy, supposedly able to
work its will efficiently and without effective social opposition'
(Evans, Rueschemeyer, Skocpol, 1985: 351). The distinction is
therefore viewed as a mere 'temptation' (ibid.: 352) which is
better avoided since 'possibilities for state interventions of given
types cannot be derived from some overall level of generalized
capacity or "state strength"' (ibid.: 353).
    This reluctance is not general, however. Classic state-minded
authors, from Hegel to Raymond Aron, could hardly avoid the
strength/weakness distinction. The issue is not completely
absent from contemporary sociology (Nettl, 1968). But, more
important — at least for us here — is the fact that the issue has
remained central in the political discourse, and more deeply in
the political culture. One could see how American diplomats
were busy rebuilding a 'strong state' in Lebanon in 1982-3, a
natural alternative to several years of civil war. More generally,

29

Arabic newspapers, Kuwaiti *diwaniyyas*, and Cairo cafés are so often places where the eternal comparisons between Syria and Iraq, Algeria and Morocco, North and South Yemen, and continuing arguments on their compared strengths, are feverishly made.

It is true that the concept is then used in a much wider meaning (which will therefore be adopted here) than the one used by political sociologists analysing the weight of the state *vis-à-vis* the society it pretends to control, i.e. its autonomy in dealing with other socio-economic actors and its capacity for influencing their behaviour. A more down-to-earth definition would certainly include this meaning, plus a view of Iraq or Syria as Arab countries, i.e., as relatively autonomous and implicitly competitive actors within the general regional framework. The state, then, means at the same time the apparatus in control of a particular society as well as the supposedly 'sovereign' international entity itself. It includes the state *per se*, plus all the resources this state can gather to compare well with other Arab neighbours.

This ambiguity in the definition partly explains why the necessary ingredients of a 'strong state' remain to be clarified, though the concept is widely used. What does it mean to say that Saudi Arabia is 'strong' or 'weak'? Its strength could easily be traced to its petro-financial resources, but also, at the same time, to the way these resources are used by one particular group of leaders. It would therefore be quite difficult, in a society which had not experienced a long democratic tradition, to explain to the 'man in the street' that the holders of political power could refrain from concentrating in their hands all the resources available to them. How to explain, for example, that an American president is at the head of a 'weak state' in a 'strong country'? How to explain the fact that in the Arab (and other Third World societies), the expansion of the state's role in society did not lead to its enhanced capacity in dealing with external challenges? How to explain that, unlike Beirut, Damascus, Baghdad or Riyadh, where political power automatically leads to the concentration of financial and economic activities in its fringes and to chaotic urbanisation, Washington and Bonn are not magnets for attracting American and German bankers and industrialists. The distinction between the country and its leader, between the public budget and the resources at the dictator's disposal, or between national and praetorian armies, is yet to be fully made in reality as well as in perceptions.

One hypothesis runs through this paper: perceptions of the state's strength and/or weakness are substantially marked, in the Arab world, by a tradition of authoritarian rule, where the military *ghalaba* (domination) has preceded and practically made possible a generally unrestrained plunder of the society's available resources. These perceptions do not seem to have really adapted to modern times, where states are, more often than not, born dependent. They are generally blurred by centuries-old ideas on the privileges and vulnerability of states and a substantial amount of confusion between the national state apparatus and those who are manipulating it. This explains the current misperception of their (and other) states' strengths and weaknesses, in an era when Khaldunian views of political authority can no longer completely account for the situation of twenty-two (by any standard) weak Arab states in a highly integrated world system.

LESSONS FROM THE 'MUQADDIMAH'

A reader of 'Abd al-Rahman Ibn Khaldun's *Muqaddimah* would easily notice his inclination — almost an obsession — to discuss the strength/weakness dilemma. When he deals in the very first pages of the *Muqaddimah* with the problem of al-'Abbasa, al-Rashid's sister, Ibn Khaldun asks: 'How did al-Rashid lose his authority and how did the state of the Barmecides rise?' He seldom forgets the vulnerability of states throughout the *Muqaddimah* and is clearly fascinated by the regular succession of dynasties.

Ibn Khaldun asserts that the rise of the state is based on the necessity of deterrence (*wazi'*) and is therefore equivalent to the appearance of a leader who enjoys superiority (*ghalaba*) over others. The persistence of that leader in power is based on the strength of blood ties (*'asabiyya*) among the people, whose defence and protection are successful only if they are a closely knit group with common interests. This strengthens their stamina and makes them feared since everybody's affection for his family and group is more important than anything else (Ibn Khaldun, 1967: 97).

Ibn Khaldun then gradually uncovers the components of state power. The first is related to the division of society into

31

several parts. The 'natural' state must possess the means to control each part on its own, and it in turn must recognise the state's power over it. This is because leadership (*ri'asa*) exists only through superiority (*ghulb*) and superiority only through group feeling (*'asabiyya*). Leadership over people, therefore, must, of necessity, derive from a group feeling that is superior to each individual group feeling. Each individual group feeling that becomes aware of the superiority of the group feeling of the leader is ready to obey and follow him. However, the superiority of the leaders' 'asabiyya over all other individual group feelings is not sufficient to build strength. Following that, the whole society must be coalesced (*iltiham*) in accordance with the new authority:

> Natural authority is derived from a group feeling through the continuous superiority over competing parties. However, the condition for the continuation of this authority is for the subservient parties to coalesce with the group who controls leadership (Ibn Khaldun, n.d. 139).

Thus, Ibn Khaldun judiciously distinguishes between two ingredients of the state's strength. There are, on the one hand, the actual capabilities of the state and, on the other, the recognition by others of these capabilities. Their recognition of this strength will make them accept it, obey it and shift their political loyalty to its possessors. This central concept of iltiham makes Gramsci's 'hegemony' have clear Khaldunian connotations, if not an identical meaning. As well noted by G. Fiori (1970: 238):

> Gramsci's originality as a Marxist lay partly in his conception of the nature of bourgeois rule (and indeed of any previous established social order), in his argument that the system's real strength does not lie in the violence of the ruling class or the coercive power of its state apparatus, but in the acceptance by the ruled of a 'conception of the world' which belongs to the rulers.

The iltiham is then the ultimate form of hegemony in its insistence on social integration by and around the ideology professed by the ruling 'asabiyya.

The larger the new iltiham the stronger the state. Ibn Khaldun does believe that strength is related to the numbers of the state's supporters. Iltiham remains necessary, however; Ibn Khaldun clearly postulates that societies which are formed of one group are always stronger than those composed of different tribes and consequently several 'asabiyyas: 'A dynasty rarely establishes itself firmly in lands with many different tribes and groups. This is because of differences in opinions and desires. Behind each opinion and desire there is a group feeling defending it.' At any time, therefore, there is much opposition to a dynasty and rebellion against it. Ibn Khaldun then points to the ease with which Egypt could be governed; because in Egypt 'Royal authority is most peaceful and firmly rooted, because Egypt has few dissidents or people representing tribal groups. Egypt has a sultan and subjects' (Ibn Khaldun, 1967: 130). The crisis is therefore inevitable when a ri'asa proves to be unable firmly to dominate other group feelings and to draw them to accept its domination now formalised into 'state power'.

Luxury and procreation are linked. Ibn Khaldun distinguishes two stages: at the inception of the state luxury adds to its strength, because it leads to more procreation. The group grows in numbers and in strength. In addition, a great number of clients and followers (*mawali*) are acquired. But during the state's final days luxury becomes the sign of weakness and senility, owing to its negative demographic consequences, because it is sought for itself, not to strengthen the group. It is in this vein that Ibn Khaldun discusses the sensitive issue of Banu Quraysh's claim to legitimate authority. He treats a matter overloaded with clear ideological implications, in a dispassionate way: 'If we try to understand the *raison d'être* of this condition (that the Caliph should be a qurayshi), we shall find that it is based on the 'asibiyya which allows protection and ambition. This is its foundation and not — as many authors have claimed — the Qurayshis' closeness to the Prophet through direct lineage' (Ibn Khaldun, 1967: 195). In other words, the Qurayshis possess the political legitimacy not forever, but as long as they constitute a strong 'asabiyya. Ibn Khaldun could not accept the idea of a 'divine right' to rule.

Compared with these pivotal blood links, attachment to the land is much less important. The preference of a group for national or religious ties over those of patriotism (i.e. attachment to a territory) would be a self-inflicted weakness. Ibn Khaldun could not contradict a respected Caliph: 'Umar said:

33

learn your lineage and do not be like a commoner, if somebody asks of him his origin he would say from such and such a village.' Ibn Khaldun rules that belonging to a locality is something which is historically alien to Arab culture and which would threaten blood ties and consequently the very existence of the state. If some Arabs have been known by their locality, this was due to superficial and passing reasons, because for them lineage remains a more important base:

> It happened not because the Arabs rejected genealogical considerations, but because they acquired particular places of residence after the Conquest. They eventually became known by their places of residence. These became a distinguishing mark, *in addition to the pedigree* (our emphasis), used by the Arabs to identify themselves in the presence of their Amirs. Later on, sedentary Arabs intermingled with Persians and other non-Arabs. Purity of lineage was completely lost, and its fruit, the group feeling, was lost and rejected (Ibn Khaldun, 1967: 100).

In another part in the *Muqaddimah*, Ibn Khaldun criticises Abu al-Walid Ibn Rushd (Averroes), for deciding that long residence in a territory would be an ingredient in one's identity: 'I should like to know how long residence in a town can help (anyone to build loyalties to his person), if he does not belong to a group that makes him feared and causes others to obey him' (Ibn Khaldun, n.d. 135).

STATE BUILDING IN SAUDI ARABIA

Saudi Arabia as a state has many reasons to attract Khaldunian attention, beginning with the desert, enclaved environment in which the state was born. Of no less interest is its continued survival at a time when so many other states in the same region have perished. In two instances, vigour indeed returned to this state following severe defeats. The first was after the Ottoman-inspired Egyptian invasion of the Arabian Peninsula and the second following a bloody civil war in which brothers fought each other and in the process destroyed their father's state. The rise of the third Saudi state at the dawn of this century, and its domination, in less than a quarter of a century of military

campaigns, of four-fifths of the Arabian Peninsula, in addition
to its victorious entry into the age of the modern nation-state at
the beginning of the 1930s, probably transcends in importance
the power of the financial and oil factors that were discovered
and exploited years after the establishment of the Saudi state's
political-military structure (Salamé, 1980).

One major factor in the emergence of a Saudi state undoubtedly lies in *a religious call.* Following the death of Prophet
Muhammad, the history of the Arabian Peninsula was characterised by tribal and regional dispersion. The *da'wa* of Muhammad ibn 'Abd al-Wahhab (1703-92) carried, in addition to the
fundamental principles attached to the Hanbali ideas, a call for
unity among competing and conflicting factions. Thus al-
Muwahhidun, the self-given name of the movement, had two
meanings. The first was explicit: to re-assert the unity of God in
the face of the idolatrous practices to which most of the inhabitants of Najd used to resort. The other was implied: it aimed at
the unity of (at least) the Arabian Peninsula by the iltiham of
the various tribal attachments, around a new tribal ri'asa.

What could this unifying link be other than religion? In the
middle of the eighteenth century nationalism as a modern ideology formulated in Europe was scarcely known to the inhabitants
of this area and even if it had reached them, it would have
required generations before it became entrenched and before its
proponents could answer a basic question, that remains open to
this day: the nationalism of which nation — Saudi Arabia,
Arabia, the Arab or the Muslim world?

Islam was actually the only available unifying factor. All
Najdis also spoke Arabic, but language is an element of cultural
unity and would hardly be useful here as a tool of political
mobilisation. Through a religious revival movement, the new
call would eventually be able to mobilise the majority of the
area's inhabitants, i.e. Sunni-Muslims, Bedouins and settled,
Hasawi and Najdi, 'noble' and not. Its political strategy was
consequently to differ from that usually followed by neighbouring religious minorities, such as the Zaydis in Yemen, the Ibadis
in Oman's Green Mountains or the Shi'a in Bahrain and Hasa.
These minorities' objective was to survive as schismatic groups
united around specific interpretations of the Book and hence
with a built-in group solidarity. It was therefore natural to see
them entrenched in islands (Bahrain) and mountains (Oman
and Yemen) as an antidote to the continuous (and generally

35

hostile) pressure of the Sunni/orthodox majority on Islamic minorities and other *milal*. For these minorities, the strategy was basically that of self-defence, and an obstinate rejection of the calls for political or cultural integration into the prevailing majority.

Wahhabism, as its enemies usually called it, had another purpose, and a much wider potential audience. Its strategy was based on offence. Its implied premisses were that the whole world should adopt Islam and that all Muslims should go back to earlier orthodox religion, as interpreted by the Wahhabi reformer along Hanbali lines. Therefore it was a call directed towards all without exception, and the movement was eager to see it adopted by every tribe, in every oasis and village, either by persuasion or coercion, or usually through a combination of the two. Thus, the internal dynamics were those of attack, invasion and intervention, without which the movement could hardly have survived. The call was for the re-establishment of 'true Islam'. It did not claim to offer a minority interpretation of Islam, it was not based on a new religion, but on a fundamentalist interpretation embodying a strong nostalgia for the supposedly original Islam: simple, aggressive and victorious. This interpretation was to prove attractive to many eighteenth-century Arabians.

One could hardly be surprised to read in a British traveller's diary of 1784: 'When I arrived at Basra, the Ottoman Wali of Baghdad, his delegate in Basra as well as other Turks, were all worried by the activities of the leader of the Wahhabis. This is because they knew that Ibn 'Abd al-Wahhab's strict interpretation of the Quranic texts was the purest and most abiding by it' (Rentz 1972: 57). While two centuries later the Lebanese traveller Amin ar-Rihani described King 'Abd al''Aziz by saying: 'Sultan 'Abd al-'Aziz is the Saudi people's *imam* in every sense. He recognises the courageous, fearful, patient, sane and foolish among them, while he is also capable of ruling over them and thus placing them in the service of God and the Kingdom of Ibn Saud' (Ar-Rihani n.d.: 87).

This duality (God and Ibn Saud) embodies another component of the state's 'strength'. A geographic region (Najd) falls under the control of a coalition led by a ri'asa. The Saudi family's rule is established over other tribal alliances in the hinterland of the Arabian Peninsula. In other words, a superior 'asabiyya was able to defeat other group feelings and later to coalesce them into one greater group feeling. The religious call acted as a cement to make this coalescence (whatever its depth) possible in such a highly segmented tribal society

Ibn Khaldun is fond of repeating Prophet Muhammad's famous saying: 'God sent no prophet who did not enjoy the protection of his people'. He relates the story of Ibn Qasi, a sufi shaykh who rebelled in Andalusia without any tribes or group feelings to support him. He was soon forced to surrender to another Andalusian call. This is what the Wahhabi call knew how to avoid by attaching itself, a few years after its inception, to a strong tribal 'asabiyya, that of the Sa'ud family. This new, by now 'ideologised', group feeling was brought about through the adoption by the Amir of Dir'iyyah, Muhammad ibn Sa'ud, and following him, by his son 'Abd al-'Aziz, of the religious reformer's views. Both father and son, and the Amirs of the family who succeeded them, embraced that call. Thus an element of strength resulted from the blending of a religious call and a group feeling, in way Ibn Khaldun would have considered ideal. Since according to him:

> prophets in their religious propaganda depended on groups and families, though they could have been supported by God with anything in existence. If someone who is on the right path were to attempt [religious reforms] in this way, his isolation would keep him from [gaining the support of] group feeling and he would perish (Ibn Khaldun, n.d. 159).

He adds, with obvious sarcasm, 'Many deluded individuals took it upon themselves to establish the truth. They did not know that they would need group feeling for that'. He compares those who are not supported by a group feeling to the foolhardy who deserve to be ridiculed:

> They did not realise how their enterprise must necessarily end and what they would come to. Toward such people it is necessary to adopt one of the following courses. One may either treat them as if they are insane, may punish them either by execution or beatings when they cause trouble, or may ridicule them and treat them as buffoons (Ibn Khaldun, 1967: 124).

The Sa'ud family skilfully used the idea of equality among

37

believers in order to mobilise the Bedouin as an aggressive force against rivals and enemies. And they were to use the politically *status-quo*-oriented jurisprudential school of Inb Hanbali to strengthen the basis of their authority, once it was established. There is no doubt that the decision (*fatwa*) issued by Shaykh 'Abd al-Latif Ibn 'Abd ar-Rahman on lending political and religious legitimacy to the strong party in any civil war, is the best example of the use of the religious Wahhabi *da'wa* in strengthening the Sa'ud authority (Helms, 1981: 76-126). The bearers of the religious call were also instrumental in collecting taxes and then redistributing them in a way which was gradually to strengthen the 'legitimate' political authority, by cementing subtle forms of economic dependence among Bedouins (bounty) and the settled population (by ensuring stability and encouraging trade).

STRATEGIC IMMUNITY AND LEGITIMACY

Engaging now in geo-strategy, Ibn Khaldun makes what he considers as a central distinction between the state's core and its more distant periphery:

> This may be compared to light rays that spread from their centres or to circles that widen over the surface of the water when something strikes it. When the dynasty becomes senile and weak it begins to crumble at its extremities. The centre remains intact until God permits the destruction of the whole dynasty. Then the centre is destroyed. But when a dynasty is overrun from the centre it is of no avail to it that the outlying areas remain intact. It dissolves all at once (Ibn Khaldun, 1967: 128-9).

In other words, the degree to which the centre is immune in the face of external challenges and threats plays a pivotal role in the emergence of the state and later in its persistence and unavoidable decay. It is not an accident that the Saudi state happens to have been born in the heart of the Arabian Peninsula. In the mid-eighteenth century, during the state's formative years, it was neither easy nor very alluring to invade such a desert space and even less to colonise it. When the British and before them other naval powers (the Portuguese, Dutch and

French) circled the Arabian Peninsula, they landed in Aden, Muscat or Hudayda, but refrained from entering Arabia Deserta. They certainly realised the difficulty of the task involved and underrated its usefulness. Similarly, the Ottomans used to move from the north to the south along two axes: the first originated in Damascus, passed through Hijaz and ended in Hudayda; the second originated in Mosul, went on to Baghdad and Basra and reached al-Hasa via Kuwait. In both cases the Ottomans avoided entering the Arabian Peninsula's heartland. They seemed content merely to encircle it along the coasts of the Gulf and the Red Sea, leaving its rugged barren centre undisturbed. Muhammad 'Ali's was the first army of modern times to invade the Arabian Peninsula, cutting across it from the Red Sea to Hasa and destroying in the process the first Saudi state. However, the Egyptian ruler was soon obliged to pull back and retreat, providing an opportunity for the re-establishment of the Saudi state, in spite of the destruction of its capital, ad-Dir'iyyah, and the presence of many Amirs in Cairo as Muhammad 'Ali's captives.

A state whose centre is located in a region like Najd would benefit from a long period of time to develop and expand without being immediately threatened by external interference. This was the case with the first Saudi-Wahhabi state, which for a period of eighty years was hardly challenged. It was located in a remote region far outside the reach of strategic naval bases or important overland routes, in the midst of the inhospitable desert, the penetration of which, even by 'legitimate' Ottoman troops, was considered utterly senseless. One might even assume that the *wali* of Basra could not easily assess the strength of the new state or the ambitions of its leaders, except after a long lapse of time. For who in the Middle East was then capable of concluding that a new powerful state had been born, and not just a new vulnerable coalition of tribes which, a few months or a few years later, would naturally disintegrate.

This asset is clearer when one compares the Egyptian experience of Muhammad 'Ali at the beginning of the nineteenth century with that of the Sa'uds, two state-building processes taking place in roughly the same era. There is no doubt that the ambitious and highly organised Albanian soldier possessed enviable instruments of power, in contrast to those at the disposal of the Amir of Najd. Egypt under Muhammad 'Ali enjoyed a surplus in agricultural production, relatively well

39

organised and well equipped military power, openness to the outside world, not to mention the experience Muhammad 'Ali himself already had in leadership and international affairs. Paradoxically, because of all these factors, Egypt did not enjoy Najd's immunity. It was permanently in danger of being conquered and occupied precisely because it was so open to the outside world and strategically located on the road to India, and on that strip of the south-eastern coast of the Mediterranean.

Galal Ahmad Amin has accurately observed that the degree of Western pressure over the different parts of the Arab world varied with the strategic importance of the country or with the raw materials it provided. Thus, while Egypt, Syria and Iraq were connected to the Western economy by the middle of the nineteenth century, the relative unimportance of the Libyan desert allowed the spread of the Sanusiyya movement. This movement survived until 1911 when the Italian occupiers destroyed it. Similarly, it was only at the end of the nineteenth century that Britain became interested in developing the agricultural resources of Sudan. Thus in the second half of the nineteenth century, Sudan experienced the rise of an independence movement similar to the Sanusi and Wahhabi movements. This was the al-Mahdiyya movement, which ruled over Sudan for thirteen years (1885-98), during which it unified the greater part of the country, eliminated the slave trade and enjoyed great popularity not only in Sudan, but also in Egypt where many Egyptians pinned great hopes on it to save them from British occupation. The strategic importance of the coastal regions overlooking the Arabian Gulf made Britain impose on their tribal shaykhs consecutive defence pacts during the last two decades of the nineteenth century. However, the unnattractiveness of the economic and strategic conditions existing in the Arabian Peninsula and Yemen allowed this region to be left on its own until the discovery of oil after World War I (Amin, 1979: 97).

Galal Amin suggests that the failure of Muhammad 'Ali's Egypt and the relative success of a state such as Japan in modernisation, industrialisation and development during the nineteenth century are to a great extent due to the relative geographic seclusion of the latter in comparison with the former's geographic centrality, depriving it of a necessary level of immunity to foreign pressure. It is indeed agreed that the location of a strategically situated state represents a source of weakness rather than of strength, when this state is not powerful enough to defend the resources and/or the services which it provides.

The relative seclusion of Najd led to yet another ingredient in the young Saudi state's strength. Abdallah Laroui points to the way nationalist forces with a fundamentalist outlook have viewed the rational reforms which the colonial powers brought to the heart of the traditional Arab state:

> it was probable or actually expected that the nationalist movement would give birth to a theory of the state, completely different from the ulama conception of authority. However, the foreign domination of authority . . . forced the nationalists to adopt the fundamentalists's view whole-heartedly. The legitimate imamate which was a utopia when authority was in the hands of Muslims, became a double utopia when real authority was controlled by Europeans while claiming the application of justice and declaring the dispensability of the revealed divine law. During the modern age the instruments of state were reformed and the economic conditions, even those of the lower classes, improved. However, the state remained alien and the society miserable (Laroui, 1981: 139).

The refusal of anything European was indeed stronger in nationalist circles than the acceptance of these modern 'benefits' of domination. Foreign powers' domination consequently had negative effects on the legitimacy of the local forces which agreed to co-operate with them. When the British Empire was helping a state such as the Amirate of Bahrain or the Sultanate of Oman to survive it was at the same time weakening these states' legitimacy. Foreign support seemed to produce an ambiguous reaction in which admiration for the ruler's craftsmanship in securing a great power's support was mixed with the idea that his rule could not survive this power's change of mind or its departure. Hence the necessity of securing the ruler's legitimacy through bureaucratic, Western-inspired achievements such as an improved health service, a modern education system, or organised police and military forces which compared favorably with neighbouring emirates' forces.

In clear contrast to the Gulf shaykhdoms or Transjordan, the Saudi state was certainly not the product of a foreign intervention, and its legitimacy was hardly based on the kind of support it was getting from Britain. Quite to the contrary, the *imara* was established despite the opposition of the external powers (the Ottoman Empire and Britain) and at their expense. Thus its legitimacy was based not so much on the Western-inspired services it offered to its citizens as on a mixture of local nationalism and religious fundamentalism which embodied a definite chauvinism. In such Arab states as Bahrain, Kuwait, Jordan and Morocco the colonial powers penetrated the local authority and, in a mimetic drive, created the structure of a modern local bureaucracy. Whether through a military government, a *Haut-Commissaire*, or a Political Resident, the British and French Governments directed, commanded, discussed and rationalised from within the local authority either as 'employees' of the prince or as his advisers. External power became a basic element in the local equation of power, which in the process restructured the local administration and increased its adaptability.

This osmosis between the two powers weakened the legitimacy of the local power, though it provided it with the ability to control its citizens and expand its bureaucracy, thereby enabling it to maintain authority in a more 'modern' way. The Saudi state, at least up until World War I, did not go through this process of penetration/satellisation which was spreading from the capital of the Ottoman Empire in Istanbul to such tiny Amirates as Bahrain. The Saudi state (like the Sanusi state up until the Italian conquest, or the Madhist state until it was militarily defeated by Gordon) remained largely outside the colonial realm and to a great extent secured a 'nationalist-fundamentalist' legitimacy. The institution-building process was much less the result of Western-inspired 'expertise' than an authentic attempt to meet the challenge of foreign forces beyond the borders of the Saudi nucleus.

A comparison with one or two other Arab states will clarify the concept of legitimacy in relation to the early contact with international powers. In his book on the rise of the Saudi state in the period between 1910 and 1926, Gary Troeller observed that relations between Britain and 'Abd al-'Aziz ibn Sa'ud barely existed, since the former did not believe that Ibn Sa'ud posed any threat to its regional interests, while 'Abd al-'Aziz was still reluctant to engage in foreign relations which could undermine his 'asabiyya. The *rapprochement* was basically dictated by the necessities imposed by World War I. This *rapprochement* did not cause Britain to intrude into this nascent desert country as was the case with Sharif Husayn ibn 'Ali in al-Hijaz. Rather, it led to an agreement specifying borders and later to Britain's gradual acceptance of the continuous Saudi expansion. Ibn Sa'ud was able to go beyond the red lines that Britain specified for him, having imposed himself on Britain as an independent and ambitious leader. This was to help strengthen his authority substantially *vis-à-vis* his Arabian rivals since, as Stinchcombe has put it, as far as legitimacy is concerned, 'The person over whom power is exercised is not usually as important as other powerholders' (Stinchcombe, 1968: 150).

In comparison, things were radically different in a country like Jordan, where Britain played an essential role in the very creation of the state. This could be explained by Britain's prior attachment to the Hashemite family and by the continuous presence of a number of British officials and soldiers in Amman. To 'legitimise' the deep British penetration of the newly established state there was the League of Nations mandate, an experience which Saudi Arabia has never been compelled to undergo. And in Amman, 'given the impoverishment of the new kingdom, both the British envoy and the financial counsellor in the administration of finance were given the right to supervise all financial affairs . . . Then the details of the general budget were submitted to the British envoy, who in turn transferred them to the British High Commissioner in Jerusalem and then to the Minister of Colonies in London to approve them' (al-Mahafdha, 1973: 38).

In this respect one could consider Lebanon, for example, as falling somewhere between the Saudi and the Jordanian examples. Meir Zamir's dual conclusion is accurate: modern Lebanon is the product of the evolution of the centuries-old Druze imara into a Maronite-dominated entity as well as of French colonial designs. His study of the state's formative years (1920-6) clearly shows that the geo-social nucleus of a state was well-entrenched in the area when the French were given the mandate over Lebanon and Syria. They played a central role in defining the new state's borders, but they did not create it (Zamir, 1985; Salibi, 1965; Harik, 1968 and in this volume).

Saudi Arabia stands out in a positive way, when compared to these two and other examples, at least as far as legitimacy based on 'authentic', non-Western-induced state-building is concerned. But should these credentials lead to the conclusion that the regime's legitimacy is endowed with a resilience that is beyond erosion?

INTEGRATION IN THE WORLD SYSTEM: THE EFFECTS

Legitimacy, when it exists, is certainly not resilient to all kinds of challenges. The first among them is the largely unsuccessful attempt at compulsory social integration. The Saudi leaders have tried to create an integrated society by bringing together different tribes whose men were militarily trained and drawn into a religious 'asabiyya. By this means, each was to become the 'brother' of the other, in spite of differences in their tribal allegiances. It has become clear that this experience did not actually succeed, as the various *hijra* (intended to mix tribes together) continued to be characterised by the domination of specific tribal cleavages. True iltiham is indeed very difficult to trigger, despite the combined and intensive use of two supra-tribal cleavages: first, the Wahhabi da'wa and then the allegiance to the modern Saudi national state.

When the creation of this state became the conqueror's exclusive endeavour, the clash with the religious zealots and the feared soldiers of the *Ikhwan* became inevitable. This clash was indeed to be a watershed in the Kingdom's history for several reasons. 'Abd al-'Aziz had first to mobilise troops to fight against the rebellious Ikhwan and to do this he cleverly used tribal cleavages as well as the settled population's fear of Bedouin extremism, thereby acknowledging the disintegration of the inter-tribal coalition between the Bedouin and the settled population which made possible the re-emergence of Saudi rule.

Abd al-'Aziz also had to call for (or at least to accept) external help in order to crush the rebellious Ikhwan. Hence the utopia of an 'authentic' state, built outside the reach of foreign powers and at their expense, was seriously undermined. The West was no longer a *kafir* enemy, but an ally in the fight against those groups who most clearly embodied the traditional religious-chauvinistic legitimacy. British financial aid was rapidly to follow military support, and the Saudi ruler's position came gradually to resemble that of his previously deposed neighbours, such as the two Hashemite kings of Jordan and Iraq or the Gulf shaykhs, surviving under, and thanks to, British protection. This integration into the world system had huge implications for the state's vision of its own capabilities and for the ways in which its survival could be secured. 'Abd al-'Aziz was to trade his imam title for a secular royal one; the country was to sign border treaties and thereby accept an imposed limitation on the spread of the da'wa; the idea of coexisting with differently-minded neighbours and with foreign colonial powers was to prevail and, last but not least, oil explorers were to be tolerated in the Kingdom.

The Bedouin were to be the designated victims of this shift in the King's political strategy:

Although the alliance of the al-Sa'ud and the Badu in the early twentieth century had fulfilled specific functions, especially the military expansion of the kingdom, it was not practical. While the al-Sa'ud emphasized the unity of 'church' and 'state' as well as the legitimacy of their own authority, they were eventually forced because of external influences to define their state on a territorial basis (Helms, 1981: 272).

The Saudis were indeed to witness a clear concentration of power within the now-royal family, and eventually within one exclusive 'House', that of 'Abd al-'Aziz (Salamé, 1982). Largely similar movements of power concentration took place in Bahrain, Kuwait or Qatar. In these shaykhdoms, however, politics were traditionally dominated by a ruling coalition between the Amir and the leading trading families. But, with oil, the Amirs were able not only to settle the ruling families' debts to the merchants, but also collectively to buy them off. 'As a result, trading families in both states rose economically, but declined politically' (Crystal, 1985: 27).

Swords and British help were to defeat the Bedouin and oil was to cut the appetite of the settled population for political participation. Studying the Iranian case, Skocpol (1982) has concluded that huge and sudden oil revenues can render states more autonomous vis-à-vis domestic social and political actors, but more vulnerable in moments of crisis. In Saudi Arabia and the Gulf shaykhdoms at least the first part of this proposition can be verified. And this trend is not restricted to oil countries, but has a special significance in those where extractive industries

45

are central in the economy (Evans in Evans, Rueschemeyer and Skocpol, 1985: 119-226).

This state 'autonomy' on the domestic level, coupled with a deepening integration in the world economic system, naturally leads rulerships to seek other bases of legitimacy, other definitions of strength: a welfare state, a skilful redistribution of resources, some form of co-optation within the new elites. While the process is taking place, these countries' political evolution remains largely unpredictable, because it is very hard to measure, at a particular moment, the extent to which these new elements of the state's legitimacy have been integrated into the political culture. Political socialisation is by definition a long-term process, and even longer in these countries where, in contrast to Iran, the ruler is reluctant radically to depart from his traditional bases of legitimacy, or to trade them completely for his new role as head of state. He will hesitate before operating such a radical shift, correctly recognising that, among his 'subjects', identification with the abstract concept of a national state remains vulnerable. The society indeed remains vertically disintegrated and rival groups may use any shift in policy to organise along old tribal or geographical cleavages, around a new ri'asa.

LEBANON: A STATE IN A SOCIETY AT WAR

For the individual, this shift is certainly not an easy process, and this can not be ignored even by the 'modernisation' school of analysis. Lucian Pye has noted that 'the stable modern state cannot be realized without a clear feeling of identity: that is, without solving the problem of the co-existence of traditional cultural forms with modern practices and factional allegiances with cosmopolitan lifestyles. It is as if the individual is torn between the two worlds without having roots in either of them' (Pye, 1962: 63).

Erich Fromm is more explicit in the description of this new psychological dilemma (1960: 29):

> The identity with nature, clan, religion, gives the individual security. He belongs to, he is rooted in, a structuralised whole in which he has an unquestionable place. He may suffer from hunger or suppression but he does not suffer from the worst of all pains: complete aloneness and doubt.

The rise of the modern state represents a real challenge to the individual, a challenge to his feeling of belonging to a group and to the security of having a defined place within it. The transfer of loyalty from the traditional group to the modern state can not be easily completed, and anyway takes place in a clearly alienating manner. It is doubly alienating when not only the form of the state is unfamiliar but when those commanding it are strangers as well. This could be due to the leader's allegiance to an external power (during the period of colonialism), or to his membership in another traditional group (much as a Shi'i would look at a Sunni-dominated state or a Berber at a state dominated by the Arabs), or to his belonging to a social group that is unfamiliar to the rest of the citizenry (such as technocrats or professionals).

Thus, suddenly, the citizen is given an identity card or a passport specifying for him a new exclusive identity. He is either Lebanese or Syrian, Tunisian or Libyan, Qatari or Bahraini. Yet a real identity crisis exists underneath this change in outward form. To quote Fromm again (1960: 177):

The loss of the self and its substitution by a pseudo-self leave the individual in an intense state of insecurity. He is obsessed by doubt since, being essentially a reflex of other people's expectations of him, he has in a measure lost his identity. In order to overcome the panic resulting from such loss of identity, he is compelled to conform to seek his identity by continuous approval and recognition by others.

The Lebanese war has harshly revealed the fragility of the state within the society, due, among other factors, to the failure of (Ibn Khaldun's) iltiham and to the lack of (Fromm's) 'continuous recognition'. The most revealing fact of this situation is the survival of the state itself, not through the strength of its internal structures but for much the same reasons as those explaining its weakness.

With the prevailing international system not favouring any geographical reformulation of existing political entities, whether through partition and division or through integration and unity, any state is in a way guaranteed its existence. And this is all the more so in sensitive regions like the Middle East because here a challenge to a state's existence might lead to a reformulation of the political map and consequently to wars that are not necessarily desirable. Regardless of internal wars, the state remains intact as a form through the support and recognition of regional and international powers. The Lebanese state, at least since 1975, is to a great extent a form without a substance.

Some Lebanese have felt that they were alien to the Lebanese identity and that this was imposed on them by external powers. Before Lebanon's independence in 1943, Muslims often expressed their desire to be part of Syria instead of being 'artificially' attached to Mount Lebanon. And when the domestic balance of power shifted after 1975, many Maronites felt that remaining in Greater Lebanon was becoming too heavy a burden for them, and was no longer the asset it had been in the days when — thanks to their higher level of education, their advanced 'asabiyya and the support France was providing to them — they had greater control over the country. Most of the Muslims before 1943 and some Maronites after 1975 think therefore that, to use Clifford Geertz's distinction, their attachment to Lebanon is not 'primordial', is not 'given', and could consequently be negotiated or even radically repudiated.

But these people also feel that they cannot really alter a *status quo* which is beyond their power. Identity is indeed a cultural product which is not exclusively shaped by those who are going to bear it. David Laitin has successfully shown that foreign powers have been able to intervene substantially in this process. Their success could be measured by the extent to which 'locals' viewed as 'authentic' and 'primordial' a cleavage which was previously identified and supported by the hegemonic power (Evans, Rueschemeyer, Skocpol, 1985: 285-316). Berber identity indeed depended on the Berbers' and Arabs' views as much as on the French strategy concerned with political cleavages in North Africa, and the determination with which this strategy was pursued. Ian Lustick has convincingly demonstrated how Israel has pursued a policy of direct control over the Arabs living within the pre-1967 borders through a mixture of segmentation, co-optation and economic dependence. The following words by an Israeli anthropologist, quoted by Lustick, should consequently be viewed more like a government programme than a mere description:

> Arabs in Israel do not constitute a united, integrated community. They are divided on many lines which tend to overlap, rather than cut across each other. There is the broad

division into Bedouin, village dwellers and townsmen, with hardly any links between those divisions. Furthermore, each of these divisions is divided internally, etc. (Lustick, 1980: 82).

As far as Lebanon is concerned, it is difficult to believe that the war has suddenly unleashed all these competing loyalties, thus leading to the collapse of the state. The Lebanese have generally known how to live 'outside the state'. Their wealth and most of their cultural and political trends have been imported. Their press was often established and/or subsidised by foreigners. The economy has been restricted to the private sector, and only with great difficulty can a popular trend be found supporting state intervention in the economy and society. Actually it was very easy for the mercantile right to destroy the only attempt aimed at giving the state a social, economic and security base: President Fuad Shihab's regime (1958-64) which vanished during the second half of the 1960s under the attack of the representatives of radical Lebanese individualism, and later under the parallel attacks of militarised sectarian forces and the Palestinians.

The Lebanese state did not fall in 1975, it continued outside society by means of the external recognition it still enjoyed. Following the failure of the Shihabi initiative which was based on some *sens de l'état*, the problem of identity was exacerbated and went on to destroy the basis of the society. States are in need of suitable political cultures which they can adopt as legitimate legal frameworks. Under Shihab, the Lebanese state, as in other Third World countries, attempted to develop this same political culture through political socialisation focusing on such concepts as national unity, religious sectarian co-existence and Lebanon as a final indisputable entity. Yet the war was also to reveal the failure of Lebanese iltiham, which was meant to rise within the modern state in defence of its borders and institutions.

The war also led to the strengthening of sectarianism as a central political cleavage. But its victory was never complete. Many Lebanese were too accustomed to 'the Lebanese idea', or too opposed to sectarianism, to be born-again Maronites or Shi'a. And sectarianism itself remained ambiguous, since the new warlords were continuously changing their strategy, stressing one day the sectarian cleavage (Maronites-Sunnites-Druzes,

49

etc.) and the religious binary cleavage (Muslim/Christian) the next (Salamé, 1986).

The Lebanese case is extreme but not exceptional. Indeed, the Arab state seems to be caught between the combined fire of sub-state and supra-state forces. Hanna Arendt points to the crisis of states in the face of greater nationalities transcending their limits (a good example being German nationalism). This is why, for example, pan-Germanist Schroener was among the bitterest enemies of the state, as was pan-Slavist Rozanov. Both looked with disdain at modern international political entities and considered them obstacles in the way of a nation's self-fulfillment. Both can inspire (and have inspired) the propagators of the Islamic nation, or those championing the unity of Greater Syria, and most importantly, the modern Arab nationalists. A 1985 editorial of *Al-Mustaqbal al-'Arabi*, probably the best scholarly journal to appear in Arabic, included the following evaluation:

> All appearances point to the spread of the phenomenon of the state in the Arab world. But, in spite of these appearances, the failure of the Arab state — despite its slogans, flag, national anthem, university, plan and national museum — in achieving true independence and in eliminating all kinds of dependence, or in liberating the occupied Arab territories in Palestine, not to mention the failure to accomplish national security on the part of all states, will sooner or later strengthen the Arab citizen's conviction that the state has failed to achieve the major objectives it has set for itself. Consequently, this same Arab citizen will be inclined to work at a national [pan-Arab] level and transcend the local state phenomenon (Hasib, 1985: 7).

The above statement approximates the idea of the state to a mere 'local phenomenon'. Any acceptance of such an attitude is a blow to the legitimacy of existing Arab states. The writer of this article, like other Arab nationalists, seeks the achievement of precisely this aim. The need to fulfil this objective is stronger among Arab nationalists than it is among proponents of the Islamic *umma* who generally seem to accept the independent existence of the current Islamic states, as long as they adopt the Islamic *shari'ah* and its laws, and seek active 'solidarity' with other Islamic countries. The aim of Arab nationalism is the

50

elimination of all existing states and their integration into one Arab state. Twentieth-century Islamism (Al-Banna, Quth, 'Awdah) is more interested in domestic politics than in bringing about the unity of the world's Muslims into one state.

Whether Arab nationalists, propagators of Greater Syria or of the Islamic unity, like it or not, they are working alongside other enemies of existing states that are also intent on undermining their legitimacy. These enemies are sectarian, tribal and ethnic movements which, in turn, also aim at reformulating the existing political map. While Arab nationalists regard contemporary states as too small clothes for the Arabs to wear, others find these same states too large or completely unsuitable. The Kurds, for example, may well believe that borders were drawn with the specific intention of dispersing them into a number of states.

Whether Kurds, Maronites, Berbers or south Sudanese, these groups often reject the states in which they find themselves. Even when they adopt a more rational and realistic attitude and recognise that existing states cannot be easily destroyed, they prefer them to be weak and fragile, allowing ethnic groups the largest possible autonomy. This autonomy must also be expressed geographically, that is, self-rule in specific regions in which these groups enjoy a demographic superiority, or as the euphemism goes in Lebanon 'de-centralisation in security and development matters'. Foreign interference is rendered easy and attractive by these separatist trends.

A short-cut remedy to all these problems is 'unity'. Anyone following the Lebanese war will recall that it was continuously said that the solution lay in the unity of the Maronites or of the Shi'a, unity of Muslims or Christians, national (Lebanese) unity, unity with Syria, or Arab unity. Too often 'unity' appears as a panacea, whatever the political cleavage. This reveals this 'remedy's' highly ideological nature and hence its extreme vulnerability. In so far as the identity remains debatable, in so far as those in control of the state have not established a strong social iltiham, unity remains an empty shell. This widespread obsession with unity is so 'tribal' (Arendt) that it becomes a sort of 'political religion' (Apter), with no real impact on the society. It probably also hinders a more rational search for state strength, outside the old Khaldunian realm.

HOW IMPORTANT IS THE ECONOMY?

Yet where does the source of strength lie? Is it found in a strong economy? Among the interesting elements in Ibn Khaldun's thinking is the place given to economic activity, as he describes the five stages of the state: the first stage is that of success; the second is the one in which the ruler gains complete control over his people. The fourth is one of contentment and peacefulness and the fifth is one of waste and squandering. The economic stage is the third:

> It is the stage of leisure and tranquillity in which the fruits of royal authority are enjoyed: the things that human nature desires, such as acquisition of property, creation of lasting monuments and fame. All the ability (of the ruler) is expended on collecting taxes; regulating income and expenses, keeping books and planning expenditure; erecting large buildings, and constructions, spacious cities and lofty monuments; presenting gifts to ambassadors of nobility from (foreign) nations and tribal dignitaries; and dispensing bounty to his people. In addition, he supports the demands of his followers and retinue with money and positions. He inspects his soldiers, pays them well and distributes their allowances fairly every month. Eventually, the result of this (liberality) shows itself in their dress, their fine equipment and their armour on parade days.

Even more interesting is his conclusion, when he says: 'this stage is the last during which the ruler is in complete authority' (Ibn Khaldun, 1967: 141-2).

Why should the economic stage be in the third position and yet be the last stage during which the ruler is in complete authority? Ibn Khaldun points out two basic factors. First, that the economy (actually economic capability) is related to actual political and military strength; thus, when superiority is achieved and the authority of the ruler is established, wealth comes as a natural bonus to whoever is in control. Second, that economic activity is not so much related to production as it is to spending. This is why this stage does not lead to more strength, but actually leads to the stage of senility. *Iqtissad*, in contrast to the usual meaning of the word (that is, to cut down on expenses), is based on spending. Its political result is not so much derived from the strengthening of the economic and then the political structure of the state, as it is from giving both supporters and enemies the indisputable impression of luxury and of an unlimited capacity to spend. This will enhance the state's authority since it is capable of buying loyalties and paying the military.

For anyone who has travelled in the Arab oil countries, this view can hardly be surprising. But one could get an identical impression in other poorer countries, as this conclusion on Syria's industrial efforts, drawn by Michel Seurat shows:

> It is not necessary to be an expert in economic anthropology to discover that a factory in the public sector there does not function like a similar one in France, as the real reason behind its presence is not the achievement of profits, as much as it is to provide a means for spending. This spending represents a part of the strategy of the political authority and provides it with a new source of strength (Bourgey *et al.* 1982: 35).

If this analysis holds in Syria, it is all the more relevant in Arabia where, historically, stable powers used to persuade long-range caravan tradesmen to take their routes through their areas. One could hardly say that this long-range caravan trade 'created' states, since it was vulnerable and therefore dependent on the level of security that was established along its routes. Hence the weakness of the vulgar 'Marxist' theory that conquerors, ambitious Amirs or established tribal leaderships were the mere tools of these merchants. These leaderships were certainly affected by this trade and very much relied on the mixture of protection and racketeering which they exercised over it. Without it, a military-political tribal power would have had less control over its troops, or would have been less influential with the area's smaller tribes, but it would not have disappeared altogether.

In modern Kuwait and Saudi Arabia no ideologised economic nationalisations took place, as was the case in Syria or Iraq. But are the consequences any different? In the Gulf countries political leadership is clearly based on 'asabiyya. This leadership has ruled from the outset that the oil is state property. But what is the state? The state was then more a cover for a ri'asa than an 'autonomous' apparatus. Money, which essentially means immense oil revenues, was controlled by the governing families, by small groups of brothers and cousins who head the ruling families and rule the rest of the people. Since oil is itself the revenue that is extracted by means of the help of external Western technology, it is not really subject to the laws of production. And one is often tempted to compare the relationship in the 1940s or 1950s between the new Saudi state and the international oil companies with the one binding its ancestors with long-range tradesmen. An enclaved economic activity was merely paying the dues for a continued peaceful expansion. For the state, the issue is not about the means of production or its actual development, nor about the identity of those controlling it. Rather, it is about the way the oil revenues are distributed, about the identity of those controlling this process, about the amount of money that is being distributed and the identity of the beneficiaries.

If this is how things stand in such countries, then it is no wonder that a country like Saudi Arabia did not and could not provide a sufficient political cover for a number of American political projects in the region. A country's capabilities do not lie only in the extraction of millions of barrels of oil per day, nor in the fact that a quarter of the world's oil reserves are found under its deserts, nor in receiving billions of dollars of revenues or, finally, in the possession of huge financial reserves. These assets would have constituted a real 'power' if they had been found in a fully developed country like Britain or France. But Saudi Arabia is a country with a small population. It is technologically underdeveloped, unable to integrate women into the work force, dependent on millions of foreign workers and possessing only one almost exclusive and exhaustible source of revenue: oil. In addition to all this, Saudi Arabia continues to be militarily weak in a region characterised by intense conflicts and the emergence of strong military forces (Iraq, Iran, Israel). Given all these facts, it cannot limit itself to the immense oil revenues if the 'asabiyya is in danger or if the ri'asa is threatened. It might even be that the present state of oil revenues is not the last stage in which these gulf ri'asas are in control. Is not the ease with which money is procured a sign of senility?

Arab political culture is rarely tuned to stock market indicators. Although there are Arab economists, the existence of Arab economic thought and its influence on society remains an open question ('Abd al-Fadil, 1983). The Arab renaissance was not characterised by a clear interest in economics. Even a figure known for his great openness to 'modernity', such as Ahmad Lutfi as-Sayyid, was not concerned with this topic. As noted by Albert Hourani, 'industry is not, in his opinion, the basis of national strength. All his emphasis is on a strong national consciousness' (Hourani, 1983: 181). In a more general summary Hourani had observed that

> the content of nationalism in this period included few precise ideas about social reform and economic development. This may have been a result of indifference, or of the fact that most of the leaders and spokesmen of the nationalist move- ments either belonged to families of standing and wealth or had raised themselves into that class by their own efforts. But it can also be explained by the liberal atmosphere of the time ... To be independent in the language of the time, was to have internal autonomy and be a member of the League of Nations (ibid.: 344).

Did this interest in the economy develop after World War II? It certainly increased for a variety of reasons, among them being: the growth of socialist thought, the process of nationalisations and socialist practices adopted in more than one country, not to mention the establishment of economics departments in a number of Arab universities. There is an increased coverage of economic affairs in the media and the establishment of a number of specialised journals and newspapers in the field. A quantitative development has certainly taken place. Yet econ- omic 'power' as an important factor to be dealt with remains largely absent from the works of political activists. For a long time, economic journalism in the Arab world was the work of foreigners or local Christians and mainly directed towards them. This was the case with *Le Commerce du Levant*, Beirut or with *La Bourse*, Alexandria. Following these came *Al-Ahram al- Iqtissadi*, published in Arabic, as well as *Al-Bayan*, *Al-Masarif* or *Al-Iqtissad wa al-A'mal*.

Yet one cannot conclude that the economic question has become an integral part of political culture. One might compare, for example, the reactions to a contemporary event such as the 1979 Iranian Revolution. At the time of its occur- rence, many Western observers began to question what type of economic and international economic relations the new regime

55

would adopt, while Arab commentators, both supporters and critics, were almost entirely concentrating on personalities, parties, or even the theological-political debate. The thousands of pages written on the nature of the 'Islamic economy' are in large part boring and scarcely informative and the reader may eventually reach the conclusion arrived at by Samir Amin, that the 'Islamic economy, in the real sense of the word, outside of a number of fundamental slogans and measures, can hardly be regarded as Islamic' (Amin, 1982a: 181-98).

Arab political culture is to a great extent the reflection of a centuries-old reality: economic and financial resources did not play a central role in the establishment of political power in the Arab world. Consequently, people still refrain from viewing them as being necessary elements of power. Wealth is the reward received by the powerful and not the source of this power. One could argue that such an un-economic political culture is the most suitable local complement to foreign economic domination.

THE (ARAB) MAN ON HORSEBACK

Ri'asa is basically achieved by military means. Following the 1967 defeat, Nasser said: 'What has been taken by force, cannot be claimed back except through force'. Did not Max Weber himself describe the Arab as 'a warrior more than anything else'? Was not Saudi authority established on the basis of repeated military campaigns initiated by a small group of armed men in their bid to control Riyadh in the mid-eighteenth century, with similar attempts being made in the nineteenth and twentieth centuries? Similarly, was not the independent Algerian state established through a popular liberation war that expelled the French *colons* and established a national state? Did not the military dominate the Arab state, with the aim of endowing it with more strength and rationality, and with an organised, modern and effective military spirit? It is not easy to link the yearning for the great Islamic conquests and the ambitions of certain current officers in their attempt to build a better future through power? Only a few years back, the parents of a would-be bride were accustomed to say that the bridegroom had to be an officer or he would not do (*Mulazim* or *mu lazim* in a Damascene accent).

Arab culture presents us with contradictory images of the military. On the one hand, there are the glorious conquests and the great military leaders, such as Khalid ibn al-Walid, 'Uqbah ibn Nafi' and Tariq ibn Ziyad, the great victories of the wars of *Ridda* (apostasy) and conquests stretching from Khurasan to Andalusia. However, this bright image of the Arab military was to a large extent replaced by another: the image of foreign mercenaries who, through the adoption of Islam, were able to become an integral part of authority and consequently transformed the Caliphate into a formal instrument in their hands. This transformation most probably began in the ninth century less than two centuries after the establishment of the empire. Turkish soldiers played an important role in the dismissal of Caliphs and the designation of their successors. They also took part in the suppression of rural and urban insurrections. A clear separation took place between the Arabs and the military, with the latter's transformation from conquerors of new lands into mere protectors of those in power.

This historical development is probably central in understanding the present ambiguity in the Arab's view of the soldier. As noted by Claude Cahen, 'The armies of conquest were for the most part composed only of Arabs'. But in the Umayyad period, the great distances separating warriors and their tribes made conquests more difficult to carry out than before. Following their successful uprising, the Abbasids formed their main army from the Khurasani troops. This meant that they put an end to the role of Arabs in war and their claim to war booty. Distrust of Arabs grew and intensified during the reign of al-Ma'mun, when he rejected any military volunteers of Arab origin. A substantial number of Arabs who used to form the army of conquest were forced into misery and returned to a Bedouin way of life. Matters deteriorated further when al-Mu'tasim imported slaves and through them created a separate force with a Turkish majority. Cahen believes that the creation of this settled army in Samarra' meant in practice the forsaking of all fighting outside the country.

All things considered, the soldiers were aliens to the nation and their conflicts were unrelated to the problems of the people. Hence, the army was perceived as an alien system and the system which provided this army with political cadres was also an unfamiliar one and unwillingly accepted by the

57

people. As for the army, it perceived that the Caliphate was incapable of doing without it and thus became even more aggressive (Cahen, 1977: 164).

There is no doubt that the first Islamic conquests still stir up a yearning for them. Yet we should also take into consideration the intervening centuries of alienation between the people and the military, in the professional, political and ethnic realms, for al-Mu'tasim's example was adopted on an even larger scale in the centuries that followed. The Saljuks, in their time, became the victims of the same slaves that used to form the bulk of the army, until the Mamluks established control in the thirteenth century under the leadership of Buyides. Following them, the Ottomans, through their domination of most of the Islamic world, fully achieved the surrender of form (the Islamic Caliphate) to the content of power (the militaristic ethnic group feeling). The two examples of the Janissaries and the foreign military aristocracy, which continued to rule Egypt in one form or another until 1952, point to the continued elimination of Arabs from the military and to the division of society into two groups: the military and the civilian population (*al-'Askar'al Ra'iyya*).

It is therefore not difficult to understand why the image of the military in the political culture was shaken. A number of those who studied Egyptian society (Edward Lane, Husayn Fawzi) concluded that there are reservations among all parts of Egyptian society about joining the army. Henry Ayrout concentrated on the inclination of the Egyptian peasant towards peacefulness and his distaste for revolution and bloodshed. In one of his moving productions, the Egyptian film director Salah Abu Seif portrays the image of an officer (Omar Sharif) who is unable to attain his position except through the help of his sister who becomes a prostitute for this purpose. In the end, however, when he discovers this, the officer kills his sister.

Leaders and intellectuals of the period prior to 1945 were rarely interested in developing the military. Al-Afghani was only concerned with finding the source of the early Muslim's strength in confronting the enemies of Islam. Muhammad 'Abduh's negative reaction towards the insurrection of 'Urabi comes as no surprise. 'Abduh's analysis of this incident remains on the personal and psychological level. He believes that 'Urabi was an Egyptian officer who revolted for the simple reason of the preference of Circassian officers over him in the military hierarchy. As for 'Urabi's later interest in the idea of calling the parliament to convene and introduce political reform, 'Abduh believes that it was only an attempt to legitimise his movement. 'Abduh's discussion of 'Urabi's movement is full of sarcasm; he portrays the Egyptian officer as a naive reader of newspapers and magazines, taking superficial political ideas from them but lacking the capacity to understand them.

Similarly, it is very difficult to find among the intellectuals of the next period such as Constantine Zuraiq or Sati' al-Husri any real interest in the problem of the establishment of Arab military potential. It seems as if the well-established remoteness between the intellectuals, attempting to speak in the name of the people, and the military continued to exist.

The picture began to change in the 1930s. In Iraq, through Bakr Sidqi and Rashad 'Ali al-Kaylani, the military entered politics by force. In Syria, Husni az-Za'im began a long series of military *coups*. In Egypt the revolution of 1952 entrenched its authority on the basis of a new military-based form of legitimacy. In Algeria, after three years of Ben Bella's rule, the military seized political power. The toppling of the royalist regime in Iraq led, among other things, to the elimination of the civil factions that had contributed to bringing down the previous regime.

The Iraqi experience prior to 1958 had embodied a novel development capable of integrating military officers — even older officers of the Ottoman army — into the new Arab political context. Of the prime ministers who succeeded each other in Iraq, many were officers who graduated from the high military academy in Istanbul: Ja'far al-'Askari, 'Abd al-Muhsin as-Sa'dun, Yasin al-Hashimi, Nuri as-Sa'id, Jamil al-Midfa'i, 'Ali Jawdat al-Ayyubi, Taha al-Hashimi and Nur ad-Din Mahmud. All the above played an important role in Iraqi politics from the creation of the state until the 1958 revolution. This made the participation of Bakr Sidqi and al-Kaylani and, after them, others such as 'Abd al-Karim Qasim, 'Abd as-Salam 'Aref and Ahmad Hasan al-Bakr, in the leadership of the state, more acceptable. Hanna Batatu counted around three hundred Ottoman officers who had entered Iraqi politics during the 1920s.

In the 1950s, the intervention of the military in politics was expanded and generalised and, consequently, its image was considerably improved. Specifically, there was a growing conviction in public opinion that the military might bring new blood into the structure of the state and in the process endow it with new momentum. The memoirs of 'Adel Arslan are full of almost continuous demands for the arming and training of the armies in all the Arab countries in which he was politically involved, particularly Syria and Iraq (Arslan, 1984). Arslan is obsessed with Ataturk and Turkey, for he perceives Ataturk as an active military man who dared to side openly with modernity and to adopt Western methods. Loyal to his people, he continuously sought to increase his country's strength. Arslan compares him with Arab rulers lacking in perception and concerned only with their own interests. He views Turkey as a model, and not once does he forget that the source of all this strength was a modern and reconstructed army.

However, Arslan remains at the level of generalities. Interestingly enough, Arslan was to become the foreign minister of Husni az-Za'im, the first military ruler of contemporary Syria. Much as Muhammad 'Abduh viewed 'Urabi's revolt, so does Arslan explain az-Za'im's rise to power. Arslan even goes further in his criticism of Husni az-Za'im, accusing him of high treason for plotting with the Americans to conclude a separate agreement with Israel. Az-Za'im came to power with a platform of army reform, following the scandals of the first Arab-Israeli war, yet he considered doing what no Syrian civilian dared to do.

The Arab military came to power with the slogan of liberation and its publicised capacity to confront the enemy. Bakr Sidqi was inclined to emphasise his role in maintaining national unity by means of his bloody suppression of the Assyrian rebellion in the north of the country. Husni az-Za'im and his allies in Damascus as well as 'Abd an-Nasir (Nasser) and his colleagues in Egypt, came to power as a consequence of the devastating results of the first Arab-Israeli war. Those who succeeded them also upheld the same slogan of liberation.

But this positive development in the image of the strong, patriotic and liberating military was accompanied by a historical deterioration in the field of liberation itself, for the military establishment did not have much success in its battle with external powers. Many examples can be mentioned: the devastating 1967 defeat against Israel, Somalia's failure in its confrontation with Ethiopia, and the failure of more than one Libyan military adventure in Africa. It is as if the Arab armies were committing themselves to the achievement of objectives greater than those they had previously set themselves, but they seemed to suffer from at least an equal incapacity to achieve them. Iraq's performance in the war with Iran is yet another example, and one might even mention here India's victories over Muslim Pakistan.

Nor is it possible to say that the politicisation of the military led to the strengthening of the state *vis-à-vis* other states or within society. There has been a slight improvement in image. There is no doubt that the Libya of Mu'ammar al-Qadhafi appears to be stronger than the Libya of the Sanusi king. The same thing can certainly be said about Syria under Hafiz al-Assad. But the question remains open. To what extent does an Arab feel that this or that state is stronger because its leaders come from the military? To what extent does he believe that the price of the presence of the military in power is comparable with what the state has gained in strength?

To what extent is this military authority identified as a patriotic and popular one? The military's rise to political power did not mean that it was being purified from all the maladies of civil society. As a matter of fact, it can be said that the maladies have survived with the military and at times have even grown in proportion. To what extent can we consider the Sudanese, or Libyan, or Somali or Syrian or Iraqi armies to be ruling their respective countries, without regarding the ethnic, sectarian or tribal 'asabiyyas looming behind them? It appears as if a number of neo-Mamluk regimes have arisen in some Arab countries. These regimes are based on old group feelings that now dominate the state and society through the army, behind the mere façade of modern institutions.

WHERE DOES STRENGTH COME FROM?

In 1905, the Arabs were amazed by the victory of Japan over Russia. How could a small underdeveloped Asian country defeat a great country that was threatening the territorial integrity of the Ottoman Empire? The Egyptian politician Mustafa Kamel found time to write a book on the subject. This war also inspired the Algerian thinker, Malek bin Nabi, to daring ideas. He compared the Arabs who approached European civilisation as consumers with the Japanese who approached it in quest of knowledge. The Japanese imported ideas, while the Arabs limited themselves to the importation of commodities. The interest in Japan which filled the pages of Arab newspapers for years after 1905 was only a reflection of the deep and basic questions that occupied the Arabs/Muslims of the *Nahda* concerning their own weakness and the strength of other nations. 'Why Japan?' asks Charles Issawi (Issawi, 1983). Why did Japan alone among the countries of Asia, Africa and Latin America 'make it' in the nineteenth and early twentieth centuries? Why not the Arabs? Why not, for instance, Iraq, whose potential was, and still is, so great? Or why not Egypt, with its homogeneous population, centralised government, substantial agricultural surplus, excellent internal waterways, long-established fiscal tradition and, by contemporary standards, urbanised society?

Galal Amin's answer is based on geo-strategic factors. Amin argues that Egypt failed in this endeavour owing to its (too-enviable) geographical location, the proximity of the European powers, and because the Suez Canal had to be established. These factors enabled the West to penetrate Egypt, tame its will and fetter it militarily and financially, with the aim of preventing it from developing on its own. Issawi's answer is based on culture: he explains that Japan is the best example of the active and successful khaldunian group feeling. However, the Japanese were able to preserve a double standard of moral superiority and of cultural inferiority, *vis-à-vis* the West. The Arabs, on the contrary, combined a feeling of moral superiority with a false feeling of cultural superiority. According to Issawi, this false feeling resulted in the absence of the 'spirit of curiosity' among the Arabs and Muslims regarding other cultures.

As the Arabs sense their senility, the modern models of power (Europe, the USA, Japan, the USSR) grow in front of their eyes. Questions relating to the reasons behind this discrepancy in power still remain. If Issawi's opinion is valid, then the current period, which is characterised by a return to fundamentalist religious slogans, is moving away from, rather than approaching, the solution he prescribes. The emphasis on the religious-cultural superiority of the Islamic religion could hardly be stronger than it is today. The 'spirit of curiosity' that Issawi looked for among Arabs to no avail is sometimes condemned as 'cultural alienation'. Why should we seek others, when the solutions to our problems are found in our Holy scripture, religion and culture? Is not the interest in the culture of others, according to the fundamentalists, the reason for our plight?

They say this while having in mind the example of Israel, which is the closest to them and the most violent and destructive. Israel appears as a supreme military power and a strong actor in international relations, rejecting all red tape and possessing a capability for continuous brinkmanship. Was not Israel established specifically by stressing its religious personality? Was it not right to do so? Israel, at least as viewed by the Arabs, is the ideal of the religious state. It contradicts all the ideologies that call for the separation of religion from the state. According to the fundamentalists, these ideologies have weakened the Arab state despite Abdallah Laroui's warning that 'the expression: *al-Islam din wa dawla*' (Islam is a religion and a state) implies a co-existence and not an integration between religion and the state . . . Islam . . . means the civilisation which developed throughout history in the Islamic nation, and not the ideology . . . the state did not transform Islam into a state religion, and Islam did not transform the state into a religious institution' (Laroui, 1981: 122).

This quotation from Laroui represents the exact contradiction of the fundamentalist attitude towards the community and the enemy (particularly Israel). It seems that a new dynamism, almost materialising in a 'war of religions', may have been established in the region. Israel is as Theodor Herzl dreamt it to be in *The Jewish State*: 'A state in the full meaning of the word, having its territories and laws, ruled and administered by Jews'. Herzl thought along two lines: that of the political system and that of the financial company supporting it, to which Herzl devotes the longest chapter in his book. Consideration of Israel as an example to be followed in an attempt to establish a strong state is growing in the writings and practices of Arabs. Are the continuous Arab defeats by Israelis driving them to adopt the ideas and terminology of the victors, as was the case with other peoples at different periods?

Despite many recent theories on the 'communalisation' of the Arab-Israeli conflict, it is still possible to believe that this conflict has and will continue to have tremendous effects on political culture. Its seeming transformation into a mere war among religions, a war of the True God against the Old One or the False One, is a frightening prospect. Arabs and Muslims may be tempted to consider the historical conditions in which

63

Israel was created as marginal, and to view it basically as a 'religious product', despite Herzl's laborious financial planning. The idea of a gradual identification of strength with faith should not be dismissed; each side can gird on its sword and join the battle, chanting: 'How can we be defeated when God is on our side?'

3

Allocation vs. Production States: A Theoretical Framework

Giacomo Luciani

Possibly nowhere more than in the Arab world is the crucial importance of the economic foundations of the state as clearly borne out by historical developments in contemporary times. The contrast between the six thousand year old record of centralised state structure in Egypt and the total lack of any stable authority structure in the Arabian Peninsula until well into the present century could not be more marked. Ecological and economic factors have conditioned the existence of state structures and the geographic reach of their authority throughout Arab history.

Thus one does not need to accept any schematic and deterministic model to point to the importance of the economic foundations of state structures in shaping the basic parameters of Arab politics. Economic realities condition the total resources that any single state structure can muster — and until only a few decades ago these resources were in some cases simply insufficient to permit the consolidation of states that, as a consequence, disappeared as fast as they arose. Second, the nature of the predominant productive processes conditions certain basic parameters of existing state structures, such as the degree of centralisation and the tendency to authoritarian rule. Finally, the nature of the sources of income of the state influences the basic rules of political life in each individual country. While this chapter will be devoted primarily to a discussion of the latter aspect, the first two aspects must also be kept in mind, as they are equally important.

In the preceding lines we have already implicitly made use of a distinction that must be defined for the rest of this chapter. In

65

English usage the term state is almost always meant to indicate an independent country as well as the structure of power and authority that exercises the attributes of sovereignty within it. In this chapter we address the question of the nature of the state only in the latter of the above mentioned meanings.

ECONOMIC REALITIES AND THE 'SIZE' OF THE STATE

A state structure will tend to be stable in history if it commands sufficient resources to guarantee its own survival. This implies primarily the ability to resist outside aggression, but it implies as well the ability effectively to exercise its authority over the territories that fall — or are generally believed to fall — under its sovereignty. The resources that are needed to enforce state authority are greatly variable as a function of structural (geographic, demographic) and political realities, and the ability to resist outside aggression is also a function of the intensity of such aggression. Thus it is difficult to say whether a given economic system does or does not offer the potential to sustain a stable state structure. Yet it is evident from Arab history that in many cases, states could be wiped out when exposed even to small-scale aggression, and in other instances states were in fact not able to exercise their authority over territories that they nominally controlled and that no other state claimed for itself.

It is only with the colonial era and the valorisation of oil resources — two interconnected developments — that state structures appear to have consolidated and extended their authority over their entire territory. In many cases, the colonial state structures were the first to effectively rule their claimed territories and almost all the state structures that existed in Arabia until World War II could only survive thanks to British subsidies. Even after World War II, a fortuitously independent Libya could not really sustain a state structure until oil exports began in the late 50s. Still in 1960, British aid and American payments for the leasing of the Wheelus base accounted for 35 per cent of Libyan GNP and substantially all the state's revenue (Luciani, 1976: 121–3).

Oil has drastically changed the picture. In most cases, it has provided the weaker state structures with abundant financial resources. In other cases, states in poor and weak countries, while not blessed with oil revenues, still manage substantially to increase their income, by encouraging migration or otherwise tapping foreign resources, both regionally and internationally. Thus today it is very rarely the case that the very existence of a state structure is endangered by the lack of resources; still, the relative importance of the resources supporting each state is greatly variable.

One is tempted to believe that differences in state income per subject (i.e. *per capita*) reflect differences in *per capita* GDP, on the basis of the assumption that the ability of individual states to appropriate a certain share of GDP is a constant in the short term. Yet this is certainly not the case for the oil-producing countries, where the causational chain is inverted, and state income determines GDP rather than the other way round. In these countries, differences in *per capita* GDP simply reflect the variable income opportunities and spending preferences of each state structure — indeed state income cannot in any meaningful sense be considered as being part of GDP until it is actually spent, and then only in so far as it is spent domestically.

CAN ONE SPEAK OF 'HYDROCARBON SOCIETIES'?

The stability of state formations is increased if, beyond being able to appropriate resources for their own ends, they also play an economic role which objectively increases the sum total of resources available to the country that they run. While this is, in itself, neither a necessary nor sufficient condition for stability of state formations, it is reasonable to expect that states that perform a useful economic function will be more easily accepted in the specific form and configuration that they take. Thus the character and behaviour of state formations is influenced by the prevailing features of economic life in the countries that they rule.

With reference specifically to the Middle East, the importance of water as long as the prevailing economic activity is agriculture has repeatedly been noted. There is, of course, Wittfogel's stress on hydraulic societies (1957: 48–9). His argument appears to us today greatly overextended, and it has been criticised from a historical point of view. Yet, it is difficult to deny, as we look at the history of what is today the Arab world, that the extraordinary resilience of state formations based in the Nile and the Mesopotamian valleys, respectively, as contrasted to the extreme variability of state definitions elsewhere, has a great deal to do with water and irrigation.

Yet the importance of water and its availability or lack of it in shaping political institutions and political life, and ultimately dictating the essential characters of state formations, does not necessarily point in the direction of Wittfogel's argument. More recently numerous authors, and especially anthropologists, have pointed to the importance of water management in shaping the social and political life of specific communities (Eickelman, 1981: 48–72).

The political impact of oil may be said to be in many ways similar to that of water, and at the same time different in a few crucial respects.

Oil, of course, is a liquid. This is more than a superficial coincidence because it means that the production and transportation of oil is best effected through the creation of an integrated network of hydraulic installations. There is an intrinsic need for centralised coordination: the latter was often provided by non-state entities in the industrial countries and internationally (e.g. Standard Oil before 1911, the informal 'understanding' between the major international oil companies thereafter, or regulatory agencies such as the Texas Railroad Commission). But in the Middle East no such entities were available indigenously and the task was viewed naturally as pertaining to the state.

Furthermore oil, just as complex irrigation, requires a 'specific type of division of labour' (Wittfogel, 1957: 22): one which clearly defines a technocratic layer that has the geological, chemical and financial knowledge necessary successfully to manage oil operations.

Another similarity is that oil, like water, is found in 'basins' and 'provinces'. While the need for integrated management is felt *strictu sensu* only at the level of the individual field, much can be gained through coordination at a higher level as well. This has had consequences over the territorial definition of Arab states: not only did certain demarcations become very contentious, but others almost ceased to be. Regions with no oil shelved the secessionist tendencies that they might have cherished in past times (Hijaz) or accepted federal arrangements with oil-rich neighbours (the United Arab Emirates); or the central location of the oil basins compensated for strongly rooted centrifugal forces. In the case of Libya, the three regions of Tripolitania, Cyrenaica and the Fezzan were effectively glued together by the fact that most oil lies squarely between them.

But there are important differences as well. A first crucial difference between oil and water is that the former does not require the mobilisation of large numbers of the population. Quite to the contrary, oil production is a highly automated business, in which few are employed, and a relatively high percentage of those few are specialised full-time labour. The vast majority of the population is not involved at all in oil operations.

A second capital point is that oil, differently from water, is of no immediate interest to the survival and well-being of the vast majority of the domestic population. To be sure, oil products are consumed, but direct access to oil is not important *per se*, as direct access to water was and still is. What is important is access to oil *revenue*, that enables the consumer to buy a wide array of goods, including oil-derived products. Thus the vast majority of the domestic population is not involved with oil either as far as production or as far as utilisation is concerned. Their interest is in oil revenue, i.e. it is mediated, and mediated by the state.

A very important corollary of the second difference is that oil is mostly utilised abroad. Be it in crude or refined form, oil has value only to the extent that it is exported. Oil is not traded domestically in the oil-producing countries. Because oil valorisation implies a relationship with the rest of the world, it tends naturally to fall within the responsibility of the state and creates solidarity among its subjects.

Thus the specific characteristics of oil production and trade may well be said to have an impact on the stability and configuration of state formations. Yet it would be a mistake to follow Wittfogel's lead and propose a theory of the 'hydrocarbon society'. There is a distinct danger of exaggerating the argument and overlooking the fact that oil, just as water, is not the only significant dimension.

The point is that in the latter decades many aspects of economic life have tended to increase the economic role and impact of the state. Independently of the ideological orientations of each government, international realities have forced individual states into taking some fundamental steps such as issuing a fiduciary monetary instrument to be used within their boundaries or adopting complex economic legislation. While in most cases foreign trade has always been regulated, the significance of such regulations has increased because of the growing importance of international trade on commonly expected standards of living. Furthermore, in most instances the state vested in itself the responsibility for the upkeep and improvement of basic infrastructures: roads, transportation, mail, telephone, power, water, etc., to the point that today hardly any economic activity is conceivable which is not in someway related to and conditioned by the active presence of the state.

The tendency towards a direct state role is, of course, very significant from the political point of view. State formations that appeared to be entirely artificial and haphazard at the time of their creation 50 years ago or less are nowadays a deeply-rooted reality which would be quite difficult to modify. Thus any attempt to portray oil-producing countries as hydrocarbon societies would be an unacceptable simplification.

OIL AND THE NATURE OF THE STATE

While we should not speak of hydrocarbon societies and states, it is a fact that oil production appears to have a strong and decisive influence on the nature of the state. It does so through its effects on the structure of state revenues and the ratio between revenues that are obtained domestically and revenues that are obtained from abroad.

The key factor in this discussion is a precise understanding of what it is that makes the difference. Sometimes, a decisive importance is attributed to the fact that oil is the source of state income and that oil revenue includes a predominant rent element (Stauffer, in Beblawi and Luciani, 1987, Chapter 1). Hence the concept of 'rentier state' which is sometimes adopted to characterise the state in oil-exporting countries. While this concept captures the essence of the problem, a certain number of clarifications are needed:

(a) there are other rent-like sources of revenue which accrue directly to the state besides oil: thus rentier states are not necessarily oil exporting states;
(b) some important flows of income containing a rent component do *not* accrue directly to the state, in which case we should not speak of a rentier state, although we may well characterise the economy at large as being rentier, in the sense adopted by Beblawi (Chapter 4) and Abdel-Fadil (in Beblawi and Luciani, 1987, Chapter 4);
(c) it is essential that the income of the state not only be in the

nature of a rent, but also be earned abroad; if it were earned domestically the nature of the state would not be substantially affected.

It is for these reasons that I prefer to propose a new categorisation that, instead of looking at the nature of the income of the state, looks at its origin, domestic or foreign. The essential impact of oil production and exports is that they free the state from the need of raising income domestically. It is oil exports that play an essential role in this respect even more than oil production *per se*: the state in a country in which a lot of oil is produced but none exported may or may not be called rentier, but does not appear to be essentially different from any other state whose income depends on domestic sources. In both cases it is the overall strength and productive capacity of the domestic economy that conditions the income of the state. On the contrary, if oil is mostly exported, and the income of the state is mostly linked to the exportation of oil, then that state is freed from its domestic economic base and sustained by the economic base of the countries which are importing its oil.

Thus if we look at the origin of state revenue, we should speak rather of 'exoteric states' — being states predominantly based on revenue accruing directly from abroad — and 'esoteric states' — predominantly based on domestic revenue and taxation. Yet a different way of looking at the same distinction may be more enlightening, and this relates to the predominant function of the state. From the latter point of view the relevant distinction appears to be one between 'allocation' and 'production' states, depending on which of these two functions — mere allocation or production and reallocation — is the necessary task of the state.

A rentier or exoteric state will inevitably end up performing the role of allocating the income that it receives from the rest of the world. It is free to do so in a variety of ways: among the various purposes for which money is spent, the strengthening of the domestic economic base may be included, but not necessarily so. Even if this happens to be one of the goals of the state, as long as the domestic economy is not tapped to raise further income through domestic taxation, the strengthening of the domestic economy is not reflected in the income of the state, and is therefore not a precondition for the existence and expansion of the state.

On the contrary, whenever the income of the state is based on

71

tapping the domestic economy through whatever assortment of fiscal instruments, the state can grow and perform an allocative function only to the extent that the domestic economy provides the income which is needed to do so. Growth in the domestic economy is one of the various 'luxuries' that the state can buy with its oil income in one case, it is an essential precondition for its existence and growth in the other. Clearly, all states aim at performing an allocative function, because in a sense this is what politics is about; and all states perform some allocative function. However for those that depend on income from abroad, allocation is the only relationship that they need to have with their domestic economy; all others ride their domestic economies.

Besides oil, other sources of income from abroad accruing directly to the state are transportation infrastructures of an international relevance and aid, be it economic, military or political — although the fact that it is sometimes in kind or tied limits the freedom to allocate it among different alternative purposes.

On the other hand, taxation on international trade is not a source of income from the rest of the world because the burden of such taxes falls on the domestic consumer or producer, not on the foreign importer or exporter. Neither are migrants' remittances a source of income from the rest of the world because they belong to the migrant, not to the state. The state may attempt to tax the income of migrants, but is in no position to do so before it is repatriated. It is only after remittances have entered the domestic economy (and generally not immediately after because of the need to encourage migrants to repatriate their income) that they can be taxed and become a source of income for the state. By then, the state is taxing the domestic economy. In fact, the importance of migrants' remittances is what imposes the distinction between a rentier economy and an allocation (or rentier) state: whenever remittances are important, this tends to give a rentier character to the economy as a whole, but the economic base of the state is not changed.

We may define allocation states as all those states whose revenue derives predominantly (more than 40 per cent) from oil or other foreign sources and whose expenditure is a substantial share of GDP.

The primary examples of allocation states are found in the Arab Gulf countries. In Kuwait, oil income alone accounted for 62 per cent of total revenue in 1982, down from 84 per cent in 1980; however, if investment income from abroad (31.8 per cent of total revenue in 1982) is added, the share of total revenue accruing from foreign sources reaches as high as 94 per cent. According to conventional standards of national accounting, government revenue reached a peak of 94.2 per cent of GDP in 1981, but fell thereafter as oil revenue declined more rapidly than GDP. Before 1982, government revenue was considerably larger than expenditure, but the difference was reduced thereafter, as expenditure increased while revenue shrank. Government expenditure reached a peak of 53 per cent of GDP in 1982, and declined thereafter. Finally, if GDP figures were to be revised in accordance with the accounting standards suggested by Stauffer, government expenditure would account for a considerably larger share of GDP (or, in Stauffer's terminology, ND-GDP). Yet, if we adopt Stauffer's approach, we should also revise government income, and define a 'permanently sustainable' income level by detracting oil rent — which would wipe out government income almost entirely. These accounting exercises are useful in understanding the nature of the relationship between government income and GDP in a country like Kuwait.

Most Arab Gulf countries are in the same position. In Oman, government expenditure was 55.5 per cent of GDP in 1978. It declined to a minimum of 40.6 per cent in 1980, and grew thereafter to reach 47.3 per cent in 1982. The Omani budget has shown a tendency to close with a deficit. Revenue from oil and grants from abroad account for 90 per cent (1982) of total revenue.

In Saudi Arabia, in a year (1984) of weak petroleum prices, oil revenue accounted for 64 per cent of total revenue and income from investment abroad generated approximately another 18 per cent. Thus the government solidly depends on income from abroad, but at the same time it accounts for a smaller share of GDP. In 1977 — when the budget closed with a solid surplus — government revenue accounted for 66.3 per cent of GDP; this ratio fell to 50.1 per cent in 1981. As expenditure overtook income in the following years, the composition of GDP also changed and starting in 1983/4 the private (non-oil) sector generated more than half of GDP.

Outside of the Gulf, Libya is likely to fall into this category, but Libya's budget is drawn very unconventionally, making comparative analysis impossible.

Finally, both Jordan and Syria fell into the allocation state paradigm, at least temporarily. In Jordan, government expenditure fluctuated around 50 per cent of GDP according to IMF statistics (1981: 52.4 per cent; 1982: 45.1 per cent); but inclusion of public independent entities would bring the ratio to an impressive 85 per cent (*MEED*, 4 January 1985: 12). In the case of Jordan, grants from abroad started in a significant way in 1979, when they reached a peak value of 54.4 per cent of total revenue. Thereafter they declined, and in 1984 they were budgeted at 24.1 per cent of total revenue. In Syria, grants accounted for 40.9 per cent of total revenue in 1979, and 30 per cent in 1981; it is however, not clear whether all grants are included in the budget. Syrian government expenditure was 38.8 per cent of GDP in 1979 and 38.1 in 1981.

In the case of Algeria, hydrocarbon revenue (including gas) accounts for a diminishing share of total revenue (67 per cent in 1981, 53 per cent in 1984) (*MTM*, 24 February 1984: 429). Government spending accounts for 84.8 per cent of GDP. Algeria is, thus, a borderline case.

So are, for different reasons, Bahrain and Iraq. In both cases oil and grants are the major source of revenue (Bahrain: 78.5 per cent of GDP in 1982; for Iraq no recent data are available), but government expenditure accounts for a relatively smaller share of GDP: in Bahrain, it was 40 per cent in 1977 and declined to 34.6 per cent in 1981, while in Iraq government revenue was 26.8 per cent of GDP in 1978 and 25.3 per cent in 1980.

Minor oil exporters with relatively large populations, such as Egypt and Tunisia, cannot be called allocation states. In Egypt, non-tax revenue, which includes oil revenue as well as revenue from the Canal, but also includes some typically domestic revenue, accounts for 23.8 per cent of total revenue, while government expenditure is 47 per cent of GDP. The latter fact is far from extraordinary: the qualitatively important fact is that this level of expenditure significantly exceeds revenue, and revenue, in turn, is largely derived from the domestic economy. In Tunisia, oil revenue in 1981 was 18.6 per cent of total revenue and pipeline fees and grants added only 0.7 per cent. Again, government expenditure was significantly larger than revenue, and accounted for 37.3 per cent of GDP (1981). In other Arab countries such as Morocco, the relative importance of foreign sources of income is even less.

Thus it is seen that the Arab world is fairly clearly divided between allocation and production states, and the former comprise countries that are not oil producers, but receive substantial income from abroad on different grounds.

POLITICAL RULES OF THE GAME IN AN ALLOCATION STATE

In what respect should we expect that the rules of the political game will be different in an allocation state?

In countries where the state is of the production type the largest part of the population derives its income from sources different from the state itself. In socialist regimes, a majority may be employed in publicly-owned industry, rather than in the more narrowly defined state machinery. Because of its need to rely on taxation (or in the case of socialist regimes, on income from publicly-owned industry), the state has an interest in expanding the income base on which taxes can be levied. Economic growth is the primary goal of the economic policy that all production states adopt: but no economic policy is neutral from a distributional point of view, and the polarisation of society into a variety of interest groups struggling to influence economic policy is a necessary corollary. Although the precise political implications of tax levying may vary according to the nature of the tax itself, in most cases the operation requires a large degree of acceptance on the part of the population. Tax evasion can be repressed if it is a marginal phenomenon, but when it becomes the rule the cost of tax collecting becomes much too high. This establishes a link between the ability to raise taxes and legitimacy, which is captured in the saying 'no taxation without representation'. Although the immediate link between taxation and representative democracy may well not exist, as countless examples demostrate, it is a fact that whenever the state essentially relies on taxation the question of democracy becomes an unavoidable issue, and a strong current in favour of democracy inevitably arises. This is the result of the fact that people will naturally be induced to coalesce according to their economic interest, and those groups that find no way to influence the decision-making process in their favour claim appropriate institutional change. The state for its part must give credibility to the notion that it represents the common good: it therefore tends to propose a national myth whose purpose is that of overcoming the conflict of interest that the very existence of the state creates or exacerbates. National myths may have a variety of specifications: their least rhetorical expression is the notion of GNP or GDP, and the stress on the goal of economic growth as seen in isolation from distributive preoccupations.

None of the above is to be found in an allocation state. The state, being independent of the strength of the domestic economy, does not need to formulate anything deserving the appellation of economic policy: all it needs is an expenditure policy. Because state revenue itself is the largest part of GDP, the simple act of spending domestically will maximise GDP growth. The only relevant problem to an allocation state is extracting the maximum potential revenue from the rest of the world: this, however, has little to do with the domestic economy. Because an allocation state only spends and does not tax, its expenditure policy can only indirectly damage some of its people; it will, on the other hand, usually be seen as benefiting everybody.

That benefits are unequally distributed is not relevant for political life, because it is not a sufficient incentive to coalesce and attempt to change the political institutions. To the individual who feels his benefits are not enough, the solution of manoeuvring for personal advantage within the existing setup is always superior to seeking an alliance with others in similar conditions. In the end, there is always little or no objective ground to claim that one should get more of the benefits, since his contribution is generally dispensable anyhow. Were this not the case, the individual would usually find himself in a position whereby he could increase his income if he left the country and sought employment elsewhere; but normally allocation states pay well. Because Exit (Hirschman, 1970) normally involves a considerable loss of income, Voice becomes a dangerous proposition and Loyalty will be popular with a vast majority of the population.

Loyalty is to the system, not to individuals in power. A lot of scheming may be expected to go on in allocation states along the time-honoured pattern of court politics, but this will seldom, if ever, develop into a truly political debate. Democracy is not a problem for allocation states. Although they may find it expedient to set up some kind of representative body to vent and control some of the resentment that even court politics generates, these bodies inevitably have a very tenuous link to their apparent constituency: their debates are followed with indifference by the public and the ruler can disband them and meet practically no resistance whatsoever. More commonly, representative bodies do not exist at all and to the need of establishing them little more than lip service is paid. Even such lip service is intended more to serve the wishes of public opinion abroad than to satisfy any substantial pressure domestically. The fact is that there is 'no representation without taxation' and there are no exceptions to this version of the rule.

It is only in the case that an allocation state fails, or is widely believed to fail, to take full advantage of the possibility of receiving income from the rest of the world that substantial political opposition may develop. While in fact opposition groups may be numerically limited, they sometimes find themselves in a position to overthrow the existing political order. The result is generally a different institutional setup, although in no way a more democratic one. The history of Libya and possibly Iraq is exemplary in this respect: in both cases the ruling family was seen as being subservient to foreign interests not just from a political point of view, but from a revenue point of view as well: they were forfeiting revenue. It is in this respect that corruption becomes important: inequality of distribution is not an issue, but if the search for personal advantage leads to a failure in cashing in fully the potential rent it develops into a very important one. The reason is that while inequality of distribution can only be corrected by benefiting some and damaging others and each individual generally is not entirely clear on which side he is going to be, mismanagement of the revenue potential of the state can be corrected by benefiting practically everybody in the country.

An allocation state does not need to refer to a national myth and, as a matter of fact, will usually avoid doing so. A national myth, when it coincides with the boundaries of the country itself, may be interpreted as a basis to claim a say in the allocation process. The patrimonial non-national state is, on the other hand, best adapted to being an allocation state, because its origin naturally restricts the number of people who have a say.

Because they do not refer to an appropriately sized national myth, allocation states may avoid having a clearly defined constituency. While this behaviour will clearly tend to perpetuate and possibly reinforce the importance of traditional segmentary politics and kin groups, the fact that most of the GNP is made of government expenditure practically ensures that few or no alternative groupings will develop. The small number of hands employed in the oil business makes it possible essentially to buy off the possibility of unions developing in that sector. Elsewhere, the lack of industrial establishments, and more generally of productive activities, will prevent a union structure and culture from developing. Unions are born in factories because the latter enclose a large number of workers that share common interests. From factories, unions can spread to other sectors and smaller establishments: but it is very difficult to start unionisation from the service sector or from a petrochemical plant. Very mild repression is all that is needed should someone fancy imitating foreign experiences.

The same is largely true for parties. As the politics of allocation states leave little ground for economic interests of citizens not belonging to the elite to be represented, parties will develop only to represent cultural or ideological orientation. In practice, Islamic fundamentalism appears to be the only rallying point around which something approaching a party can form in the Arab allocation states; plus of course the government-inspired parties, wherever they exist.

In actual practice, the distinction between allocation and production states becomes blurred at the margins. Algeria is becoming less and less of an allocation state, while Egypt and Tunisia do enjoy some income from abroad and thus are not purely production states. Apparently, the only differences is in the degree of budget tightness: if money is available, there is less concern for return on unit spending; as money grows scarcer, results are expected of projects that are undertaken. It is impossible to differentiate sharply between states that undertake industrialisation as a tool for political control and states that do so because they expect positive economic returns and increased revenue.

Yet the fact remains that even limited revenue from abroad dramatically improves the state's ability to buy legitimacy through allocation and increases regime stability. Iraq since the early seventies and Algeria almost since independence have had remarkably stable power structures. The major example to the contrary seems to be Iran: but there the Shah was more preoccupied with promoting aggressive industrialisation, even at the cost of exacerbating class conflict, than with buying political support. His successors have done little in the direction of democratisation, but their concoction of populism, Islamic revival and appropriate use of oil money to buy consensus at the retail level (taking care of the poor, improving life conditions in the rural villages) seems to be working quite a bit better than most observers expected. Plus, of course, there is the gruesome rhetoric of war.

ACTUAL POLICIES AND THE NATURE OF THE STATE

The case of Iran clearly demonstrates that the nature of the state is not a rigid determinant of government policies. The latter may well diverge from what we would expect on the basis of the analysis of the nature of the state. If policies do so, they may be expected to be unstable, as they will lead to economic and/or political contradictions which will eventually force their change. Thus the proposed distinction between allocation and production states is far from being an easy tool that allows us to predict which policies are used, but may improve our understanding as to whether policies currently being enforced are likely to be stable or not.

It is specifically important to recognise the existence of allocation states and the fact that they constitute logically coherent political systems which can display considerable stability if the appropriate policies are adopted. The latter are not the same as those that we would deem appropriate for production states.

Much of the literature on the Arab political system suffers from the assumption that there is but one 'modern' model of state, and stability can be gained, in general, only through 'modernising' policies. This approach does not explain genuinely 'reactionary' mass movements, such as in Iran, and leads to endless paradoxes. Witness Michael Hudson's concept of 'modernising monarchies': a monarch ruling a patrimonial state is not exactly what most people would call 'modern' — in fact, they often call it 'traditional' or 'feudal'. Something must be wrong there: a modernising monarch should be expected to promote democratisation and gradually evolve into a ceremonial head of state in the northern European tradition. Yet these monarchs and ruling families, although they love modern technology and use computers and jets, have apparently no intention of sharing their power or changing their role.

The concept of allocation state makes it possible to overcome the paradox. The ruling patrimonial monarchies are neither traditional nor feudal. Feudal they never were; traditional they may be in the sense that they have a tradition, not in the sense that they are the same thing as 20 or 30 years ago. Appearances may not change much (in fact, they have changed quite a lot) but the substance is entirely different: those 'traditional' rulers today head complex and sophisticated allocation states. It so happens that the patrimonial form of government is very well adapted to the specific character of allocation states and vice versa; it is, on the other hand, particularly ill suited to the characters of production states. But democracy, which has advantages in the case of production states, has strong disadvantages in the running of allocation states.

Allocation states are neither better nor worse than production states from a moral point of view, and they are neither more nor less modern. Each has its own rules of the game and evolves along a different path. There is no reason to expect that eventually they will converge towards some kind of standard modernity.

ON RELATIONS BETWEEN ALLOCATION AND PRODUCTION STATES

Relations between allocation and production states are not easy. Each group projects a different model of international relations, according to its specific interests and security preoccupations.

To neighbouring production states, the resources that are available to allocation states are a source of frustration and envy. To them, the best solution would be to wipe out the allocation state altogether, and appropriate its sources of income. This is, however, impossible and nobody quite expects things to go this way: but somehow this fundamental tension remains latent and permeates all relations between the two types of political formations. Allocation states, on the other hand, naturally tend to project internationally their characteristic pattern of buying consensus at home: thus they propose themselves as sources of income to the neighbouring production states, and in doing so, initiate a process that may turn the latter into allocation states. But while production states are interested in appropriating income and allocation states are ready to share theirs, this will not lead to harmonious coexistence, because the question of who is in control is inevitably left open.

The balance of the game depends on the relative importance of the financial resources that the allocation states have available relative to the military potential and economic needs of the production states. If the latter feel stronger, as in the fifties and early sixties, they will propose a model of inter-Arab relations based on a pan-Arab ideology that has clear revolutionary undertones and proposes the dissolution of existing separate state structures. On the other hand, when allocation states feel stronger they will propose again a pan-Arab ideology, but one in which the Islamic component dominates and the revolutionary one does not exist and inter-Arab affairs are primarily seen as cooperation among independent Arab heads of state.

In the phase of production-state hegemony, the Arab world was dominated by Egypt, which is by far the most important political formation in this respect. Whenever production and economic growth are seriously the main problem of Arab politics, Egypt moves in to the fore. But military defeat and economic disaster coupled with growing oil prices seemed to change the definition of power in the Middle East: there was, as Kerr writes, 'the new belief that power grows, not out of the barrel of a gun nor out of the appeal of a revolutionary leader or movement, but out of an ample state Treasury' (Kerr and Yassin, 1982). Thus Egypt lost the lead and Saudi Arabia took it over again using arguments that were extremely appealing, including to the Egyptian leadership. After an attempt at acquiring its share of the oil income in the least expensive way by exploiting Qadhafi's Nasserite enthusiasm through the union in 1972–3, the Egyptian state was confronted squarely with the prospect of turning into an induced allocation state, subservient to the wishes of Saudi Arabia. But, apart from pride, this solution was barred because the money that was being offered was simply not enough to guarantee the ability to buy domestic political consensus in a complex and populous country such as Egypt. In order to establish a stable induced allocation state in Egypt one needs considerably more money than the Saudis were willing to offer, and Sadat turned to the USA, which he expected to be both willing to provide abundant aid in the short term and capable of opening new development prospects in the longer term. With Mubarak, the importance of domestic production, industrial growth and exports are being stressed anew. The country still relies heavily on income from the outside world, but the state perceives itself as being a production state.

Syria and Jordan provide the best examples of induced allocation states. These countries are crucial to the security concerns of the Gulf allocation states, because they are in the front line facing Israel, because they — singly and together — hold the keys to keeping the PLO under control, and finally, because they may be useful, in quite opposite ways, in containing Iran. This allows the two countries to extract very considerable income relative to their size, while at the same time being almost totally free of interference in their domestic policies. Yet an induced allocation state is not a stable formation: its very existence may be seriously undermined by international developments or by the weakening of their purveyors of funds.

Allocation and production states project two conflicting models of regional integration. In this sense, while they both are inevitably attracted by a pan-Arab national myth, the real content and meaning that each attaches to this myth is different. After the demise of the Nasserist approach proposing political unity with no intermediate steps — in essence, an attempt to wipe the traditional Arab monarchies off the political map — today Arab unity is sought through gradual processes of regional integration. To the production states, the main objective of this integration is the acquisition of a wider economic space that would allow their industrial sectors to benefit from economies of scale. The production states are aiming at a kind of regional cooperation that will regulate migration, liberalise trade and financial flows within the region and establish protection vis-à-vis the rest of the world. They are interested in mechanisms that will generate a preference for financial placements within the region, rather than in the global markets. Although the specific situation of the Arab region is in many ways different, they are attracted by the European model, whereby political unity is sought by creating an economic framework within which private contacts and initiatives are allowed to multiply, up to a point when the region would be effectively unified and political unity would cease to be controversial.

The allocation states have a completely different set of interests and goals. Because they are structurally dependent on imports for almost all consumption and investment goods, they are extremely reluctant to give preferences to any other country and attach priority to being able to shop freely. For the same reason, they wish to be able to invest their suplus funds anywhere in the world. De facto they need immigrant labour, but do not wish to formally acknowledge this by signing treaties with the countries of origin. In their present investment plans, access to the markets of industrial countries is much more important than protected access to a regional market. To them, regional cooperation and integration is more of a political and security affair. Regional integration is a framework for cooperation among sovereign governments and the individual citizen or corporation is not expected to play much of a role. The purpose of this intergovernmental cooperation is to defuse and solve local conflicts and improve security conditions. The final goal is not at all some form of political Arab unity, but rather the survival of the allocation states. The pan-Arab national myth then becomes the ideological cover that legitimises a certain degree of interference in the domestic affairs of other countries in exchange for grants and subsidies. Ideally, integration as pursued by the allocation states includes only primary or induced allocation states.

THE LONG-TERM EVOLUTION OF ALLOCATION STATES

The concept of allocation state does not seem to offer a clear evolutionary pattern. It is possible that, being influenced by the opinion and counsel that emanates from the rest of the world, some of the allocation states will seriously pursue a process of diversification of their domestic economic base and gradually turn into production states. Their political orders may also gradually evolve and today's patrimonial rulers may slowly develop ways that are typical of Scandinavian monarchs.

On the other extreme, we may imagine a situation in which the allocation state continues unchanged until the last drop of oil is exported. At that point, the state may simply fold up and the country be deserted, most citizens having accumulated enough of a fortune to allow them to live elsewhere. Today's oil capitals may be turned into ghost towns whose role would be restricted to issuing passports and providing diplomatic protection to a largely expatriate body of citizens. Such states would not face a security threat because they would interest nobody: just as Liechtenstein or San Marino, they would not need to worry about their defence. Once the likely duration of oil reserves is considered, plus the possibility of accumulating financial assets that would allow the state a theoretically permanent source of income, this scenario is not to be ruled out for some of the less populated countries in the Gulf, possibly even for Libya.

In an intermediate case, the allocation state is confronted with greater demands than it can accommodate and gradually turns into a production state. We may expect this to be the case for both Algeria and Iraq. These are not patrimonial states anyhow, thus a transition in the nature of the state may occur with less political trauma.

The point is, that since oil, which is the main economic foundation of the allocation state, is a depletable asset, allocation states are necessarily a passing phenomenon. But how fast in passing? As things stand today, they can all count on another five or six decades of good life. And that is a long time.

CONCLUSION

This chapter discussed the question of the economic foundations of the state in the Arab world and underlined the importance of factors that are traditionally recognised in literature — such as conditions for water supply — as well as other factors, such as conditions of oil production and more generally the increasing role of the state in economic life. Attention was focused on the sources of revenue of the state and a distinction was proposed between allocation and production states. Of course, economic conditions do not explain all aspects of the behaviour of a state and economic factors cannot be reduced to the simple dichotomy of allocation versus production state. This is one analytical tool that may be added to others in order to achieve a better understanding of Arab realities.

The proposed distinction might be relevant outside of the Arab world as well. Oil then ceases to be the primary factor: still, in many countries the state primarily depends on income from abroad rather than from its own citizens. While aid-giving is an important dimension of today's international relations and a necessary instrument to spread development, the fact that it may generate induced allocation states is possibly not sufficiently recognised. The growing importance of international realities is allowing an increasing number of power structures to become essentially independent of their natural domestic constituencies: whoever has power has access to foreign resources that effectively elevate him above most challenges from within. Most frequently, commentators underline the instability of the developing countries, but in many cases it is the stability of some obviously rotten and unpopular regimes that should surprise us. Stability may, in fact, mean political immobilism, which is seldom for the better: what is frozen is not necessarily peace, but conflict; not freedom, but oppression.

4

The Rentier State in the Arab World

Hazem Beblawi

INTRODUCTION

The concept of a rentier state has gained renewed interest with the advent of the oil era and the emergence of the new Arab oil-producing states.

In a celebrated passage, Adam Smith distinguished between rent and other sources of income: wages and profit. 'Rent', says Smith, 'enters into the composition of the price of commodities in a different way from wages and profit. High or low wages and profit are the causes of high or low price; high or low rent is the effect of it' (Smith, 1960: 412). A rent, it is to be remembered, is not merely an income for landlords, but generally a reward for ownership of all natural resources. 'Mines, as well as land', affirms Ricardo, 'generally pay rent to their owners and this rent, as well as the rent of the land, is the effect and never the cause of the high value of their produce' (Ricardo, 1962: 590). The same applies to all natural and differential endowments: location, climate, etc. In its general usage, the term 'rent' is reserved for 'the income derived from the gift of nature' (Marshall, 1920). Rent in this broad sense exists in all economies, abeit in different degrees.

It is not the purpose of the chapter to discuss the economic concept of rent and its various forms: rent/quasi-rent, scarcity/ differential rent etc. In modern economic analysis an efficient management of resources would call upon rent as much as on other factor prices. No value judgement is implied, rent is an economic price or factor income like any other price.

It remains true, however, that social scientists — including economists — suspect a difference between 'earned' income and effortless 'accrued' rent. Religious ethics, and then the capitalist instinct for work salvation, helped create a long tradition of hostility against non-earned income.[1] This was reflected in a deep-rooted mistrust of the economic profession against rent and rentiers. Classical economists — Malthus apart — and later Marx have few kind words to say about rent and rentiers. Rentiers as a social group were thus assaulted by both liberal and radical economists as unproductive, almost anti-social, sharing effortlessly in the produce without, so to speak, contributing to it.

A rentier is thus more of a social function than an economic category, and is perceived as a member of a special group who, though he does not participate actively in the economic production, receives nevertheless a share in the produce and at times a handsome share. The distinguishing feature of the rentier thus resides in the lack or absence of a productive outlook in his behaviour.

It is important to emphasise here that it is the social function of the rentier rather than his legal status of private ownership, that is usually evoked with undertones of discontent. The contrast between the rentier and Schumpeter's entrepreneur is striking as well as instructive. Dynamic, innovative, risk-bearing, Schumpeter's entrepreneur is the antithesis of the rentier.

Such stereotype rentier is, of course, a caricature. In fact 'pure rent in the strict sense of the term is scarcely ever met with; nearly all income . . . contains more or less important elements, which are derived from effort invested' (Marshall, 1920: 350).

The emergence of the new oil states in the 1970s and their promotion to the forefront of world trade and finance resuscitated the concept of rentier economies. A windfall wealth of unprecedented magnitude in such short time revived the idea of unearned income, hence the epithet of rentier economies. The impact of the oil phenomenon on the role of the state and on economic behaviour in general has been so profound in the Arab world during the seventies as to justify special treatment. The concept of a rentier state is chosen for lack of better concepts to characterise the prominence of the oil economies in the Arab region.

A RENTIER STATE: ELEMENTS FOR DEFINITION

The purpose of an attempt to define a rentier state is not to reach an abstract notion of such a state but to help elucidate the impact of recent economic developments, in particular the oil phenomenon, on the nature of the state in the Arab region.

Certain characteristics should be kept in mind in view of the definition of a rentier state in our context. First, there is no such thing as a pure rentier economy. Each and every economy has some elements of rent. A rentier economy should be defined as one where rent situations predominate. This, of course, is a matter for judgement.

Second, and this is very important, a rentier economy is an economy which relies on substantial *external rent* (Mahdavi, 1970: 428). The externality of the rent origin is crucial to the concept of a rentier economy. The existence of an internal rent, even substantial, is not sufficient to characterise a *rentier economy*, though it could indicate the existence of a strong *rentier class* or group. A pure internal rent cannot be sustained without the existence of a vigorous domestic productive sector. In such a case, a rentier class is only one face of the coin, the other face would be a productive class. Internal rent is no more than a situation of domestic payment transfer in a productive economy. An external rent, on the other hand, can, if substantial, sustain the economy without a strong productive domestic sector, hence the epithet of a rentier economy.

Third, in a rentier *state* — as a special case of a rentier economy — only few are engaged in the generation of this rent (wealth), the majority being only involved in the distribution or utilisation of it. The distinction between generating wealth and its utilisation is not always clear. It can, however, be accepted that the creation of wealth is the cause of all other activities and the utilisation is only the effect. It is true that interactions always exist between various activities, blurring the cause-effect relation. In the case of the oil-producing countries, the role of oil revenues is so overwhelmingly obvious that it can be approximated to be the cause of other activities.

A rentier economy is thus an economy where the creation of wealth is centred around a small fraction of the society; the rest of the society is only engaged in the distribution and utilisation of this wealth. The respective roles of the few and the many can hardly be overstated for the concept of a rentier economy.

87

Accordingly, an open economy with high foreign trade is not a rentier state, simply because it relies on the outside world, even if it generates its income from natural endowment (e.g. tourism) in as far as the majority of the society is engaged in the process of wealth generation.

Fourth, a corollary of the role of the few, in a rentier state the *government* is the principal recipient of the external rent in the economy. This is a fact of paramount importance, cutting across the whole of the social fabric of the economy affecting the role of the state in the society. The role of the government as the principal recipient of the external rent is closely related to the fact that only few control the external rent. In fact, the 'economic power' thus bestowed upon the few would allow them to seize 'political power' as well, or else induce the political elite to take over the external rent from them without major political disruption. A predominantly rentier *state* will accordingly play a central role in distributing this wealth to the population. This brings us close to a distinction proposed by Giacomo Luciani, that is, between productive and allocative states (see Chapter 3).

Having characterised the main features of a rentier state, it is important to emphasise that the choice of such a concept is based on the assumption that such an economy creates a specific mentality: a *rentier mentality*. The basic assumption about the rentier mentality and that which distinguishes it from conventional economic behaviour is that it embodies a break in the work-reward causation. Reward — income or wealth — is not related to work and risk bearing, rather to chance or situation. For a rentier, reward becomes a windfall gain, an *isolated* fact, situational or accidental as against the conventional outlook where reward is integrated in a *process* as the end result of a long, systematic and organised production circuit. The contradiction between production and rentier ethics is, thus, glaring.

It is also assumed that the pre-eminence of the oil countries has not only brought to the fore a contradiction between production and rentier ethics, but more seriously, has meant the prevalence of the rentier economy. A decade of the oil era shows that the whole of the Arab world, oil rich as well as oil poor, is becoming a sort of oil economy with various undertones of rentier mentalities. This development has affected the role of the state in the whole Arab world.

THE OIL STATES: MULTILAYERS OF RENTIERS

The Arab oil states represent, it has been said, the example *par excellence* of rentier states. With oil exports' revenues, the Arab oil states depend on external rent. Oil revenues represent more than 90 per cent of budget revenues, 95 per cent or more of exports. Also, only a small fraction of the population is involved in the generation of oil revenues, the rest being engaged in the use of the oil wealth. No more than 2 to 3 per cent of the labour force is engaged in the production and distribution of the oil wealth, which adds 60 to 80 per cent to the GDP, as conventionally measured. Nevertheless, this fact does not preclude genuine productive activities outside the oil sector. Finally, oil revenues (rent) accrue directly to the state or the government. The Arab oil states thus correspond to our definition of rentier states. The role and the nature of the state has been greatly affected by this fact.

The state or the government, being the principal rentier in the economy, plays the crucial role of the prime mover of the economic activity. Rent that is held in the hands of the government has to be redistributed among the population. Special social and economic interests are organised in such a manner as to capture a good slice of government rent. Citizenship becomes a source of economic benefit. Different layers of beneficiaries of government rent are thus created, giving rise, in their turn, to new layers of beneficiaries. The whole economy is arranged as a hierarchy of layers of rentiers with the state or the government at the top of the pyramid, acting as the ultimate support of all other rentiers in the economy. It is important to add here that the rentier nature of the new state is magnified by the tribal origins of these states. A long tribal tradition of buying loyalty and allegiance is now confirmed by an *état providence*, distributing favours and benefits to its population.

The conventional role of the state as provider of public goods through coercion — mainly taxation — is now blurred in the Arab oil states by its role as a provider of private favours through the ruler's benevolence. Public goods and private favours have thus gone together in defining the role of the state.

With virtually no taxes, citizens are far less demanding in terms of political participation. The history of democracy owes its beginnings, it is well known, to some fiscal association (no taxation without representation). The government's budget in

89

the oil states remains a one-sided document, an expenditure programme, a promise to spend money and distribute benefits to
the population with virtually no levy on them in terms of taxes
or similar impositions.

Kuwait was probably the one to introduce into the Gulf area
the concept of distributing part of the oil wealth to the population which eventually evolved into that of the welfare state. The
shrewd Sheikh Abdullah al-Salim of Kuwait made the fundamental decision that he (the state) should share part of the oil
rent with the population. The role of the government was thus
defined as being primarily a partial distributor of oil wealth
among the population. In his quest to create vested interests
among notable Kuwaiti families round the new states in the early
1950s, Sheikh Abdullah al-Salim introduced the system of
government land purchase, at prices hardly related to market
value. No more than a decade or two later, the same system was
adopted by other Gulf states: Qatar and UAE. In Saudi Arabia,
the practice of land gifts was already in force since the 1920s and
1930s. With the annexation of Hijaz in the pre-oil era, the
pilgrimage royalties (another source of rent) gave Ibn Saud the
means to distribute favours (land). The government continued
to grant land to relatives, ministers and anyone else it wished to
favour. The recipients sometimes sold their land to private
developers, but the biggest and most generous buyer was always
the government itself (Field, 1984: 99). The early relationship
between oil revenues and land speculation — the proper domain
for rent and rentier — can be seen here. Later developments, as
we shall see, made land as well as shares a prosperous source of
rentier speculation.

Of course, governments in the oil states outgrew their role as
distributors of favours and benefits and embarked on the
modern function of providing public goods and services to their
population. Governments are providing their populations with a
wide range of genuine public goods and services: defence,
national security, education, health, social security, employment, an impressive network of infrastructure, etc. The level
and quality of these public goods and services are usually
adequate, sometimes excellent. They are also provided free or at
very low cost to the beneficiary. However, the original sin
remains, sometimes open but mostly latent, thus vitiating the
provision of these public goods. It is reported that 'if a prince
heads a ministry or some other government department, it is

accepted that he is entitled to draw on the budget of that department or take a share of its spending in major projects' (Field, 1984: 101–2). To a certain degree, all government contracts are seen as royal favours. Their origin as part of the ruler's benevolence does not fail, thus, to exhibit their peculiarities.

The distinction between public service and private interest is very often blurred. There seems to be no clear conflict of interests between holding public office and running private business at the same time, and it is not infrequent to use the one to foster the other. Sometimes high-ranking public officers (ministers) take the trouble to form their private businesses under the names of their sons, brothers or similar *prête noms*. In fact, huge development projects, joint ventures, agents, tenders and awards of hundred million — sometimes billion — dollar contracts have provided opportunities for those in public office to use their positions for private gain (Beblawi, 1982: 216). The practice varies from one oil state to another; it is most conspicuous in Saudi Arabia and least apparent in Kuwait. In Saudi Arabia, contracts are given as expression of royal gratitude. Contract brokers, commission fees for the ruling elite, lobbying the royal family, etc., are not unusual practices in the Gulf areas. Some names earned notorious reputations in this respect; Adnan Khashoggi, Mahdi Tajir, Princes Muhammad Bin Abdel-Aziz, Muhammad Fahd, Sultan Bin Abdel-Aziz are only the most visible (Field, 1984).

The government not only distributes benefits and favours to its population, but it is also the major and ultimate employer in the economy. Every citizen — if not self-employed in business and/or not working for a private venture — has a legitimate aspiration to be a government employee; in most cases this aspiration is fulfilled. Though utterly free enterprise oriented, the number of government employees in the oil states is only matched by socialist-oriented states. Civil servant productivity is, understandably, not very high and they usually see their principal duty as being available in their offices during working hours (*Al Dawam*).

If governments are the principal rentiers in the Arab oil states, they are by no means the only ones. Trade and business professions in many cases consist in no more than taking advantage of special situations entrusted to them by law or fact. Merchants are favoured by existing laws. It is the law in oil states that foreign companies may sell their products only through local agents. Most states insist that foreign companies should also take local merchant partners if they want to operate on their soil. In any case, foreign companies find it difficult to deal with local bureaucracy without local partners or sponsors (Field, 1984). The big trading houses, the family conglomerates that are involved in all business matters owe their wealth, in one way or another, to some rent situation. Being a sales agent if the classical road to business and hence to wealth. Big family names in the oil states are intimately related with one or more brand names; e.g. in the car distribution business we have Alghanim with GM in Kuwait; Juffali with Mercedes in the truck business in Saudi Arabia, and Bisher and Al-Kazmy with the same company in Kuwait; Futtaim with Toyota in Dubai and Al-Sayer with it in Kuwait; Galadari with Mazda in Dubai . . . The list is long indeed ('Arabian Trading', *Financial Times*, 23 January 1985).

Not only should distribution agents be exclusively nationals but also the practice of most professions and trades be restricted to nationals. This legal restriction has been established to counter the well-known shortage of professional and skilled labour. The result is the appearance of a peculiar function, that of the sponsor, *al-kafil*. This is someone, a national of course, who offers his name to expatriates to exercise various trades and professions under his name, in return for a share of proceeds (rent). The *kafil* mentality, where citizenship is becoming a sort of financial asset and hence a sorce of income, transcends national/expatriate relations, to become, even among nationals, a normal feature of everyday life. For example, in Kuwait, during the euphoria of the stock market, it was the habit of the government to allocate a certain number of shares for each Kuwaiti citizen in new public shareholding companies. A very active trade in 'citizenship' (*ganaci*) took place, where those not interested in buying their shares would sell their rights — as attested by the citizenship certificates — to others. Citizenship is not only an affective relation between man and his homeland, it is also, or primarily, a pecuniary relation.

Oil rent thus gave rise, in turn, to a secondary wave of rent generations: second order rents. Two areas seem to distinguish themselves as rent centres: real estate and stock market speculation.

Land, it was said, has played a major role in the process of trickling down oil money from governments to private individuals. The readiness of governments to purchase land at higher prices sustained ever-growing prices for real estate. A very profitable business was created round land speculation with some very active brokers. Government was always prepared to act as the ultimate buyer.

The ingenuity of some land brokers soon introduced a very powerful instrument to keep real estate prices high even in face of credit squeezes, liquidity shortages and/or government's momentary reluctance to inject money into land purchase. This was the so-called forward market or post-dated cheque system. Kuwaiti brokers masterminded these new techniques and extended them imaginatively — and dangerously — to stock market transactions. Growing prices for real estate and stocks cannot be sustained indefinitely unless they are matched by a growing injection of liquidity to back up demand for these assets. Sooner or later there comes a time when liquidity is not forthcoming and the market comes to a halt if not a collapse. This is where the role of the forward transaction which provides the market with a new instrument for credit creation at the disposal of the speculators, bypassing the banking system, comes in. Each speculator becomes something of his own bank, capable of adding to liquidity by issuing his own IOUs which are more or less accepted in the market (real estates, stock market). In final analysis, liquidity is created through bank intermediation in the exchange of obligations. With forward transactions and the issuing of post-dated cheques, speculators assume the role of informal banks and pay for their deals by increasing their own liabilities.

A forward deal is a spot deal with credit, where the buyer gets the commodity (shares, land, etc.) at the time of the transaction and pays forward with a post-dated cheque with a premium (an interest rate or rather a usury rate) which can vary between 50–200 per cent per annum. At maturity, he can either roll over the cheque with another more attractive premium (an offer which the other party usually cannot refuse), or if his creditor refuses the offer, he can just borrow from the market by buying another commodity (shares) on a forward basis (another post-dated cheque to a third party) and selling it on the spot market to get the cash to pay his first creditor. The game can continue indefinitely in as far as dealers are prepared to accept each other's post-dated cheques. In fact, there was a general tacit agreement to continue the game, with everyone issuing and receiving post-dated cheques at the same time. Cheques were rolled over and every second new cheques were added to the market thus giving the illusion of ever-growing fortunes. These were the rules of the mirage wealth creation or the big casino later known as Soukh el-Manakh. A money machine — the dream of all speculators — was invented and nothing could stop the attractiveness of Soukh el-Manakh. Young graduates left their jobs for the new gold mine, early retirements took place, 'creative' companies invested heavily in the stock market, thus scoring huge profits and offsetting their losses in their normal lines of business. Even off-shore bankers and more sober institutions and professionals were tempted by the new phenomenon. New companies were created every day, giving rise to new share-offerings on the market and accordingly fresh opportunities for new wealth. Social life was also transformed: politics was no more a subject for discussion, and even gossiping, a favourite pastime, was fading away. The new and almost only talk of the town was centred on share prices and the new shares coming on to the market.

The end of this fancy world is well-known to all. The Soukh el-Manakh dream turned into a nightmare. In July 1982 some dealers, sensing the imminent difficulties of the market, began to cash their cheques ahead of time. A minor crisis was thus turned into a full-scale crash. The age-old adage that what goes up — artificially — must come down, was finally vindicated in Kuwait (Beblawi and Fahmi, 1984: 173).

The government role in the development of this speculative activity can hardly be overestimated. Not only did governments indirectly help speculations, but in many instances were directly involved in supporting speculative markets. When the Kuwaiti stock market faced its first setback in 1976/7, the Kuwaiti government was prompted to bail it out. Even in 1982, when the Kuwaiti government refused to repeat the role it played in 1976/7, it compensated the so-called small investor — defined as one owed no more than KD 2 million ($6.75 million): no small reward for speculators. In both cases, a number of key members of government and parliament were deeply involved in the stock speculations.

The juxtaposition within Arab oil states of a rentier economy and a productive economy is paralleled by the coexistence of two social communities: nationals and expatriates. Expatriates are called upon to help fill the gap in available manpower in oil states. More often than not, these expatriates assume productive activities to satisfy the growing needs of the society. They earn their living by the work they do. The relationship work-reward is actually maintained in their case. Rent economy, on the other hand, is normally confined to nationals; the privileges it conveys hardly extend to expatriates.

The contrast between the two communities is striking as well as revealing. Nationals live more in a rentier economy and associate with its financial manna all the political rights of citizenship. On the other hand, although earning their living in a more productive manner, the impact of the rentier economy on expatriates is far from negligible, giving rise to serious corruption of the productive system and work ethics. Even if they form the core of the productive manpower, expatriates nevertheless remain alien to the body politic. Though they serve the country, live — and also die — on its soil, they are not part of it. Expatriates are thus part of the labour force but not of the society. The material life of expatriates is usually comfortable and by no means comparable to the living conditions in their homeland. Their emotional life is, none the less, unstable, terribly wanting in security and lacking a sense of belonging.

The political cleavage between the two communities widens as the economic rent to citizens increases. Restrictions on exptriates' professional mobility as well as their political integration increases with the increase in the oil wealth. The contrast between the less abundant years of the 1960s and the more affluent 1970s is very significant. Regardless of the vocal rhetoric of Arab nationalism, in the 1970s the political elite in the oil states, no matter whether right- or left-wing, advocated a narrow local nationalism and restirictive benefits to expatriates.

THE NON-OIL STATES: SEMI-RENTIERS WITHOUT OIL

The Arab non-oil states are by no means rentier states in the sense previously outlined. The predominance of the oil phenomenon on the whole region is, however, such that many non-oil Arab states are showing increasing signs not dissimilar to those witnessed in oil states.

Let us first draw attention to the fact that because of oil wealth, the whole Arab area — oil rich as well as oil poor — has assumed strategic value in the world chessboard. The area as a whole, particularly neighbouring countries, have gained location rent.

Military and political aid to preserve and/or introduce super-powers' — as well as mini-powers' — influence in the area, is a major source of external rents to many states. Otherwise remote and poor states (e.g. Somalia) would hardly receive alternately Russian and American aid. In the 1960s Egypt received the highest Soviet aid to a foreign country, to become, together with Israel, the highest American aid recipient in the 1970s and 1980s. Syria, Jordan and South Yemen are other examples.

Rhetoric aside, inter-Arab aid was related, to some extent, to its effect on the stability and tranquillity of oil rent in oil states. Very often Arab aid to fellow Arab states was used in much the same way as domestic redistribution of oil revenues: to buy allegiance or rather avoid trouble. Pan-Arabism and Arab money were, to a great extent, and in different hands, the stick and the carrot, used to bring about a very subtle equilibrium in sharing oil rent. By conferring and/or withholding super-legitimacy over individual states, the advocates of pan-Arabism used their political clout as a source of financial aid. By distri-buting and/or promising aid, the carrot in the hands of the oil states helped them buy peace and stability. Arab finance was thus more a counterpart than a complement to pan-Arabism. It is no wonder, then, that Arab financial flow to Arab brothers coincided with the retreat of the pan-Arab system after the 1967 war, which 'marked the Waterloo of pan-Arabism' (Ajami, 1978/9). In the wake of the October 1973 war, it was Sadat and Assad — 'revisionists' or 'correctionists' of the pan-Arab doctrine — who obtained Arab finance. With the decline of Egypt's role in mobilising Arab public opinion, particularly after Camp David, the Baghdad Summit relieved the Arab oil states of their financial commitments to Egypt, shifting them to more assertive Iraq, Syria and the PLO. The subsequent Iraq-Iran war proved to be quite a drain on their treasury. The Baath party, which is in power in both Iraq and Syria, though two competing factions, is notorious for its unscrupulous and ruth-less practices vis-à-vis its opponents. Some oil states — Kuwait and UAE for example — had the privilege of actually experienc-ing firsthand such practices when a number of attacks and/or bombings took place on their territory. They had, of course, the tact and discretion to turn a blind eye to these 'accidents'. But the message is clear.

External location rent is also evident in so-called transit countries (Mahdavi, 1970). Suez Canal revenue and oil pipeline royalties are major revenue sources to some countries, e.g. Egypt and Syria.

Workers' remittances are becoming one of the major foreign exchange sources in some non-oil states. Yemen is a well-known example where remittances represent more than 85 per cent of GDP. Workers' remittances are becoming the biggest single source of foreign exchange in Egypt as well. In Syria, Lebanon, Tunisia, Algeria and Morocco, workers' remittances play a very important role in their balance of payment adjustments. It is not easy to equate workers' remittances to external rent. From the worker's point of view, he is earning his income at the cost of effort and work. From the recipient country's point of view, remittances are, nevertheless, more akin to aid or non-requited money transfers.

All told, various elements of external rent play an increasing role in non oil Arab states. In Egypt, for example, it is estimated that about 45 per cent of its GDP is represented by exogenous — read rent — elements in the form of oil revenues, workers' remittances, foreign aid, Suez Canal revenue and tourist expenditure. It is also to be noticed that most of these revenues accrue directly to the state or the government. The epithet of semi-rentier state is, thus, not far-fetched.

The semi-rentier nature of non-oil states is not without its effects on the role of the state and on citizens' behaviour. Government favours are now embodied in a welfare doctrine. Subsidies of all kinds pervert the economic system. A huge bureaucracy, sort of a new rentier class, is getting a substantial slice of the government's accrued rent. Though individually very low-paid, civil servants as a social group are a very expensive element in view of their contribution to the country's productivity (it is often thought that they contribute negatively to the growth of the economy).

It is also interesting to see how each source of external rent has bred its own chain of second-order rentiers. In Egypt, for example, a prosperous trade has been developed around workers' movement to the Gulf. Also, money dealers have grown immensely to process workers' remittances. American aid helped create a flourishing consultancy — legal, technical, economic, etc. — business to prepare proposals for aid consideration. A new social class — lawyers, consultants, financial analysts, lobbyists, brokers, etc. — is on the rise everywhere.

Finally, when not direct recipient of the rent, the state, because of its external origin, quite often tactfully courts the rent earners. Suffice it to observe tax exemptions and other incentives given to workers' remittances, foreign banks, tourism, etc. Governments do their utmost to sweeten their normal coercive practices. They are willing to appeal and not to impose. Economic liberalisation, *infitah* or whatever, is everywhere.

CONCLUSION: AN OIL ARAB ECONOMY

It seems from the foregoing that the oil phenomenon has cut across the whole of the Arab world, oil rich and oil poor. Arab oil states have played a major role in propagating a new pattern of behaviour, i.e. the rentier pattern. Oil as the primary source of rent in the Arab region has generated various secondary rent sources to other non-oil Arab states. To the first-order rentier oil states is thus added a second-order non-oil rentier strata. The impact of oil has been so pre-eminent that it is not unrealistic to refer to the present era of Arab history as the oil era, where the oil disease has contaminated all of the Arab world. Be it oil revenue, or workers' remittances, or strategic location, or *el-kafil*, or Soukh el-Manakh, they are all consequences of the oil phenomenon, and have been accompanied by a serious blow to the ethics of work. Income is no longer a reward of serious and hard work, it is very often related to special circumstances, chance, location, etc. In a word, we are living in a rentier universe which has affected both the state and the citizen.

NOTE

1. 'The religious valutaion of restless, continuous, systematic work in a wordly calling, as the highest means to asceticism, and at the same time, the surest and most evident proof of rebirth and genuine faith, must have been the most powerful conceivable level for the expansion of that attitude toward life which we have here called the spirit of capitalism.' Weber (1958: 127).

5

Policies for Development: Attitudes toward Industry and Services

Michel Chatelus

INTRODUCTORY REMARKS

The purpose of this chapter is to investigate industrial structure and policies and the extension of the service sector in Arab countries in the light of the production versus allocation states paradigm. Starting from the simple distinction between those Arab states where allocation prevails (those states able to live from oil revenues), and those whose spending capacity depends both on the country's production and on the state's capacity to raise taxes on this production, we discuss whether this two-way distinction may be utilised as the central tool of analysis, or whether it is only one among several criteria and determinants of the situation in the Arab states. The varying impact on the state building process in the Arab world, of the allocative opportunities and productive constraints mix, will be the central theme of the chapter: the principal issue remaining is the appreciation of the relative weight to be attributed to each of them if we wish to understand the successive stages of the industrial and service growth in the Arab states.

Our objective is hence to analyse, evaluate and explain, not to present a complete description of the industrial and service sector in the Arab world. It is necessary here to clarify a potential source of ambiguity. We do not believe in the existence of such an entity as 'the Arab economy'; for only political arguments can be called upon to support this concept; economic realities do not offer convincing proof (Amin, 1980; Brahimi, 1978; Sayigh, 1982). We shall refer therefore to a diversified set of Arab economies, using different regroupings of the concerned states depending on the aspect we intend to study. In this perspective, the gathering of all states in a single group may be a meaningful approach to dealing with basic trends and influences whenever their consequences concern all states, equally affected by the same environment and subject to identical pressures and constraints.

The first part of this chapter will present an analytical background and discuss the main hypotheses relating the distinction between the allocation/production states to their attitudes toward industry and services. Keeping the main distinction as a useful analytical reference, we will note the necessity of introducing more complex criteria to explain state policies. The second part will examine the industrial development process in the light of the state's regulation of domestic and external revenues sources. The service sector will be the object of a similar analysis in the last part of the chapter.

ANALYTICAL BACKGROUND AND MAIN HYPOTHESES

Allocation or production states: a paradigm revisited

Starting from the simple allocation/production paradigm, we are led to successive revisions and qualifications in order to cope with the growing complexity of relations of Arab states to oil rent. Various alternative definitions have been utilised to classify Arab states, and a rapid glance at some of the most widely used expressions may facilitate the understanding of the underlying hypothesis. We find distinctions between surplus and deficit Arab countries, between oil rich and poor states, between production and circulation economies, rentier and recipient states, oil dependent and tax dependent states, etc.

In current IMF publications, Arab countries are divided into three groups, all of them under the major heading 'developing countries': a first list of 'oil-exporting countries' comprises Algeria, Iraq, Kuwait, Libya, Oman, Qatar, Saudi Arabia and the United Arab Emirates; in a second list we have 'non-oil countries', classified as 'net oil exporters', namely Bahrain, Egypt, Syria and Tunisia; the other Arab countries belong to the residual group of 'net oil importers' (International Monetary Fund, 1984; World Bank, 1984). In the often quoted statistical tables of its yearly *World Development Report*, the World Bank re-groups oil countries with high income (Kuwait, Libya, Oman, Saudi Arabia and the United Arab Emirates) in a specific group, while other Arab states, whether oil exporters or not are ranked in the lengthy developing countries table, according to their *per capita* GNP (ECWA, 1984). All those groupings are drawn from one simple assumption: the pertinence of a dualistic approach to the analysis of the behaviour of states, with a fundamental contrast between allocation in oil-rich states and production in other states. A slightly modified approach is presented in a recent report by the UN Economic Commission for Western Asia (ECWA, 1984): it proposes to divide Arab countries into three groups: in a first group we find oil countries with small populations, i.e. Gulf countries and Libya; a second group consists of oil countries with relatively more diversified resources and larger populations (Algeria and Iraq); all other Arab states are in a third group. The fundamental reference in such a grouping remains unchanged.

Observing the political economy of state industrialisation in the Arab Middle East (Chatelus and Schmeil, 1984) we suggested a generalisation of the rentier state hypothesis (another name for the allocation state paradigm) to the great majority of Arab states. Induced allocation effects in non oil states are just as determinant as direct allocation in oil countries. Simply delineating rent as an income not originating from the productive activity of the concerned unit, the flows and dimensions of which are not directly linked to the beneficiary's activity (i.e., any income the amount of which is determined for the most part by decisions the concerned unit cannot control), we distinguish 'production economies' and 'circulation economies'. Rent economies are an ideal type of the latter: individuals, groups, even the state, compete for the control of rent. In that view, most economic activities are to be considered as means of ensuring income circulation, rather than production-oriented behaviour. Arab states exemplify to a large extent this ideal type. We are struck, indeed, by the overwhelming importance of oil as a rent for the whole region. For major producers, oil is a quasi-exclusive source of original income depending to a great extent on non-national decision centres. Most activities are therefore 'subsidised' by products of oil revenues. For non-oil countries — even when a genuine productive sector exists — a growing part of economic activity is linked to oil money produced through labour and capital movements. The incongruity

101

between 'resources' and 'uses' in national accounting terms is much higher in most Arab countries than in developing countries in other parts of the world. The resource deficits of Middle Eastern states such as Egypt, Jordan, Syria or Sudan are just as massive and cumbersome as oil surpluses have been for a long time for Saudi Arabia, Kuwait or the United Arab Emirates.

In this context, the role of the state is paramount: it is the unavoidable instrument of resource allocation whether in liberal or socialist regimes. Paradoxically, the state plays an even more determinant role in the economic activities of liberal countries through budgetary expenditures (in Saudi Arabia, public spending accounts for over half the GDP), state-controlled or state-supported enterprises, food subsidies, administered prices, etc.

In most Arab countries, a growing part of the population depends for its living, either directly or indirectly, on unrequited transfers. Money comes from expatriate relatives, patrons or tribe elders, or state allocations. There is at best a tenuous link between individual income and activity. *Getting access to the rent circuit is a greater preoccupation than reaching productive efficiency.*

Anti-productive biases both influence economic behaviour and distort economic choices. Economic behaviour is biased in a rent-dominated economy by individual or even corporate group tendencies competing to increase their share of the circulating income. Given that goal, productive activities are not efficient. They stand as second-best choices for groups of individuals who are more or less excluded from the rent circuit. In most cases, handling productive activities is the 'privilege' of expatriates, immigrants and minorities. Reluctance to do productive work is a widespread attitude among dominant groups. In any case, most people have not much to gain from the risks and pains of active work when they get easier benefits from rent sharing through sponsoring, import trade, brokerage, or real estate and housing speculation. Economic choices are distorted by the contradiction between rent-controlling political strategies which aim at stability and the unavoidable emergence of new social values which a successful economic strategy would necessarily imply.

The case of industrialisation is a good example of this contradiction which compels economic agents to follow the path of what we call a 'failure-oriented policy'. In that respect, industrialisation policies are less committed to selecting objectives (giving them priorities, implementing those goals), than to selecting appropriate *means* (of spending money, distributing income, providing power, hegemony or rent control). A global view on the very limited successes and major failures of industrial policies in Arab states, oil rich or not, in the late 1970s, seemed to confirm the generalised rentier state paradigm. Even though Arab rulers pay lip service to industrialisation, their allegedly consistent industrial strategies hardly go beyond spending programmes. No real answers are given to such fundamental questions as linkage effects, economies of scale, labour training, market size, or insertion in the world economy.

Despite some remarkable exceptions (such as the Bahraini dry dock and aluminium plant), there is little or no coordination between industrial perspectives in the various Middle East Arab states. Competition for prestige or leadership often leads to redundant projects. Optimal allocation of resources on a regional basis is not a determinant preoccupation. Most 'productive' investments reveal a preference for infrastructure, public works, construction, and expensive 'big projects' that are vulnerable in an unfavourable economic environment.

Confronted with the major problem of building domestic order and regional stability, the Arab states tend to use economies as a way of solving strategic puzzles. It is the very industrialisation process which contributes to state-building rather than the state which helps to build a national industry. The strategy of industrialisation is therefore part of a strategic plan.

If the above analysis is pertinent, the generalised rentier hypothesis may significantly improve our understanding of attitudes toward industry in most Arab states. Useful as it may prove, it none the less accounts for only a part of the overall picture, just as the simple two-way distinction throws light on only another part of the same picture. Actual conditions prevailing in the Arab world reflect a more complex reality, calling for less simplifying assumptions than were used at the height of the oil boom. Disparities within each group of states tend to enlarge, reducing the explanatory contribution of any single classification criterion. Similar attitudes are observed in states belonging to the production or to the allocation category, while policies concerning external revenues and their utilisation reveal striking contrasts within a given category.

Political turmoil in the Middle East, the changing world economic outlook, depressed markets for oil and oil-related products, reduced income for pure allocation states, justify the introduction of new parameters in the model, differently affecting various Arab states. State policies have to integrate a growing number of unfavourable factors, and so do private economic agents' behaviour. The adjustment process will differ from one state to the other. Production and allocation still constitute a basic reference, with a special mention for the generalised allocation hypothesis; however, the analysis of the actual situation requires the introduction of new criteria and the abandonment of a simple, single, clear-cut distinction between two types of states. As oil income dwindles and the first stage of an infrastructure-dominated investment policy comes to maturity, allocation states deeply need precise policy guidelines, while the nature and consequences of the induction process in states receiving transfer income is greatly modified.

A reassertion of the role of the state and its implications for allocation attitudes

New constraints and changing attitudes may be observed through the evolution of the role played by the state in Arab economies. Many countries have inherited a strong public sector and a high level of state intervention in the working of the economy. Three levels of 'state presence' in the economy may be distinguished (Chatelus, 1984: 101): as a builder of infrastructure, the state creates the necessary conditions for the effective working of a productive system, whether public or private. This is a case of the 'philosophy of infrastructure development' (Bowen-Jones, 1984).

At a second level, the state behaves as an allocative agent. In the Gulf it distributes to the great majority of nationals at least part of oil revenues: it is a question of survival. In oil-poor countries it has to establish and maintain some sort of allocation policy (through food subsidies, for instance).

At a third level, the state directly competes with the private sector by taking direct charge of productive activities and acting as the major economic agent, especially through a system of public enterprises or state-controlled business concerns. In most Arab countries, whether capitalist or socialist, the public sector dominates industrial production, investment and employment.

The present state of affairs in the Arab world produces a trend toward the privatisation of the economy, which has important implications for the attitudes toward industry and services.

The relaxation of economic controls, the 'opening' of the national market to foreign goods and capital, the sale of public shares to private interests, or the new emphasis laid upon the introduction of market considerations and efficient managerial attitudes in the public sector, are some of the expressions of a general tendency affecting, with a varying intensity, most Arab countries. The wide range of concerned states extends from Saudi Arabia to Algeria and Egypt. Privatisation may be analysed in a certain sense as a move towards the reconsideration of allocative and circulation attitudes by direct or induced rentier states. Since massive allocation of income by the state is limited by economic constraints, governments will try to reach a more satisfactory balance between available resources and distributed income.

Evidence of such a tendency is apparent in the public expenditure commitments and budgetary measures adopted in several Gulf states. In short, there are currently some *major reconsiderations of salient features of the welfare state*. In Kuwait, we observe deliberate attempts to remove the welfare mentality to which the population has been accustomed by long growing oil revenues: for instance highly subsidised gas and oil prices were increased sixfold in 1982/3. The prices charged for electricity and water may well be increased significantly; they are currently sold much below cost, which encourages waste (in 1982/3, the subsidies on those items reached almost 800 million dollars.) It is also reported that ministers talk increasingly about the possible introduction of charges for medical care which is now absolutely free. In Saudi Arabia, there have been cuts in the subsidies paid in petrol, electricity, water and certain foodstuffs, though the amounts involved have not been great. In the UAE, charges for medical care for non-nationals were introduced in May 1983. (Non-nationals have to buy both a yearly medical card and cover the costs of major operations.) Unprecedented talks about income tax are reported. It would be premature to conclude that 'the end of the welfare state' is near, but proper consideration should be given to the multiple signs of economic pressures on the largesse of the allocative state (*Financial Times*, 23 Feb. 1983 or 25 April 1985).

In 'non-oil' countries (or should we call them production states?), the objective of political survival, supported by induced rent income, has for many years fed an uneasy but somewhat manageable compromise between limited domestic resources, increased needs and a minimum level of mass consumption. Subsidies for popular consumer goods, especially food and kerosene, have become the omnipresent political means utilised to limit wage escalation and ensure a minimal redistribution toward the lowest income groups. Today few, if any, states escape the 'subsidy trap'. Under IMF pressure (or more plainly under financial necessity), recurrent attempts have been made from Morocco and Tunisia to Egypt and Syria to reduce the food subsidy bills. This burden can absorb up to 30 or 40 per cent of budget allocations, as is the case in Egypt.

The immediate political upheaval provoked by increases in basic food prices (especially bread and edible oil) gives full credence to the notion of 'allocation policy for survival'. 'Bread riots' have deeply shaken Morocco, Tunisia, Egypt and Sudan. Algeria alone was able to reduce significantly subsidies on basic commodities, by including food price increases in a broad wage revision and economic reform package. Unfavourable economic effects (waste, budget deficits, high import bills, low prices for local producers) and perverse social results (subsidised goods do not necessarily reach the highly needy, especially in rural areas) impose upon governments in one form or another a reduction of the food bill by reducing the gap between food costs and food sales prices. This is not only a necessary constraint of any 'privatisation policy' (which some attack as an 'IMF dictate'); it is a critical issue which conditions any improvement of the working of the economic system. All countries are concerned. Clearly there is a trend toward less allocation in allocation states and a growing burden of allocation constraints in would-be production states.

States and production: changing attitudes in the Arab world

New conditions in the world economy leave little choice to the Arab states: the necessary shift in the economic structure toward more productive activities and the reduction of dependence on external income should cease to be a mere ritual invocation: new sources of diversified income have to be found. Efficiency in production and a better control over allocation-induced attitudes are urgent necessities for all states. Signs of changes in attitudes responding to this challenge are multiplying, although the burden of the past still decisively influences the present poor performances of the productive sectors in both oil and non-oil countries. The privatisation drive and the trends toward less direct allocation revenues do not imply a reduced role for the state. On the contrary, in efficient production economics, the role of the state is paramount.

A brief glance at some of the 'new industrial countries', such as Korea or Taiwan, reveals the magnitude of the place occupied by the state in a successful industrialisation process. The nature and content of the state intervention, the specificity of the economic planning process, help, by contrast, to delineate the reasons of the reduced efficiency of state intervention in most Arab 'pro duction states'. Several aspects of state intervention in a country like Korea are worth observing as illustrative examples of this contrast. The state determines the objectives of the country's economic strategy and the content of the leading (interrelated) industrial choices through an efficient long-term planning process. Therefore, planning does not appear as the expression of the state political vision of economic development through a catalogue of projects, but as an instrument of guidance and stimulation for all concerned economic actors. Global planning is complemented by sectorial programmes. In Korea, for example, successive programmes have been devised for ship-building in the 1960s, for machinery and equipment and nuclear energy in the 1970s, and for electronics in the early 1980s. When necessary, the state invests directly in the recommended activities and creates appropriate institutions to help and follow-up plan implementation. We should also mention the importance of the channelling to industry of local financial capacities and the crucial role attributed to technological formation and the development of a national engineering capacity. *The state emerges as an active engine for industrial growth*, not only through the industrial projects it promotes, finances and controls, but through the overall impulsion and cohesion it brings to the industrial sector (Courlet and Judet, 1981).

In the Arab context, such a prescription requires drastic changes in attitudes and rapid solutions to several urgent problems. In entering the world market for high technology — high capital products, such as petrochemicals, aluminium

107

derivates or fertilisers, Arab industries cannot rely on excessive subsidies and state privileges. They have to be fair competitors, in order to avoid tariff barriers in Western countries. Regional cooperation, such as it develops between members of the GCC, requires well-monitored projects of proven feasibility. Joint ventures with foreign firms have to break even in a reasonable period. All these requirements imply a favourable economic environment created by the states, and a new type of industrial policy.

In the domestic economies, the heart of the argument is to be found in the consequences on consumption of the increases in oil income and purchasing power created throughout the region by the wide circulation of oil-linked revenues. Not only do growing food dependency and soaring food imports highlight the demand for more to eat and a better diet, but a great number of consumer goods have become very common even in low-income countries (Egypt or Yemen, for instance). The greatest part of those increased consumption needs was satisfied through growing imports as long as sufficient rent income was available. Public spending has been the most powerful channel to encourage private consumption (including budgetary subsidies). Under the prevailing conditions, state spending thus creates supplementary demand much more rapidly than state investment and public production can match by a corresponding increase in supply.

The only possible answer is for the state to support private production activities; such support can be understood as a direct consequence and natural outcome of public spending. Populist inclinations in such countries as Egypt, Algeria, Syria or Iraq are less and less compatible with developmentalist attitudes (implying high investment ratios and massive capital accumulation). With declining external income to pay for imports and the irreversibility of new consumption patterns, the necessity to meet growing consumption needs imposes on the Arab governments new alternatives or combined attitudes toward the production sector. They may try to stimulate positive responses from the private sector through various policy measures: profit rehabilitation, credit facilities, tax exemptions, relaxation of controls, etc., and/or they may aim at increased efficiency in the public sector.

Concerning the first point, in recent years, most governments in the Arab world, whatever their past or present commitment to socialism or state control, have conceived and implemented specific measures to encourage private production and stimulate the initiatives of independent producers. From the official recognition of the 'non-exploitive character' of small-scale private property in Algeria (Bernard, 1984) to the adoption of credit facilities, tax exemptions, customs duty facilities, etc., numerous cases of policy measures in favour of private initiative and investment can be noted. Saudi Arabia encourages light industries by reducing almost to nil land acquisition costs, and providing long-term per cent loans and almost cost free electricity. Not surprisingly, Qatar, Kuwait and the Emirates have adopted similar policies of 'subsidised privatisation' (as an intermediate step between direct state intervention and pure market activities).

Small and medium size enterprises are a favourite target for any private sector investment policy, as they appear both politically safer than powerful companies and economically complementary to large public sector undertakings. Most development plans or economic programmes pay due tribute to the essential functions to be fulfilled by those enterprises. In the Gulf countries, substantial achievements have been recorded in Saudi Arabia, where the fourth plan (due to start in 1985), will be 'above all a plan for the Saudi private sector' (*Financial Times*, April 1984). Several hundred enterprises run by small entrepreneurs already exist, mostly in food processing, building materials and mechanical work. A qualified observer speaks of 'the great surge towards industry witnessed in Saudi Arabia in the past three years'. In Qatar, Bahrain, Kuwait or the UAE, similar efforts to encourage local businessmen to take over joint ventures or to launch new enterprises (partly making use of the output of national industries: aluminium, steel, chemicals) have met with uneven but not totally insignificant responses. Cooperative developments within the Gulf Cooperation Council countries should be of great aid. Presently, the products of private industry represent 3 billion dollars of savings in imports in GCC countries (Daddab and Mihyuddin, 1984).

'Small is beautiful' seems to be the motto behind the scenes in the recent economic measures adopted in Algeria where two kinds of small businesses have been encouraged: local public enterprises and private sector activities. Their extension is a priority objective in the third quadrennial plan; several specific laws were passed in their favour in 1981 and 1982. Jordan,

Morocco and Tunisia, among others, have multiplied measures favouring small and medium sized firms. Though Moroccan private capital is conspicuously reluctant to invest in industry, Jordan and Tunisia have obtained encouraging results. In Syria and Iraq, legal dispositions encouraging private industrial investment have met with very limited success so far; this is because the would-be entrepreneurs have doubts about the governments' political conversion to the ideological legitimacy and economic efficiency of private enterprise.

On the other end of the economic spectrum, the whole system of state capitalism and state control over the main productive activities, often through bureaucratic and highly inefficient public enterprises, is under critical examination: direct (but partial) answers are expected from the restructuring of the public enterprise system. Algeria aimed at breaking feudalities by dismantling the giant 'sociétés nationales' and fragmenting them into smaller independent entities, easier to control and to manage efficiently. The underlying idea is that smaller companies should prove more sensitive to preoccupations of efficiency, escape the excess costs of huge state monopolies and invest personal responsibility in their managers. In Egypt the abolition of the general organisations by law 111 in 1975 was considered a step toward more effective responsibility on the part of company heads (Waterbury, 1983). The absolute necessity of improving the performance of public enterprises is a recurrent theme in the political and economic literature of all countries with a large public production sector. Algeria's President Chadli and Prime Minister Brahimi have often insisted in public in the last two years on the low productivity and lack of efficiency of the public sector. In October 1984, President Chadli asserted that (public enterprise) 'profits were legitimate as long as they were genuine profits' (*Le Monde*, 19 Sept. 1984). A 1980 report on Syria mentioned a debate on 'whether the private sector should be given a greater role either directly or indirect *through the public sector adopting some of its techniques* to gain efficiency' (McDermott, 1983). In Sudan, rehabilitation plans for big farm projects and sugar factories strongly rely on the adoption of market incentives and privately oriented management criteria: for example, it is recommended that tenants of public land be charged for inputs and their incomes be determined according to their effective production. In Algeria, one of the main targets of the 1980–4 plan is decentralisation, for political as well as managerial reasons. The introduction of competitive behaviour between enterprises in the public sector is often presented as a means of improving productivity and increasing efficiency (such proposals are often made in Egypt and Algeria).

The trends we have just decribed do not invalidate the Middle Eastern Arab states paradigm (extended with some qualifications to Maghreb countries) of circulation and allocation dominated economies. However, they did add two important perspectives. The first is the fact that political survival cannot be guaranteed any longer by a skilful allocation policy dominated by a few oil-rich states; production aspects are becoming increasingly important. There is an urgent need for state legitimacy based on efficiency in the productive sector, rather than on its position in the allocative circuit. Second, the increased role of market forces and private agents reacting to government stimuli and price incentives will not necessarily provide Arab economies with the desperately needed efficiency in private and public management. Allocation biases remain extremely influential and legislative changes cannot, by themselves, change economic conditions: the final outcome has yet to be determined.

ATTITUDES TOWARD INDUSTRY: AIMS AND ACHIEVEMENTS

Industrial objectives in a political perspective

In many countries of the region one can observe the prevalence, from the late 50s to the mid-70s, of an industrialisation ideology which privileges political considerations over purely economic conditions and constraints. When oil resources are available, they temporarily strengthen the policy toward industry. The declared ambitions of several important states, often newly independent or having just achieved total emancipation from Western control, are to establish the economic basis of autonomous growth: the political process of state building is closely connected to the economic-political process of establishing an industrial infrastructure. Disappointing results recorded in the manufacturing sector clearly point to the unfavourable consequences of such overdetermination by political considerations (the allocative aspect of which is evident). We may tentatively distinguish four categories of states, according to the amount of money they can allocate to industry, the past and present importance of value added manufacturing activities and the intensity of allocative influences on productive choices.

The most significant and controversial category is constituted by *'pure' allocation states*, essentially the six members of the Gulf Cooperation Council (GCC) on the Arabian Peninsula: Bahrain, Kuwait, Oman, Qatar, Saudi Arabia and the United Arab Emirates. They claim to diversify their economy through industrialisation and the development of productive activities, spending part of their oil income on huge infrastructural works and large industrial projects. Until recently, there was little or no coordination between concerned states (even within the United Arab Emirates) and duplication was conspicuous whether in infrastructure (seven international airports within a hundred mile range) or in plants and manufacturing units: aluminium smelters, fertiliser and petrochemical plants, dry docks, etc., seemed to multiply and lead to harmful competition. With the limitations imposed by a shortage of labour, relatively small markets and the strong dependency of most projects on the availability of free oil and gas, the authenticity of the claim for 'diversification by industry' has, of course, to be questioned. To a large extent, oil states tried to buy legitimacy through conspicuous spending on spectacular industrial schemes.

When the oil glut led to the reduction of the Gulf States' revenues, the greatest part of the expensive basic infrastructural work had been completed (water desalination plants, electricity generators, transportation networks, gas collecting installations, etc.), paving the way to the much hoped for 'exchange of assets' (Kerr and Yassin, 1982: 167), where industry would replace oil as a major source of income. A first wave of big industrial projects has also recently been completed: refineries, fertiliser complexes, aluminium smelters, steel mills are now realities in Qatar, Bahrain, Saudi Arabia and Kuwait. There are technical successes, and a few financial successes as well: ALBA (Aluminium of Bahrain), QASCO (Qatar Steel Company) or QAFCO (Qatar Fertiliser Company), the HADEED steel mill in Saudi Arabia, and fertiliser units in several states. There are also numerous cases of abandoned projects, delays, overcosts and low-capacity utilisation, due either to changing economic conditions and suddenly depressed markets, or to technical and manpower difficulties.

Qatar and Bahrain represent particular cases, where value added in manufacturing accounts for a sizeable share of GNP. Bahrain's industrial achievements benefited from regional cooperation and Arab joint ventures actively supported the well located, small and oilless state's industrialisation policy. A limited but dynamic industrialisation process is now working in Bahrain, with a second generation of industrial projects, including important private investments, due to mature in the coming years. Income from manufacturing accounts for 10 to 15 per cent of GNP. Qatar also displays industrial realisations making a systematic use of gas as cheap feedstock and fuel, and absorbing surplus capital. Qatari long-term development plans have established the customary heavy industry units: fertilisers, steel rolling, petrochemicals and cement. The list of first-generation massive projects has apparently now been completed and much attention is now paid to the expansion of Qatar's second tier of industrialisation (downstream activities) and to the encouragement of greater participation of the private sector in industry. Industrial income reaches 10 per cent of total GNP.

The contrast between Qatar and Bahrain on one side and Kuwait on the other, illustrates the wide range of attitudes in allocation states. Industrial ambitions of Kuwaiti ruling elites have always been limited, and cautious plans for industrial diversification have been shelved in the recent period in response to the reduction of oil income and in order not to exacerbate the expatriate labour problem. With the apparent indefinite postponement of a large-scale petrochemical project which had been adopted in principle in 1982, oil refineries and a fertiliser plant remain the only heavy industries in the country (we should however remember that half the petroleum exports are now refined products). Allocation attitudes and the 'rentier state' mentality have thus been recently reinforced by the evolution of the environment. A choice has been implicitly made (and is now more overtly uttered) not to develop a heavy industry base from which to derive downstream manufacturing industries. Earmarking part of the oil revenues for a Fund for Future Generations, Kuwait has given preference to investment abroad: 'good will' allocations through direct aid to Arab countries and the Kuwait Fund for Economic Development, regional investment through participation in joint ventures in Gulf countries and other Arab countries. Due to the early start of the Kuwaiti economy, a number of industrial enterprises produce intermediate and consumer goods. Manufacturing contributes from 5 to 7 per cent of GNP. Increased competition, the recession in the Gulf and the aftermath of the financial crisis of Soukh el-Manakh, will impose a drastic revision in the management of existing industries and the adoption of more efficient methods; few existing indutries presently meet the criteria for survival. Kuwait state policy toward industry clearly reveals the limitations of productive efforts in a pure allocation context (investment income is half the size of oil income). With local specificities (especially in Dubai), the United Arab Emirates and Oman display a similar trend in their attitude toward industry.

Saudi Arabia, another pure allocation state in the original stage, illustrates the obstacles which must be overcome in order to implement an efficient policy to reduce dependence on oil, and establish a productive industrial sector. Present achievements do not offer clear-cut answers concerning the possibility for an oil state to escape the allocation trap. A long-term development policy, aiming at the rapid industrialisation of the kingdom, was adopted in the mid-70s. Beside the construction of several big petroleum refineries, Petromin (a specialised state institution) was charged with the building, operation and marketing of the products of a number of huge industrial projects. These projects respond to two principal criteria: they utilise the country's huge hydrocarbon (especially gas) resources, and they do not require abundant manpower. Over-ambitious schemes elaborated during the frantic years of the oil boom had to be reconsidered. A manageable, although sizeable programme for ten major industrial units (not including refineries), eight of which are in the petrochemical sector and two in iron and steel production, was adopted and implemented. Two specifically conceived industrial sites in Jubail and Yanbo were built to house the petrochemical projects (and later the second-generation industries). Major Japanese and American firms are SABIC partners in joint ventures (except for one project which saw the withdrawal of Dow Chemical). Those foreign giants will have the responsibility for the bulk of the marketing of the new products (ethylene, methanol, low-density polyethylene, urea, etc.) which are already on stream or were due to be in the first part of 1985. Saudi Arabia is adding 4 to 5 per cent production capacity to the world chemical output. When three petroleum refineries presently under construction are completed, the first stage of Saudi industrialisation will be achieved. We are thus entering the decisive stage: the development of a second generation of intermediate industries oriented toward local and regional markets (and not exclusively exporting on world markets), utilising part of the output for heavy industry and establishing links with the dynamic but vulnerable private sector manufacturing consumer goods. The crucial test will be the ability of industrial enterprises, both public and private, to live on their own with decreasing state support and to face increasingly fierce competition. Saudi industry, like other Gulf states' industry, remains to a large extent the expression of a spending process depending upon allocative attitudes. It has yet to prove itself capable of becoming a genuine source of income, alternative to oil income.

In a second category, we will place states long dominated by a *strong industrialisation ideology*: Algeria, Libya, Iraq or Syria. They put high hopes in the emancipation potentialities of a voluntarist economic policy, as part of a strong reaction against colonialist domination. In the case of Iraq, Algeria and Libya, oil income is a unique and important source of investment finance. In the case of Syria, the meagre surplus has to be enlarged by transfer revenues. Nationalised enterprises and heavy investment in basic industries are the preferred instruments of the state political commitment to industry.

We can briefly examine the Algerian case as a good illustration of the potential achievements and the harsh constraints of such an approach. Algeria's strenuous post-independence efforts to conquer economic independence as a key to political independence led to the construction of a strong industrial basis, financed by oil revenues. The Algerian experience has attracted much attention and given rise to extremely divergent appraisals (Thiery, 1982a). The price paid for forced industrialisation has been heavy: a slow increase in individual income and consumption, particularly a complete neglect for the housing sector and public utilities; a soaring imported food bill, a consequence of the virtual collapse of the agricultural sector; poor management and reduced capacity utilisation in big state-controlled complexes unable to extend the expected backward and forward linkage effects. Bureaucratic controls and political rigidity led to quasi-stagnation of industrial production in the early 80s. An allocation-induced attitude paradigm applied to Algeria points to the disturbances introduced by the existence of oil income: excessive importance given to political criteria at the expense of economic considerations; extremely high investment rates (over 40 per cent of GNP) extending capacity beyond efficient utilisation; underestimation of the dismal performance of agriculture as long as the growing food bill could be settled with the hydrocarbon rent. On the positive side of the balance sheet, Algeria can claim a more sensible use of its oil and gas resources than that observed in other oil states, fewer social inequalities (although they might be increasing), a potential ability to assess past performances and to take care more efficiently of agricultural needs and decentralisation necessities. An optimistic point of view may consider Algerian shortcomings and the high cost of developing gas reserves and building heavy industry bases as the unavoidable price of a learning process — the *entrance fee* a state has to pay to master a development process; dividends come later. A more sceptical perspective will reluctantly accept such an emphatic assertion and consider that allocation-induced biases have ruined Algerian potentialities and that oil has been 'the worst thing that could ever happen to Algeria'.[1]

Egypt is in a category by itself, although the same political attitude as found in the preceding group prevailed in the Nasser era. The 'industrialisation of Egypt' is less felt as a political choice than as a 'must', the desirability of which stems from the necessity to create employment opportunities and to increase a desperately small *per capita* income. Furthermore, the Egyptian industrial potential was not negligible in the late 60s (it exceeded probably that of all other Arab countries together), while the financial resources available for industry were dramatically insufficient. One specificity of the Egyptian case today lies in the ambiguities of the state attitude toward the appropriate means to encourage and finance industrial expansion, while the industrial objective remains unquestioned (which is not necessarily true of the states in the first group). The *infitah* policy (Kerr and Yassin, 1982; Waterbury, 1983) undoubtedly reinforced allocation induced behaviour in the Egyptian economy, with skyrocketing manufacture and food import bills and a rapid increase of the share of external income (worker remittances, Suez Canal tolls, oil revenues, tourism, foreign and Arab capital) in GDP. The recorded foreign investment in industrial projects, either in free zones or in joint ventures with Egyptian private or public capital, is rather disappointing. The greatest part of foreign capital has been allotted to financial and tourist services, real estate and speculative construction. The present development plan (1982–3 to 1987–8) allocates a sizeable amount of money to industrial development, with high priority for food, clothing and housing in order to reach self-sufficiency by the year 2000. Another priority is for non-oil exports, expected to rise by 13.5 per cent a year, to offset the anticipated decline in oil income. The public sector still accounts for three-quarters of the industrial investment under the five-year plan (about $7.5 billion), and for two-thirds of the production. There is, however, an obvious allocation aspect in the attitude of the state toward public enterprises: they are used as a means to re-distribute income to the people through below-cost prices and excess employment. The recent reorganisation of the public sector in 1983 went only halfway toward an authentic reassertion of the role of the public sector as a means of efficient produc-tion. The main question is the degree of compatability between the extreme dependence of the Egyptian economy on external resources and its conversion to productivity, efficiency and com petitive attitudes in the industrial sector. It is a source of concern to notice that the most convinced opponents of this dependency upon external resources are also the most reluctant to give the public sector the autonomy and the financial means allowing it to become the stronghold of Egyptian industrial expansion. How long is it possible to allocate through the public sector revenues it is unable to earn?

We find in a fourth category countries where a *limited state commitment to industrialisation* ideology does not prevent *an active and often efficient industrial policy*. Tunisia, Morocco, Jordan and, with limitations, pre-war Lebanon may be num-bered in this category. Industrial exports account for a sizeable part of total exports; medium and small-sized enterprises expand in a favourable environment. The nature of the relationship between the state and the emergent category of 'bourgeoisie d'affaires' is open for discussion. In the three countries (we exclude Lebanon), natural mineral resources are the basis for an export sector developed through public investment. A growing part of the phosphates output (in all three countries) or potash (in Jordan) is processed in heavy installations within the country. The manufacturing sector, strictly speaking, is largely private and the share of export in manufacturing value added is significant: either exports to regional markets (Jordan) or in the framework of some sort of international division of labour (Morocco and Tunisia). In order to reduce unemployment and lessen dependence upon mineral exports, industrialisation has been recently stressed as a priority, especially in Tunisia. Although external revenues are important in these countries (particularly workers' remittances in all three, oil in Tunisia, grants and aids in Jordan), allocation biases are certainly less predominant than in the other categories of states: a major step toward a production economy has been accomplished.

From attitudes to achievements: Arab industry in perspective

The present dimension of the industrial sector in the Arab countries accurately depicts the ambiguities and contradictions of the Arab states' attitudes toward industry in the last 25 years. Global figures of industrial output should, of course, be taken with caution, but they offer us a general perspective.[2] Starting at a very low level of industrial development in the late 50s (except in the case of Egypt), the rates of growth of the manufacturing sector in Arab states were high in the 60s and 70s, as compared to the average of developing countries; and an increase in the annual rate of growth was recorded in most countries for the period 1970–80 as compared to 1960–70 (such is the case for Egypt, Algeria, Morocco, Tunisia and Jordan). Among countries which achieved an annual rate of growth of manufacturing value added (MVA) exceeding 10 per cent during the years 1970–2, are Libya, Jordan, Algeria, Tunisia, Morocco; Egypt is not far from this score with 9.2 per cent. The ECWA region as a whole reached a 7.6 per cent annual MVA growth rate in the 1960s and 10.7 per cent in the 1970s (in constant prices). These encouraging results should not however lead us to overestimate the absolute and relative weight of industrial achievements in Arab countries. The share of the manufacturing sector in total GDP reaches only 8.2 per cent in the ECWA region and 8.6 per cent in the Arab world. In 1982, the manufacturing sector exceeded 10 per cent of GNP in four countries only: Egypt (27 per cent), Morocco (16 per cent), Tunisia (13 per cent) and Jordan (13 per cent). Only in Egypt is the value of industrial production large: about $4.500 million; Saudi Arabia ($3.568 million) and Morocco ($1.960 million) are the only other countries whose industrial production exceeds $1 billion. The percentage of manufactured goods in total exports is sizeable in four countries only: Egypt (8 per cent), Morocco (28 per cent),

Tunisia (23 per cent) and Jordan (43 per cent).

In terms of employment, attitudes toward industry are sharply contrasted in pure allocation states as opposed to other states. In the former, concerns about the growing number of expatriate workers have affected the drawing up of industrial policy and lowered industrial ambitions (especially in Kuwait). The 'exchange of manpower for hard currency' (United Nations, 1983), a paramount dimension of the allocative attitude, has been strongly questioned from the manpower exporting country point of view as well. Manufacturing, in any case, is not a great labour user, particularly in the heavy industry projects where labour requirements are minimal. In the other categories of states, employment objectives are essential, and the recent drive to encourage the private industrial sector has its roots in the urgent necessity of increasing 'genuine' employment. Official statistics of the workforce in the manufacturing sector should be carefully scrutinised, as an increase in the number of wage earners may be the mere consequence of an allocation bias in the industrial policies: a measure of growing inefficiency. State enterprises, for instance, are often overstaffed and labour redundancy expresses political and social constraints on the productive sector. This has long been the case in Algeria, Syria, Iraq and Egypt. The recent evolution towards more productive behaviour and efficiency-oriented management implies drastic cuts in subsidised employment, and an increasing demand on the private sector to create new jobs (Algeria openly admits this perspective). Very little is known about employment in small companies and in the 'informal sector'. Empirical studies, however, convey the idea that the informal sector is much more dynamic and efficient than is generally expected, for instance in Tunisia or Morocco. The role of the state in taking into account and fostering this form of private entrepreneurship must be analysed.

A brief glance at the sectoral distribution of manufacturing activities confirms the contrast between oil economies and the other economies. The chemical industry, in its early stages of development, accounts for the bulk of recent massive industrial investment, concentrated in a few allocation states. With the recent coming on stream of the major petrochemical projects in Saudi Arabia, this tendency will be strengthened. In 1980, value added in chemical manufacturing in the Arab world had already reached $8.5 billion, half of which was in Saudi Arabia. The weight of petroleum-linked fertilisers and chemical intermediate products exported (mostly on the world market) will increase in the future, thus reinforcing productive activities in allocation states; this does not necessarily imply successful diversification. In other countries, the traditional 'big three' industries of developing countries take the lion's share of manufacturing value added: food; textile, clothing and leather products; building materials. Food industries, according the ECWA estimates,[2] represent around 10 per cent of Arab MVA. They are concentrated in a few states like Egypt, Algeria, Morocco, Syria and Iraq and are almost totally oriented toward the domestic market. If we add Tunisia to this group of countries, we will find the great majority of the clothing and textile industries, which rank third in Arab manufacturing with around 14 per cent of MVA. The only other manufacturing sector worth mentioning is iron, steel and metal working, which suffers however, as does the Arab manufacturing sector as a whole, from the weaknesses of backward and forward linkages. Either export-oriented for a few very specific projects of an extroverted nature (aluminium smelting, oil refining, chemicals), or limited to a small domestic market for traditional consumer goods, Arab manufacturing lacks an intermediate and equipment sector. The bulk of capital goods and heavy engineering products are imported, while agriculture (long neglected), cannot provide the food industry with the basic agricultural raw materials it transforms.

In conjunction with the necessary steps to reduce the structural industrial imbalance, Arab industry has to improve its efficiency and to modify the nature and scope of state intervention in the productive sector. We have already dwelt upon the imperative reconsiderations of state attitudes and of the allocation content of industrial policies. We may briefly present the essential consequences for the industrial situation, either in allocation states or in production states. The end of the almost limitless oil funds available for all industrial enterprises implies drastic changes for the business community in Gulf countries. The trend in Gulf economies is well summarised in a recent study of the Saudi economy; 'In effect, the Saudi economy is becoming more normal. The government argument is that the days of the 30 to 100 per cent profit margins were bound to end at some point and that if the kingdom is to become a diversified modern economy, its companies must operate as companies do elsewhere' (Field, 1985). Similar comments are presented on the evolution of the economic situation in Kuwait, where 'the only industry that is going to succeed at this time is one that is well managed, with operating costs well trimmed, local tastes researched and the final product well marketed' (Evans, 1985). These efficient management constraints are not limited to oil-rich countries hit by depressed oil markets; we find them in all countries, and they concern public enterprises as well as private businesses.

At the same time, as some allocative aspects of industrial activities are questioned or suppressed, state support to industry is needed more than ever, and government, which continually encourages the private sector, remains the main locomotive for growth, in Saudi Arabia, as in Algeria, Egypt or Jordan. The main change concerns the forms of intervention and its general outlook: industry is less and less a channel for spending money with little concern for the productive result. The states' new interest in efficiency and competitiveness leads to more articulate industrial policies combining national preferences, financial incentive and, when possible, reduced direct subsidies. In many cases, cheap finance is available for business enterprises; for instance the Industrial Bank of the Emirates makes loans for industrial projects at 4.5 per cent with a three-year grace period; in Kuwait, industrial loans are set at 5 per cent and in Saudi Arabia at 2 per cent. Barter deals are increasingly imposed on foreign contractors who have to find suppliers and must propose local industrial counterparts in order to be awarded contracts. (Of course, this is more favourable to domestic industries than the better known barter agreements where the contractor gets petroleum in payment.) Pressures are also exerted on foreign companies for a rapid increase in the share of nationals — both qualified workers and staff — in their total payroll. Protectionism is not excluded, it tends to become part of a more active policy; the necessity to ensure competitiveness on regional or even world markets is now part of the picture, and direct support through subsidies cannot be the only answer.

Arab industrial growth will depend very much in the future on the capacity of the Arab states to coordinate their activities and to fully endorse *the regional and international dimensions* their industrial sector requires. The constraints of economic rationality and financial balance will thus increasingly limit allocation-induced attitudes in industrial policies. From that point of view, regional integration is important to both oil and non-oil countries. Until recently, the creation of Arab joint ventures was the most visible form of Arab cooperation. A first step was taken by the Arab Economic Council of the Arab League, which created the Arab Potash Company. Later on, the Council for Arab Economic Unity (CAEU) set up four industrial projects in Jordan, Iraq and Syria, and the Organisation of Arab Petroleum Exporting Countries (OAPEC) has been active in promoting joint ventures among its member states (for example, it created the giant ship repair drydock in Bahrain). The concept of Arab joint ventures provides, however, only a partial answer to integration needs in the Arab world. Because it was based primarily on political considerations, the creation of the Gulf Cooperation Council (GCC) in 1980 did start a new era in Arab economic cooperation. The coordination of economic plans and industrial projects, the systematic search for complementarity, the gradual establishment of a common market between the six member states, will strongly influence governments' attitudes and compel them towards realistic industrial polcies. The second generation of industrial projects in Gulf countries will not stand a chance of success if the market is not extended to the whole peninsula at least. Concerning the international market for petrochemicals and other export oriented products, it is important to avoid competition between Gulf countries, and to compensate for the consequences of cyclic fluctuations as much as possible by coordinating investment decisions. Each single state has to take into account other states' projects and this is a limit to prestige investments devoid of real economic sense.

There are *no equivalent moves* in other parts of the Arab world, and no sign that GCC may expand to include other ('production'?) states. The present industrial situation in non-oil countries, however, brings into focus the importance of regional coordination to overcome the high unit costs and low efficiency due to the insufficient size of individual domestic markets. The reduction of external revenues accruing to the states of the region will diminish their import capacity as well as their ability to allocate growing subsidies to inefficient local producers in order to satisfy local demand. The only sensible way out, hence, will be a regional approach to the problem of mass production of consumer goods in local industrial establishments; this implies more cooperation and less allocation. Turning to the intermediate goods sector and the new production lines required in the near future, each individual state has to give up its exclusive point of view in order to implement a regional design. Purely political considerations and predominantly allocative use of available funds will cease to be valid criteria as concerns industrial policies.

ATTITUDES TOWARD SERVICES: ALLOCATION THROUGH SERVICES AND PRODUCTION OF SERVICES

The evidence of different attitudes in production and in allocation states should be more striking in the case of services than in industry. The basic idea is that extending the number and the quality of services provided to the people is the foundation stone of an allocation state and the condition for its survival, while production states severely limit, for financial reasons, the quantity and quality of services they offer. Although this might appear self-evident, this statement still needs analysis and qualification. A conceptual clarification is required, in order to distinguish among very different types of services, displaying analytical links of various forms with the productive economy. The complex relations between states' financial and economic situations and their attitudes toward services will then be briefly considered.

Services: a meaningful economic category in the light of the production-allocation paradigm

The term itself is full of ambiguities. Figures in national accounts are rough estimates and may be misleading as 'all branches of economic activities which do not belong to the agricultural sector (agriculture, forestry, fishing, hunting) or to the industrial sector (mining, quarrying, manufacturing, construction, water electricity and gas), are registered as services' (World Bank, 1984). The economic nature of services, treated as a 'residual' sector, is thus extremely vague and uncertain, and further hypotheses must be introduced in order to analyse the place and role of services in the economic system. At any rate, a systematic distinction between productive and unproductive sectors is of limited validity, for the notion itself is questionable. There are, on the one hand, services which are the products of a

123

spending process: their quantity and their quality will thus depend directly on the amount of money allocated to them. There are, on the other hand, services which can generate money and increase the flows of revenue in the economic circuit. Whether initial 'productive work' is a prerequisite for the existence of both categories is an important but metaphysical question not pertaining to our present study. Delays and time lags may have a decisive impact on the issue: services which are money-absorbing in the short run, and the expansion of which requires an allocative capacity, such as education or health, may prove eminently favourable to production in the long run. The generalisation of such concepts as 'human capital' or 'investment in human capital' to analyse the extension of these services, as well as the dubious productive value to be attributed to giant prestige infrastructure or oversized industrial projects, point to the weaknesses of the basic opposition between productive and unproductive characteristics of an activity.

The analysis of services and attitudes toward services in the production-allocation states hypothesis leads us to utilise a fundamental distinction between *income-generating services and income-utilising services* (nothing to do with the usefulness of the services, but everything to do with production and allocation attitudes). The main income-generating services are transportation and transit activities, tourism, financial services, part of housing activities, research-development and engineering services, etc. The most important income-spending services are educational services, health and social services, the supply of subsidised goods, personal services, etc. Commercial activities or housing services may be considered, depending on the situation, as income-generating or income-spending.

Some significant trends in the production and allocation of services in Arab states

Despite the aforementioned limitations in the use of global figures, statistics on the growth rate of the service sector in a group of Arab countries provide useful information on the general evolution. Taking countries for which we have comparable data, we observe a firm tendency during the period 1970–82 for services to grow at a higher annual rate than GDP. In Egypt, Sudan, Morocco, North Yemen, the gap reaches 3 to 4 points per year; Saudi Arabia's situation is similar, while the difference is much greater in Kuwait, Libya and most probably in the United Arab Emirates. Some countries where we have identified a stronger propensity for industrial growth — Algeria, Jordan, Tunisia — display a different picture: the growth rate for services does not exceed that observed for GDP[2] (World Bank Development Report, 1984: ref. 3). Looking now at the share of services in GDP, the situation is changed, especially if we utilise non-oil GDP to calculate the ratio in oil rich states. The share of services is close to 50 per cent in most non-oil-dominated states: Egypt, Sudan, Morocco and Syria, the major exception being Jordan where it reaches 64 per cent. In oil countries, the ratio of services to non-oil GDP reaches 70 per cent in Algeria and exceeds 80 per cent in Kuwait, Saudi Arabia and Libya.

The main differences between 'pure allocation states' and the other states fundamentally rest on the absolute amount of money they have the capacity to allocate to certain types of services. There are no clear indications of significant divergences in the structure of public expenditure between the various categories of states, but in oil-based economies, public expenditures are a much greater part of total domestic expenditures and, of course, total income *per capita* is much higher: for example, Saudi public expenditures in fiscal year 1982/3 ($71 billion) well exceeded twice the Egyptian GNP of 1982 ($26.4 billion). Great amounts of money are thus allocated to education, health and various aspects of general welfare. This allows the citizens of Gulf countries to benefit from free (and even subsidised) education, subsidised electricity and water, often subsidised housing, and other health and welfare advantages which have often been described. A particular characteristic of many of these allocative services rests on their 'imported' nature: foreign employees far exceed the number of local workers in most services, particularly education and health: 100 per cent foreign staff is not uncommon. A striking example of huge spending expressing the importance of allocative attitudes is manifest in the developments in the higher education field. Each Gulf country, with the exception of Oman, has established at least one university; there are seven in Saudi Arabia. The Saudi government has spent $2 billion on the King Saud University project near Riyadh, which will handle over 20,000 students (in 1985). There are almost 100,000 university students in Saudi Arabia, and $7 billion was spent in 1984 for the seven universities. The cost of financing nationals' studies abroad has to be added to local spending on education in Gulf countries. With the lack of finance in non-oil countries, despite the high priority granted to education (10 per cent of public expenditures in Egypt and Jordan, between 15 and 20 per cent in Tunisia and Morocco) (IMF, 1984), the creation of a mass education service meeting minimal quality criteria has often failed to get beyond a purely symbolic stage.

Expenditures on health absorb a much smaller part of public expenditures in most non-oil countries: on average they do not exceed one-third to one-fourth of spending on education. The ratio is higher in oil countries where state expenditures on health are more than half those on education: these countries record an extremely rapid decrease in the number of inhabitants per doctor (utilised as a measure of improvement in the health sector); the reduction is tenfold in Saudi Arabia between 1960 and 1980, and 15 times in Oman. In Kuwait and the United Arab Emirates, we find a ratio of fewer than 1,000 inhabitants per doctor, a figure quite comparable to that found in Western industrialised countries. The situation is less favourable in other countries. But there are striking contrasts between Morocco, for instance, where the situation is bad — indeed worse than it was 20 years ago — and Tunisia where it has much improved. Surprisingly enough, Egypt, which has for years implemented a policy aiming at the satisfaction of the basic needs of the masses, displays a ratio of 970 inhabitants per doctor, which compares favourably to the ratio we find in oil countries; finding adequate financing to maintain such services and improve their quality will certainly represent an increasingly difficult challenge for the Egyptian authorities.

Not all developments in the service sector concern costly activities with little direct influence on domestic sources of income. There have been important improvements in the transportation sector in the Arab world, particularly, but not exclusively, in Gulf countries. This applies first of all to port infrastructures which have ceased to be the crucial bottleneck they were for a long time. Due consideration has also been given in many countries to the expansion and improvement of roads and even railways, and to connections with neighbouring countries. National shipping fleets have been developed by Kuwait, Saudi Arabia, Iraq and Algeria. Transit activities are a valuable source of income for Jordan, Dubai in the United Arab Emirates and even Kuwait (where re-exports account for more than 80 per cent of non-oil exports). Tourism is a major source of foreign exchange and its contribution to the solution of unemployment problems is significant in Egypt, Morocco, Tunisia and increasingly in Jordan. Activities of this kind, however, as well as the development of luxury housing bought by Arab capital, or certain transit revenues, while generating additional income in the concerned countries, may reinforce allocation attitudes there, as their flows escape national controls and increase dependency upon external revenues.

Some oil countries have looked for diversification in financial activities, and are building a network of investment companies, banks and insurance activities in order to create financial centres partially replacing Western financial markets for local capital. Bahrain took the lead in 1975 by launching an offshore banking market. The volume of business steadily increased in the late 70s and early 80s, reaching $61 billion in August 1982. Since then, the market fluctuations have expressed the changing situation of the oil revenue outlook. More specifically, the financial policy of Saudi Arabia exerts a decisive impact on Bahrain's OBU (Offshore Banking Unit) results. The Offshore Banking Centre contribution to Bahrain's income is not negligible. Kuwait's ambitions and real capacities to become a regional financial centre have been shaken by the Soukh el-Manakh crisis and its lasting aftermath. Egypt and Jordan in the other group of countries, have also stressed the development of banking facilities: the Amman Financial Market is a small but efficient realisation. The near future will bring an answer to the crucial question concerning development in the financial sector: has Arab finance acquired the skills and the strength it needs to become an autonomous source of income? Or is it still a mere by-product of oil revenues, an allocation device unable to outlive the reduction in those revenues?

This brief overview of major tendencies in the service sector provides an incomplete perspective on the multiple developments in the last ten years. However, it confirms the main arguments of this study. Oil states allocate considerable amounts of money through services which constitute a basic instrument for self-assertion and claims for legitimacy. The financing of a welfare state, the benefits of which may be restricted to nationals, is a major component of allocative attitudes, while the economic rationality of service extension has been long

127

neglected. In other states, the extension of services meant to improve social conditions and satisfy basic needs has been limited by lack of resources, although part of induced allocation income is financing budgetary expenditures on social services. Income-generating services try to attract an increased share of regional oil revenues.

Recent trends in the region point to the need to reconsider oversimplified assumptions about such contrasting attitudes. Facing declining oil revenues, and anxious to reverse the unfavourable consequences of allocative attitudes toward industries and services, allocation states try to foster income-generating services, and to limit the expenses due to their welfare policies. They tend also to reduce subsidies on free or low price goods and services. They will increasingly found their claim for legitimacy on the usefulness of their spending and on the long-term perspecitives of an authentic diversification away from direct oil revenues. The other states, under political constraints and strong popular pressure, have little choice but to maintain and extend the provision of allocative services: free education, minimal health facilities, public utilities and low-price housing, food subsidies, etc. Such demands have been encouraged by the relative abundance of induced oil income in the past, whatever the level of production-linked resources. With such constraints on allocation, production states will have to prove increasingly productive in the future.

Clearly, the simple two-way distinction between allocation states and production states is increasingly confused, even when applied to the attitude toward services.

NOTES

1. To quote the remark (off the record) of a former senior manager of Sonatrach.

2. The World Bank and ECWA are the main sources for statistics. Very scarce data is available for Iraq and Syria in the recent period. The figures utilised to analyse the main trends concern Algeria, Egypt, Jordan, Kuwait, Libya, Morocco, Saudi Arabia, Tunisia and United Arab Emirates. ECWA members are the Arab countries of Asia and Egypt (for the recent years).

6

Arab Bureaucracies: Expanding Size, Changing Roles

Nazih Ayubi

Few can fail to notice the process of bureaucratisation that has swept the Arab world since the 1950s. 'Bureaucratisation' means two things: (a) bureaucratic growth, i.e. expansion in public bodies of the sort that can be measured by increases in the numbers of administrative units and personnel as well as the rise in public expenditure, including in particular, wages and salaries; and (b) an orientation whereby the administrative and technical dominate over the social. Generally it is a tendency that goes very much in the direction of centralisation, hierarchy and control.

Both aspects of bureaucratisation have grown substantially in the Arab world in the last 30 years. The remarkable thing is that this has happened in all states. For the purposes of this study, the Arab states are classified along three scales: 'old' vs 'new', large vs small, rich vs poor. A fourth scale — 'radical' vs 'conservative' — should not be forgotten, although it is of less significance at present to the issue at hand.

It is possible to argue that the expansion and role of the public bureaucracy are affected by the position of any particular Arab state along these three scales. Given that we could not cover all Arab states in detail, the study has concentrated (without excluding others) on Egypt on the one hand, and three Gulf states (Saudi Arabia, Kuwait and the United Arab Emirates)[1] on the other. These were chosen to represent 'extreme types' on the three scales: Egypt is old, large and poor, while the Gulf states are on the whole new, small and rich. The choice is also useful in that in the 1960s Egypt was usually characterised as 'radical' and Saudi Arabia as 'conservative'. Two 'intermediate' cases — those of Jordan and Syria — are also touched upon briefly in order to provide the chapter with more of a comparative nature.

129

EXPANDING SIZE

It is remarkable how extensively and rapidly the bureaucracy has expanded in practically all Arab countries, even though the relative weight of the various causes of this expansion has differed from one type of country to another. Four criteria are used to measure bureaucratic growth: increase in the number of administrative units, increase in the number of public employees, increase in current government expenditure and, within that, increase in the wages and salaries of the employees. In considering the extent of bureaucratic growth, these four criteria should be taken together in the sense that a relatively limited or slow increase in one category at any particular stage should not distract the analyst from observing the phenomenon of bureaucratic growth in its totality; i.e. as represented by a combination of all four factors together.

EXPANSION DESCRIBED

The dynamics of bureaucratic growth in a number of Arab countries will be described before we investigate possible reasons for expansion.

Bureaucratic growth in Egypt

The disproportionate group of Egypt's public 'establishment' is not a new phenomenon. However, with the 1952 revolution, the public bureaucracy grew more rapidly and extensively under the impact of the regime's policies to expand industrial activities, welfare services and free education (Ayubi 1980, Chapter 3). This growth was particularly striking after the 'socialist measures' of the early 1960s, which involved widescale nationalisation of industry, trade and finance, worker participation in management and profits, and an extensive programme for social services and insurance. Thus from 1962–3 to 1970, Egypt's national income increased by 68 per cent, resting on an increase in the labour force of no more than 20 per cent. Yet at the same time, posts in the public bureaucracy increased by 70 per cent and salaries by 123 per cent (Ayubi 1980, pp. 218–32). Thus far, the rate of bureaucratic growth had substantially exceeded the rate of growth in population, employment and production.

The main irony, however, is that in the 1970s, and indeed following the adoption of the economic open door policy in 1974, the impetus of institutional growth continued under its own momentum even though the role of the government and the scope of the public sector were starting to diminish in importance. For example, the 1975 budget indicated that current expenditure accounted for 66.2 per cent of the total financial outlay of the budget, while wages and salaries accounted for 10.5 per cent (Ministry of Finance, *The State Budget*, 1975). Indeed, considering governmental outlays in the period from 1973 to 1978 as a whole, one finds that salaries more than doubled while current expenditure trebled during this time.

In terms of manpower, in 1978 the public bureaucracy — *i.e.* the civil service and the public sector excluding enterprise workers — employed over 1,900,000 persons. If state companies are added, the public 'establishment' at the beginning of 1978 was employing about 3,200,000 officials and workers (CAOA and Ministry of Finance, 1978 and 1979). At the beginning of the 1980s, the still-expanding Egyptian bureaucracy looked even bigger. It employed 2,876,000 individuals in central and local government as well as in the public sector.

One of the main problems about bureaucratic inflation that has occurred since the adoption of *infitah* is that it has happened at a time when the public economy as a whole and state industry in particular are not — given the reorientation of policy and the changing role of the government — expanding fast enough to make these increases in personnel and expenditure a rewarding exercise. It is therefore probable that bureaucratic inflation will increasingly represent a strain on national resources. One of the unhealthy aspects that accompanied this inflation in public expenditure was the decline in the percentage of such expenditure on economic activities from 35 per cent in 1962 to only 22 per cent of the total outlay in 1976. Other problems to emanate from bureaucratic growth include excessively slow action, very low remuneration and as a result, extremely poor performance.

Bureaucratic growth in the Gulf

Compared to Egypt, the origin of whose bureaucracy goes back thousands of years and whose formation in modern form dates back over a century, the bureaucracies of the Gulf have been created from scratch. Their main expansion has been an outcome of oil wealth,

131

which moved the states towards large-scale social welfare programmes and ambitious economic development plans.

Saudi Arabia

The Saudi bureaucracy was initiated in the 1950s and its growth has been remarkable in the three decades it has existed so far. The number of ministries has grown from four to 20, and over 40 public authorities and corporations have been established since 1950.

Civil service employees, who numbered no more than a few hundred in 1950, increased to about 37,000 in 1962–3, to 85,000 in 1970–1 and to over 245,000 in 1979–80. The ratio of public employees to the total population in the early 1980s was approximately 3.5 to 4 per cent, which is admittedly not excessive, but government civil servants represented 10 per cent of the total labour force and 13 per cent if one counts non-career personnel.

The oil boom manifested itself in a massive increase in revenues which jumped from $2.7 billion in 1972 to $22.6 billion in 1974. This was immediately followed by large increases in expenditure. Between 1973 and 1982, salaries and benefits, as well as current expenditure, grew thirteen-fold (*The Statistical Yearbook*, 1981–2). Without doubt, the expansion in public expenditure in Saudi Arabia has been most impressive.

Kuwait

The handful of administrations and directorates that existed in the early 1950s developed into ten departments in 1959. These were turned into ministries in 1962, when three more were added, making a total of 13 ministries. By 1976, the number of operating ministries had reached 16 in addition to two ministers of state (Marouf, 1982, pp. 32–9). Furthermore, a number of higher councils have been created (for Petroleum Affairs, for Housing Affairs etc.) and over 25 public authorities and corporations.

The numbers of government employees grew rapidly: from 22,073 in 1966, to 113,274 in 1976, to 145,451 in 1980. According to official figures, government employees represented 12.5 per cent of the population and about 34 per cent of the total labour force of Kuwait in 1975.[2] In 1979 the Amir of Kuwait expressed the view that some 65,000 civil servants in Kuwait were unnecessary and a World Bank report on Kuwaiti public administration suggested a total freeze on all new appointments.

Government expenditure also soared. Between 1973 and 1979, domestic expenditure increased by 388 per cent and salaries and wages by 242 per cent (Central Bank of Kuwait, *Economic Report*, 1978). It is estimated that nearly 39 per cent of government expenditure can be classified as organisational: this includes the substantial incomes provided to the head of state and the Amiri Diwan as well as more standard expenses such as the Employees Bureau and supplementary allocations.

United Arab Emirates (UAE)

The first federal government was formed immediately after the Union was declared in 1971, with Abu Dhabi as the main sponsor. In 1968 Abu Dhabi had some 20 government directorates, which increased to 25 by 1970. The first council of ministers of Abu Dhabi, which was formed in 1971, included 15 ministers, but this was abolished in 1973, and replaced by a federal cabinet with 28 ministers. Abu Dhabi also established an executive council to run its own affairs. Public authorities and corporations were set up, including the Abu Dhabi Steel Works, the General Industry Corporation and the Abu Dhabi Investment Authority.

In 1968 the Abu Dhabi administration employed 2,000 officials. By 1970, their number had doubled and by 1974 it reached 5,352, of which 37 per cent were UAE citizens, 42 per cent were other Arabs and 21 per cent were foreign nationals (Rashid, 1975). Eight years later, the number of public employees in Abu Dhabi had jumped to 24,078 (AIPK, 1983, p. 358).

Public employment on the federal level quadrupled between 1972 and 1982, from 10,500 to over 40,000 (Arabian Government, 1983, p. 213). The explosion in numbers of public employees is the most dramatic among the three Gulf countries studied, given the country's minute population base, its recent independence and the fact that the oil boom more or less immediately followed its formation. The UAE is representative, but in an extreme way, of what happened in other desert states where the local human base could not support the required expansion, leading therefore to heavy reliance upon expatriate labour. In the Abu Dhabi bureaucracy (which is the largest and most established within the UAE), a ludicrous 83.6 per cent of all officials are foreign nationals.

There are several indications that the state bureaucracy may have stretched itself beyond its capabilities. In 1983, this country, which ranks among the highest in the world in terms of *per capita* income, ran up a budgetary deficit which forced it to defer payment of salaries to public employees for a number of months. As the budgetary deficit was expected to increase in 1984, the Ministry of

Finance and Industry forbad the creation of new public posts for non-citizens in the following financial year (*al-Watan*, 7 May 1984).

There has been a vast expansion in public finances in the UAE since the oil boom. The federal budget, which is mainly financed by Abu Dhabi, quadrupled between 1971 and 1974.[3] Between 1973 and 1974, for example, Abu Dhabi's budget more than doubled. Payment for national and federal ministries accounted for nearly 40 per cent of the total (Aziz, 1979, pp. 55–70). In the Abu Dhabi budget for 1976, expenditure on both Emirate and the federation continued to grow; expenditure in 1977 was 74.8 per cent of the total, rising to 84.3 in 1982.

Bureaucratic growth outside the Gulf

Bureaucratic inflation followed the same pattern outside the Gulf. Where there were fewer than ten ministries at the time of independence, there were more than 20 by the 1980s (22 in Jordan, 24 in Syria). Public sector organisations proliferated: in Syria in the early 1980s there were 60 public organisations (*mu'assasat*) and 25 public corporations; in Jordan, there were about 38 public organisations of various descriptions.

In 1982, Syria had 440,000 public officials in the civil service and public sector (excluding the armed forces, police and security). Compared to a total population for the same year of 10,788,000, the ratio is one in 25, or 4 per cent (Syria Minister of State, 1984). Related to a total labour force of 2,174,000 in 1979, this means that civilian public employment represented 20 per cent of total employment (Syria, Central Statistical Office, 1981).

Jordan's 1979 census records a population of 2,152,000, of which the labour force constituted 18 per cent. In 1982, 59,000 people worked for the government (excluding casual workers) (Public Statistics Department, 1982; *al-Khidma al-Madaniyya*, June 1983). Thus government officials represented 2.75 per cent of the population and 14.9 per cent of the labour force.

Current expenditure came to over half of the total outlay in Jordan's 1981 budget; of that, 21 per cent went on salaries and wages (State Budget Department, 1981). In Syria, current expenditure amounted to 57 per cent of total outgoings. Of that, about 18 per cent went on salaries and wages (*Statistical Yearbook*, 1984).

WHY THE EXPANSION?

Reasons for bureaucratic expansion are multiple. Some is due purely to demographic growth and to the need to supply services for increasing populations. But as the percentage of public officials within the population in general and the labour force in particular tends to be higher than in many other societies, one has to examine other causes. The following seem to be of particular importance: traditional prestige of public office (for long associated with powerful foreign rulers); strong belief in the developmental role of the bureaucracy; the relationship of public office to creating the contacts vital for private business; and possibly the impact of the Egyptian model, both as an example and through the role of the large number of Egyptian officials working in many other Arab countries.[4]

Some of the reasons for bureaucratic growth are entrenched in the social and political conditions of the society. Most important is the expansion in formal higher education that is in no way related to the economic needs and manpower requirements of the society. Under pressure from people aspiring to higher social prestige, and the belief that qualifications lead to economic development, the Middle East has witnessed a strong case of what one expert has called 'diploma disease'.

This tendency, which reached alarming proportions in Egypt, has caught up with even the small city states of the Gulf, where everybody is racing to build yet another new university, regardless not only of whether the market needs graduates but even of the availability of students. In Egypt, where there are three times the number of engineers that are required by the country's industrial base, and where only 20 per cent of agronomists work in agriculture, where can the remaining graduates go but into the public bureaucracy, where they do very little but drain the public purse. The share of wages and salaries in Egypt's total expenditure has risen steadily over the past 20 years.

Proportionately, too much attention has been given to formal higher education in comparison with technical education and vocational training in all Arab countries. In most countries of the world, educational expansion has in fact followed, not preceded, industrial development (the only possible exception is Japan, where the two went more or less hand in hand). Muhammad Ali's experiment in nineteenth century Egypt to expand higher education without a similar expansion in on-the-job training resulted in virtually no real industrial development and the country had to start almost from scratch in the inter-war period. All Middle Eastern countries are currently making the same mistake, with high ratios of university graduates and relatively low levels of industrial development. One important outcome is to inflate public bureaucracy, with too many controllers, inspectors and supervisors but few functioning personnel to control, inspect or supervise.

Another major reason behind the expansion in the size (and role) of the government bureaucracy in some Arab countries is associated with the growing *rentier* nature of the state in these countries, mainly as a consequence of the oil boom. The description is meant to indicate that a dominant or significant proportion of the national income is derived from rents rather than from the productive (mainly commodity) sectors of the economy; these revenues mostly go to the state, which takes charge of their allocation and distribution. Palmer, Alghofaily and Alnimir (1984) maintain that:

> 'Rentierism' is not only an economic phenomenon. Rentier criteria . . . also possess concomitant cultural-behavioural characteristics that make it difficult for the rentier state to increase its productive capacity and to maximise the economic and political advantages at its disposal.

The rentier nature of the oil-rich states like Saudi Arabia, Kuwait and the UAE is obvious enough. The percentage of oil exports to total exports in these countries ranges between 90 and 99 per cent; the percentage of oil revenues to total government revenues ranges between 85 and 99 per cent; oil's contribution to GDP in turn is to a large extent related to government expenditure, which is almost totally dependent on oil revenues. It one excludes the direct and indirect impact of oil, it is clear how weak the economic base of the society is (Abd al-Rahman, 1982, pp. 67-8).

The fact that oil revenues accrue to the state before they are distributed has made the economic role of the state in the oil-rich countries extremely powerful, in spite of the anti-socialist rhetoric of the governing elites. Saudi development plans may extol the virtues of free enterprise, and the advisers to the Saudis may assure us that the rapidly growing role of the Saudi government in the Saudi economy is viewed as only a 'temporary evil', but the fact cannot be concealed that the government sector was responsible for over 62 per cent, or nearly two-thirds, of GDP (as expenditure) during the third plan (KSA, *Third Development Plan*, p.29). In 1976 the share of government in total consumption was 59.8 per cent, the share of government purchases in GDP was 33.3 per cent and the share of government in Gross Fixed Capital Formation was 69.6 per cent (Mallakh, 1982, p. 276). As Usama Abd al-Rahman (1982, p. 40) observes, 'The government's hegemony over the economy is large — possibly exceeding government hegemony in most developing countries, and not differing very much from the hegemony of government in countries following a socialist path'. Another writer has tried to reconcile the two contradictory aspects by concluding that the government has in effect 'become the senior partner in a system of Islamic state capitalism' (Long, 1976, p. 56).

For the rulers of the oil-rich states, the bureaucracy serves as a respectable and modern-looking method of distributing part of the revenues. Unlike traditional, straightforward handouts, bureaucracy provides a more dignified way of disbursing largesse, camouflaged in the language of meritocracy and national objectives. And sure enough, the Gulf bureaucracy is, in spite of all its paternalism, a redistributive instrument that provides people of lesser status and income with opportunities for social promotion through state education and bureaucratic careers.

The creation of jobs in the 'oil state' becomes almost an objective in its own right, with little regard for what these recruits should (or can) do. This explains, among other things, the high numbers of illiterate and other poorly educated nationals who tend to be employed by the bureaucracies of the oil-rich states. It may also partly explain why many officials are not in their offices for much of the time. According to studies made by the Saudi Institute of Public Administration, 75 per cent of officials arrive at work late, 69 per cent often leave the office for private business, and 51 per cent are frequently absent without leave; when the employee is actually at his desk, only 48 per cent of his time is spent on his official job (al-Yamama, 9 to 15 March 1982, pp. 4–7).

Foreign and local advisers who recommend things like job descriptions and reductions in the number of jobs, are often mistaken: the inefficiency may be at least partly intentional. Even before the oil bonanza, one analyst observed:

Some of the inefficiency is deliberate, because civil service appointments are viewed as a vehicle for distributing oil wealth among the citizenry and as a means of giving idle Kuwaitis a job. Consequently, most offices are grossly overstaffed; five people are commonly employed to do work that one could perform (al-Marayati, 1972, p. 290).

137

Public employment is also perceived to be a political safety valve; and this does not apply only to oil-rich states. The government in Egypt, as much in Saudi Arabia, cannot fail to see, for example, that most members of the militant Islamic groups are either university students in their final years or newly graduated. Public employment may be regarded as one way of reducing their anger, and if not of co-opting them, at least controlling them through attendance requirements and official tasks. Little wonder that the most extreme among these militant groups (such as *Takfir* in Egypt and *Ikhwan* in Arabia) dissuade their followers from working for the government (Ayubi, 1982–3).

Even the growing number of foreigners in the bureaucracy of the oil states, which is often regarded as a potential political risk, is not without its rewards. It gives locals the opportunity to command and supervise a respectable number of subordinates (who are, further-more, frequently better qualified and more experienced than their superiors). This is bound to represent an element of satisfaction for the native officials and to lessen possible antagonism between them and their rulers, by emphasising instead the citizen-expatriate dichotomy. The assignment of technical tasks to outsiders in the oil states fits the established tradition and represents an element of continuity. Nomadic societies have traditionally assigned technical jobs to slaves, minorities and outcasts, keeping for the insiders — in addition to the pastoral activities — the honour of carrying arms (Gellner, 1981). Given that only Kuwait has military conscription and that various foreign military advisers now work for the Gulf states, one wonders whether the oil boom is moving the Arab away from even this time-honoured function?

The oil bonanza, superimposed upon a bedouin society, has produced a rentier economy, with a dominant state sector and a sizeable commercial sector.

The oil boom's effects on Egypt have tended in the opposite direction. The erosion of Nasser's populist regime and the reverberations of the oil boom led to the emergence of an inverted-rentier economy characterised by the state's shrinking economic role and fast expansion in the commercial sector. The country has depended increasingly in the last decade on revenues that are not production-based and in particular on the remittances of workers in the oil-rich states. Muhammad Duwaidar (1983, p. 160) writes:

At the expense of the productive sector (in agriculture and industry) Egypt is becoming more dependent on income: income from oil, income from their overseas labour force, income derived from the Suez Canal and from tourism, and income from interest payments, as investors look for high returns on capital instead of turning to entrepreneurial activity.

Jordan and Syria have also become increasingly dependent on these sources of income, especially worker remittances, and Syria is adopting its own mini open-door policy. Although the Egyptian government has earned considerable revenue since 1973 from oil and the Suez Canal, income from tourism has benefited primarily the private sector, while remittances from people working in the oil-rich states have helped the private sector — in the absence of taxation — almost exclusively. Put differently, the state is richer in the Gulf, and society is richer in Egypt.

Because wealth does not translate immediately and automatically into power, the state in Egypt remains much stronger than the society. This was made clear during the seventies: the bureaucracy that had been expanded and strengthened mainly for development purposes under Nasser, was used for control under Sadat. By the same token, the state in the Gulf is not becoming stronger as fast as it is becoming richer. Institution-building is much more recent in the Gulf and is being implanted in a society in which primordial loyalties (familial, tribal, regional and sectarian) are stronger than they are in Egypt.

This, however, is to anticipate an aspect that will be examined more closely elsewhere in this study.

ROLE IN DEVELOPMENT

Marx explained that bureaucracy survives by projecting an image of serving the general interest. In the Middle East the bureaucracy does the same, but it also projects the image of being the main vehicle for development.

Middle Eastern leaders called upon the bureaucracy not only to fulfill the conventional law and order functions, but also to be involved in industry, trade, education, culture and so forth. The literature of the fifties and sixties was full of praise for the potential for progress of the public bureaucracy — for many people it represented an orderly alternative to the agonies of a social or cultural revolution. The direction of development administration was clear: expand and consolidate departmental-type administration, involve the bureaucracy in national comprehensive planning, in extensive industrialisation programmes, in urban construction and in a fast-expanding system of conventional higher education.

Discovering — usually half way along — that bureaucracy is probably ill-equipped to deal with this heavy load, the authorities declared that in order to have successful development administration there must first be effective administrative development. Since administration is regarded as a science that has reached its maturity in the West, administrative development was to a large extent regarded as an exercise in the transfer of technology, and the modernisation of administration was regarded as the solution to most of its problems (Wickwar, 1963). The fifties and sixties were also the heyday of technical assistance (both national and international), concentrating first — in the Middle East — on Turkey, Egypt and Iran, and then proceeding to the rest of the Middle East.[5] A combination of the ideas of such people as Fayol, Taylor and Weber, with their underlying concepts of economy, efficiency and rationalisation, were presented — sometimes in the simplified form of POSDCORB — as the *passe partout* 'science of administration'.

It is unnecessary to go out of one's way to illustrate the hold that the ideas of such authors, particularly those of Max Weber, had and still have on experts on administration in the Arab world. All one has to do is to pick up any piece of writing by any reputable Arab expert on administration, and there it is. Of course, there is nothing wrong with referring to these writers: the problem is that the exercise often not only begins with them but ends with them, and makes no reference to the relevance of their ideas to an Arab society.

Guided by this 'science of administration', improvements were introduced in the functions of personnel, budgeting, planning, organisation and training, changes that were usually confined to the central secretariats and the capital city. The line agencies, functional departments, sectoral units and operating levels of organisations — the real carriers of development — did not benefit as much (Islam and Henault, 1979, p. 259).

The cost, inefficiency and authoritarianism of an omnipotent bureaucracy afflicts most Middle Eastern countries. As in many other countries of the Third World, dependence on a central bureaucracy as a vehicle for economic development has given rise to the irony that it is the societies which lack good administration which are the ones to establish the most comprehensive and complex array of administrative controls over every aspect of investment, production and trade (Weinstein, 1981, p. 120). Egypt under the open door policy — as I have illustrated elsewhere — is a very good case in point, for even while trying (or claiming) to liberalise the economy, the bureaucracy continues to play a domineering and obstructive role (Ayubi, 1982b). Even the bureaucracy of a presumably shining example of a welfare state, such as Kuwait, does not always rise to the level of expectations. In a study on government services in Kuwait, 65 per cent of all respondents thought that the performance of the administrative machinery was poor, 30 per cent thought it was moderate and no more than 5 per cent thought it was good (al-Salim, 1982, p. 51).

Middle Eastern bureaucracies have not, on the whole, succeeded in solving the development problems they have been called upon to solve. Poverty persists, although it has often been modernised. Technology-intensive industrialisation has failed to create a sufficient number of jobs to absorb a rapidly expanding labour force, and the so-called trickle-down effect from the modern industrial sector to the poor in general and to the countryside in particular remains negligible. In short, the quality of life for the majority of the population has remained abysmally low with many of the basic needs for food, water, shelter, health and education still unsatisfied. Nor has the administration managed to reform itself and improve its own performance as an instrument of service.

Practitioners and experts alike are not prepared to accept much of the blame for the poor performance of the administration. It is always somebody else's fault: the politicians for interfering too much (but sometimes for not interfering enough, through a 'lack of political will'); the financial or technical resources (*imkaniyyat* in Egyptian terminology) for being meagre; or the whole population for not possessing a rational culture.

ORGANS OF CONTROL

Part of the reason why central, monocratic types of administration are favoured in the Arab World is the useful control functions that this type of bureaucracy can serve. This is why other types of organisation are not tried, and why, when they are adopted within programmes of administrative reform, they are used only as techniques void of power-sharing devices.

Rulers become impatient with the Weberian-style 'machine bureaucracy'[6] because its narrow minded, routine-bound instrumentalism seems incapable of confronting developments needed for

141

innovations and mobilisation (Mintzberg, 1979, pp. 314–47). But its elaborate hierarchy and strict chain of command is also an invaluable instrument of control. They feel bound to criticise the dysfunctions of the monocratic-type bureaucracy that they inherited from the colonial period,[7] but they know that its control qualities should never be eroded. Most leaders in Arab countries now want (or say they want) development; but many want power too, and in most cases power is the more immediate and pressing of the two objectives. According to Chackerian and Fathaly (1983, pp. 202–7):

> Part of the superficial attractiveness of machine bureaucracies is that they cope quite well with hostile political environments. Power is centralised in the administrative apex and this arrangement provides clear responsibility for administrative action and quick response to *political* threats.

Rulers continue to lament the inefficiency of machine bureaucracy, but they overlook the fact that it is their obsession with control that lies behind its survival and strength.[8] Arab rulers appear to prefer a system of administrative authority in which all power emanates from a single political leader and where the influence of others is derivative in rough proportion to their perceived access to him or their share in his largesse. They often subject their bureaucracies to frequent and unpredictable transfers of administrators. Shifting people around is a continuous reminder of how those in superior positions can intervene on whim and at will. Ministries fight for funds with other units of government, not as a means to pursue particular programmes but as an on-going test of their standing in the bureaucratic pecking order. The often-criticised overlapping of jurisdictions may also be politically functional from the ruler's point of view. To ensure competition among a leader's subordinates, they are endowed with roughly equal power and given overlapping areas of authority. Absence of defined responsibility fits the system's informal modes and enhances the leader's flexibility to choose among personnel and policies (Weinbaum, 1979, pp. 3–7). An element of tolerated corruption goes a reasonable way towards ensuring the official's loyalty. Not only does he benefit but he is always under the threat that the authorities may decide to put a stop to that tolerance and apply the law.

Should it come as a surprise, given the Arab rulers' obsession with the control functions of bureaucracy, that security organisations tend to be the most 'efficient' public organisation in most Middle East countries.

The top and middle administrators themselves — given their cultural and social background — are likely to be just as power conscious. A study of 52 executives from six Arab countries (Egypt, Jordan, Kuwait, Lebanon, Saudi Arabia and the UAE) showed that out of a range of seven decisions, 22 per cent are likely to be the executive's own decision, 55 per cent a consultative decision (discussion with a small selected group followed by his own decision), 13 per cent a joint decision and only 10 per cent a decision based on delegation. There is even less power-sharing, more autocratic behaviour in organisational decision-making (Muna, 1980, pp. 47–60).

If subordinates oppose the Arab executive's decision, he is most likely to pull rank and go ahead in spite of the opposition. In situations where the executive opposes a decision that the subordinate favours, the power tactic most often used is inaction — freeze it or give it time to die. The Arab executive is so frightened of losing power if discussion is allowed and managerial conflict is tolerated, that he usually seeks security in what appears to be complete subordinate compliance. As one Egyptian executive said, 'If a leader, whether on the national or organisational level, does not suppress opposition, people (including my employees) think he is weak and he loses respect'[9] (Muna, 1980, pp. 63–8).

It is hard to imagine that anything but a monocratic, hierarchical bureaucracy could suit the inclinations of such a power-conscious executive. It is no wonder administrative reform based on power-sharing, participation and delegation, tends to die a speedy death almost as soon as it is tried in the Arab world.

Even when rulers and executives are prepared, under popular pressure or expert advice, to consider some measure of reform that involves delegation and decentralisation, they will tend to apply it in such a way that it is robbed of its participatory ethos. In Egypt, the introduction of a system for management by objectives (MBO) in the mid-seventies was unsuccessful since, among other things, the executives though of it more as a means of increasing their managerial power than as a way of achieving a high level of consensus among the employees over the policies and programmes of the organisation (Ayubi, 1982a).

Bureaucracy vs Bedoucracy

The dynamics of bureaucratisation are quite easy to comprehend in a hydraulic society with old state traditions like Egypt. They are more difficult to understand in bedouin societies, that are known for autonomy and individualism. 'Bedoucracy' and bureaucracy seem to be completely at odds with each other. As Ernest Gellner (1981, p. 77) explains, bureaucracy is the antithesis of kinship. They have been developed to deal with completely different sets of problems. Arid-zone tribalism is a technique of maintaining order which dispenses with the specialised enforcement agencies that are associated with the state (and, in a way, *are* the state) (Gellner, 1983, pp. 439–40). Yet the opposites are partly reconciled by *petrocracy*.[10]

Through the creation of a bureaucracy, the rulers of the oil states are paying the citizen — by way of lucrative government employment — in return for a cessation of the old tribal wars, for tacit acceptance of the political supremacy of one tribe or fraction of a tribe (the royal or princely family) over the others. What the central administration does for the modern urban sector, the system of local subsidies achieves for the rural and nomadic areas. This can be likened to a system of indirect administration that recognises the traditional authority networks of the bedouin and incorporates them in the state structure.

The taxation function is thus reversed in the oil state: instead of the usual situation, where the state taxes the citizen in return for services, here the citizen taxes the state — by acquiring a government payment — in return for staying quiet, for not invoking tribal rivalries and for not challenging the ruling family's position.

The relationship that is being established between the official and the state is quite complex. On the one hand he knows that the state (or more specifically the ruling family) needs his acquiescence; on the other he knows that he needs a public post not only for the financial benefits it offers him but also for the contacts it provides (which are indispensable for the conduct of private business). In the short run, the official is tempted to feel that he is in the stronger position, that the state needs him more than he needs the state and that he can bargain with the state over the price of acquiescence.

Given this feeling and given the abundant oil reserves accruing to the state, the official is bound to think that he receives a meagre price for his service to the state. An empirical study conducted on 614 Saudi officials indicates that 79 per cent of the respondents were dissatisfied or neutral as far as their pay was concerned: the petrodollar flood has obviously created very high pay expectations (Chackerian and Shadukhi, 1983, p. 321).

In the long run the individual is likely to be caught up in the web of organisational relations and eventually submit to the grasping hand of the state. For he has nothing to offer the state, in return for his salary and benefits, other than power over himself.

There is much evidence to suggest that most Arabs either have no alternative but to rely on the state bureaucracy or feel they cannot do without the wages, benefits and subsidies with which it supplies them. Such unilateral services offered by the state bureaucracy to meet the important needs of the populace provide those in control of the state apparatus with what Peter Blau calls the penultimate source of power — its ultimate source, of course, being physical coercion (Blau, 1964). This partly explains why governments of the oil-rich states, although hardly liberal and democratic, have on the whole managed to rule with less physical coercion than many governments of the oil-poor Arab states.

Hierarchy in organisation has two aspects. The first is as a channel for occupational mobility, with related status and economic rewards; the second is as an instrument of control (Chackerian, 1983, p. 94). When an Arab takes a government job because it has prospects, he cannot escape, at least in part, the control that it will have on him. Available empirical evidence tends to support this: the Arab *is* learning to obey. In Saudi Arabia, for example:

While government workers are not highly motivated, they do seem to be responsive to demands from superiors. Hierarchical information flows are quite effective, but decisions are made at the top of the hierarchies regardless of competence (Chackerian and Shadukhi, 1983, p. 321).

Learning to obey indicates that the control functions of bureaucracy work successfully. But to respect hierarchy is not the same as becoming an 'organisation man'. The bedoucracy, with its emphasis on family and kin relationships, has survived into the petrocracy with its superficially large, complex and 'modern' (i.e. formal-rational) arrangements, and this has given rise to a new variety of state organisation that we may call a petro-bedoucracy. Al-Awaji (1971, p. 187) explains the resulting conflicts within the bureaucrat most eloquently:

145

. . . Because he wants to maintain his position both with his kin, friends and neighbours, and with his superior or superiors, he either evades the issue to avoid possible conflict, or exploits it to his advantage. While his loyalty to his particular group is largely an emotional one, his loyalty to his superior and his organisational mandate is for expediency. Where there is no conflict between personal goals and those of his organisation or superior, his opportunism remains unrevealed. This may occur when a bureaucrat is able to satisfy the demands of one interest without violently offending the other. In such a case, he is an exploitationist. He can be boldly corrupt when the formal rules are flexible, or legalistic when this best serves his interests.

Nevertheless, in most cases, he is escapist. When the conflict is so sharp that it endangers his position at the office and/or at home or before his friends, he is most likely to evade it. The typical situation is when the interests involved are vital to both his particular group and to his supervisor or the formal regulations of his agency.

The existence of conflict should not be taken to mean that bureaucratic organisations will not develop: bureaucracy may co-exist with kinship, and bureaucratic organisations can be held together through patronage. The case of Jordan illustrates that the two apparent opposites can be blended rather well. Concerning the Gulf region, Amir al-Kubaisi has coined the term *sheikhocracy* to describe the behavioural outcome of the juxtaposition of the attitudes of the sheikhs who act the bureaucrats' role, and the bureaucrats who act the sheikhs' role (al-Kubaisi, 1982, pp. 152–4). Another use to which the rulers may also wish to put the bureaucracy is to maintain the *status quo* by co-opting the intelligentsia and other aspiring groups while blurring the class issue, under the guise of the bureaucracy's universality. Under the banner of 'meritocracy' people from a wider pool are recruited into the bureaucracy, which establishes the impression that social mobility is possible without the need for conflict. This takes the heat off potential class conflicts and allows the state to control the situation. In populist regimes (for example, those applying a strategy of 'developmental nationalism', such as Egypt under Nasser), a kind of 'Bonapartism' may emerge as the rulers declare that 'we are all workers', while trying to use the bureaucracy as a means for 'creating their own class' (Ayubi, 1980, Ch. 5 and 6). In the petro-bedoucracy, the bureaucracy seems to represent a vehicle by means of which the privileges of the royal entourage can become entrenched and class confrontation avoided altogether, sometimes in the name of the egalitarian ethos of the nomadic society and sometimes in the name of the brotherhood of Islam.

And sure enough, Arab officials have proved to be politically docile. They have not on the whole formed special trade unions. Those who join a professional (technically specialised) syndicate have usually been more of an asset to the government than to fellow members without government jobs — this is particularly the case with the professional syndicates in Egypt.

In situations like these, 'bureaucratic politics' are likely to assume a relatively important role. A job in the bureaucracy for an individual or one of his relatives represents access to sources of allocative and distributive power. Influence over decision-making related to important national or local projects represents one of the few available channels for 'participation' in the public affairs of the society.

In conclusion, one can say that the deficiencies of Arab bureaucracies in offering services and promoting development are not due simply to the lack of knowledge on the part of Arab officials. The rigidity, formality and arbitrariness of the bureaucracy is in no small measure the outcome of its use as an instrument of power: most Arab rulers find in the machine bureaucracy a useful control device, and most executives find it a means of acquiring authority and exercising influence. Most Arab rulers and executives want to see their bureaucracies play a part in developing their countries, but in their real order of priorities, power often comes before development.

NOTES

1. Three countries are chosen to represent the new, small and rich category of state so that, given the paucity of data, they can complement each other. It goes without saying that, although they share salient characteristics, there exist several differences among them.

2. Three per cent of the population and 17 to 20 per cent of the labour force is considered usual in many countries.

3. Bahrain dinars were later replaced by the United Arab Emirates dirham. One Bahrain dinar = 10 UAE dirham.

4. In the early 1980s, a million to a million and a half Egyptians worked in other Arab countries (Auybi, 1983, 'The Egyptian brain drain', *Journal of Middle East Studies, 15*). Many were in administrative and technical jobs, of which a significant proportion were employed in government.

5. The level of American technical assistance in Iran was by far the

largest and the relationship the closest. One of the earlier projects lasted from 1956 to 1961, cost over $2.3 billion, and involved about 26 advisers to each of the Iranian ministries except foreign affairs and war. The majority of such advisers, who remained in the country until 1978, had little knowledge of the local environment or culture. They spent most of their energy trying to change local practices without understanding why they existed. It is hardly surprising that, with the exception of the police, these advisers were not on the whole successful in transferring their techniques across cultural boundaries (Seitz, 1980, 'The failure of US technical assistance in public administration: the Iranian case', *Public Administration Review, vol. 10, No. 5*).

6. The 'machine bureaucracy' is a term used by Henry Mintzberg to connote the type of bureaucracy first described by Max Weber. The operating work of such a bureaucracy is routine, often simple and repetitive and hence easily standardised. If the tasks of the organisation, however, require a high degree of innovation and call for a flexible response to frequently occurring and not easily predictable changes (as is the case in developing countries), standardisation is not as easy, and other types of organisation would be needed to face the challenge.

7. Both the Ottomans and the European colonial powers had been more concerned with control than with development, and relied on authoritarian administrations to achieve their goals. As Arab countries gained their independence they retained the ex-colonial administrations more or less intact, and whenever they introduced changes, they drew their inspiration from the French or the Egyptian models, which are both strongly control-oriented (Alderfer, 1967, *Public administration in newer nations*, Praeger, New York, pp. 5–62).

8. In the literature on organisation there are two orientations in studying control: one that views it mainly as a technical managerial device for enduring efficiency in fulfilling organisational goals, another that views control mainly as the ability to use power *vis-à-vis* others within the organisation. Although the two senses are not mutually exclusive, we are more interested in the second, as it is more relevant to the subject of the state (compare Dunsire, 1978, *Control in a bureaucracy*, Martin Robertson & Co, Oxford, pp. 21–72).

9. It is interesting to note that this statement came from an Egyptian. Muna's study (1980, *The Arab executive*, Macmillan, London, pp. 56–7) found that executives from Egypt shared less of their decision-making power with their subordinates than executives from the other five countries. Among these executives from Saudi Arabia showed more power-sharing in departmental decisions than the others. Could this be a reflection of the hierarchical traditions of the hydraulic society in the case of Egypt, and the egalitarian traditions of a bedouin society in the case of Saudi Arabia?

10. The term 'bedoucracy' is adapted from Muhammad al-Rumaihi. It is meant to imply that in spite of modern technology and equipment, the Arabian administrator is still predominantly a traditional nomad in his way of thinking and patterns of behaviour (al-Rumaihi, 1977, *Muawwiqat al-tanmiya*, Kazima, Kuwait, p.137). The term 'petrocracy' is our own coinage, but inspired by the title of Usama Abd al-Rahman's book *The petroleum bureaucracy and the development dilemma* (Abu Shikha, Nadir,

1983. *Al-Tanzim al-idari* [administrative organisation in thirteen Arab states], Amman: Arab Organisation for Administrative Sciences.) It is meant to indicate a system whose politics as well as economics are dominated by the 'oil factor'.

7

Social Structure and Political Stability: Comparative Evidence from the Algerian, Syrian and Iraqi Cases

Jean Leca

The classic question of political sociology is concerned with the relations between the evolution of the social structure (the guiding principles for the allocation of scarce and valued resources; the identity, permeability, strength and wealth of beneficiary and deprived groups) and the political formula (the process of coercion, compromise and legitimacy which functions in a global collectivity). It is generally assumed that a causal relationship, functional or systemic, exists between the social constellation of interests (who benefits and who loses?) and the authority's moral order (who has the right and the power to master the political process? Who has the duty or the obligation to obey? What are the contents of the rules and the outcome of policies?)

For the past fifteen years most of the political Arab regimes can be considered as stable. Can the evolution of the social structure, both forming and formed by the nature of the government, provide part of the explanation for this stability?

POLITICAL STABILITY AND SOCIAL STRUCTURE: A STATIC MODEL

The concept of social structure can be used in a very abstract fashion to identify patterns of inequality, whatever they are. However, it is misleading if it rests on three concepts derived from the sociology of bourgeois society: (i) *the autonomy of the economic sphere* unified by the market with access to economic resources conditioning other resources, (ii) the *horizontal stratification* constituted by unequal access to the private ownership of the means of production, (iii) the *superposition* of units of analysis of the economic *structure* and of units of analysis of *action*; not only do socio-political actors behave in general in conformity with economic interests as they see them (which in itself is quite commonplace) but political groups are, to paraphrase Lenin, 'the nomenclature of the social classes'.

Whatever their value in bourgeois societies, none of these concepts hold good in Arab societies (Bill, 1972; Eisenstadt, 1964; Chatelus and Schemeil, 1984; Batutu, 1985). Although they may apply to some historic situations or to specific substructures, they cannot be drawn on as part of a general paradigm. To throw light on this enigma it is not necessary to look to culturalist explanations or to dependency theories even though both have their value. Suffice it here to mention the long history of weakness in autonomous economic institutions (cities, feudal principalities, etc.) during the period of modernisation (Issawi, 1982, p. 170) and, in recent history, the importance of the economic role of the state, holder of oil rent, purveyor of employment, initiator of industry, instrument of investment, consumption and distribution of revenue (Chatelus, 1982; Batatu, 1984 and Beblawi and Luciani, 1987). Where the economy is one of circulation more than production, access to rent is a more important principle of social structuration than the owner-ship of the means of production (though this is not so for real estate and commercial capital).

Three phenomena follow: (i) the importance of the political process (and of the state) in the constitution of social classes (for Egypt, see Waterbury, 1983, pp. 323 ff) and not only in their representa-tion; (ii) a social articulation, complex determination and rating of categories and social functions, not exclusively manifest in occupa-tion (Van Nieuwenhuijze, 1965, p. 77); (iii) the existence of multi-level identifications and the difference between classes and groups (ethnic and religious factions or local groups and clientele groups), with the latter more pertinent than the former to an understanding of social interaction (Bill, 1972). Since access to distribution is one of the principles of social structuration, and in consequence one of the issues at stake in the social struggle, group action is more immediately seen as normal and instrumental than class action.

The notion of social structure does not then imply the concept of a civil (i.e. bourgeois) society directly applied to the Arab world (Leca and Schemeil, 1983). Nor is it necessary to reduce the society to its kinship or corporative structure or to an ensemble of compound and decomposed groups (sometimes known as 'non groups' in anthropological language) connected by clientele relation-ships or lopsided friendships and dominated or crowned by a palace

151

of ethnic clans, army officers and bureaucrats. Social mobilisation modifies the mosaic of solidarities without superseding the class, ethnic or factional action as the transformationist model would have it (Hudson, 1977, pp. 7–16).

The ideal *static* model of the relationship between social structure and political stability can thus be outlined, at least in the socialist republics of our study. Peripheral middle classes (non-bourgeois, coming from small rural cities) take state power and install a politico-economic formula based on the redistribution of wealth and political control of the economy. Agrarian reform, planning and expansion in the public sector, industrialisation and social spending are its main ingredients. This combination is only a variant of the big trade-off in the democratic capitalist states between equality and efficiency, analysed by Arthur Okun (1975). The allocation of revenue resources is only a way of avoiding confrontation and reinforcing the social stratification of those governed. Economic efficiency is not officially rejected. It is seen only as the outcome of political efficiency. Thus the growth of a new salaried middle class and a commercial and industrial private sector linked to the state is favoured. The difference between these states and the traditional monarchies (Heller and Safran, 1984) is that the new educated middle class is considered supportive of the regime and a factor in maintaining stability so long as resources are sufficient and their distribution accepted as equitable (that is, responsive to the different expectations of classes and groups).[1]

The trade-off with the new middle class has been important in the socialist republics, although it has never been presented as such. Whereas in Tunisia the government of Hedi Nouira was explicit about its strategy, in Algeria, on the contrary, the 1976 National Charter attributed the leading role for the future to the working class. Nevertheless, if we take our examples from socialist countries, it is because, despite their differences, the three regimes are sufficiently similar to test dynamically the model outlined.

SOCIAL CHALLENGES TO POLITICAL STABILITY: THE SPLIT IN THE MIDDLE CLASS AND THE DILEMMAS OF REDISTRIBUTION

(1) The 'new middle class' (NMC) is a vague concept which has borne the wear and tear of time quite well (Halpern, 1963; Bill, 1972; Turner, 1979; Heller and Safran, 1984). It does have

problems: (a) it is a *vague* concept which postulates a unity of position and condition of socio-professional workers competent in modern techniques, in whatever sphere they find themselves (administration, the army, enterprise or commerce), and attributes to them a common will for political modernisation; (b) it is an *elastic* concept which can just as well apply to menial jobs as to the upper civil service, to small entrepreneurs as to intellectuals; (c) it is a *residual* concept which rests on negative characteristics (neither the traditional merchant middle class, nor the big landowners, neither landless peasants nor proletariat;[2] (d) finally, it creates confusion between that middle class which formed the original political base for the regime, the peripheral middle class of the small rural towns, and that produced by the expansion of salaried employment, of consumption and of education. But these weak points are only the reverse side of a very fertile concept for which a better substitute has yet to be found.

The problem is the question of the destiny of this class. Can it remain an element of stability, dependent on the state for its reproduction but able to avoid and temper the resentment of the lower urban and urbanised classes and the dwindling peasantry, considering especially its lack of consumer ostentation, its austere habits and the authenticity of its cultural behaviour? It is possible that this middle class, modest and prosperous, ambitious and puritan, is only a fantasy in the minds of a leadership dreaming of Max Weber or Werner Lombart, or of Gambetta's new strata. Yet it is not a total figment of the imagination. The problem is that it sometimes tends to pay more attention to the religious opposition than to the nation state. Or is it possible that this class might split into an upper level of public and private managers and businessmen and a lower level of badly paid and barely committed salaried public employees (Waterbury, 1983, pp. 360–2)?

A double influence operates then, on the dual base of the patrimony (through continual access to oil revenue, foreign aid and international trade circuits) and the private ownership of the means of production and exchange. Neither of these bases of structuration necessarily obeys the same fundamental logic. The first rests on a commonplace logic, endogenous to groups: the patrimony is a sure and certain way of maintaining the family groups' social level, without running the risk of intergenerational downward mobility if the professional opportunities of one generation are lost for the next through rivalry or loss of palace favour. The second can be the result of a state strategy attempting to transfer onto the private sector the responsibility for meeting demands, creating employment and mobilising potential savings when its financial difficulties (debts, a fall in the oil income) no longer allow it to do without a bourgeoisie. But it is a risky strategy.

(2) Redistribution means that the NMC has that much more of a chance of being a stabilising group both when it benefits extensively (if not equally) from the resources accruing from oil revenue or foreign aid and also when state revenue stretches to cover classes with rising expectations. In a paper devoted to a comparison between Iranian and Nigerian social movements, Burke and Lubeck (1987) have convincingly argued that a regime's capacity to convert its oil wealth into collective goods and to co-opt the potential opposition determines its power to resist the challenge posed by popular Islam and cultural nationalism. In fact, the contrary would be surprising: whatever the source of wealth (annuities, industrial production or circulation), there is no reason why Muslim Arab societies should be spared the Tocquevillian tendency towards equality (i.e. refusal of excessive social rifts formerly considered natural); indeed, the opposite is more likely. Every spring must trickle through and water the entire social fabric. Not that great wealth is illegitimate (even Boumedienne's Algeria treated itself to a Messaoud Zghar). But if it becomes the negative symbol of the frustration of the excluded, that is if the social structure presents itself as a form of opposition between a predatory and corrupt group and all the rest (lower middle class, peasant smallholders, artisans, underemployed urban dwellers), popular protest could unite all those not belonging to the NMC and even its own frustrated members (those excluded both from the constitution of the patrimony and the private ownership of the means of production).

States redistributing wealth to the NMC can then find themselves facing a double challenge:

(a) The challenge of contradictory tendencies in redistribution. This is jointly rooted in rising expectations and the demand for equality, but the groups expressing such goals do not have the same objective. The upper middle class, who have received the first benefits, will be anxious to improve the standard and quality of their consumption while at the same time assuring their own reproduction by passing on material (notably real estate) and intellectual capital to their offspring (education for professional opportunities). The rest of the population wants the same things but on a lesser scale, which modifies the nature of the demand. A job, preferably salaried to give a minimal base income, and eventually a start in small scale business, is the basic demand of those whose inadequate education (second rate diplomas and wasteage in the school system) bars them from the positions and returns that meet their minimal expectations. This is followed by a demand for the mass consumption of basic produce subsidised by the state. In the first instance, then, the state must enlarge and diversify the patrimonial and consumption market, in the second it must do the same thing in the labour market. It is not clear whether both can be done at the same time, since the jobs created to satisfy the latter do not necessarily produce the benefits which would satisfy the former, nor do they do so for the same people.

(b) The tendency toward opening the economy to the private sector appears to be an attempt to respond to this bottleneck. Could not the private owners of enterprises, commerce and services at one and the same time mobilise potential savings, create employment, develop disposable income and respond to the demand for consumption? Private entrepreneurs supported and protected by the state (but paying taxes to it), benefiting from a protected domestic market, in part through the state monopoly on foreign trading (although this is also an inhibition for entrepreneurs), are perhaps the dream solution of the socialist regimes. This only partially corresponds to the dependent development formula applied to Brazil by P. Evans: a non-agrarian class alliance among the industrial technocrats, the capitalists from protected industry, the state bureaucrats and nearly all urban consumers (Evans, 1979). As we shall see later, the regimes in our study can integrate farmers or at least rural dwellers.[3] In any case, in so far as the regime does not need to resort to exporting manufactured goods (because it can make do with exporting its hydrocarbons) and in this way can avoid the destabilisation of its political base by side-stepping direct confrontation with the international market, the creation of a bourgeoisie directly dependent on the state and oriented towards the domestic market can be a stabilising factor. But even if this bourgeoisie is a real entrepreneurial bourgeoisie there is a political price to pay. It is the manifestation of the social structure and inequalities by drawing attention to privileges (instead of concealing them within the state apparatus), especially if foreign debts and foreign bank pressures result in cost-cutting in the public sector, preventing it from playing out the residual redistribution role which it played with the creation of a public employment that was unproductive of anything but minimal social satisfaction.

ALGERIA 1962–1985

The social base of the politico-economic formula: class links and class constraints

The Algerian politico-economic formula may be summarised by two characteristics: (a) *the combination of rationalities:* an economic rationality which demands the constitution of a self-supporting economy that must therefore be integrated and surplus-producing; and a political rationality which looks to the state to maintain a high level of allocation (in employment, consumer goods, social services) in order to transform political sovereignty into a means of satisfying social expectations; (b) *the constitution of an autonomous national society* which can superpose the political community and the economic community, in other words, lay the basis for a social structure on activities of production and exchange situated on the national territory. Hence there is an absolute priority accorded to state-sponsored industrialisation, the development of an administrative apparatus and the public services (see Benhouria, 1980; Benachenhou, 1982; Benissad, 1982; Lawless, 1985; Bennoune, 1985; and on agriculture, Mutin, 1980; Bedrani, 1982; Chaulet, 1984 and Pfeifer, 1985).

These two characteristics may perhaps be explained by the class nature of the Algerian state. By this term we do not mean the existence of a class link between a group clearly situated in the production process, and sectional or state elites, the latter recruiting from among the former. The hypothesis of a class link is simply not applicable to Algeria if one takes as a criterion of class the private ownership of the means of production and exchange. The urban and rural Muslim middle class studied by Ageron (1980) which was made up of middle-scale landowners, tradesmen, small industrialists and salaried executives and which constituted about 4 per cent of the population in 1954, participated in the FLN's decision-making process but did not itself hold a dominant position (see Quandt, 1969; Michel, 1972; Zartman, 1974 and 1984; Harbi, 1975; and Entelis, 1982).

Hardly anybody still maintains that the petty bourgeoisie has taken power. On the other hand a class link is plausible in two other senses of the term. It can refer to a political class whose members, regardless of their place in the economic division of labour and quite often without any fixed place therein, have a common investment in the political struggle because it is this that determines the ensuing socio-political structures. But it must be recognised in that case that the class link becomes tautological, since the state does not recruit from any distinct group but, rather, is that group, and constitutes it,[4] or on the contrary, since it is the political resources of the state which alone can permit the creation of a socio-economic group.[5]

Class link can also refer to a group which is characterised first of all by its place in the cultural division of labour: in this sense Colonna (1983) could speak of the emergence between 1954 and 1962 of a literate petty bourgeoisie possessing as its principal capital a scriptural competence (in Arabic or in French, both lay and religious) and establishing itself at the centre of the political process. The objectives of the nationalist struggle were identified from then on with the particular interests of this group and the forms of struggle with the least costly means to achieve its objectives. The same is probably not altogether applicable to the whole political class (cf Harbi, 1975 and 1980), to whose diversity of origins and social trajectories Colonna herself draws attention, but it could well be interesting to extend the hypothesis of new cultural mediators to the decisions of economic policy. A highly-planned public sector economy makes the owners of technical knowledge and other organisers (the mameluks of modernity, to paraphrase Gellner, 1974) more functionally indispensable than the owners of the means of production. However, the class link cannot be here a principle of intentional action since in 1962 these mameluks who had graduated from institutions of higher education were still few in number in Algeria.

In fact, the principle which determines the relations between Algerian leadership and the social structure is not a common position in the production process but, rather, for the most part, a common distancing from the central economic positions of bourgeois society such as large landowners, industrial and commercial bourgeoisie, and salaried industrial workers. And with reason: these classes were weak, foreign or defeated as political classes. Industrialisation was set in motion by actors who saw in it above all a political goal and a political means to legitimise their power (particularistic interest) but also to fulfil their mission (ideological interest) in response to the class constraints weighing upon them.

In effect, class nature can also refer to the existence of class *constraints* which limit and induce various choices. With the exception of external constraints, the only (though heavy) constraints weighing upon Algerian decision-makers came from those whose access to the state as distributor of resources represented the

157

expected and indispensable outcome of the liberation struggle. This access was the goal which limited the composite social base of the FLN, including small peasants and agrarian bourgeois or merchants; these two groups were, however, too lacking in cultural capital (in the case of the former) and in political and material strength (in the case of the latter: Algeria has no equivalent of the Tunisian Tahar Ben Ammar in its nationalist history) to obtain access to the state on its own terms.

In one sense, the decision-makers were under no internal constraint because no group was capable of opposing a legitimate project for a modern economy to the 1962 programme of Tripoli, but for the same reason the state could do nothing but redistribute foreign property, educate, allocate and, if possible, produce because it was there for that. After it produced independence, the production of a modern society was a necessary corollary, not only in the minds of the technocrats (who were in any case few in number) and of the politicians, but also for their clients, consumers of abandoned estates, of self-managed allotments and of public employment. What was thus one of the state's resources also acted as a constraint upon it: in order for Albert Hirschman's tunnel-effect to have full play, it was necessary that a large number of passengers got on the economic and public administration train (Hirschman, 1973). The result was an impetus towards exuberance (still using the terminology of Hirschman, 1968) of state-sponsored industrialisation. In this sense class constraint(s) pushed the state to regard industry more as a political instrument (of sovereignty and distribution) than as an economic instrument (of production and accumulation).

Algerian agriculture was not the subject of active policies until

Table 7.1: Algeria: share of agriculture and industry in labour force, Gross Domestic Product, planned public investment (in %)

	Labour force		GDP		Public investment		
	1	2	3	4	5	6	7
	1965	1983	1965	1984	1970	1977	1980–84
Agriculture	67	26.9	15	8	10	5.9	11.8
Industry (and hydrocarbons)	12	30.4	34	42	53	56	48.3

Source: 1 and 2: *World Tables: Social Data*, vol. II, World Bank, 1983; 3: *World Development Report*, World Bank, 1983; 4: *General Report on the Five-Year Plan 1980–84*, MPAT, 1985; 5 and 6: National Statistics Office, Algiers; 7: *Presentation of the Five-Year Plan 1980–84*, MPAT, 1980.

1980, because the rural world, source of legitimacy, was not the source of power (Colonna, 1980; Leca, 1980). The countryside was more the missionary field of agricultural production. Rural dwellers, who made up a significant section of the government, were not or were no longer farmers. Such sons of impoverished farmers as Ben Bella or Houari Boumedienne saw the countryside through their fathers' eyes: a distressed place offering neither new jobs nor surplus, and what is more, the site of respectable but archaic behaviour.[6] As for the rich countryside of colonial Algeria, which should have formed the capital for self-managed farming, the social movement to reclaim colonial land was quickly transformed into a policy objective led by political activists whom the peasants supported without committing themselves to production, which was made more and more difficult by the bureaucratisation of management (Blair, 1970).[7]

The Algerian social compromise

The Algerian social compromise may be summed up thus: oil revenues and access to foreign loans have permitted the generalisation of salaried employment, the creation of jobs without any corresponding extension of production and the reinforcement of managerial or bureaucratic activities. For instance, from 1967 to 1978 Sonatrach's employment tripled, while its output remained constant: in the fast-growing construction and public work sector, the value added by each worker had decreased by half from 1967 to 1982.

There has been a significant drop in unemployment in all sectors of activity. In 1966, 35 per cent of the active male population was unemployed, 23 per cent in 1977 and 11 per cent in 1984, showing

Table 7.2: Working male population of Algeria according to professional status (%)

	1966	1977
Employers	0.58	0.50
Independent	24.22	21.59
Co-operative workers	–	3.49
Seasonal workers	32.26	10.54
Full-time employees	35.15	60.00
Domestic workers	6.62	2.81
Non-declared	1.17	0.33

Source: *Statistical Annual of Algeria*, 1979.

Table 7.3: Growth in employment in selected sectors (per thousand jobs)

	1967	1982
Industry	123	468
Construction and public works	71	552
Transportation	53	148
Trade and service	321	542
Government services	306	752
Agriculture	874	960

Note: Figures given here are different from the figures supplied by the 1980–84 Plan usually quoted by the international organisations.
Source: *General Directory of Statistics*, Statistical Series for 1967–1982, October 1984.

a sustained growth rate in employment of about 4.5 per cent per annum from 1967 to 1982. But the anticipated doubling of the active population between 1983 and 1999 as a result of demographic growth and of the entry of women into the labour market will necessitate an annual growth rate in employment of 5.5 per cent, a difficult objective.

Disposable incomes (salaries and profits) grew faster than productive capacity and the growth of imports and led to strong inflationist tendencies and a growing balance of payments deficit. Between 1967 and 1982, gross household incomes increased in real terms by 4.3 per cent annually while domestic consumption increased by 5.7 per cent annually. It was at this price that the economic system was able to function without coming under pressure from workers; but the incomes which they receive come not so much from values which they have created but rather from a part of the oil revenue.

Even though the purchasing power and standards of living of industrial workers have deteriorated (Thiery, 1982b; Bernard, 1982), the organisation of the socialist management enterprises (Gestion socialiste des entreprises), the enactment of the general statute of the worker (Statut général du travailleur), the relative security of employment and the absence of pressure from state management to increase profitability, have up till now prevented the formation of broad social protest movements. Social tensions have taken the form of strategies of withdrawal from the workplace (see for example, Safir, 1985), of fairly tough local strikes, but not of an autonomous political class movement (Sraieb, 1985). The workers' movement may thus be represented as forming part of the state, legal society

160

or 'hadara', thus reinforcing the position of the left bureaucracy (Benkheira, 1985). In any case, there has been no development of a 'class-for-itself' movement with ideological and organisational autonomy. None of the massive social protest movements that Algeria has known (for example the Kabyle movement in 1980 or the demonstrations of marginalised youth in Oranie in 1982 or Constantinois in 1986) has presented such a character, even when these have resulted from a process of social differentiation.[8] Nor has Algeria experienced the degree of urban eruptions suffered by Tunisia, Morocco or Egypt as a result of massive rises in the prices of foodstuffs or (in the case of Morocco) the abrupt closing-down of educational establishments.

The system of distribution has not however prevented the crystallisation of social inequalities. One could even maintain that it has encouraged them, whatever the original intentions or the particular strategies of the social actors involved. The growth of nominal incomes has increased consumer demand, but the low productivity of the national productive system has not been able to provide the goods to meet this demand. In this vacuum, the most profitable branches of industry (construction, light industry, commerce) have grown stronger, in the sectors where public invest-ment (of which 80 per cent is earmarked for hydrocarbons and heavy industry) has been lowest (see Benachenhou, 1982). Such a process has not led to the creation of a cosmopolitan sector connecting foreign and Algerian enterpreneurs, which is forbidden by the official ideology and by the state monopoly on foreign trade, but to the growth of a national sector constituted by the mobilisation of family savings through informal banks which lend at very high interest rates (between 25 per cent and 40 per cent) (Liabes, 1985, p. 136). Between 1967 and 1980 the purchasing power of manual workers stagnated or rose only slightly while that of private entrepreneurs increased by 56 per cent (Thiery, 1982b, pp. 190–1). This indication of the vigour of the private sector became a major subject of debate at the sixth session of the Central Committee in December 1981: 'the state sector supports and reproduces private capital at all levels of the economy: in the distribution of wages, by protecting the market, by subsidising commodities, the state contributes to the structuration of an internal market and encourages the creation of a clientele . . . the restructuration of public enter-prises and the role and function of private capital in economic development are dialectically connected' (Liabes, 1984). Algeria thus seems to have entered a new phase.

The private sector and the social structure since 1980

A study of Algerian private industry in 1972 concluded with the following observation:

> the private bourgeoisie of provincial and rural origin can rely only upon limited resources. It therefore orientates itself towards the nationalised sector and administration. It seeks to develop relations with senior state officials who can protect the interests of the private sector. (Peneff, 1981, p. 162)

This bourgeoisie, politically and culturally dominated and enjoying few marriage links with senior state officials, yet fulfilling economic functions for a small but demanding clientele and even recuperating exiles from the political class, has seen its social status evolve: the private sector is now the symbol of upward social mobility for workers who wish to become self-employed and for families planning their matrimonial strategy. A sociologist specialising in the El Hadjar steel plant writes:

> A private sector employer has today become someone who is looked up to, a 'maqla' with a high social visibility, who lives in a rich villa in the old colonial quarter, who marries off his children in sumptuous ceremonies and contributes to the building of a mosque. He has nothing in common with even a senior executive of El Hadjar, exhaused by the management of a complex organisation, living in a low rent building. In the early years of the El Hadjar site an employee of the National Steel Corporation would have been considered a good match by parents in search of a son-in-law. Nowadays matrimonial alliances have changed their objective, and nothing can match a good private capitalist. (El Kenz, 1983, p. 252)

Furthermore, the growth of the private sector has been encouraged by numerous regulations since Boumedienne's death.[9]

But it is nevertheless the case that the private sector creates few jobs in comparison with the public sector. From 1967 to 1982 public employment (including the administration) rose from 46 to 61 per cent of total employment, including a rise from 28 to 31 per cent of agriculture, 42 to 74 per cent of industry, 41 to 67 per cent of building and construction, 20 to 75 per cent of commerce, but from 71 to 51 per cent of transport. From 1979 to 1982 non-agricultural

Table 7.4: Growth in total non-agricultural employment, 1980–1982 and 1982–1984 (per thousand jobs)

	1980	1982	1984	Growth 1980–2	Growth 1982–4	% 1980–2	% 1982–4
Public sector (excluding administration)	889	1,033	1,217	144	184	16.1	17.8
Administration	660	752	842	92	90	13.9	11.9
Total public sector	1,549	1,785	2,059	236	274	15.2	15.3
Private sector	635	676	737	41	61	6.4	8
TOTAL	2,184	2,461	2,796	277	335	12.2	13.6

Source: *Maghreb-Machrek*, 1986b (from Bouzidi, 1984 and *The Second Five-Year Plan, 1985–1989*, Alger, MPAT).

private employment (employers, employees and self-employed) rose by 9 per cent, employment in the public sector (excluding administration) by almost 20 per cent and employment in administration by more than 15 per cent (Bouzidi, 1984). In 1983 the non-agricultural public sector employed 1,920,000 people, or 73 per cent of the total non-agricultural workforce (compared with 70 per cent in 1979) and had created some 489,000 jobs between 1980 and 1983 (compared with 82,100 for the non-agricultural private sector), in other words, nearly 86 per cent of new non-agricultural employment.

Table 7.5: Non-agricultural private employment as of 31 December 1984 (per thousand jobs)

	Total	Self-employed	Salaried workers
Industry	127	41	86
Construction and public works	206	31	175
Commerce, transport and services	404	275	129
TOTAL	737	347	390

Source: *Maghreb-Machrek*, 1986b (figures from *The Second Five-Year Plan 1985–1989*, Alger-MPAT).

One can see from these figures (which are probably not completely reliable) that the private sector is very diverse and includes a large number of self-employed (some of whom are probably undeclared employers). According to the manpower statistics, the percentage of salaried workers is on the decrease. The private industrial sector is made up of businesses with a small workforce (except, relatively speaking, in the mechanical and textile industries). Only one private industrial enterprise employed more than 500 workers in 1982, while 4,700 out of a total of 5,700 companies employed between 1 and 20 workers (Hadjseyd, 1985); investment tends to be on a small scale and material is often obsolete, especially in the textile and food-processing industries. The National Statistics Office in its 1982 manpower survey registered for the private sector (both urban and rural) for 1983, 36,168 employers (of whom 9,860 were rural), 331,160 full-time workers, 106,170 seasonal workers and 756,900 self-employed. The structure of the sector is not very conducive to a class struggle between employers and workers.

On the other hand, although the private sector receives only a tiny part of industrial investment (2.3 per cent in 1981) it employs 25 per cent of the population and realises 34 per cent of the added value (in the agro-alimentary branch these figures are 4 per cent, 34 per cent and 57 per cent respectively and in textiles 6 per cent, 45 per cent and 51 per cent (Amirouche, 1985). Monopoly profits on the market, the possibility of reducing the costs of production thanks to the low price of raw materials and intermediate products acquired from the public sector (Benachenhou, 1982; Semmoud, 1982), the virtual absence of social expenditures and the choice of payment systems (generally by the hour rather than by the month) create favourable conditions for the realisation of profits and the artificial inflation of added value.

In the course of the first Five-Year Plan, workers' incomes rose slightly (by about 3 per cent annually) while the incomes of the

Table 7.6: The development of incomes between 1979 and 1984 (in billions of dinars)

	1 1979 (in DA 1979)	2 Forecast 1984 (in DA 1979)	3 Actual 1984 (in DA 1984)	4 Actual 1984 (in DA 1979)
Wages and salaries	40.5	65.0	76.6	51.4
Agriculture	2.5	3.0	7.0	4.7
Non-agricul.	25.0	42.0	43.5	29.1
Administration	13.0	20.0	26.1	17.5
Non-salaried revenues	18.0	25.4	45.0	30.2
Agriculture	5.5	7.0	11.0	7.3
Non-agricul.	12.5	18.4	34.0	22.8
Transfers	8.8	15.5	19.7	13.2
Gross household incomes	67.3	105.9	141.3	94.8
Disposable incomes	—	—	131.4	88.1
Consumption	56.0	84.6	121.7	81.6

Sources: columns 1 and 2: *Presentation of the First Five-Year Plan 1980-1984*, MPAT, 1980; column 3: report on the results of the first plan in *Presentation of the Second Five-Year Plan 1985-1989)*, MPAT, 1985; column 4: *idem*, using the indicator for the increase in consumer prices established by the International Financial Statistics of the IMF and reproduced by the *Quarterly Economic Review, Algeria* 1985 annual supplement, p. 15. It is this only a rough calculation which must be subject to prudent interpretation.

self-employed rose much faster (14 per cent annually). The presentation document of the second Five-Year Plan was probably not mistaken in its conclusion that 'in the course of previous plans the incomes of private entrepreneurs rose faster than had been forecast, thus contributing to inflationist tendencies and social inequalities'. These latter will no doubt be all the more manifest since non-agricultural salaried incomes have risen less rapidly than expected.

On the other hand, global consumption has increased less rapidly than forecast; and significant reduction in hydrocarbon resources which has led to a fall in investments and a serious disequilibrium in the balance of payments (*Maghreb-Machrek*, 1986a), has obliged the government to reduce domestic demand by about 5 per cent in an attempt to contain the external deficit. Such a contradiction, following a period of increased consumption, could make disparities of income a more sensitive issue. In fact, the statistics for consumer spending reflect both a general rise in the standard of living of the urban population (there have been increases for example in leisure and especially transport expenditures) and a widening of the gap in the quality of consumption. Habitations with up to seven people per room and consumption of subsidised commodities on the one hand, contrast with individual houses built 'at the initiative of the citizen', i.e. constructed on public land sold off cheaply by the state, on the other. Private habitations have multiplied in five years with the construction of over 100,000 units, while public housing fell 40 per cent behind target between 1980 and 1984, as 250,000 instead of 400,000 planned units were built.

The private sector is therefore developing, although it is still subject to control. The party, or a section of its leadership, is not prepared to allow the economic rationale of profitabiity (some would call it speculation) to gain precedence over the political rationale which governs distribution and social power. This is why there is a tendency to contrast the 'bad' private sector which is mercantile, speculative and remote from political power, although still the object of state subsidies, with the 'good' private sector, which mobilises savings, contributes to the growth of the standard of living, and combines the puritan and austere features of the nineteenth century Western bourgeoisie with the will to serve the national interest (Belaid, 1985). Echoing this attitude, certain employers (e.g. 'Parole du Privé', *Actualité-Economie*, June 1984) in the 'good' private sector emphasise their participation in the national effort, their complementarity with the public sector, and their acceptance of the state's monopoly of foreign trade, provided that a certain flexibility, and state aid for exportation in the form of subsidies, may be forthcoming. But above all, they insist on the need for autonomous organisation of their sector, presented as a means of eliminating its 'bad' side and establishing a decision-making partnership with the state. Still more interesting is the presentation of such re-structuration as the most appropriate organisation for *both* sectors, public and private. Here perhaps is manifested one of the guiding ideas of a section of the political elite: to make of the good private sector the instrument for rationalising the public sector so that it becomes more efficient, while however leaving the state in charge of access to profit and redistribution.

The rural classes and social stability

For its part, agricultural production has registered a decline in the socialist sector (self-managed lands and lands of the agrarian revolution) (Cote, 1985). As a result of the liberalisation of land transactions following the 1983 law, 500,000 hectares were shifted from the socialist to the private sector.

While large in comparison with its two North African neighbours, Algerian socialist agriculture has nevertheless declined, to the profit of a private middle peasantry which has a preponderant role in the production of meat and vegetables. Some of the agrarian revolution's co-operative structures have moreover been partially or wholly eliminated. One must nevertheless be wary of attaching too great an importance to legal distinctions between private and public sectors (the same applies for agricultural employment vs industrial and service sector employment) as a mechanical principle for the constitution and location of classes. In an important thesis which throws some light on the social basis of Algerian political stability, Claudine Chaulet emphasises the role of the family in explaining why the Algerian peasantry were quite willing to accept industrialisation while rejecting its apparent corollary, the industrialisation and intensification of agricultural production. As a result, the latter has stagnated in terms of absolute value. Indeed, many rural families, especially in the socialist sector, include sons working in industry, and fathers close to retirement as agricultural producers (not to mention sons who, as teachers and office workers, come to get produce from the farm) (Chaulet, 1984).

It is no longer a case of the extended autonomous family on its own lands, but rather the maintenance of cohesion among brothers,

167

and between conjugal units formed by brothers who are equal before the law. Wherever this cohesion has endured, it has given rise to two kinds of adaptation. Less frequently there have been associations of capitalist families covering several sectors, without however engaging in intensive agricultural production; more usually subsistence-oriented agricultural labour is combined with the salaried workforce and more of a non-agricultural nature. The rural family thus modifies the effects of urbanisation and industrialisation by contributing to the subsistence of a labour force mobilised by industry while at the same time benefiting from the support of non-agricultural employment.

The land is thus the repository of the family which looks to external sources of revenue to improve its standard of living. In this way oil revenues have been transformed into purchasing power produced by workers but not into new means of agricultural production. The social hierarchy that has been created is not founded upon the capacity to extract an agricultural surplus, that is to say upon the ownership (whether private or state-owned) of the means of production, but upon the relationship to apparatuses (both public and private) which distribute goods and services and determine the capacity to consume and accumulate. The relationship between the privileged clients and those excluded from redistribution may be more important that the relationship between owners and workers or small peasants (Chaulet, 1984, pp. 1048–55).

The combined impact of the extended family strategy and of differentiated access to the state's politico-economic circuits leads, according to Chaulet, to a triple rural class structure: (a) a rural bourgeoisie based on agricultural and more especially non-agricultural businesses, stronger in commerce than in agricultural production; (b) permanent workers on self-managed estates, unskilled full-time workers in the non-agricultural sector living in the countryside, co-operative workers and the small peasantry, constitute a rural proletariat who, because of familial cohesion and their relative security of employment, do not feel subject to the same exploitation as the isolated urban workers (but are more sensitive to inequalities of distribution), and are not antagonistic to either the state or the rural bourgeoisie; (c) a sub-proletariat with neither family support nor any secure source of income and belonging to no collectivity of kinship or of production, who may even be formal owners of a small plot of land, but are excluded (in particular by educational selection) from access to stable employment and services.

The development of the first two classes, in the context of a decline in agricultural production and expanding in industrial and commercial activities, tends to be a factor of support for the state (this is an optimistic interpretation which is not shared by Von Sivers, 1984). In any case, the stagnation foreseen in overall employment and the crisis of agricultural production are pushing the state to put forward (in a rather contradictory fashion) two recovery strategies: (1) incentives for autonomy in the utilisation of resources (and possibly even in the banking sector), which would tend to encourage the privatisation of agriculture, is a strategy imputed to the private bourgeoisie which has begun to be put into practice. It includes indemnities for landowners whose property was national-ised in the agrarian revolution, land transfers and broader provision of productive goods and credit to the private sector; (2) the inculca-tion of new techniques, the rationalisation of financial management, and the constitution of specialised workers' collectives, constitutes a strategy pioneered by state technocrats. It leads to an industrialisa-tion of agriculture through a network of state farms controlled by engineers and technicians. The restructuring of the socialist sector is tending in this direction. The paradox is that if one accepts the analysis of Chaulet, there is no reason why the first strategy should particularly suit the rural bourgeoisie, which is obliged to confront the market, unless it receives exorbitant guarantees (complete liberty of wages and prices, and very broad tax exemptions as in Morocco), and still fewer reasons why the second strategy should suit the rural proletariat. If one is to go beyond a socially satisfying *status quo* (whose only fault is to be insufficiently productive), the first strategy remains the less improbable.

THE 'CORRECTIVE' MOVEMENT IN SYRIA: 1970–1985

In many respects the politico-economic formula in Syria is embedded in an external regional context and an internal social context[10] that is very different from that of Algeria. Baathist ideology makes Syria a province of the Arab nation, which conforms with the history of this province under the Ottoman Empire and as part of the United Arab Republic from 1958 to 1961. This might be of symbolic importance if it were not that the Palestinian and Lebanese situation induces the regime to devote nearly half its budget to military expenditure, a situation that in 1985 allowed a contraband traffic into Syria amounting to about 10 per cent of all its imports, to the profit of the army stationed in Lebanon. Unlike Algeria and Iraq, Syria does not have major oil resources[11] but it does have access to its own resources (i.e. not extracted from the society) from the Gulf and most likely also from Libya and Iran by virtue of its position as a frontline state in confrontation with Israel. Such resources covered more than 50 per cent of the budget in the late 1970s and only slightly less than 50 per cent in the mid-1980s, in loans and grants for both military and economic expedition (Longuenesse, 1985, p. 9; Chatelus, 1982, p. 254). Because of this, Syria evidently lives beyond its strictly national (or 'local' in Baathist language) means.

Table 7.7: Spending-production balance (in billions of Syrian pounds at 1980 constant prices)

	1980	1981	1982	1983
Total consumption	45.5	55.8	53.6	56.6
of which private	33.6	43.4	40.0	42.7
Administration	11.9	15.5	13.2	13.9
Total investment	14.1	14.4	14.8	16.3
of which public	9.0	8.9	9.2	10.9
private	5.0	5.5	5.6	5.4
Total spending	59.6	69.0	68.4	72.9
GDP	51.8	57.1	58.9	60.8
External net contribution	7.8	11.9	9.4	12.2

Sources: Compiled and simplified from the Central Bureau of Statistics, *Statistical Abstracts;* Economic Intelligence Unit, *EIU Regional Review, The Middle East and North Africa 1986.*

Syria is therefore in some ways an oil state by transference. But unlike countries with stable transfer economies, dependent only on market fluctuations, like Algeria or Iraq until the outbreak of war in 1980, Syria is influenced by fluctuations in the international political market, which in some way explains the strange variation of investment levels in the development plans, from over 40 per cent after 1973 to about 25 per cent in the 1980s, of which 18 per cent goes to public investment. The result is an almost total inability to develop a coherent industrial policy, a question we shall return to later.

The internal context can also be characterised in three respects. The most obvious is the salient and socially legitimate, although officially ignored presence of religious, sectarian and factional identities such as the Alawis who, with about 10 per cent of the population, were formerly a sect class (according to Batatu, 1981a) and today are the central faction of Hafez al-Assad's rule. This does not mean that the ruling group either acts first and always in Alawi terms or that it does not find support and make alliances outside of this group. But the sect class faction occupies a disproportionate place for its numbers, and its group feeling allows it to respond impressively on behalf of the regime. There is also along tradition of town/country opposition that cannot be identified, as in Algeria, with colonialism vs nationalism. There, the decline of traditional cities, e.g. (Constantine, Tlemcen, Nedroma) has, in Algeria, made conquest of the city the symbol of national rule rather than a form of revenge against the very feeble traditional urban bourgeoisie. In Syria, this bourgeoisie and the landowning class were the social base of the parliamentary and dictatorial regimes prior to the union with Egypt of 1958 and the Baath seizure of power of 1963 (Picard, 1980; Batatu, 1981a). This in large measure was a victory for the 'peasant hordes' and for the ruralisation of towns over the landowning oligarchy and old town-based bourgeoisie (Van Dam, 1979, p. 99). Meanwhile, among the political elites these long established classes were supplanted by sons of the peasantry and the middle class of the small towns (Maaoz, 1973; Van Dusen, 1975; Drysdale, 1981).

The differences between the Syrian and Algerian process stems neither from the nature of the social base nor the nature of the new regime's elite, but rather from the type of political culture, perhaps more 'Khaldunian' in Syria where the notion of holding state power and wielding it in the interests of one formerly excluded group has remained stronger. The divergence is especially due to the balance of power the struggles provoked. The power of urban elements and the strength of the industrial middle class, antagonised by the radical measures of the Baathist regime in 1966, precipitated the corrective movement in 1970, which continued to promote the countryside but did so with the aid of, and under the control of, the state (Metral, 1980, pp. 314f) which instituted for the first time an open policy from which the urban and Damascene private sectors benefited (Batatu, 1981a, pp. 339–40).

The importance of the rural economy can be seen in its share of the GDP and the labour force. As elsewhere, agriculture in Syria is in decline but even so in 1983 it accounted for 19 per cent of the GDP (as against 29 per cent in 1965). The agrarian labour force represented 33 per cent of the total in 1980 (as against 52 per cent in 1965) (World Bank, 1983, 1985). The rural world is made up of

Table 7.8: Landownership and distribution (as % of surface)

	10 ha	10 to 100 ha	100 ha	State lands
1913	25	15	60	–
1945	15	33	29	23

Source: Hannoyer, 1980, p. 288.

medium-sized holdings which had increased in number in the first half of the century.

The agricultural economic growth of the 1950s which marked the rapid development of capitalism in agriculture (Metral, 1980, p. 298) paved the way for the entry of the peasantry into the political arena and also for the first agrarian reforms in 1958, 1963 and 1966 under the Baathists (Garzouzi, 1963; Keilany, 1973; Metral, 1980; Springborg, 1981). But even as these reforms weakened the landowning class and increased the role of the state in agricultural policy and the control of inputs and markets, they did not noticeably develop the agrarian public sector (agrarian reform co-operatives and state farms) which held only 23 per cent of all cultivated land. The small and middle peasantry, beneficiaries of agrarian reform, retained their autonomy through the interplay of control and assistance which links them to the state: 'the development of market crops raised the monetary income of the peasantry and was accompanied by a rise in the standard of living . . . and by a new dependence' (Metral, 1980, pp. 316–17). The second aspect of the class structure worthy of mention is the numerical importance of the traditional urban petty bourgeoisie.[12] Independent workers and traders increased in number between 1960 and 1970 while medium-sized businesses decreased and the industrialised public sector became greater and more concentrated. (Longuenesse, 1979, explains it by reference to the material advantages offered by these occupations and the mechanisation of medium-sized enterprises which reduced their labour needs).

These characteristics of Syria in the 1970s explain the greater commitment of the state to agriculture where there was politically productive capital to be made,[13] and perhaps also the resistance of towns heavily populated by the petty bourgeoisie. They do not, however, contradict the schema outlined at the beginning of this chapter: the heavy engagement of the state in political industry, a large and meagerly productive administration and public sector that none the less provides jobs (more than two-thirds of the non-agricultural jobs,

Table 7.9: Class structure of Syrian society in 1960 and 1970 (active population)

	1960	%	1970	%
Industrial and commercial bourgeoisie	19,750	2.2	10,890	0.7
Rural bourgeoisie	39,640	4.5	8,360	0.6
Working class	159,720	17.9	257,380	17.6
Agricultural proletariat	183,720	20.5	130,400	8.9
Traditional petty bourgeoisie				
— productive	51,300	5.8	103,350	7.0
— non-productive	59,600	6.7	112,740	7.7
Salaried intermediate (or middle) strata	132,530	15.0	234,930	16.0
Small peasantry	243,460	27.4	608.540	41.5
TOTAL	888,720	100.0	1,466,590	100.0

Source: Longuenesse, 1979.

exclusive of internal commerce), a growing if dominated private sector, a rural class interplay whereby the mechanism of access to the state is as strategic a factor as the ownership of soil and the control of the means of production.

The political industry, the bureaucracy and the public sector

The political rationale or the politico-military industry has been much more strongly emphasised in Syria than in Algeria (Chatelus, 1980; Scurat, 1982; Rivier, 1982; Sadowski, 1984).

The regime's politico-military functions in the region permit it 'to mobilise resources extending far beyond meagre profits of an industrial sector renowned for its lack of productivity' (Rivier, 1982, p. 119), but as we have seen, there is another side to the coin. Such external dependence can oblige the regime to cut its investments since it cannot contain either its military spending or its consumer subsidies, again only underlining the political rationale. This all works towards one end result: the economist cannot notice any strictly economic logic (for example, a heavy industry or an import substitution policy, Chatelus, 1980, p. 230) but he cannot miss the decrease in added value per job and in capital productivity (Longuenesse, 1985, p. 12). Costs become excessive, there is an underemployment of production capacity due to maintenance

173

deficiencies and the dire lack of skilled workers, production units are implanted without any overall plan (Hannoyer, 1980; Seurat, 1980).

But here the sociologist may discern a social reproduction rationale. 'The primary justification for a factory is not the goal of showing a profit but the releasing of funds which in reality are themselves a source of power', thus symbolising the real presence of the state and providing employment, notably bureaucratic, in disproportionate measure (Seurat, 1982; Longuenesse, 1985 speaks more positively of the effects of this industrial policy). The evolution of the redistributive nature of the Syrian economy may be inferred from the gross domestic production structure.

Table 7.10: Evolution of the gross domestic production structure (as %)

	1970	1977	1983
Agriculture	19	16	18
Mining and manufacturing	25	22	17
Building and construction	4	7	7
Wholesale and retail trade	23	25	26
Transport and communication	8	7	7
Finance and insurance	7	6	5
Social and personal services	2	2	2
Government services	12	15	18

Source: Compiled by the author, see Table 7.7.

The relative decline in the value of industry and the growth of commerce and administrative services allow us to legitimately suppose that this distribution of revenue develops more rapidly than does production itself.

The politically induced and economically irrational creation and distribution of credit-jobs (Batatu, 1984, p. 13) has a dual effect: in the lower echelons, it increases the number of those who owe their jobs to somebody and thus are placed under a personal obligation; and in general it holds all those dependent on the state for their livelihood and opportunity for social advancement. Batatu (1984) points out that from 1960 to 1979 the number of state employees, including manual workers, leaped from 34,000 to 331,000, and argues that almost a quarter of the total population are in this situation and so eventually are members of the trade union organisations linked to the ruling power (Longuenesse, 1985, p. 12). In the upper echelons, the interplay of factional and clientele interests transforms the public sector into a prebendal system (Sadowski, 1984; Longue nesse, 1985). The lower echelons and the upper echelons enjoy a virtually dialectical relationship; bound together ideologically and materially in defence of the public sector,[14] and all the more so since the lower echelons express themselves through trade union representatives, themselves partially dependent on the ruling power. They oppose one another in the recurring quarrel (in 1980 and 1985) over corruption and the bourgeois state, a quarrel periodically reactivated or simply tolerated by the leadership.

It is difficult clearly to analyse this type of crisis. When it becomes the object of toleration or official discussion, then its significance shifts from the original context to its presentation, organisation, and rival interpretations by rival groups. Not only does one man's efficient manager become another man's parasite but we can also discern a double entanglement, of politics and the economy on the one hand, of class, community, regional and factional interests on the other. The entire process conceals a multitude of strategies, of which some of the participants themselves are perhaps unconscious.

In 1985, the critique of the public sector and its functioning was undertaken by the trade unions and it is unthinkable that their discourse was not at least tacitly permitted by the president. It recalled certain themes of Algerian trade unionism in 1976 (Leca and Vatin, 1979, pp. 74ff) as well as the first critiques made in the post-Boumedienne era: the public sector, in particular, made massive use of imported goods with their consequent wastage and sold themselves to imperialism rather than developing the national potential. But Syrian trade unionsn went further, accusing public sector managers of seeking personal gain, a practice encouraged by the regime itself. Did this indicate a turning point towards the privatisation of the economy? The overall context would suggest a contrary interpretation: in criticising managers for their corrupt, anti-national practices, trade unionists had no intention of holding private bosses up as an example. Instead, when faced by a crisis, those in power stage-managed a scenario, about class struggle between workers and managers; the latter then became scapegoats from whom the leaders disassociated themselves and to whom they issued a warning by way of the union mouthpiece. This is state of affairs familiar to Algerians which confirms the earlier observation that the workers' movement is part and parcel of the state. This lower-upper opposition allows both symbolic and real causes to be found for the economic irrationality of public sector management when it becomes impossible to handle the crisis by increasing salaries because of the lack of finances (Longuenesse, 1985, p. 19). Upper managers are kept in a state of insecurity, thus perpetuating the clientele relationship.

The private sector

Since 1970 the private sector and its bourgeoisie have retained an important, although overshadowed, role which is why the political problems they pose in Algeria have never reached the same dimensions in Syria (a thorough study is still in progress: see Longuenesse, 1979; Amin, 1982). Class constraints weighing on the corrective movement were relatively simple: restore the confidence of domestic capital and of the bourgeoisie and petty bourgeois Sunnite merchants without losing the support of the peasantry and the wage and salary earners. A mixed political economy demands that socialist redistribution be upheld and maintained while at the same time a capitalist opening of the economy should be effected. Even though private investment (which remains stationary) equals about half the public investment allocated to the planning programmes, the private sector is in a minority in industry, both in terms of the value produced and size of labour force, and is only preponderant in real estate and domestic commerce, where speculation and the circulation of capital are necessary. Sunni traders benefit from this limited opening, which explains for some why, since 1978, the Muslim opposition has been unable to mobilise sufficient support (Ahsan, 1984). From this point of view the difference between the public and private sectors is not fundamental but only a means by which the regime can harness potential social and religious opposition.[14] But the high inflation rate (officially estimated at 20 per cent per annum), which does not bother the commercial and speculative sector, deeply affects urban workers in administration and industry.

The state which numbers these groups among its political base, or at any rate among its class allies, is doomed therefore to look for resources to transfer in order to maintain price and salary levels. In a sense, there is certainly a class struggle in the pure Marxist tradition over the question of salaries but it does not set the bourgeoisie against the proletariat for the control and exploitation of productive labour. Rather, it is the battlefield at the grassroots level and at top levels for the allocation and distribution of state resources.

Agriculture and the rural classes

As with Algeria, agricultural policies and problems are less important for present purposes than are certain aspects of the class structure after ten years of reforms. In Syria too, the reforms are marked by a combination of more flexible market mechanisms and intense state planning, since the state controls both water and credit, and the private sector holds almost 80 per cent of the cultivated land.

Françoise Metral posed the classic question in the conclusion to her 1979 article: 'kulak' (predominance of concentrated private farming) or 'collectivisation'? Posing the choices between support for high performance private ownership in the name of production, or for the co-operatives in the name of equal redistribution (Metral, 1980, pp. 321–2) or for the sake of political allegiances and control (Hannoyer, 1985, p. 28).

It is virtually impossible to answer this question fully given the wide diversity between regions in Syria (Metral, 1985). Two important examples come from the Euphrates and the Ghab (Hannoyer, 1985; Metral, 1985) where transferred oil rent gave impetus to ambitious projects. In the first, a fundamental difference seems to emerge between the rural bourgeoisie, who mastered their irrigation needs to become the main source of agro-industry production, and the lesser peasantry, bereft of capital and machinery and dependent on co-operatives in which they invest little economical labour but a good deal of political work (the playing out of factional and tribal conflicts destined to reap clientelist gains, especially jobs outside the village). Moreover, both strategies — class interest and political allegiance — can combine when the independent farmer shares in the running of a co-operative. What is more, neither group is stable.

Some members of the rural bourgeoisie may be downgraded whereas a lightweight peasant weaving his way through the local power network could turn any economic advantage to his political gain. The administration too has a dual rationale: centralised and rationalised management of economic resources where engineers are often much in evidence, and political, clientelist management of finance conceded to clans (and called misappropriation by the press). The agricultural enterprise becomes a means of forming a clientelist political base, thereby contradicting its own objective of intensifying production (Hannoyer, 1985). The end result is mystifying to the observer: has the state prepared the way for a class of private farmers to entrench themselves? Is this a state-assisted campaign which turns peasants into semi-urban workers? Is it a

177

rationalisation of production by engineers? Still, these are not the most important questions.

More interesting is the fact that in a climate of relative economic efficiency (but starting at a fairly high level of productivity), the interplay between peasant family strategies and clientelist tribal distribution networks has opened new avenues for mobility and promotion to a great number of rural dwellers (Hannoyer, 1985, p. 29). So long as transferred resources allow the socio-political logic (allegiance and access to state resources) to win over the economic logic (production and bourgeois class interest), then the Syrian countryside remains a stable, if not legitimate, base and so it will remain as long as the number of those excluded from communal property and distribution networks does not increase excessively.

A study of Ghab shows similar mechanisms at work. Access to the state and army gives room for manoeuvre. Crops not provided for in the plan can be grown; allotments can be extended; external funds can be acquired (loans and paid jobs). As is true in Algeria, family brotherhood is again the key factor in all of these strategies with a double objective: diversify one's source of income and enlarge one's circle of contacts sufficiently to penetrate the state apparatus. In both examples, the mechanism for the transfer of state resources to private operators (Metral, 1985, p. 58), and the mixed social structure with its three components (independent farmers, salaried peasants or members of co-operatives and the state apparatus) are sources of support for the state in so far as class inequality is not sensitive enough an issue to cancel out the tunnel-effect mentioned above, and as long as demographic growth can be absorbed elsewhere than in agriculture (by emigration, trade, bureaucracy, the army or militia). As is often the case, the countryside is a support base for the state as long as it finds extra resources to supplement its means of production, and as long as its human surplus is transferred elsewhere. The problem evidently is to know if such a situation is durable. From this point of view, Iraq is in a better situation since it is the only one of three examples to import hired labour (estimated at one million) outright; but since 1981 Iraq, to all intents and purposes, has been living in a war economy.

IRAQ 1963–1985

The structural likeness between Iraq and Syria is evident in any comparison of the division of labour between agriculture and

Table 7.11: The labour force in agriculture and industry, 1960–1980 (as %)[1]

| | 1960 | | 1970 | | 1980 | |
	Syria	Iraq	Syria	Iraq	Syria	Iraq
Labour force (%) in agriculture	54%	53%	51%	47%	33%	42%
Labour force in industry	19%	18%	21%	22%	31%	26%

Note: 1. The Iraqi figures offered by Sader (1982, p. 270) show quite a different picture. The agricultural labour force would have dropped from 52 per cent (in 1973) to 30 per cent (in 1977), the industrial one would here leap from 8.7 per cent to 20.1 per cent during the same period. Obviously, the bases of calculation are not the same. In any case, the similarity between Syria and Iraq is well established.
Source: *World Tables: Social Data*, vol. II, World Bank, 1983.

industry (with a deviation in the figures for 1980).

To be more precise, as the ever indispensable Batatu notes, the ethnic and religious structure is the same only reversed. Among the Muslim population in Iraq, 52 per cent are Shi'i, 20 per cent Sunni and 18 per cent Kurds, while in Syria 63 per cent are Sunni and 12 per cent Alawi.

> Thus the core of the ruling element of Iraq also consists of a kinship group (closely related members of the Begat section of the Abu Nasir tribe), rests essentially on members of a minority sect (Sunni Arabs) and on country rather than city people (on middle and lower middle class families from the country towns of the Arab north-western parts of Iraq) and reflects the balance of forces in the army rather than in the country at large (the relative strength of the bloc of military officers originating from the country town of Takrit). (Batatu, 1981a, p. 344; for details see Batatu, 1978 and 1985)

As in Syria, the centre of power tends to fix itself around a tightly welded minority benefiting from the divisions among the Shi'i majority. Its ambition is not primarily Sunni but Arab, and Saddam Hussein has tried to widen his partisan base to Shi'is (Batatu, 1981b). None the less, he still depends on his particular identity for survival. He does not pursue a national class interest but, as a member of the peripheral middle class, he perceives problems in the same light as other sections of that class. Batatu (1985, p. 389f; see also Hudson, 1977, pp. 276f) detected here a factional-clientele logic consistent with the development logic of the entire middle class benefiting from the state, at the heart of which a higher class of state bourgeoisie is distinguishable (members of the commercial socialist sector whose members increased tenfold from 1970 to 1981).

The public sector and the private sector

When compared to Syria, Iraq shows a greater state hold on the economy, notably in agriculture and commerce, with the private sector being dominant only in the transport and communication, and construction sectors. These sectors have, since 1981, shown less growth in the GDP, but the fall in oil revenue caused by the war and the unreliability of Iraqi data make comparisons difficult.

Table 7.12: Public sector and private sector in certain economic sectors of the GDP (%)

	1980		1981		1982	
	Public	Private	Public	Private	Public	Private
Agriculture	46.9	53.1	53.1	48.7	52.7	47.2
Manufacturing	62.9	37.1	54.6	45.4	59.2	40.8
Construction	12.2	87.8	6.4	93.6	6.2	93.8
Transportation and communication	28.8	71.2	27.5	72.5	24	76
Trade	59.3	40.7	55.4	44.6	56.2	43.8
Subtotal	52.7	47.3	53.3	47.7	50.0	50.0
Mining and quarrying	99.7	0.3	98.6	1.4	98.7	1.3
Total	81.4	18.6	67.4	32.6	61.2	38.8

Source: Springborg, 1986.

In his essay, Springborg (1986) suggests a rapid growth in the private sector although, again, the figures must be corrected to allow for the decline in the oil sector.

These observations, confirmed by the respective share of each sector in gross domestic fixed capital (about 80 per cent for the public sector and 20 per cent for the private sector; as against 91 per cent and 8 per cent in 1979, because of the fall in oil investments), demonstrate a moderate growth in the private sector. The private sector is made up of small and medium sized enterprises, the vast majority of which employ less than 10 workers. As in Algeria, their share in added value (31 per cent for the entire industrial sector in

1977) and employment (30 per cent in 1978) (Sader, 1982, pp. 273–9) is more important than their share in investment. The large enterprises are to be found in the public sector although there is an appreciable number of private firms employing over 250 persons — more so than in Algeria — (20 as compared to 80 public sector companies), with the private firms going from an average of 500 to 700 employees between 1981 and 1982 compared to about 1,500 for those in the public sector (Springborg, 1986).

Infitah in agriculture

After the classic agrarian reform period in the 1970s, which placed about half of all cultivated land in collective farms and co-operatives by 1975 (Nyrop, 1979; Springborg, 1981), the Saddam Hussein government gradually changed direction. The number of collective farms diminished, many co-operatives were abolished, ownership ceilings were relaxed, usufruct rights were transformed from the state to private leasees, controls over recipients of agrarian reform land were progressively reduced and rents at low rates were granted by the government to Iraqis and other Arab nationals after the passage of law 35 in 1983. Credit has been more generously extended to private farmers, which enables them to purchase machinery; producers were given direct access to public wholesale markets or licensed private shops, and a joint venture was established to deal with the marketing of fruit, vegetables, and later on of field crops (see Springborg, 1986 for numerous details, except the statistics on agricultural land ownership, not released since 1979). The result has been growth in the private and traditional sector and stagnation in the public sector, which produces fixed crops at controlled prices.

This situation can be explained by two types of class constraints. One is upper middle class demand for more produce, even at higher prices and thus their reliance on the private sector, while the public sector continues to supply subsidised basic produce to the lower class. The other constraint is the need to satisfy the desire for social promotion felt by agents of the commercial socialist sector whose access to credit and inputs permits them to develop enterprises either parallel to, or together with, urbanite entrepreneurs. Hence, 'the symbiotic relationship between public and private sectors in which the latter exists by servicing the former, frequently provides the network in which the crucial contacts are made. Occasionally, these

181

personal networks extend upwards into the political elite' (Spring-borg, 1986). Other groups may be observed in the rainfed regions: contractors, suppliers of machinery and equipment who receive about half the harvest, have fewer links with the national elite and are as yet only an amorphous group of supporters of the regime, more tied to the president himself than to the party. This verifies Hopkins's (1984, p. 7) hypothesis of a third wave of agrarian trans-formation. From the initial modernisation of large landholdings, followed by collectivisation or redistribution of land, to the constitu-tion, with the blessing of the state, of a new private sector whose agents benefit economically and derive a political power base from their enhanced role.

CONCLUSION: CLASS SOCIETY, CLASS POLITICS AND SOCIAL UPHEAVALS

The foregoing account tends to bring Algeria and Iraq into line with each other, although the former is still well behind. There is the same overwhelming presence of an industrial public sector, the same political grip on the economy intent on redistribution and control, the same trend towards private sector development although only to quite a moderate extent (even though the private sector role in Iraqi agriculture seems more pronounced and so far at least there is no Algerian equivalent to the Buniyah family). Morever, the Algerian private sector exports very little and therefore the correlation between its growth and fluctuations in foreign trading as observed by Springborg in Iraq does not exist in Algeria. Springborg's hypotheses can then, with certain qualifications, be accepted.

(1) The single party power base is compromised by an extension of the private sector despite the attempt, more successful in Iraq than Algeria, to create joint ventures between the public and private sector. One-party systems are both ideologically and materially too fused to the public sector to find common ground with the employer interests of the private sector. Nor is it certain that the private sector is the consolidating base of Chadli Bendjedid's personal power (as Springborg maintains is the case with Saddam Hussein) and even if this were the case, any leader, no matter how authoritarian or sultanic, would find it difficult to overcome party resistance once he had lost his charismatic base or religious legitimacy).

(2) It is possible that the Arab political economies are evolving towards a centrist position. Those with a dominant public sector

whose state infrastructure is well-established tend to grant greater freedom of action to the private sector (Zartman, 1982, p. 31). The Gulf states, which from the start lacked autonomy *vis-à-vis* the traditional structure, are building state apparatuses that go beyond tribal and family relationships (in order to satisfy New Middle Class demands). This implies a rapid expansion of the public sector.

Secular patrimonial authoritarianism is more easily supported by a mixed structure which combines public and private sectors than it would be by a purely state economy (whose inefficiency would dissatisfy the emerging classes) or by a strictly private economy (which, by rendering visible the social structure of the groups, would exacerbate social conflicts and make them less easy to handle). The state can create classes but it is not necessarily able to give them political strength.

(3) One final hypothesis of Springborg's seems debatable however: 'an infitah class would itself constrain the ruler's options . . . A complete infitah leading to enhanced class solidarities and conflict would provide politically precisely what he does not want.' Hence the need for a mixed economy: 'Such an economy blunts class distinctions, thereby inhibiting the formation of firmly based political movements and thus perpetuating the very authoritarian rule that has presided over its development.' This logic is implicitly bound to the fact that the creation of classes leads to class action, action by groups identifiying themselves politically in terms of class and demanding political autonomy *vis-à-vis* the state. Corresponding to the economic market opened by the establishment of a private sector there should exist a political market opened by the establishment of class groups or factions. There is no empirical proof of this. The private sector growing up in the shadow of the state (and thanks to the public sector) certainly has an interest in gaining freedom of economic action, more access to credit and fiscal facilities, the freedom of cross-border traffic, but why should it have to undertake open political action when it can try to obtain all this at less cost to itself by remaining entrenched in bureaucratic or palace politics where the informal network of family, regional, and factional solidarity is at the heart of the game? It can, it is true, by virtue of its very existence, provoke class conflict and drive the workers and the excluded to demand freedom of political action which the bourgeoisie itself may not need. But as we have seen, the structural conditions for such class mobilisation do not exist either in the agrarian or the industrial sectors (given the rural class composition and the size of private enterprises in industrial life). What is more,

183

the workers too, like the bourgeoisie have their demands (jobs, housing, subventioned low-price consumer goods, free medicine, educational opportunities) and these are also gained by way of bureaucratic and palace politics, or sometimes with local strikes or riots in the towns (although this is scarcely ever seen in Algeria) and not through any autonomous politicisation. The notion that a class structure, by simple virtue of its existence in the body politic, might destabilise populist-authoritarian regimes is related to the paradigm (erroneous in my view) of bourgeois society where economic and social relationships are meditated by citizenship and represented by political relationships in the public arena.

A society in which the social and economic relations are determined by the political ones and where the citizen does not enjoy autonomous political rights, but only the possibility of putting pressure on the bureaucracy through membership in a community or power group, might never experience the effect of the class structure binding the regime's roots so long as they are free from strong international constaints.

(4) The combination of bureaucratic authoritarian coercion and redistribution of wealth is not, for all that, a stable formula. Political action carried out by private factional, ethnic or religious groups is not always manageable. Moreover, the structure just described can also encourage another form of mobilisation. The most usual interpretation of Islamic or Islamist protest movements is as follows: secular nationalism supported by the new strata (New Middle Class intellectuals and the working class) is no longer a dominant force; Islamic ideology offers serious competition in that it both recuperates and dialectically surpasses nationalism. This Islam-based politics expresses at the same time (a) the desire for autonomy from foreign imperialism which is felt as a yoke of cultural aggression and material exploitation; (b) a revolt against the state which is seen as manipulative, corrupt and corrupting; and (c) the affirmation of a personal and collective identity, a bringing together again of spheres which bourgeois society separates (public/private, religious/political, economic/moral). This ideology finds its social base in the small towns and among those of a rural background, among young people who are relatively well-educated and politically informed, living in areas of rapid urbanisation (Etienne and Tozy, 1979; Ibrahim, 1980; Kepel, 1984 and 1985; Hermassi, 1984). Other commentators note that this social base is made up of certain segments of the lower middle-class whose leadership is a social mix including, among others, members of the rural elite (Ansari, 1984

and Chapter 9, Dawisha and Zartman, 1987). In Algeria it is the rural middle class, and most especially its urbanised offspring, who are seen as the potential bearers of an Islamic ideology that can connect socialism and the sceptical and ecumenical Islamism of the state, and that in the rural world can supplant the tradition of self-reliance and abstentionism *vis-à-vis* the state (Von Sivers, 1984).

This contemporary Islamism, whatever its social content (e.g. whether or not it is favourable or hostile to the private ownership of the means of production) presents certain characteristic traits: an all-embracing ideology, egalitarian in the abstract and anti-individualist in practice, whose religious code is its root and source and not simply an instrument used for political ends. Such a common experience of resentment and frustration (in the economic, intellectual and symbolic spheres, giving three homothetic social categories) could be considered as progressive (Davis, 1984) or, on the other hand, a branch of the fascist family tree (Arjomand, 1984) (which is by no means a contradiction in terms). It does however form a relatively identifiable social unit through its symbolic content and by way of its organisation. It rejects partisan or institutional intermediaries and favours recruitment via family bonds or personal contacts in loosely organised and often very fragmented groupings. This does not prevent the unleashing of vast social movements for urgent material demands (often enough protest demonstrations against rises in food prices) and directed against the figureheads of corruption ('Western' shops and bourgeois districts, in the name of a religious code of justice which calls for an Islamic 'moral economy' (Burke, 1986)).

These movements are sometimes described as the revolt of the petty bourgeoisie (Fischer, 1982). This is most likely true in certain specified cases. But the essential seems to lie elsewhere; the redistributing state with its ever-increasing social weight has created a structure conducive to a total calling into question of its power (and that of the elites, groups and classes who seem to benefit the most). When there are no longer sufficient resources to provide for and satisfy those expecting minimal gratification (the impoverished peasantry, the urban sub-proletariat, unemployed skilled workers, those with decreasing spending power) the state becomes the target of manifold discontent which no class ideology can really express: the excluded (from many classes) in their turn reject the system that no longer has the means to integrate them into the allocation process.

From this point of view, the emergence of the private sector has a triple social significance, over and above the necessity for increased production (always a reason to justify a productive, non-parasitic, private sector). It is firstly the strategy for advancement of an upper middle class associated with the state. It is also, perhaps, an expression of the state's wish to indemnify itself, i.e. by offering up intermediate targets to social protest movements. But it renders the social structure and the social inequalities more visible.[15] The stratification of society and the privatisation of the state (Camau, 1984) are criticised together. The private sector, instead of coming to the aid of the authoritarian state, can in this way make it more fragile.

NOTES

1. The lack of resources can be smoothed over by the migration process. This aspect will not be dealt with in this paper, in spite of its utmost importance (cf. on Maghrebian migrations to France, Garson, 1981; Moulier-Boutang et al., 1986 among many others; on inter-Arab migrations, Birks and Sinclair, 1980; Ibrahim, 1982; Serageldin et al., 1983; Centre d'Etudes et de Recherches sur le Moyen Orient Contemporain, 1985). It is difficult to assess its relevance to our problem. It is likely that migration mitigates social tensions in the countries of emigration, and increases the supply of money and consumer goods available in the domestic markets, thus favouring the circulation process. Some studies show evidence of their positive impact on upward social mobility (Sabagh, 1982). More important, it is likely that they enhance cultural and confessional identities instead of class identities (Longuenesse, 1986).

2. For example Batatu, 1985, p. 386: 'By "middle class" I mean that composite part of the society which is plural in its functions but has in common an intermediate status or occupies a middle position between the propertyless and the proprietors and which includes, among other elements, army officers, civil servants, members of professions, merchants, tradesmen and landowners.'

3. On the seemingly opposite side, Morocco fully integrates the landowning bourgeoisie within the political formula (Leveau, 1984 and 1985). Benefiting from a favourable tax system, the landowners play an important role in supporting the regime. Morocco has no oil to export and has to rely on exports of citrus fruit to make up for the imports of wheat and oil.

4. In this particular case, it may be worth noting that the classical dispute in Western sociology, opposing instrumentalist to autonomist theories of the state, evolves in a peculiar way. Here the state is both totally autonomous (as an apparatus) since it is not manned nor manipulated by members of a specific economic class; and totally instrumental (as a process), being utilised by the political class (though not for its sole benefit) and being barred to anyone else.

5. Such a hypothesis is not groundless. But if the class link in reverse reminds us that the state can create classes, such a metaphor alone cannot

explain why the political class has made specific economic choices, leading to the creation of bourgeois classes. Mohamed Harbi is one of the few to have addressed the issue: emphasising the consensus among the rulers (populist culture and ideology, bureaucratic organisation and behaviour) in spite of their diverse class origins, he bases his explanation of their economic choices on 'the internal necessity . . . driving them to concentrate more and more power and to mold the national society to their own profit' (Harbi, 1980, p. 379).

6. The 1973 census of agriculture determined that 75 per cent of the farmers needed an additional source of income to make a living. In 1972 the Charter of the agrarian revolution pointed out that 425,000 farmers and their families (making up 72 per cent of the agricultural labour force) were below the subsistence level should they rely only on their holdings, 64 per cent of the farms occupied 29 per cent of the arable land, 13,000 farmers possessed more than 50 hectares (1.5 per cent of the farmers for 22 per cent of the arable land). Half of the private farmers did not use a metal plow, 10 per cent used fertilisers and 26 per cent used mechanical means (Mutin, 1980). In 1978, six years after the beginning of the agrarian revolution, the private farmers cultivated 60 per cent of the arable land and utilised only 23 per cent of the agricultural machinery. All those phenomena form a system. Private investment has none the less increased, in particular in aboriculture. That is probably due to the migrants' money (Karsenty, 1975, p. 141).

7. See also the policy of importing cereals which enabled the government to keep the producer prices artificially low while satisfying demand. By combining low retail food prices with low producer prices, the state was able to subsidise food consumption without excessively burdening the budget. Such political rationality did not extend, however, to other products (meat and vegetables) the prices of which skyrocketed. (See a more detailed account in Bedrani, 1982, pp. 111–64 and in Cleaver, 1982).

8. Can we interpret those movements in terms of class basis and class action in the classical sense? To some extent, Roberts explains the Kabyle movement by the dissatisfaction of the Kabyle bourgeoisie (Roberts, 1983) and Von Sivers attributes the religious resistance to the private peasantry (Von Sivers, 1984). It may also be so, but here the class is masked to such a point that it is almost impossible to pinpoint a political class consciousness of any sort.

9. For example the Act of 1985 regularising the illegal occupations of building sites, regulations encouraging private investments (Acts of August and December 1982 and decisions of December 1983 on private investment in petrochemical and heavy industries), fostering access to credit, providing facilities for importation, and granting fiscal advantages to the productive private sector (all the budgetary acts since 1983).

10. The terminology is not fully adequate: (1) the demarcation of domestic, regional and international contexts is particularly fuzzy; (2) the very notion of society is debatable in so far as it carries along several prejudices springing from the sociology of Western societies (cultural unification, class or group identities exclusive of cultural and communal identities, economic and social integration through the national market system). Cf. on the Syrian societies under the French mandate, Weulersse,

1946, and on the contemporary period, Seurat, 1980, pp. 89, 119, and Michaud, 1981.

11. Syria's oil exports have made up 60 per cent of export revenues since 1974. Syria is also an oil importer since it cannot refine its own oil.

12. E. Longuenesse uses 'traditional' to point at the petty bourgeoisie (for example, the tradesmen and shopkeepers, in the usual Marxist terminology) and to differentiate it from the clerks and non-manual wage earners, part of the intermediate middle class. By 'traditional' she does not mean the traditional corporations in decline. This explains why, in her figures, the 'traditional petty bourgeoisie' (14 per cent of the labour force in 1960) is larger than the craftsmen (4 per cent, Halbaoui, 1965).

13. That does not preclude the impoverishment of a part of the peasantry. The rural world is in decline but, as Batatu has appositely pointed out,

if, therefore, in the long drawn out conflict between city and country, the city has been more and more overshadowing the countryside and growing in size, power and significance, the original city people themselves have been falling under. Even so, the city is having the final say, in as much as in the country people who are on the top of the heap now, are themselves being urbanised and transformed into citizens. (Batatu, 1981a, p. 338)

14. The opposition between public and private sector is accurately depicted as the complementarity of two forms of economic domination, rather than as a contrast between public and private interests (Hannoyer and Seurat, 1979, p. 38; Longuenesse, 1985, p. 27).

15. There are few quantitative analyses of social inequality. Samir Amin states that inequality is growing without always differentiating the absolute decline in the living standards of the poor masses from the relative gap between upper and lower strata (Amin, 1982b, pp. 30–3 on land ownership and 120–32 on the overall issue. Most of the figures cited do not go beyond 1975).

8

Arab Military in Politics: from Revolutionary Plot to Authoritarian State

Elizabeth Picard

> Stoop, Romans, stoop
> And let us bathe our hands in Caesar's blood
> Up to the elbows, and besmear our swords;
> Then walk we forth, even to the market place,
> And, waving our red weapons o'er our heads,
> let's all cry, 'Peace, freedom, and liberty!'
>
> Julius Caesar, III

Twenty years ago, for someone who studied Arab politics either on the local, the regional, and even more on the national level, armed forces appeared to play a central part in the system and to stand at the core of analysis. A first reason for this importance was to be found in the dramatic tension on the international scene in the Middle East and North Africa at that time: the last episodes of a long struggle for national liberation were being acted out, such as the Suez triple aggression (1956), the Algerian struggle for independence (until 1962) and finally the departure of the British from the Gulf. Moreover, the rising warfare between Israel and its Arab neighbours and the catastrophic Arab defeat of June 1967 contributed to stress the special importance of armed forces in politics. When reading a periodical like *Dirasat Arabiyya* in the late 1960s, one would find in nearly every issue an article dealing with such topics as 'the revolutionary army' or 'the popular war for national liberation' (Allush, 1968; Abu Uras, 1969).

Arab armies appeared even more central for the study of Arab politics on account of their growing concern for civilian affairs and their various involvements in governmental processes. Since the first aborted attempts in Iraq, the Bakr Sudki coup in 1936, (Batatu, 1978, p. 337), Rashid Ali al-Kaylani's revolt in 1941 (Batatu, 1978, pp. 451–61), there had been a long series after World War Two in Syria, soon followed by Egypt's Free Officers in 1952, and by many others.[1] As a result, military intervention in politics had become commonplace in many Arab states, actually with a much higher frequency than in most Third World countries during the 1950s and 1960s.[2]

Even when erratic and bloody, as was the Iraqi 1958 revolution against the Hashemite monarchy, military coups were looked upon rather positively at that time. They were explained by an urgent need for authority in countries where the state was still embryonic and the public services defective. They were praised because of the disciplined and hierarchical character commonly attributed to armed forces. Many observers stressed the assumed penchant of the officers for modern technology and consequently implied they might authoritatively convey their various qualities to their citizens as a whole. Armies were also deemed to operate mainly at a national-state level and consequently to have the capacity to reinforce their country's cohesion. To summarise, armed forces were seen by many a scholar, be he an Arab,[3] a Westerner[4] or even a Soviet,[5] as a strongly modernising instrument, a major agent for change and renouncement of tradition, especially because the new generation of officers who initiated most of these coups came from a more rural and less privileged origin than their elders.

This 'new middle class' with its main tool, the armed forces (Halpern, 1962, p. 278), was considered bound to set up a state-controlled economy and to give an impulse to the process of intensive industrialisation in order to substitute nationally-made products for imported products, a process then considered key to Third World development. The military would also be able to prescribe a new citizenship and to encourage such values as secularism and political participation, in the sense that Lerner praised in those years: Nasser's Egypt, Iraq after Qasim's revolution, Baathist Syria and, soon after, Boumedienne's Algeria were the paramount examples of the successful intervention of the military in Arab politics.

The reaction against such a positive view of the armed forces in the Arab world was not long to come. Both the rather negative performances of the new military regimes and the criticisms which arose regarding the so-called modernising capability of the officers when they became involved in politics decreased appreciation of the army.

The years 1967–70 represented a dramatic turn in Arab history: after the June *naksa*, leaders had to comply with a very new situation and adopt a lower path. They shifted from the nationalist, socialising and triumphant rhetoric which had prevailed for a decade or more, to pragmatism and a withdrawal towards more limited state interests. A new moderate style had to be found, and the model became Saudi Arabia. As for the flamboyant officers who had allegedly prepared the Syrian citadel for the 'decisive battle', and such a charismatic leader as Nasser, not only had they failed to repel the Israeli attack or to make the slightest gains for the Palestinians in whose name they had mobilised and disciplined the masses, but on the domestic scene, they had met serious setbacks in their policy of authoritarian nationalisation, of extensive agrarian reform, of industrialisation, and finally in their stiff control of state apparatus and bureaucracy. Their attempt at imposing social development had fallen short of the masses' expectations as well as scholars' predictions.

Thus, beyond each country's special character and peculiar events, beyond the unbearable burden of a state of continuous warfare against Israel, even beyond the strengthening ties of Arab state economies with the capitalist world system, stands the major issue of the role of the armed forces in the state-building and nation-development processes at work in the Arab world.

During the 1970s, various studies appeared in Western countries, which stressed the internal rivalries and continual feuds among Arab military elites, their communal and clan cleavages and alliances, resulting in a costly and endless series of plots and coups reflecting the mosaic social structure of Middle East Societies.[6] Once freed from the conservative monarchies as in Egypt and Iraq, or having got rid of colonial rule as in Algeria, or of patrician oligarchy as in Syria, the new authoritarian governments led by the military had no other destiny than to become the stage of rivalries between coteries of officers: the Free Officers in Cairo, Qasim's followers in Baghdad, then the Revolutionary Command Council and, in Damascus, the famous and secret Baathist Military Command. In each of these countries, officers would perpetuate their domination over the civilian masses in the very tradition of the Ottoman Empire when *askaris* were opposed to *reayas*, and they would primarily concentrate on internal adjustments and negotiations between factions.[7]

In the meantime, the debate on the nature of the military regimes in the Arab world had lost much of its importance in the Arab Middle East and the Maghreb. The main concerns had become the oil and post-oil era economy along with the cultural heritage, the

191

Table 8.1: Arab armed forces (1966–84)

	Population		Active military duty			Paramilitary			Reserves
	1974	1984	1966	1975	1984	1966	1975	1984	1984
Algeria	16.4	21.7	65,000	63,000	130,000	8,000	10,000	25,000	100,000
Egypt	36.6	47.2	180,000	298,000	460,000	90,000	100,000	140,000	300,000
Iraq	10.7	14.9	80,000	101,000	640,000	10,000	19,000	650,000	75,000
Jordan	2.0	2.6	35,000	37,000	68,000	8,500	22,000	20,000	35,000
Lebanon	3.1	2.7	10,800	15,200	20,300	2,500	5,000	7,500	–
Libya	2.2	3.5	5,000	25,000	73,000	–	23,000	10,000	40,000
Morocco	16.8	23.3	35,000	56,000	144,000	3,000	23,000	30,000	
Saudi Arabia	8.7	10.0	30,000	43,000	51,000	20,000	32,000	45,000	
Sudan	17.4	23.2	12,000	38,600	58,000	3,000	5,000	7,000	
Syria	7.1	10.4	60,000	137,000	362,000	8,000	9,500	38,500	
N. Yemen	6.3	7.5	–	20,900	36,500	–	–	25,000	
S. Yemen	1.6	2.2	10,000	9,500	27,000	–	–	45,000	
Tunisia	5.6	7.0	20,000	24,000	35,000	5,000	10,000	8,500	

Sources: M. Janowitz, *Military institutions and coercion in the developing nation*, pp. 36–42; International Institute for Strategic Studies, *Military Balance 1984–5*.

turath, and national identity. As for the issue of military participation in politics, it gained a new dimension which requires the adoption of a new perspective when we want to discuss it in the mideighties.

TOWARDS THE STABILISATION OF ARAB MILITARY REGIMES

As far as Arab military are concerned, a first important change relates to size: armies have grown considerably beyond the numbers that they used to have when their officers initiated their coups. The Syrian army, for example, counted only a few thousand men at the time of the Palestinian war and of the first coup by Husni Zaim, and thirty to forty thousand when the Baathist revolution took place in 1963. It is ten times larger in the 1980s (see Table 8.1). This growth is not only significant in itself, it is also impressive when related to the country's population and, secondarily, to the part of the state budget allocated to defence expenditures, even without taking the 'special expenditures' into account.

Another change lies in the general professionalisation of the armed forces in the Arab world, and their renunciation of previous formulas such as guerrilla or revolutionary armies. Arab armies carry armaments which are among the most sophisticated in the world, like the Mirage 2000 in Egypt, the Mig-27 (which has not been deployed yet in the USSR's European allied countries) or the SAM-5 in Syria. They also undergo intensive training in order to maximise skills and knowledge and to meet the challenge of this new weaponry. In 1985, conscripts in the Egyptian army were 66 per cent high school graduates, 14 per cent university graduates and 20 per cent vocational school graduates (*New York Times*, 24 February 1986).

In Algeria, the decision to turn the revolutionary army into a professional one was taken by Colonel Boumedienne as early as 1962 (Quandt, 1969, p. 219). His accession to the state presidency in 1965 and his suppression of Zbiri's rebellion in 1967 were further steps in his move to break with the National Liberation tradition in order to rebuild a monolithic National People's Army that he might more closely control. Difficulties in confronting the Moroccan troops during the first Saharan war in October 1963 also played a part in Boumedienne's decision to reinforce the Algerian military capability and to provide it with more weaponry and funds.

193

Similarly the June 1967 defeat led the Baathist leaders of Syria to feel the need to entrust the country's defence to skilled officers rather than to highly politicised ones, and to stress better preparation of troops and equipment.[8] This new trend had no miraculous result but clearly improved performance, as could be noticed from the Algerian stand during the war of October 1973, from the length of the Egyptian–Israeli war of attrition in 1969–70, and from the substantial steps taken by the Syrian army on the Golan Heights during the first days of October 1973. As for Iraq, it seems that the Irani attacks on Fajr 4 (1982) and Fajr 5 (1984) induced its leader Saddam Hussein to reshuffle the military command in order to keep 'political' (Baathist) officers off the battlefield and let competent officers reorganise the army and especially the air force.[9]

This move towards a professionalisation, or a re-professionalisation of Arab armies should not be interpreted as a return of the military 'to the barracks'. After all, General Mustafa Tlas who has been in charge of Syrian defence for nearly 16 years, warned the world at the time of the neo-Baathist radical coup of February 1966 in which he had taken a minor part, 'We will never surrender power to civilians' (Picard, 1979a, p. 58). As far as Arab armies are concerned, there is no evidence of any link between an increase in professional skill and a de-politicisation, as argued by Huntington (1969). The precarious loyalty of the highly professional Jordanian armed forces to the Hashemite throne (Haddad, 1971, pp. 47 ff) seems to have been secured at the price of large exclusions. The Saudis perpetually seek to maintain a balance of power between their paramilitary units and the national military establishment. If they were compelled to enlarge these forces, to train them and to give their command more initiative in order to resist an Iranian threat in the Gulf, they might not only have to face a military lobby in their administration but possibly an eruption of the officer corps onto the political stage (indeed, rumours of various attempted coups have already been heard). In Morocco the army combines high professional standards with a persistent tendency to interfere in politics.

Rather than deal with these three traditional personal authoritarian regimes, however, this chapter deals with four Arab countries that have ranked high in military coups: Syria, Egypt, Iraq and Algeria. In the 1980s their armies play a decisive or even a central part in politics, and their strong involvement in civilian affairs clearly distinguishes them from the three traditional states or from the Tunisian presidential regime,[10] or even from the party dictatorship in the PDRY. Libya might have fitted in this set, although it is rather a charismatic-leadership regime — curiously close to Tunisia — rather than a military one. As for Sudan, the country shows that no military dictatorship is settled for ever.

The counterexample offered by Sudan stresses the impressive longevity of the four regimes under discussion. Syrian Baathists came to power as early as 1963, and General Assad in November 1970. The authoritarian state established by Nasser in 1954 succeeded in institutionalising its succession process, from one *rais* to the next, as did the Algerian regime. Saddam Hussein, who has been a member of the Iraqi Baathist command since 1968, raised himself to supreme power in 1979. Of course, longevity does not necessarily mean stability. Numerous failed coups and rebellions are known to have taken place within the Syrian armed forces since 1970: at the beginning of 1972 and in July 1973, with Jadid supporters; in March 1976 when 30 senior officers tried to stand against their country's intervention in Lebanon; in December of the same year, during the festivities of Aid al-Adha; in January 1982, a large plot involving several Alawaite air force officers was discovered.[11] A similar record can be listed for Egypt in 1972, 1974, 1981 (in Mansurah, a few days before Sadat's assassination) and, to a lesser extent, for Algeria and Iraq. But on the whole, the endurance in power of more stable military groups clearly indicates a change of trend for the Arab military regimes and requires a reflection upon the causes and meaning of such longevity and apparent stabilisation. Among the issues at stake are the nature of the state dominated by armed forces; the role of the military towards the society of the country; and their growing participation in the domestic economy. All three issues raise the question of the role of armed forces in Arab politics, whether it is either conservative or modernising, and the extent of their commitment to the public good. Analysis is based on scarce information and dubious facts: where the military is concerned, even on the political stage, suspicion and secrecy become the rule.

ARMED FORCES AND THE STATE

It is altogether striking and enlightening to discover the variety and the looseness of the terminology used by academics to describe the regimes of the Arab states where the military have successfully engineered a coup and happen to share in the political power: it includes 'military dictatorship', 'army-party rule', 'military olig-archy' and 'civil-military coalition'. Such variety not only relates to situations changing according to place and time; it also reflects a controversial appraisal of the role of armed forces in politics as illustrated by the examples under discussion.

The longevity of the Syrian and Iraqi regimes cannot be ascribed to the peaceful operation of democratic processes. It is founded upon authoritarian, if not dictatorial, power. Competitive processes which characterise open societies are excluded in such a way that these regimes must be described as 'authoritarian personal' regimes supported by armed forces (Picard, 1979a, p. 52). The first national authority in revolutionary Syria was a National Revolutionary Council Command which appointed itself in the days following the 1963 Baathist coup. Its 15 members were officers only until July, when Baathist civilians replaced the Nasserist military members who had been removed. Its chairman was of course military General Amin al-Hafez, and officers never accounted for less than 20 per cent of its total membership. As for the governments since 1963, the military steadily held 15 to 25 per cent of the ministerial portfolios (Van Dam, 1979).

Since the revolution, sensitive ministries like Defence and the Interior have been their constant prerogative, but they have often taken charge of the Ministry of Agriculture at times when rural structures were undergoing fundamental change, and sometimes even the prime ministry. It is more difficult to appraise the part they played within the Baath Party, which is nevertheless essential. During some periods, senior officers have accounted for a third of the members in the National (pan-Arab) Command and in the Regional (Syrian) Command. Even after the decision was made at the Kisweh military meeting of April 1965 to restrain the respon-sibilities of the esoteric and powerful Baathist Military Command and to limit the participation of the military in the RC to three of its eleven members, those three still managed to secure their hegemony through civilian alliances (Van Dam, 1979, pp. 31–51).

The influence of the military also spread down the party to its lower levels from the very first months of the revolution, with nine new military branches were authoritatively created by the BMC. The army's overwhelming influence is summarised by the multiple civilian functions of General Hafez al-Assad, its commander-in-chief, who is president of the State, and secretary-general of the Baath and of the National Progressive Front since 1971.

Through a formal reading of Iraqi institutions, the 'civilian' character of the political regime in Baghdad is frequently contrasted with the hegemony of the military in Damascus. However, such a contrast fades before the high state positions occupied by army officers and the importance given by Saddam Hussein to the apparatus of repression and coercion. Five officers, and no civilians, sat in the first Revolutionary Council Command, the first executive body after the 1968 Baathist coup. Until 1973, the military held all the key state positions: the presidency of the RCC, the prime ministry, the ministries of Defence and the Interior, the secretary-generalship of the Baath, and naturally the army command. Afterwards, the growing influence of the civilian wing of the party around Saddam Hussein — who was appointed general in 1976 — cannot conceal the strong reliance of the regime on both the regular and the 'popular' army (*jaysh ash-shab*) (*al-Thawra*, 6 January 1976; *New York Times*, 11 January 1981), a tendency which has been accentuated since the war with Iran. As a whole, the move observed in Baghdad as well as in Damascus in the mid-seventies to transfer key positions in the Baath Party and the government from officers to civilian technocrats, in an attempt to set the conditions for a successful economic liberalisation (Picard, 1979b, p. 665; Springborg, 1986, p. 33) has been slowed down in both countries: in Iraq, because of its deepening involvement in the Gulf war, and in Syria after the intervention in Lebanon and the extension of an internal state of warfare. This stresses opportunely the fact that a major cause for Arab military intervention in politics and the main reason for the stay of the armed forces in power are to be found in an external threat to state security.

Has a similar secularisation of political power occurred in Egypt and Algeria? The five years of the Nasserist revolution and the period of Ben Bella's rule were marked by harsh competition between the military and other rival groups: revolutionaries, intellectuals and technocrats (Abdel Malek, 1962, pp. 178–9; Quandt, 1969, p. 110). The historical importance of armed struggle in Algeria's accession to independence had conferred a major political role on officers, either from the guerrilla or professional armies. At the time Boumedienne replaced Ben Bella with the support of a reshaped army, the Revolutionary Council, then the upper executive body in the country, counted as many as 22 officers from both armies out of 26 members. Another institution, the National Liberation Front, the only official party, barely had any formal existence, in spite of the resolutions of the Soummam Congress in 1956 and of the text of the National Charter (1963),

197

both guaranteeing its pre-eminence over the military. But the move had already begun and the homogeneous coalition of professional military men and technically competent administrators under Boumedienne (Zartman, 1970, p. 342) turned year after year into a more technocratic group, while the FLN's role expanded slowly. From the mid-seventies on, the military command has been mainly devoted to the custody of the state and of its legitimacy. During the FLN Congress of January 1979 following Boumedienne's death, it demonstrated its influence in the designation of Chadli Benjedid as his successor. The continuing importance of the National People's Army was well illustrated by the accession of the highest ranking officer to the state presidency, and then to the office of secretary-general of the FLN (Entelis, 1982, pp. 108–9). But this primarily conservative mission no longer implies that the military outnumber the civilians in key government positions nor that they have authority to initiate Algerian state social and economic policy.

As the power of decision lies mainly in the executive, and because the command of the executive is a necessary condition for military control of society, the proportion of the military inside the executive can give an indication of its role and importance in the state. The figures available for Egypt indicate that army officers occupied 20.6 per cent of the ministerial portfolios under Nasser, with a peak of 51 percent in 1961. This percentage fell to 7.5 under Sadat (Cooper, 1982, p. 209) and after 1971, the military had charge of only certain ministries: Transport and Communications, War, and War Production. The demilitarisation process took place in two stages. First, after the Yemen debacle in 1963 and the June 1967 disaster, Nasser lost confidence in his army and tried to rely more upon the progressive forces and the Arab Socialist Union, the party in which the military were not eligible for membership, unlike in the Syrian and Iraqui Baath. Later, the election of a new assembly in October 1971 and the publication of the October Working Paper in April 1974 clearly showed Sadat's intention to demilitarise the polity and institutionalise a civilian power, a decision strongly supported by most segments of the political class. At the same time, when the Egyptian army recovered its lost honour by nearly securing a victory on the Canal, it was eliminated from central points of political influence on the national as well as at the local levels, in an apparent agreement to send the military permanently back to the barracks (Waterbury, 1983, p. 376; Cooper, 1982, p. 223). However, the demilitarisation process should not be overemphasised; a clear indication of its limits was given by the nomination of Hosni

Mubarak, the commander-in-chief of the army, to the position of vice-president of the state, a sensitive position for communications between the government and the armed forces, and by his accession to the state presidency after Sadat's assassination. Another indication is the growing popularity of the Defence Minister, General Abu Ghazala, a potential rival for an executive power weakened by Egypt's hopeless predicament.

Such attempts at demilitarising the political system in Egypt and in other Arab states are meant to initiate stable civilian patterns of government and to codify the revolutionary process in order to balance the country's power centres successfully. In various public addresses as early as 1966, Nasser argued about the necessity of codifiction (*taqnin*). Actually he, and Sadat after him, developed an important legislative and institutional apparatus both at the local and the national levels, thus contributing to the renewal of political institutions such as the legislature, various political organisations and parties, and local government. The Algerian move on the same path was impressive after Colonel Boumedienne had strengthened his hold of the state: in 1976 he ordered referenda on the National Charter and the new Constitution, and in the following year, presidential and legislative elections. Afterwards, a party congress of the FLN was convened in January 1979, while the local and regional assemblies (*assemblées populaires communales* and *assemblées populaires de Wilaya*) were revived (Entelis, 1982, p. 108). As in the succession from Sadat to Mubarak in Egypt, the transmission of presidency from Boumedienne to Benjedid took place through an institutional process in an apparently cohesive and stable mood. This confirmed at first sight the thesis of the capability of a military regime to bring about a 'state of institutions', as Sadat's October document put it: it was up to the holders of power openly to determine its rules and procedures. There were to be clearly designated mechanisms for making decisions in such a way that the danger of arbitrary and coercive interference would be eliminated.

But once they have attained power and set themselves up as arbitrators, how qualified are the Arab military to work out such a project? The political processes at work in each of these four cases after new institutions have been prescribed lead to questions about the meaning of value of such institutionalisation. In Egypt, for example, the new government chosen by Anwar al-Sadat following the legislative elections of 1976 took so little account of electoral results that it was as if they had no meaning for the president.

Indeed, do elections, 'platforms' (*manabir*) and pluripartism really mean much for a population whose participation in the electoral process approximates 20 per cent and whose lives, for the most part are lived outside the political (and economic) system? Given such weakness and mediocre pervasiveness of the institutions, the likelihood of military intervention, or of the strengthening of military rule can never be dismissed, should the social situation or the regional balance further deteriorate. The mutiny by police conscripts in February 1986 was overcome through massive action by the regular army. Order was restored but no negotiation followed, nor any political debate on the real issues at stake: the extreme poverty and the crisis of identity of the Egyptian people.

In Algeria, structural and especially demographic problems are not as serious. The country did not undergo mob riots in January 1984 as its Tunisian and Moroccan neighbours did. It offers a rather successful image of transition to a civilian and liberal regime. However, the army remains strongly influential in the civilian decision-making bodies, in the government and even in the party. It has a tendency to react authoritatively to political or social contests and to rely on repression rather than on dialogue, as the events of 1985 proved, when a group of lawyers who had established an association for the defence of human rights were severely sentenced.

Another example of the limited effect of an imposed institutionalisation is the Iraqi National Assembly, elected in June 1980 after ten years of delayed promises by the regime. The method of selecting the candidates, described as a process of 'controlled democracy' (Baram, 1981), gave the new parliament a merely symbolic function. But the extreme example of contradiction between institutionalisation and reinforcement of coercion is Syria. The country has experienced tremendous institutional development since November 1970: not only was a new Constitution promulgated in 1973, but people's representation was set at the national level (*majlis ash-shab*) as well as the regional (*majlis al-muhafaza*) and local (*majlis an-nahiyya*) levels. Ever since, these assemblies have been duly renewed through elections, while throughout the 1970s and 1980s the Baath party and the Worker's Union (*Ittihad al-ummal*) have held regular congresses. Competition for nominations as delegates has become more intense, and the delegates of their congresses more often reviewed in the national press than under the previous secretive neo-Baath regime (1966–70). The government has been enlarged to about 30 ministers, nearly half of whom come from 'independent' back-grounds and have no official connection with the political leadership in the Progressive National Front. The judiciary and administration have been considerably expanded, thus increasing the number of institutions to which an individual might refer in order to escape arbitrary treatment. Judged purely by this record, the military regime of General Assad seems to have been successful in improving political communication and participation, and in promoting a stronger relationship between the citizens and the state.

What does such a 'return to democracy' initiated by the Syrian authorities really mean? The Syrians have gone to the polls nearly once a year, but the turnout in the elections has decreased as regularly as the government's success has grown (Picard, 1978). Notwithstanding the fact that many of these institutions have been created purely for international purposes,[12] they can only result in bureaucratic overdevelopment and ideological indoctrination as long as they are not accompanied by a reduction in state coercion. In Syria, emergency laws promulgated in 1963, at the beginning of the revolution, have never been lifted. Despite presidential promises, arbitrary arrests, kidnappings and imprisonments are frequent and have even increased since 1976, when personalities of the higher military command became the target of attacks by opponents. A limiting clause concerning the Progressive National Front restricts political activities in the army and the university to the Baath party only. Another clause in the 1973 Constitution assigns more than half of the 195 parliament seats to 'representatives of the workers and peasants', which means to appointed militants of the popular organisations affiliated with the Baath. Even more, political practices frequently diverge from the law, when they do not contradict it altogether: elections are engineered by state agents in order to eliminate disturbing candidates and secure favourable results. The press of the progressive parties allied to the Baath in the PNF is freely printed but not displayed in public newsrooms; as for the opposition press, it is totally forbidden. Even the semi-official Baathist periodicals are censored (*Le Monde*, 20 April 1979). Finally, in an ambitious attempt at destructuring the civilian society, the military regime dissolved the main professional unions, including those of the physicians, engineers and lawyers, for having criticised the repression of Islamic militants and the lack of democratic liberty, and replaced them authoritatively in early 1980.

Of special significance is the amazing growth of paramilitary forces in the Arab military regimes in their stabilising and institutionalising phase since 1970 (Janowitz 1977, ch. 5, p. 17). These paramilitary units were created to reinforce and combat together with the regular forces. In Iraq, the *Jaysh ash-shab* is linked to the Baath party and recruits larger numbers than the army, around 600,000 men. It was long dedicated to internal security and 'peace-making' tasks, especially in the Kursish areas, until the war with Iran, when it was sent to the battlefront. In Egypt, the Ministry of the Interior heads some 300,000 members of security forces. Algerian gendarmes number 25,000. The strategy of multiplying and diversifying armed forces has even been adopted by other Arab authoritarian regimes such as Saudi Arabia whose White Guard numbers 45,000 men, nearly as many as the regular army.

In Syria, the regimes' militias underwent tremendous growth owing to the development of political sectarianism and to the seizure of power by Hafez al-Assad's fellow Alawite officers. His brother Rifat's militia, the Defence Companies (*saraya l-difa*) mobilised as many as 50,000 men until February 1984[13] and included armoured companies, a mechanised brigade equipped with T72s, missiles and paratroop units. It had serious rivals such as General Ali Hydar's 15,000-strong 'Special Forces' or Adnan Makhluf's Presidential Guard. Each established its own intelligence and acted independently. At times, militias would operate out of the country's boundaries, in Lebanon, but it is rather the regular army which intervenes on the domestic stage, along with the police and the militias, hence a long list of military operations in Syria's streets, from the shelling of the great mosque in Hama in January 1965 to the devastation of that town in February 1982.

Reflecting upon the longevity of some Arab military regimes, one should thus consider the huge technological progress of their armies and wonder whether the 'stability' which has been remarked on since 1970 does not owe much to an increasingly pervasive state machinery and especially state police: today, the seizure of the radio building and the broadcasting of a *communiqué no. 1* are no longer enough to ensure the success of a revolutionary coup. A bloody battle must be fought, whose outcome is far from certain, as shown in the fighting between rival militias in Damascus from February to May 1984, or the uprising of the Security Forces in Egypt in February 1986.

THE MILITARY AND SOCIETY

In view of such circumstances, the hypothesis that Arab armies are especially effective at carrying out the autonomisation of the state appears highly disputable. So, too, is the description of their intervention as 'praetorianism', under the pretext that the army has a central role that leaves it free to induce constitutional changes and to take governmental decisions (Perlmutter, 1974, p. 4) and that this is consistent with the Ottoman tradition and necessary for industrialisation and modernisation (Perlmutter, 1974, pp. 27, 52). If the military succeeds in controlling society and in exercising power over it, this power should not be mistaken for the true authority of the state (Haddad, 1971, p. 33). In the long run, military rulers will have to seek popular consent, they will need to secure their legitimacy and to enlarge their social basis, lest they be regarded not as state rulers but as a mere clique, a gang (*jamaa*) as Michaud (1983) once described the military regime of Syria. A full understanding of the political role of the military in the Arab world thus requires an examination of the attitude of the military towards society as a whole, and of the special linkages between the officers in power and certain parts of society.

In order to gain the legitimacy which will allow it to implement its authoritarian decisions and to feel free from the hegemony of any social group, the military aims at representing the nation as a whole, on the ideological as well as on the social stage. It does not rely so much on the so-called historical and highly controversial legitimacy of the kind granted by the *hadith* tradition: 'obey those who wield power'. It rather claims a revolutionary legitimacy, gained through political struggle or, in the case of Algeria, through armed struggle. In many circumstances, this legitimacy proves strong enough to resist the erosion caused by the regime's mediocre achievements on the regional as well as the domestic level, and to survive internal feuds between rival factions. It has even benefited from the involvement of the military in the defence of its country, as all four states have had to fight on their borders since the beginning of the revolutionary period: Egypt and Syria against Israel, Algeria with Morocco, and Iraq in the Gulf war. Another way of strengthening its legitimacy is by acting as an authentic instrument for organising socio-economic goals, such as implementing agrarian reform, participating in public works, educational campaigns or emergency rescue (Leca and Vatin, 1975, pp. 398f).

The legitimising process of the military regime and the conveyance of patriotic values to the nation as a whole, operated through military service (Devlin, 1982, p. 237). Universal conscription was set up in Iraq, in Syria and in Algeria shortly after the

203

revolution, and both Iraq and Syria gradually renounced the *badal*, a system which allowed fortunate conscripts the option of paying in order to escape their military duty. In Algeria, the conscripts serve for six months only (Table 8.2). In Syria, because of the permanent tensions both on Israel's eastern front, and in Iraq, since the beginning of the war with Iran, they are kept in the army for several years. Military service in Egypt also lasts several years but conscription has been kept selective because of the rapid growth of the population and the low educational level among the rural masses. Both the army and a teaching career in the government schools offer a way out from impoverished origins. It is well known, that in Iraq as well as in Syria,[14] many of the revolutionary officers were recruited among youngsters from modest origins, the 'village generation' (Van Dusen, 1971). In Algeria,

> The ANP has a popular base, drawing largely from the lower social strata: 'sons of *fellahin* and sons of workers'. But social origins are less important for the ANP than social change; the army is composed not of workers and *fellahin* but of their sons (Zartman, 1970, p. 246).

But beyond the ability of the army to provide individual educational opportunities and upwards mobility lies the issue of the extent to which it can mould individuals into a common process of political socialisation. In other words, does the country depend on mobilisation for conscripts to develop their identities as citizens and soliders? Does conscription offer a national tradition, common values, and a set of relations between the state and the citizen? In

Table 8.2: Arab states and military service

Country	Conscription	Length of service
Algeria	General	6 months
Egypt	Selective	3 years
Iraq	General	2 years
Jordan	Selective	2 years
Lebanon	General (never effective)	
Libya	Selective	
Morocco	General	18 months
Saudi Arabia	Selective	
Sudan	General	not implemented
Syria	General	30 months
N Yemen		
S Yemen		2 years
Tunisia	Selective	12 months

the states of the Arab world, such common national values are still very weak. National solidarity competes with and overlaps clan, communal and religious solidarities, thus obstructing army attempts at conveying a national ideology and a unified political culture. And, on the other hand, the persistence of authoritarianism and military regimes is in itself an impediment to the development of any kind of political culture (Khuri and Obermayer, 1974, p. 55).

Even Arab nationalist ideology, as put forward by the military, is burdened with flaws. While Baathist regimes have put themselves forward as propagators of pan-Arabism, especially through their stance on the liberation of Palestine, their ambitions emerge purely on the nation-state level, as mere Iraqi or Syrian ambitions (Hurewitz, 1969, p. 423). They dedicate themselves to the defence of their state and the recovery of its lost territories, and they mobilise the population within the state borders. Hence the limited objectives of the October 1973 war, the Syrian attempts at recovering the Golan, or the launching of a war against Iran by Saddam Hussein. An even more conclusive demonstration was offered by the deterioration of the relations between Damascus and Baghdad in 1974–5, and again after the brief episode of the failed merger of the two Baathist states from October 1978 to July 1979. Not only had both countries rival economic interests as far as oil and commercial transit or the division of the Euphrates' waters was concerned, the process of unifying the two branches of the Baath party and the armed forces in both regions (*aqtar*) of the Arab nation also presented a threat for the leadership in each country: members of the party national command in Damascus would have had to yield to Michel Aflaq's historical leadership in Baghdad, while the militias should have surrendered to a unified regular army authority. Such a process was very soon seen as a menace to the hegemony of the military in each country; it had to be avoided, and a plot was uncovered in Baghdad, which put an end to the negotiations (Picard, 1979c, p. 9).

Have Egypt and Algeria been more successful in using the army as the backbone of their national cohesion? Have they been able to escape the contradiction between their Arab identity and their nation-state identity, and find their way through the contradictions? The choices of Anwar Sadat when initiating the October war, or opening peace negotiations with Israel in 1977 appear to indicate the greater homogeneity of Egyptian society and cohesion in the country's army, that it is capable of representing all the nation's strata, both urban or rural on a national level (Vatikiotis, 1961, pp. 44–68).

However, the failed coup of October 1972, the attempt in April 1974 by Takfir wal Hijra involving cadets at the military academy, and Sadat's assassination in October 1981 at the very moment he was presiding over the annual military parade in celebration of the October war, challenge the indications of reinforced cohesion by disclosing the existence of an Islamic contest in the midst of the Egyptian armed forces.

In Algeria, Colonel Boumedienne's policy (Criscuolo, 1975, p. 206), resumed after his death by Colonel Benjedid, clearly aimed at reinforcing the army's cohesion and capability in order to turn it into a modern professional force, but also to use it as the central apparatus in the state-building process and the protection of the state. The integrity and homogeneity of the Algerian state are less endangered by border conflict with Morocco or by short-lived uprisings in Berber areas, than by the family and regional cleavages which split the political and economic leadership into rival groups, such as the Oujda group which dominated the state under Boumedienne. Of course, Algerian society should not be compared to the mosaic diversity of the Arab East, but its social cleavages threaten the country's stability whenever they permeate the armed forces, and they are carried by military officers into administration, party and government, or into private business. Civilian conflicts then turn into open armed interventions: although little is known about the abortive coup against Chadli Benjedid in June 1979, in which senior officers might have been involved along with top civil servants, it is an indication of the extension of the cleavages and rivalries within civilian society into the military command.

It is interesting to compare Algeria with Iraq as regards the position of armed forces towards national identity and the state-building process, as well as their links with the various segments of society. Although Iraqi armed forces became involved in civilian tasks and responsibilities, they still acted primarily as the defender of the land and state legitimacy. Confronted with an external threat such as the Iranian invasion of national territory during the Gulf war, the Iraqi army succeeded in maintaining cohesion, even if it lacked the mystical impetus of the Iranian *basijin* and *mujahidin*. Desertions and cases of insubordination did occur, especially among the Kurds, but on the whole, no major dissension appeared either among the conscripts or at the command level, between Sunni Arabs (20 per cent of the country's population) and the Shia (55 per cent). One might eventually conclude that where there is a threat to the national entity, and in spite of the artificial character of the 'colonial'

206

borders, the army does play an efficient part as the catalyst of a superior common interest. Such a conclusion might even apply to the Syrian army, however surprising it may seem at first sight. In June 1982, confronted with the invasion of Lebanon by Israel, its Sunni as well as its Alawite brigades fought in the Shouf mountains and the Beqaa valley without restriction. While the battle was soon lost by the Syrian air force and on the diplomatic scene (Schiff, 1984), armoured and infantry units kept on resisting valiantly for what was unanimously regarded in Syria as a national (Syrian) issue.

However, such cohesion in the face of an external threat does not prevent the Iraqi armed forces from being caught in communal conflict and civilian ideological dissent. Recent Iraqi history offers a long record of struggle, eliminations and changes of leadership inside the country's military and political command: in 1970, General Hardan al Takriti was mysteriously murdered after he opposed his country's intervention on the Palestinian side in Jordan. In 1973, the army was shaken by the Nadhim Kazar plot and rebellion (Batatu, 1978, pp. 1093, 1094). One year before Saddam Hussein ascended to power in July 1979, 39 officers were executed in Baghdad on the charge of having reorganised Communist cells in the army. On the whole, the tight control of the Baath, the army and the security services by a small group originating from the Sunni area of Takrit is evidence that the military dictatorship is permeated by civilian cleavages; power imbalance does not come so much from an uneven regional distribution of key positions as from the impact of clan and family ties on the economy of the state and eventually the nature of its society.

Of all examples of an hegemonic army being drawn into the process of civilianisation, the most obvious is the Syrian case. Before independence, troops and officers were mainly recruited along communal lines. The French mandate purposely kept Sunni Arabs out on account of their nationalistic tendencies, although they were more than three-quarters of the population, and chose to rely on ethnic and religious minorities. After independence, the army was opened to all, but the new generation of officers were attracted to the political parties that were competing at the time for the leadership of the young republic: the Baath, the Communists, the Muslim Brotherhood and the Syrian Social Nationalists.[15] The incorporation of civilian political conflicts within the army and the failure to organise it efficiently resulted in 1949 in the shift of controlling power in the state from the civilian leaders to the military. But once Baathist officers had triumphed over their rivals from other

207

progressive parties in July 1963, they were not a homogeneous and cohesive group, even though they unanimously called for socialism and Arab unity. Their cleavages and internal struggles reflected Syria's regional and communal diversity. Kurds and Christians were almost completely barred from military and political command after the United Arab Republic (1958–61). In 1964–5 came the turn of the Sunnis, then the Druse and the Ismailis in 1967. The confrontation and successive elimination process between military 'parties' reached down to clan and family divisions within the Alawite community itself, with the elimination of Jadid in 1970, Umran's assassination in 1973, and finally the battle among the brothers, cousins and relatives of Hafez al-Assad and all his lieutenants, in the Rawdha district of Damascus in February 1984 (Batatu, 1981a, pp. 331 ff).

An army which devotes so much of its strength and activity to internal feuds is no more able than the armies of more homogeneous countries such as Egypt and Algeria, to fulfill its task of guarding the state and standing for national unity. Syrian officers had entered politics in the 1950s and 1960s through personal and conspiratorial networks, relying mainly on secrecy and selective coercive control. Once in power, they could not escape involvement in civilian linkages; they enlarged their networks into factions and were drawn into bargaining and negotiations in order to protect their access to state, material and symbolic benefits. They were compelled to rely heavily on paramilitary units in order to control those sectors of the civilian population that were not incorporated in their political bargaining (Janowitz, 1977, pp. 45–6). Thus, in spite of the institutionalisation mentioned earlier, every part of Syrian public life fell under direct control of the military who became the brokers (*wasta*) between the state and the people for any kind of public transaction, thus eradicating the civilian society they had wanted to shape.[16]

While in Egypt and Algeria the army stands to preserve the unity of the state and contributes to the construction of national identity through governmental and political institutions, as long as it is able to silence its internal divisions, in plural societies such as Syria, and Iraq to a lesser degree, the hegemony of armed forces over the polity is far from having a strengthening and unifying effect or promoting democratic institutions. It freezes political debate and turns it into a struggle between factions, which can be resolved only by coercive means. It has created an immobile and oppressive society.

MILITARY REGIMES AND ECONOMIC DEVELOPMENT

Among the central objectives of the Arab military regimes and among their primary justifications for using coercion over their people, was the need to accelerate economic development. In a move inspired by Atatürk's experience in Turkey, they intended to initiate an intensive industrialisation process through public enterprises in order to eliminate the old elites — especially the urban industrial bourgeoisie that had presided over the Egyptian economy for several decades, that had grown rapidly in Syria during the 1950s, and that was present even in Iraq. The state was to become the main and nearly exclusive agent of economic decisions, through a series of seizures and nationalisations which would give it the necessary legal and economic means.

As far as the military is concerned, such a project involves two corollaries. First, the capacity of armed forces to bring about national development through their internal modernisation process and through cooperation with civilian elites. Secondly, their ability, once they become an hegemonic group in power, to free themselves from their social origins and thereby to secure the autonomy of the state.

A dramatic statement must be made from the start: the military in the Arab world are budget devourers. Since the extension of the war with Iran, Iraqi military expenditures as a proportion of GDP are particularly high (Table 8.3), and Syria is close behind. The contrast made earlier between these two military regimes on one hand, and bureaucratic regimes controlled by the military on the other, shows up here again: Egypt devotes 'only' 8.56 per cent of GDP to national defence; Algeria has an even lower level. The

Table 8.3: Gross Domestic Product and military budgets (1982) ($m)

		GDP	Defence	%
1	Iraq	34,600	8,043	23.25
2	Syria	18,467	3,210	17.38
3	Saudi Arabia	153,099	21,952	14.33
4	Jordan	3,831	542	14.21
5	Morocco	14,697	1,328	9.03
6	Egypt	29,141	2,495	8.56
7	Libya	28,520	709	2.50
8	Algeria	43,584	847	1.94

Source: *Military Balance (1984–5)*, International Institute for Strategic Studies, London.

question is how massive expenditure on arms and equipment dedicated to destruction can have a constructive effect on these countries economies. Answering it requires consideration of alternative uses to which their financial resources might have been put. But Egypt since its 1979 peace treaty with Israel has not altered its public investment policy or its economic priorities. It is also often suggested that the army serves as a training ground for technical and administrative skills. Thousands of young men either belonging to the professional army or recruited as conscripts come into contact with modern technology and management: a basic skill such as driving is taught to hundreds of young Iraqis every year in the barracks. In Damascus, the army weekly *Jaysh ash-shab* offers a regular review of the different kinds of technical and professional education provided by the army for the conscripts.

The counter-argument is that much weaponry is relatively simple to import and to operate (Murad, 1966, p. 46), and that military training does not really offer the type of education relevant afterwards in industrial management or agricultural machinery. Furthermore, the rigid military ethics and authoritarian pattern of decision-making lessen the soldier's ability to adapt to his own society. In the field of civilian technology and management, choices that have to comply to complex social requirements benefit from a relaxation of the military's political influence and supervision (Owen, 1983, p. 144). The low level of military educational efficiency is also shown by the fact that so many young Egyptians and Algerians are unemployed after leaving the army, while young Syrians have to emigrate to the Gulf to be able to acquire useful knowledge and skills.

It must also be remembered that in these four states, as in most countries of the Arab world, the army is a different world with its security of employment, standardised patterns of work, housing and other economic advantages. In Syria, the military earns four to ten times more than its civilian counterparts. Officers' privileged positions do not predispose them to innovation nor to social, political or even technological change, but rather to caste consciousness and conservatism. Another handicap is the lasting domination of the 'political' officers over the 'professionals', since civilian divisions have permeated the armed forces. It led to disastrous consequences on the Iraqi army's performance during air battles in the Gulf war. It still burdens the Syrian military where any officer, especially the Sunnis or Christians, with serious technological and professional ability has to be supervised by another, closely related to the regime.

Could officers become part of a dynamic development process in their country's economy, while insisting on stability and hierarchy, and closely controlling their own corps? First, their number and influence in the civilian field should not be overestimated: although figures are not available for all four countries, it appears that officers have not filled many technical and administrative posts and constitute only a small part of those elites termed 'strategic' in the development process. In Egypt, for instance, the importance of the military in the managerial elite was never very great, and soon declined (Ayubi, 1980, p. 248; Owen, 1983). At the height of military influence in the Egyptian economy and polity, around 1967, officers accounted for 2 per cent of the 18,000 top-level civil servants. Syria's state and bureaucratic elites further clarify the role of the military: when they enter civilian positions, they taken charge of political rather than technical functions; they command, decide, organise, and even maintain order. Most gravitate to the Ministry of the Interior, where they can dedicate themselves to protecting the state and regime, with special emphasis on order and hierarchical transmission of 'revolutionary' values. The dichotomy suggested by the title of Entelis's study of the Algerian elite, *Technocratic rule, military power*, points to military who do not directly contribute to the good of the economy. Although officers enter the civil administration, government, national enterprises and private companies with their managerial skill and professionalism their influence generally results in the perpetuation of a meddlesome, complex and often inefficient bureaucracy.

Because of the growth of their armies and the diversification of their requirements, the military has recently turned to economic procurement, entering as a major partner in the industrial world, international and domestic services, and commercial networks. The growth and size of the Egyptian army's stake in the country's industrial and building enterprises has become a frequent subject of criticism in the national press. Officers coordinate government departments, run industries and public works enterprises and even administer land reform. No survey has been published so far on the Egyptian army's global economic participation, but the intensive development of its arms industries in vast plants at Saqr and Abou Zabal is an indication of the Egyptian military's increasingly diverse economic production.

The Algerian military does not appear on the frontlines of business, possibly because large state public enterprises like the Sonatrach and its offshoots are difficult to challenge, and the private

211

sector is still small and insecure. However, the army's own industries and suppliers are extensive and productive, under military management. In Iraq and in Syria also, the armies have become first rank entrepreneurs. They started out by producing military supplies like equipment and uniforms, moved into manufacturing that required special skills and imported technology, and soon enlarged their range of activities to produce consumer goods such as construction equipment and aluminium window frames, and even bottled mineral water. From there, they have diversified into public works, road and house building, poultry farming, and even the cultivation of thousands of acres of newly irrigated state land along the Euphrates. Army officers control economic empires and employ tens of thousands of civilians, whose pay is better than in either the civil public sector, or the private sector. They share successfully in their country's economic growth, especially by running its most technologically advanced and economically productive units.

When the time comes to evaluate the impact of the military-managed sector, its effect on other enterprises appears questionable despite the economic success. Not only do military enterprises transgress the law by escaping the social and monetary constraints which burden other companies, they often fail to respect employment laws or observe either import restrictions or the financial rules of the currency market. The most famous example in Syria is the *Sharikat al-Iskan al-Askari* (Milihouse), a contracting firm headed by Major Bahloi (Jarry, 1984), which in five years has become the country's leading enterprise. In Iraq, the equivalent is the Saddam Military Establishment for Prefabricated Housing. But alongside the fact that Milihouse manufactures quality products, delivers them on time and earns large profits, the distorting effect of its methods on the social and financial balance of the country cannot be easily dismissed.

The revolutionary military which seized control of the state has tended to base its management on political rather than economic logic. The Egyptian 1962 National Charter and after it the Baathist 'Theoretical Perspectives'[17] of October 1963 proclaimed 'the abolition of the feudal system' to be the first revolutionary priority. The new leaders would do away with the old, exploitative bourgeoisie. Secondly, and only secondly, came the need to set up import-substitution industrialisation (ISI) under state control. An investigation into the decision-making process regarding important moves such as nationalisation of trading and industrial companies in Syria or Algeria often reveals that the decision was made as a reaction to regional or domestic events, like Nasser's challenge to the Syrian

Baath, or a feud between Algiers and Paris, or even internal competition within the group of military leaders. Although dealing with economic matters, the officers respond mainly to ideological necessities because this aim is to impose a new system. Besides this, they pursue personal, family and clan interests and often impose strategies likely to benefit themselves when dealing with public affairs.

Many state-owned industrial plants in Syria are less dependent on local or national requirements than on the amount of expenditure at stake, and above all, on the identity of the partners involved. Rather than developing the state sector, the role of the 'strategic elites' and especially of the officers who hold civilian functions, lies in allocating the benefits of government operations. Their purpose is to enlist politically devoted clients from the state bureaucracy, who benefit from the patronage process in which goods and services are traded for loyalty and obedience. The Syrian press[18] regularly denounces these petty or powerful clients as 'parasite' (*tufayliyya*) bourgeoisie.

Patronage was a feature in Syrian politics long before the revolution but it became more extensive under the military regime, especially under *infitah*, the economic liberalisation. Theft of public property, bribery of civil servants, graft and nepotism have become commonplace. These informal practices are today an integral part of a new political order, in which authority, or rather power, is the main means of acquiring material and symbolic goods. The supremacy of strength and coercion at state level, which is the prerogative of the military, has led to the embezzlement of the revolutionary Baathist programme: the party slogan *Wahda*, *Ishtirakiyya*, *Huriyya* (Unity, Socialism, Liberty) has been turned by popular derision into *Wahda*, *Ishtirakiyya*, *Haramiyya* (Unity, Socialism, Banditry).

Being in charge of the external security of the state, the Syrian army has extended its control to the country's foreign trade and imposed a tax on all imported goods and equipment. Not satisfied with regular commerce, the military heads a vast smuggling network across the Lebanese and Turkish borders,[19] which provides an extensive income and has become an essential part of the country's economy: to suppress it would hurt production and lead to a dangerous shortage of consumer goods. In July 1984, General Assad officially condemned these practices and ordered the restoration of regular control over trade at the Lebanese border and the arrest of a dozen junior officers, along with a general, accused of illicit trafficking in construction material. His purpose was not so much to forbid the trade as to check members of the military caste competing for hegemonic position. Finally, while a high-ranking officer, General Ibrahim Salameh, was arrested in Damascus (*Le Monde*, 14 August 1984), and an ex-minister of the Interior was indicted in Egypt in May 1983 during a similar anti-corruption campaign,[20] the economic basis of the military power remained untouched.

Illegal profit and scandalous abuses by the military (and technocratic) elites have not been as important in Algeria as they have been in Syria. Does this difference allow us to make a distinction between 'production states' and 'allocation states' when the influence of the military on their country's economy is at stake? Nothing is more questionable: Iraq, which turned into an archetypal *rentier* state in the middle of the seventies never underwent the distortions and prevarication known in the Syrian system although the costs of industrial production are generally 50 per cent higher than in the West (Stork, 1979, p. 145). A more convincing explanation lies in the balance between the technocratic and the military elites in the key state positions. In both Algeria and Egypt, the technocrats were successful in containing the officers and confining them to the role of guardians of the state, as well as in keeping control of the decision-making processes. A similar balance prevailed in Iraq until the Gulf war propelled the military to the fore. Syria's armed forces, however, have always kept a strong hold on civilian power.

General Assad's regime even succeeded in the uncommon strategy of turning its regional policy into a major source of income. Since the Arab summits following the October war, Syria has been granted an annual subsidy from the Gulf oil states. This allocation was decided on in order to underwrite the military effort of confronting Israel, and was raised to nearly 2 billion dollars a year at the Baghdad summit of 1979 following Egypt's defection. In some years, the amount received by the Syrian regime represented half the state budget, and it rapidly became indispensable to match the level of expenditure of the country. The subsidy's main object was to allow Syria to maintain a new strategic balance with Israel on the eastern front, but the country came to depend on its relationship with the other states in the Arab East: in 1976, the oil states' aid was drastically cut as a reprisal for Damascus' military intervention in Lebanon, and again in the 1983, because of the Syrian confrontation with the PLO in the Beqaa and around Tripoli. In the meantime, the Baathist military has become a master at playing on political and military tensions on their borders, with Iraq in 1979 and 1985, with Jordan in 1981, and even in Lebanon. Each crisis allows it to take advantage of its Arab financial protectors and to receive a new subsidy to reward its political compliance. Because the allocations come from abroad, because a part is given direct to high-ranking officers and often registered on 'special budgets', it further escapes official governmental supervision.

In all four countries, members of the ruling elite have reacted to the intervention of the military in their countries' economies and to their regimes' uneven achievements. They have stressed the necessity of reinstating populism by complying with socialist ideas of redistribution. These requests and criticism come mainly from civilians, members of the parties which inspired their revolutions: Baathists in Syria and Iraq, militants of the Algerian FLN, or of the ASU in Egypt. The extension and regulation of the allocation process, they claimed, would have helped civil servants, skilled workers and peasants alike, and enhanced a class formation process. The authoritarian military regimes instead chose to reinforce state capitalism by linking the state sector with the newly flourishing private sector. This choice was strongly influenced by the evolution of the international balance of power in the region after 1973; it was encouraged by the surplus capital provided by the oil booms of 1973 and 1979. On the domestic front, it meant the estrangement of the leaders from the classes from which they came and their alliance, instead, with bourgeois entrepreneurs.

The *infitah* period has allowed private contractors to increase their share in the national economy, in domestic and foreign trade, in housing, in the production of consumer goods and even in agriculture. Their cooperation with the military has facilitated the obtaining of permits, credit and raw materials; together with the officers, they have shared in ventures and eventually tightened their economic links through matrimonial strategies. In Algeria, criticism was raised of the new wealth of high-ranking officers as well as civil servants dealing with private business and foreign trade. In Egypt, the connection between Anwar Sadat and the famous contractor, A. Osman Ahmad, aroused much popular suspicion. In Iraq, the manager of Maktab Khalid, a major public building contractor in charge of the construction of Baghdad's new airport and several military bases along the front was known to be married to a close relative of the Iraqi Minister of Defence, Adnan Khairallah, himself the brother-in-law of Saddam Hussein (Springborg, 1986, p. 44).

215

In Syria, Alawite senior offices have extended their hold on trading and building companies. The best known of all, Rifat al-Assad, has been involved in trade with a Damascene businessman, Muhammad Ali, who had to leave for France suddenly when the Prime Minister General Khlaifawi set up a Committee for the Investigation of Illegal Profits in July 1977. Rifat also supervises imports into Syria of cement from the Shikkan plant in Lebanon, which belongs to his friends, the Frangiahs, and is involved in the hashish trade in the Beqaa valley. In order to secure his business, he has extended his matrimonial strategy towards other Alawite officers, the ruling Saudi family, and the Damascene bourgeoisie. As such, he is a paramount example of military patronage.

The categories involved with the military in power are less the 'new middle class' from which the officers themselves originate and recruit their new members, than a coalition of old and new land-owners, merchants and contractors. Due to the personal, familial and communal nature of their ties with the military command, they are unable to coalesce into a social class — an *infitah* class — which might have made up the main basis of the state. On the contrary, the officers' strategy is to play their various segments against each other, and to oppose them to the mass of state clients, in order to hold into their own power. Still, the military regimes have succeeded in staying free from class hegemony. But in the long run, their strategy fosters the upper bourgeois interests while weakening the state-building process.

Few of the features of military intervention in Arab politics described here should be considered specific to the Arab world. 'Oriental' society is not uniquely fated to rule by armed despots estranged from the masses. These characteristics are common to many underdeveloped countries, bound in economic dependency and impeded by weak institutions. The intervention of armed forces results in temporary stability which can be considered as positive, although it hampers the establishment of regular institutions for discussions and decision. Because of military oppression, the alter-natives appear to be primary solidarities and religious eschatology. In that respect, the kind of response Arab tribalism and Islamic fundamentalism offer to the suppression of society by the coercive state is not much different from the various African, South American and even Eastern European responses.

It is the history of the region itself which gives the intervention of armed forces in politics its specific features, and which help explain the transformation of a revolutionary plot into a lasting authoritarian military regime, the officers' abuse of coercive power in a society they had intended to transform, and their appropriation of their country's economy. Except for Egypt, which enjoys a better record of civilian institutions, most Arab states were founded only recently. Most have endured colonialism and still resent its violence through the perpetuation of the war with Israel — which is central in the analysis of the Syrian regime. The sudden and fragile changes in their economy resulting from oil wealth have conveyed to their leaders a feeling of overestimated strength — it led Iran to military adventurism and the interruption of its demilitarisation. And finally, they have to balance their moves towards modernisation and democracy with the preservation of their societies' culture and values — Algeria's slow steps towards institutionalisation illustrates the difficulties. However, the growing population and the continuing pressure for social change in the Arab world are issues which no military regime can resolve politically, unless it chooses to work towards its own dissolution.

NOTES

1. E. Beeri who in 1969 wrote on Syrian and Egyptian experiments, comes back to the subject in the disenchanted and critical article published in 1982 in *Middle Eastern Studies, vol. 18, no. 1*, 'The waning of the military coup in Arab politics'.

2. M. Janowitz (1977), *Military institutions and coercion in the developing nations*, University of Chicago Press, (Chicago), p. 88: of the twelve Arab countries with modern armies of a professional type, the military constitute the political ruling group or military oligarchy in four. They are actively involved in civil-military coalitions in six.

3. An example quoted by F. Khuri and G. Obermayer, (1974), 'The social bases for military intervention in the Middle East', in C. MacArdle Kelleher (ed.), *Political-military systems, comparative perspective*, Sage Publications, is from B. Aridi (1968), 'The role of the army in the process of development' (in Arabic), *al-Siyasa al-Dawliyya*, vol. 4, no. 13, 77–87. Aridi argues that 'the army is the most advanced institution in society and therefore capable of changing it'.

4. The thesis, apparent in most contributions of J. Johnson, (*The role of the military*) also appears in J.C. Hurewitz (1969) *Middle Eastern politics: the military dimension*, Praeger, New York, and in many others at the time.

5. The role of the army in the development of 'backward societies' and its class nature were discussed in the Soviet periodical *MEIMO 3* (1966) pp. 57–70, quoted by H. Carrere d'Encausse (1975), *La politique sovietique au Moyen-Orient*, Fondation Nationale des Sciences Politiques, Paris, p. 163.

6. A brilliant example of such treatment of Arab politics was given in I. Rabinovich's well-informed book, *Syria under the Baath, 1963–6: the*

217

army-party symbiosis, Shiloach Institute, Tel-Aviv (1982). Recent writers, such as N. Van Dam, 1979, do not escape the tendency.

7. The leading supporter of this thesis is A. Perlmutter in his polemical work (1974), *Egypt: the praetorian state*, Transaction Books, Brunswick, (New Jersey).

8. C. Wakebridge (1976), 'The Syrian side of the hill', *Military Review*, vol. *56*, *no. 2*, pp. 20–30. An American officer, Wakebridge visited the Syrian Southern Front and Q.G. in Qatana with United Nations Forces (UNDOF). For an Arab denunciation of the 1967 defeat and responsibility of the military regime, see M. Khalil (1969), *Suqut il-Jawlan* (The fall of the Golan), Dar al-Yaqin, Amman.

9. In July 1982, following the loss of Khoramshar, Saddam Hussein eliminated eight members of the RCC. At the time, reports spoke of unhappiness in senior Iraqi ranks and of a reshuffle in the military command because of 'negligence and incompetence'. Another reshuffle took place after Fajr 5 (*Washington Post*, 30 July 1984).

10. In a recent article, L. Ware stresses the 'highly professional qualities of the Tunisian army' which never 'mounted a coup nor fomented a revolution' and is mainly 'dedicated to defence'. He also interestingly predicts that 'when Bourguiba leaves office or dies . . . Destourianism cannot help but undergo a final and irrecuperable dilution (so that) the military can be expected to intervene on a regular basis . . . (But) as it lacks elite experience, the Tunisian military is unlikely to adapt a formal political and ideological structure of its new position of power'. It is, thus, bound to follow the authoritarian military regime pattern of failure. L.B. Ware (1985), 'The role of the Tunisian military in the post-Bourguiba era', *Middle East Journal* vol. 39, no. 1, pp. 40–2.

On the other hand, the trial in September 1983 of 19 military men for their membership in the Islamic Liberation Party, a fundamentalist movement founded in Jordan, raises questions about concern over fundamentalist penetration in the Tunisian army.

11. Such information can be obtained through the London biweekly *Arab Report and Record* until 1981, then in daily newspapers such as *al-Ray-al-Amm* (Kuwait) and *al-Sharq al-Awsat* (London).

12. Just as domestic political measures are bound to reinforce foreign and Arab legitimacy, so foreign policy is used as a means of strengthening internal legitimacy. See Chapter 11 in this volume.

13. They reached the peak of their power at the time of Assad's illness, June 1984. See A. Drysdale (1985), 'The succession question in Syria', *Middle East Journal*, vol. 39, no. 2, p. 248.

14. 'I did not choose the army career by vocation. I would have become an engineer, but my family's income did not allow me to enter university,' said Colonel Abdel Karim Jundi to E. Rouleau. Quoted in 'La Syrie Baathiste ou la fuite à gauche', *Le Monde*, 13 October 1966.

15. During this period, Egyptian Muslim Brothers were infiltrating the Egyptian Army. Mitchell, R. (1969) *The society of the Muslim Brothers*, Oxford University Press, London, pp. 148–60.

16. Recent cinematographic works such as *al-Hudud* (To the frontiers) and M. Melhem's beautiful *Ahlam al-Madina* (Dreams of the city), or novels like N. Sulayman, *al-Misalla* (The obelisk), Dar al-Haqa'iq, Beirut,

display the overwhelming presence of the military in Syrian daily life. In *al-Misalla* (1980), the group of young heroes who belong to various political parties such as the CP, Nasserist groups, the Palestinian Resistance, and even official Baath, is constantly under the intelligence network's control and influence.

17. *Bad al-Muntalaqat al-Nazariyya* (Theoretical perspectives) is the document adopted in October 1963 at the Sixth National Baath Congress at a time when Baathists were in power in Damascus as well as in Baghdad. It is still a fundamental charter for both Baathist branches.

18. In the party dailies such as *al-Baath*, *al-Thawra* and *Tishrin* and even more frequently in the union's weekly, *Kifah al Umma al-Ishtiraki*.

19. According to Y. Sadowski, 70 per cent of Syrian annual imports, (1 to 1.5 billion dollars worth of goods), are smuggled from Lebanon: Y. Sadowski (July-August 1985) 'Cadres, guns and money — eighth regional congress of the Syrian Baath', *Merip Report*, p. 6.

20. General Nabawi Ismail, who had already fled to the United States with his family.

219

9

Opposition as Support of the State

I. William Zartman

In seeking to explain the reasons for the survival of the Arab state, one must come to terms with the problem of opposition. Since some opposition can be assumed to be a natural condition for any political system, the absence of opposition in Arab politics would provide both an explanation of state survival and a condition to be investigated. Overwhelming or persistent opposition, at the other extreme, would indicate a weak state. All political life goes on between these to extremes. Totalitarian regimes seek to eliminate all opposition, but are never successful for long. Overwhelming opposition is its own undoing, since if successful it becomes the government and weaker opinions are relegated to the new oppositional minority. Pure harmony and pure anarchy do not exist in anything but the short run, and are consequences rather than conditions (i.e. dependent rather than independent variables). This chapter faces the paradoxical challenge of using opposition as the independent variable to explain the durability of the Arab state in the 1970s and 1980s.

The picture drawn thus far carries implicit assumptions which may be less intuitively acceptable than those initial notions. It would appear that any government would seek to move from the extreme of oppositional majority to approach as closely as possible the opposite pole of total support. The conceptual ways of doing so are clear: it can physically eliminate the opposition, it can remove its causes and grievances, or it can co-opt its members. Yet not only is the goal impossible to reach in its totality, as has been seen; it is also impossible to attain even partially. Downs (1957) and Arrow (1951) have shown the impossibility of satisfying a constant majority in theoretical terms on a 'flat' surface — when there are merely many differences of interest and opinion. It is even more striking in

220

a developmental context where the nature of socio-political change introduces another dimension that makes the construction of consensus out of the traditional and modernised sectors impracticable. There will always be significant opposition anywhere, and even more in developing countries than elsewhere. Even if the government tries physical elimination, opposition, like the soldiers of Hercules, will continue to appear in new forms and places.

The other implicit assumption is the Western notion of democratic alternance between incumbents and opposition (Dahl, 1966, 1973; McLennan, 1973; Ionescu and de Madariaga, 1968). A democratic political system is held together by the restrained efforts of the ins to stay in and the outs to get in, with everyone following the rules because each has an interest in being guaranteed a chance to get back in from an out position. But democratic alternance is not a characteristic of Arab politics. Instead in the period under focus — the decade and a half of the 1970s and 1980s — the predominant characteristic of government is the presence of one socio-political group and no chance of alternance. Opposition is neither undercut, co-opted nor eliminated. It is used, and it tends to acquiesce to this use, for some reason other than the expectation of finding itself in power on the next occasion, electoral or otherwise.

One conclusion might be that opposition in such cases is merely the dupe or puppet of power, but this argument is not convincing. Such an interpretation gives more credit to the incumbents and less to the opposition than is warranted; there are too many valid politicians in the opposition to be dupes, and too little monopoly of wisdom for government to practise consistently successful puppetry.

Instead, the argument proposed here is that an understanding of opposition is to be found in the notion of role complementarity. Both government and opposition have interests to pursue within the political system, and this complementarity of pursuit reinforces the state. Neither uses the other, but each serves the other's interests in performing its own role. Thus, stability in the contemporary Arab state can be explained not only by the government's handling of opposition but also by the opposition's handling of itself and of government. This theme will be explored in this chapter, using a number of different states — Morocco, Egypt, Tunisia — as case studies.[1]

Whether authorised or unauthorised, opposition need not be restricted to political parties. Additional forms need to be considered: corporatism and functionalism. In addition to political parties and often more effectively, corporate and functional groups express opposition in the Arab world. When opposition parties are not authorised or when the political system is opened up to pluralistic forms, corporate groups are often the surrogate for or transition to formal opposition parties. Thus another assumption about opposition, drawn from another world's experience — the assumption of an identifiable partisan form — needs to be dropped to be realistic in the Arab world. Instead, opposition exists through a spectrum of formality, from some internal and informal fractions through organised surrogates to formal parties and informal movements inside and outside the authorised political system. Some of these forms are outside the present inquiry, since factions within a ruling group do not pose the same paradox nor do they have the same role. Furthermore, opposition does not take on the same significance and activity in an unorganised or informal form. The following discussion will take into account the oppositional status and activities of corporate groups as well as parties, but it will require some degree of organisational formality for the angle of role complementarity to be pursued.

The focus on formal organisation should not obscure the equally important matter of social base. Organisations are important only to the extent that they represent something. However, social basis is only a measure of reality in this analysis, not a term of the analysis itself. There is no indication — at least initially — that role complementarity demands any particular social sources of opposition or that social sources come into play at all in any way other than simply as a grounding for the power and existence of incumbent and oppositional organisations. Some incumbents and oppositions will be socially specific, representing identifiable social groups or activities or even classes, whereas others will be general and broadly representative. Indeed, some will compete for the same social clientele on the basis of things such as ideological, regional or personal appeals. Unlike some other structural analyses, this discussion focuses on the political, and assumes that in the Arab world of the 1970s and 1980s social structure is not the prime explanatory variable.

Like any structural explanation, this study assumes that stability — the condition to be explained — is found in some sort of balance, here seen as complementarity. It is important to emphasise that stability is not assumed: instability is as much to be accounted for as stability. The cases that follow will test, and hopefully show, the usefulness of this approach.

MANIPULATED PLURALISM: MOROCCO

Morocco is a centralised political system, with much power held by the king. The central figure is imbued with both traditional and modern legitimacy (to use Weber's concepts) and also with a charisma that is closer to its original religious meaning that to a merely personal transitional attribute. The king manipulates his support through a mystical bond which he cultivates with his people and through his control over the political elite. However, both of these activities are complicated by the fact that the nationalist movement also shared political legitimacy at the time of independence in 1956 and left its legacy to its successors, the political parties and national organisations, notably labour and student unions. Although parties and organisations have left their nationalist sources of legitimacy behind them as a quarter century has passed since independence, they have been given new life over the past decade by the fact that the king has found them to be useful to the functioning of the system. Thus parties and organisations have established a role in providing members of the political elite and in helping to mediate ties between the king and his people. This role is not to the king's liking, no doubt, but it is tolerated because the events of the preceding decade (1963–72) showed that without such organisations of support, the system was vulnerable to direct challenges from within and without.

However the king has also established limits to the power of mediating organisations of support (and demand). They are expressed in his graphic phrase, 'I will never be put into equation'; that is, king and party should not be equal centres of power but rather, parties must be subordinate to king and pluralistically competing and self-limiting. At the same time, other elements of support must be directly under royal control. A segment of the political elite must be directly dependent on the king, without independent sources of power such as party organisation, and a segment of the population — primarily rural society — must be directly supportive of the monarch, their representatives being spokesmen of support rather than spokesmen for demands (Marais and Waterbury, in Debbasch, et al., 1970).

After 1973, the king began to recreate the polity, using the same elements of support which had been weakened and disorganised during the previous period — parties, army and networks of his own authority. Parties were brought back into activity in a painstakingly negotiated structure of roles which Abderrahim Bouabid has labelled

223

'limited democracy' (Rousset in Leca *et al.*, 1979). But, having learned from the previous period the lessons about the destabilising challenges that political parties with autonomous sources of power can bring, Hassan worked to tame the mass parties of the nationalist movement and confront them with patron parties under his sponsorship. Pluralism is in the Moroccan pre-constitutional political norms and is written into the Moroccan constitution to counterbalance the centralising effects of the monarchy. The king has always worked in various ways to replace the unity of the nationalist movement with an array of political organisations from amongst which he could pick his instruments of government.

Therefore, except at times of a government of national unity (i.e. national coalition, not single party), some parties would always be left in opposition. Some of them consider opposition status to be simply a time of reserve duty 'at the disposition of the king' but other see themselves in permanent opposition (until the millenial day when the nature of the system changes). Indeed, some can be recovered from the opposition personally with an appropriate government job, like Justice and then Prime Minister Maati Bouabid, formerly of the UNFP, but at the cost of being disowned by the opposition party. Still others constitute the disloyal opposition, rejecting the entire polity and suffering its rejection as well. Morocco therefore has a broad polity, widely (even if not universally) considered to be legitimate, and a wide spectrum of oppositions, most of them out of power for a very long time. It is thus an appropriate place to begin inquiry about the opposition's role in stability.

The most important of the parties is the Istiqlal, the venerable descendent of the nationalist movement, for a long time Morocco's largest as well as oldest party, with a coherent articulated structure and philosophy. Although the Istiqual was on the oppositing side in 1959–60 and then again after 1963, it began a new era a decade later when its president and spiritual leader Allal al-Fasi died. The Ninth Party Congress of 1974 set out a programme based on national integrity, public liberty and economic reform that was in many details close to the existing Five Year Plan (1973–7), soon to be cancelled because of the Saharan campaign. When the regime's policy of liberalisation brought an invitation to the Istiqlal to return to power, the response in 1976 was more of a justification of cooperation than a declaration of demands that the party would bring to the new coalition (Rousset in Leca, 1979, p. 204f). The party's position is generally known to cover concerns of territorial recovery, economic nationalism, guarantees for organised participation in politics and parliamentary responsibility in government, Arabisation in culture and education, and welfare economics. With the death of al-Fasi, and the king's decision to share some power and responsibility in government, the two major obstacles to Istiqlal participation in government were removed. Neither of them concerned specific substantive demands. In a system in which legitimacy is attached to cooperation between monarchy and nationalist movement, association in government increases the attractiveness of the party to its constituents (and vice versa, as demonstrated popularity increases the party's claim on association in government).

Yet mobilisation and participation are part of the Istiqlal's day-to-day activities with its constituent activities with its constituents. This activity resembles party life reported in an earlier period (Ashford, 1961) and previous electoral campaigns (Leveau, 1976; or Santucci and Benhlal, in Leca, *et al.*, 1979), although there are few studies of the current period (Sehimi, 1979, 1985 on elections; and El-Mossadeq, 1981 on party life). Demands and discontents are raised in party cell meetings and electoral campaigns, and to some extent are passed on upwards. While it is likely that such transmission is not very important for the general nature, shape and functioning of the political system, it is also likely that the fate of individual demands is important to individuals and constitutes the grains of sand that comprise the edifice. At the same time, demands do not constitute the entire edifice. Much, and perhaps nearly all of the business at party cell meetings, as well as at higher levels, involves purely supportive participation, including reiteration of points that are already part of party and government programmes, attacks on the opposition, patriotic and nationalistic declarations, or simply association with party rituals. After all, a person is a supporter of the Istiqlal in part because he feels that it best handles his particular concerns (demands) but also because of regional and family connections with the party and because it is good to be associated with a party that enjoys the Istiqlal's relation to government (support).

Istiqlal alternance between government (1960–3, 1976–83) and opposition has trade-offs and implications for party interests in terms of both support and demands. Internally, there is a trade-off between the two; demands are expressed only within the basic decision to support the regime, but support is accorded only as long as it is compatible with the basic positions (demands) of the party. This sequence is unexceptional, no doubt, until it is added that it does not

225

result in a continually recycling decision but rather in long-term commitments. Once it is decided that association in government is compatible with basic positions, the decision to support becomes a limitation on the expression of day-to-day demands. But when the decision is to oppose, the party is freed to reaffirm its demands in their full integrity. Participation in power compromises, as Al-Fasi knew it would, and opposition permits integrity. Participation also restrains the other participants, and that is the second trade-off. In providing support for the monarchy, the Istiqlal ties the king to its basic demands, and in voicing opposition it constrains him by showing up his deviation. Paradoxically, either position effects the Istiqlal policy of making the national integrity Saharan issue the bottom-line criterion for membership in the polity, thereby limiting the king's room for manoeuvre in international negotiations.

The Istiqlal is a waning party in Morocco, one that has suffered as much from participation as from opposition. Both positions have worked to discredit the party. Participation has shown its programmatic ineffectiveness, and opposition has shown royal disfavour. Programmatic ineffectiveness was the cause of the Istiqlal split in 1958–9, when royal restraints on socio-economic programmes made the party's left wing restive and finally led it to break away to form the National Union of Popular Forces (UNFP). Royal disfavour probably accounted for the Istiqlal's loss of voters in 1976–7 (after 13 years in the wilderness), and in 1984 (after a shorter time — a year out of power), despite the intervening six years in the government coalition. In the Istiqlal case, opposition has served party interest in integrity at the price of party fortunes. At the same time, it served government (royal) interests as well.

Undecided on the borders of the polity are the National and Socialist Unions of Popular Forces (UNFP and then USFP), the opposition parties, and also the labour unions and students, whether in their organised form of the National Union of Moroccan Students (UNEM) or not. In general, the undecided have the greatest interest in unhindered demand articulation and mobilisation, although they have also special roles in defining the limits of the political system and special meanings attached to their mobilisation mechanisms. These points will be developed in the following discussion.

The newly formed UNFP was the primary partner in the government of 1958–60, after which it entered into permanent opposition. In July 1972, however, it split into two factions over the question of whether any collaboration with the regime was possible. Although the hardest line was taken by the Rabat section, under

Abderrahim Bouabid, it gradually came around under the pressure of police measures and then offers of collaboration by the king and in 1975 became the USFP with participation in the political system, leaving the Casablanca section under Abdullah Ibrahim with the original party name and no role to play. The USFP joined the 1974 government with a Ministry of State and participated in the diplomatic campaign for the recovery of the Sahara and in the pre-election negotiations, but it could not reach an agreement to participate in government after the elections and has remained more or less the loyal opposition. During 1980 it rejected basic decisions of the regime, notably the constitutional amendments on the regency and the duration of parliament, and withdrew from participation in the by-elections of 1981 and from parliament itself after the expiration of its original mandate in the middle of the same year. In 1981, its leaders were jailed for a year for criticising the king for weakness in the Saharan policy, but in 1984 the same leaders were offered participation in the government, which they rejected. They then joined a government of national unity to guarantee the 1984 elections and emerged the largest of the non-government parties in the ensuing vote. But they continue to opt for opposition, having already undergone a second split in 1983 over the issue of whether to join the national unity government. Its opposition has, therefore, been accentuated to the point of straining the notion of 'loyalism', reinforcing its role as a boundary marker for the system.

Like the Istiqlal, the USFP is a real party, with ongoing constituency relations and functioning cells in contact with the party hierarchy and with their elected representatives. Its programme is socialist, and its local cells have their own ideas about their demands as well as about the degree of support the party should give to the regime and about the meaning of socialism (Benhlal, in Leca et al., 1979). The USFP is wracked by continual debate on its relation to the system; 'support' is much less certain and more fragile than 'demand', and the party is made up of many factions and sections which take different positions on the question of the relation between the two. Thus, in a sort of Moroccan Watergate, with Moroccanly different consequences, the USFP was defeated in a major electoral battle in the Souss in 1977 by unnecessarily foul means piled on top of fair. The USFP congress of the following year had to keep a rebellious rank and file in line behind its policy of loyal opposition by means of a firm organisational hand. When the monarchy then extended the life of the national assembly whose initial election the USFP had challenged, the party could only hold itself together by taking a further step out of loyalism into opposition and withdrawing from the assembly.

Nor did it hold together in 1983 when a minority withdrew in protest against association with government. Although its participation in guaranteeing the elections won the USFP a sizeable increase in votes, pressure from the members led to the party to decide 'to remain in opposition for two or three years rather than join in an incoherent government coalition'. Yet, to the extent that it supports the system, the USFP puts the monarchy into a dilemma, either of whose outcomes gives the party some satisfaction. If the king wins on the Saharan issue, the party benefits along with the rest of the country. But if the king is tied to an unshakeable goal with insufficient means to attain it and ends up weakened and vulnerable, the USFP — unlike the parties of the government — is not unhappy. The king has long played the USFP beyond all patience and credibility, never offering full association in government, always harrassing the party with police controls, and continually dangling the lure of participation in power before the leaders' eyes until the party cracks as a result (Barrada, 1980). Events that weaken the monarch and make the USFP more useful to it — such as the events of the constitutional breakdown (1963–72) and some conceivable outcomes of the Saharan affair — could work to the party's benefit. Yet as the decade of emergency showed, the cost of such an evolution in the political system is tremendous for the party in personal terms, for the monarchy does not allow itself to be weakened without weakening the other participants in the ring at the same time. The USFP has lived under repression and has been able to mobilise its membership under adverse conditions.

If the USFP's support role therefore results in a trade-off different to those available to sometime government parties, its demand role also involves a paradoxical exchange. The USFP is remarkably successful in achieving its demands, which it does only at the price of authorship, by 'ghostwriting' royal programmes. For example, while repressing the party for the plot of March 1973 and restricting civil liberties, the king undertook a programme of Moroccanisation of foreign-owned land and of the service sector, introduced a limited programme of labour participation in capital ownership of certain industries, and other measures, all part of the (then) UNFP platform. Again, in 1980, the king announced a reduction in poor people's rents by a third, while the USFP was calling for the simple freezing of rents. When the party and related unions heavily criticised ministerial decision on higher education, the king (after a number of intervening steps) cancelled them. None of these measures, or others like them, have produced the procedural move which the party would prefer: a frank invitation to share power, to carry out programmes and to meet demands in the name and to the credit of the party. Instead, the king takes the credit for the measures. But the origins of the demands must certainly not be lost on UNFP members. Morocco is a political system in which initiatives come from the opposition but are enacted by the government in order to undercut the opposition's appeal.

Opposition on the outer fringes is organised under the name of the Front. The Front was the alliance between the Movement of 23 March growing out of the protest riots of 1965 in Casablanca and the 'Onward' (*ila al amam*) Movement which broke away from the Party of Progress and Socialism (PPS) — the authorised incarnation of the Communist Party (PCM) — in protest against its compromise with the government. The Frontists grew out of the republican element of the nationalist movement, as represented by Mahdi Ben Barka, who was assassinated in Paris by Moroccan Interior Ministry figures in 1965. They were typically members of the student movement, the National Union of Moroccan Students (UNEM), in contact with Communist organisations. Frontists were arrested in the early 1970s, sometimes tortured or liquidated, and then for the most part amnestied in 1980. By 1982 some were back in prison again. In subsequent trials, ties were alleged between Frontists and the protest riots of July 1981 and January 1984. Frontists were therefore the organised tip of an iceberg of unknown and varying size (Degenhardt, 1983). The key position of the Frontists, which put them beyond the political pale, was their rejection of the struggle for national integrity in the Sahara. Without that issue, they might have merely been subject to harrassment, albeit serious at times. However, they also opposed the regime on many other issues, so broad in nature that the Frontists basically rejected the form of the political system instead of simply imposing specific demands on it. They never sought collaboration within the system, on whatever terms.

Yet even Frontists were useful to the system, for they provided volunteers through whom the regime could show the limits of participation and the fate of total opponents, and once it had made its point it could also use them, through amnesty, to show both control and magnanimity. Thus even outside the system, the Frontists had a role to play, and they played it well.

Another element of opposition are the labour unions,[2] though

229

each in a slightly different position with regard to the political system, since each is related (in a different way) to a political party — the General Union of Moroccan Workers (UGTM) to the Istiqlal, the Moroccan Labour Union (UMT) to the now-defunct UNFP, and the Democratic Labour Confederation (CDT) to the USFP (Eqbal, 1966; Forst, 1976). The Istiqlal dominates its union, the UMT dominated its party, and the CDT and USFP look on each other as equals with 'relations of . . . constant, privileged, . . . independent, militant . . . solidarity' (*Liberation*, 14 December 1978). Unions are active in Morocco and enjoy a good measure of freedom. They are an effective means for mobilisation of participants and the articulation of demands, and the government responds to their protests and pressures — never adequately by labour's standards, of course — as part of a bargaining process. Much of the recurring labour agitation concerns labour's demands for a sliding pay scale indexed to the inflation rate. In general, the government responds with a one-time pay rise and measures (including an Economic and Social Council in 1980) to maintain constructive contacts between government and labour. Labour demands are of two types — primary demands over wages and conditions of employment, and secondary demands for the revoking of punitive measures taken by the government against over-intense pressures for primary demands, such as arrest of strikers. These two levels allow for flexibility and face-saving in mobilisation and response.

In general, however, Moroccan labour unions operate within the polity, for they are aware of their vulnerability to the unemployed taking over their jobs. Both government and opposition are also aware that the real challenge comes from an event such as the 1965 Casablanca riots, when organised political forces were outflanked by anomic movements. Even the 1981 riots, which were union (CDT) instigated but got out of hand, point up the threat of anomic protest. The anomic threat is another of those paradoxical trade-offs which characterise Morocco. It brings government and unions together against a common danger but it is also brandished by each against the other in bargaining over labour demands. After the 1981 and 1984 riots, the king required all candidates to the September 1984 elections to be members of a party. Henceforth, opposition was to be organised and organisations were to be responsible, thereby enlisting them in the government job of control. With a common interest in avoiding anomie, government and unions bargain over demands, in support of the polity.

Yet the line between supporters and opponents of the polity is not sharp, as USFP behaviour indicates. Moreover, a link between organised and anomic demands exists among students, where the meanings of mobilisation, participation and demand are most complex of all. There are a number of ties between students, student unions, teachers unions and the main labour unions. Students are regarded by labour as natural allies, a vanguard which cannot be allowed to get too far ahead of the mass. The National Teachers Union (SNE) is a branch of the CDT and is one of the most radical of the unions, the instigator of the 1981 protest. UNEM is an established political organisation; banned in 1973, it was readmitted to legality in 1978 and is the most radical of the legal organisations in Morocco, wavering on the outside fringes of the polity. Mobilisation for demands not only exists within groups and organisations, but spreads from one to another because of overlapping membership in the education sector. Furthermore, the mobilisation cycle is an annual event. It begins soon after the opening of the calendar year (in the middle of the school year), and continues throughout the semester, mixing various types of demands and mobilisation groups — teachers, students, parents — both in secondary and in higher education. Vacations in the spring and summer provide cooling-off periods where life can return to normal without the protesters losing face. Demands here are on three levels: primary and secondary levels covering education and low-and-order grievances, and then residual demands against the political system in general, concerning its nature and existence (a point Hodges, 1981 confuses).

Strikes — the normal expression of demands — in this sector are thus different from strikes in the regular labour sector, and are met by a different response. On one hand, strikes are a frivolous 'panty-raid' type activity clothed in the form of serious political statements. On the other hand, strikes in the educational sector are a continual boundary-drawing device in which both sides of the line of legitimacy test their strength. It must not be overlooked that this aspect is not just a one-off test — the year's redrawing of the boundary that will hold until the sides have regrouped to meet again in a new tenporal context; it is also a crucial socialisation process for new elites and counterelites — new participants in the confrontation of *siba* and *makhzen*. Students are versed in distrust of authority and political cynicism, but they are also trained in observing encounters with the political system (whether they find its nature to their liking or not). Student leaders grow more and more radical in their job, as increasingly stiff government opposition to their demands drives them to increasing opposition to the political system (opposition to primary and then secondary demands confirms their residual demands). In the end, radical leaders are purged from the political system, moderate students are co-opted into the system, and the lessons of the fruitlessness of fighting the system are conveyed to succeeding age levels or generations of students until a new generation which has not observed the cycle appears. In this cycle, the fortunes of the parents, their attitudes towards the system, and their rapport with their children also has a role to play. Morocco in the early 1980s appeared to be entering into a new cycle: the reappearance of the UNEM began a series of spring semester protests in 1979, 1980 and 1981, each slightly more intense and each mixing political and educational demands.

In the process, demands and discontents are not always well handled. As long as they can be subordinated to ongoing discussion about support, demand activity can be routinised or can be mobilised behind the continual manoeuvring over new role definitions. The Moroccan polity has a remarkable ability to keep its participants' hopes high, their demands dulled and their support cynical or at least self-interested. Each group, by playing its role, supports the polity in its way.

CONTROLLED PLURALISM: EGYPT

Egypt, too, is a centralised polity, governed by a royal household or palace elite as much as Morocco is governed by its *makhzen*. Within this republican palace, power is highly centralised in the hands of the president, who combines a high degree of institutional legitimacy and political skill — both in using his institutional power and in making the right policy decisions that keep the loyalty of his lieutenants and followers. There is pluralism at the level of the lieutenants, who have their own sources of power and bring their followers along with them, but who are totally at the mercy of the president for their positions. Conceivably a group of lieutenants could coalesce and react to their removal with enough weight to overthrow the president, but that has not happened since the uncertain days of 1954. There is considerable institutional pluralism under the centralised palace, including not only a highly articulated and entrenched bureaucracy but also a functioning parliament, many corporate groups (labour and professional syndicates), one or more armies, and, in the current period, political parties.

After an interregnum of factional pluralism in 1970 to 1971, the current period began with the 'corrective revolution' of 1971 which eliminated the internal opposition faction. Since the party (the Arab Socialist Union — ASU) was the organisational basis of that faction, it was natural that it be reorganised, opened up and then broken up under the controlled pluralism of President Anwar Sadat. Elections took place in 1972 with an enlarged party, in 1976 with three official 'tribunes' (*manabar*), in 1979 with competing parties, and in 1984 with competing parties under the new leadership of Hosni Mubarak. Throughout this evolution, one party remained dominant, the structural heir of the ASU, known as the Socialist Democractic Party of Egypt (1976–8) and then the National Democratic Party (NDP) thereafter. Scattered about this large central core was the opposition (Waterbury, 1983; Hinnebusch, 1985). During the time of the tribunes, the competitors of the Egypt Party were the Socialist Liberals on the right, the Progressive National Unity Party (PNUP) and the Nasserites on the left, and the unorganised independents, taking over the tribune of Nasserism. On the right, the old nationalist movement, the Wafd Party, appeared in new form in 1977 and then disappeared under official harrassment the following year, before it ever stood for elections. Subsequently the PNUP was nearly displaced by the Socialist Labour Party (SLP) on the left. The empty space on the right, at first co-opted by the NDP itself, was occupied under Mubarak by the New Wafd.

The decision to authorise an opposition came with Sadat's October paper in 1974 as an important part of the new regime's self-image of liberalisation. This thrust was crucial to the appearance that the regime was seeking to cultivate as a government of *laissez-faire* pluralism, but those appearances in turn were imperative to its public appeal in response to a popular thirst for relaxation of the Nasserist mobilisation and for time to absorb Nasser's social changes. Appearances were also important externally, where the government was seeking political forms that would help its appeals to Western sources of support and cared little about making itself attractive to the Communist countries. Finally, the government acted the way it did because it believed in its course, both negatively and positively. Sadat reacted against the perceived failure of the unitarist system of which he was earlier a part (political actions are frequently taken in rejection of a previous model rather than in sound analysis of a proposed one (Quandt, 1969; Zartman, 1980)). But there was a positive element as well: Sadat expected that opposition would be both constructive and manageable, a contribution but not a threat to successful and popular government. Moreover, pluralism at the government level was necessary to his view of father-like unity as the head of state. Paternally, the president would orchestrate his pluralism, and adjudicate his opposition. There were also more manipulative reasons for wanting an authorised opposition, the most important of which had to do with the delimitation of the polity. Although there is no *a priori* evidence, subsequent behaviour supports the common use of the opposition as a border marker for the authorised system. Opposition was subject to two sorts of control: 'unfair' competition with the massive official party (ASU — Egypt Party — NDP), and direct efforts to break or restrain the party over a specific oppositional action. Both can be viewed as efforts to use the opposition as an indicator of the limits of authorised action. Elections were less and less free and fair since the open elections of 1976; the opposition fluctuated and then declined (18 per cent in 1976, 21 per cent in 1979, 13 per cent in 1985). Rally breaking, ballot stuffing, newspaper seizures and harrassment, and eventually the legal requirement of 8 per cent of the total (not district vote) to qualify for elections (when the SLP received 7.1 per cent) all worked to define the polity as a consensus system and the opposition's role as an official devil's advocate (Dessouki, 1984).

Direct efforts to break the opposition parties also stake out the limits of the polity. The self-dissolution of the New Wafd in June 1978, official pressure for the SLP to do the same in 1981, and the harrassment of the informal opposition from the appearance of the National Coalition in the spring of 1980 to the police round up of September 1981 were all reactions to sweeping criticisms of government and its policies. They were designed to indicate that specific opposition in policy debates may be acceptable but opposition across the board, and particularly against the hallmark policies of the government such as the Peace Process, *infitah*, and communitarian cohabitation, was out. Although Sadat paid for his policies, the definition of the authorised political system has remained under Mubarak. Moreover, use of the opposition to delimit the polity had a threat value that was useful in diplomacy. Opposition was used to show Israel and the US the limits of Egypt's room to manoeuvre (Waterbury, 1983, p. 272). It was probably less useful against domestic third parties in bargaining, but was of some utility in counterbalancing the right and the left. Sadat used and indeed encouraged Muslim religious spokesmen both against the Coptic revival and against Muslim fundamentalists outside the authority system. All of these efforts to play parts of the opposition off against each other — both within and between parts of the political spectrum — failed in the end, but helped maintain dynamic stability for a while.

Lastly, opposition was useful in defining the position of the government on that spectrum. What is involved is a symbolic game that may not fool everyone, but since the basic mode of definition is by distinction or contrast, symbolism does have operational consequences. Initially, the official tribune was placed squarely in the middle of the road, but the 1976 elections gave it practically no official opposition to the left and only a timid Liberal Party to the right. However, instead of being a left-centre party defining itself against right-wing opposition, the Egypt Party found itself facing real and outspoken opposition from the unorganised left of the independents. The party reorganisation of 1978 and the elections of 1979 changed that, by providing an equally outspoken but organised (and therefore controllable) opposition from the SLP on the left, with the rightist opposition of the New Wafd stillborn. The government marked its new orientation by defending itself against the left, rather than by coming to terms with its vocal but formally impotent opposition. Ultimately this broad strategy, too, was unsuccessful, since Sadat was surrounded by informal opposition from all sides and was shot from the right.

The Mubarak regime shifted its position and its opposition. The 1984 elections eliminated the left and gave the government party an opposition from the right, forcing it either to defend itself against the right as a centre-left party or to come to terms with it as a centre-right party. The first has been the strategy of Mubarak, as it was of Sadat. Whether successful or not, it is an example of the ultimate use of the opposition to define the government (Ottoway, 1984).

In sum, opposition was useful to the government for many reasons, just as long as it was under control. But Sadat's government overestimated the leeway it had in exercising that control, and eventually succeeded only in channelling opposition into the terrorist group, a support group, and a climate of opinion (Waterbury, 1983, p. 387). To complete the analysis, a number of complementary questions need to be examined: under these conditions, what was the interest of the opposition in playing their particular roles? What kind of expectations did they hold? How complementary were the roles, and how did that complementarity break down? In dealing with these questions, distinctions can be made among four different opposition groups: tame opposition, vocal opposition, corporate opposition and unauthorised opposition, as well as a few groups that floated among these forms. If the rest of the discussion proceeds in the manipulative terms of interest, roles and uses, it must be remembered that, basically, people entered different forms of opposition because of what they believed, and their actions fit the strength and direction of those beliefs. Opposition, whatever its form, was self-satisfying. Those who opposed only a little and were cowed in the process pretty much accepted the government position, whereas those who undertook unauthorised activity and ran its risks believed very strongly that the government was wrong. The first answer then to the question of motivations accepts action (or inaction) as the prima facie test of beliefs.

Tame opposition disagreed only a little with the government, criticised only a bit, and was easily co-opted. The Liberals, for example, were content with a chance to state their position and to contribute in the process to the diversity of power. Their expectations may have been greater individual visibility in opposition than in government, or a greater chance of being bought off than of being rewarded. The NPUP and some parts of the SLP were in the same position (Hinnebusch, 1984d). The role of Mahmud Abu Wafia, Sadat's brother-in-law, who organised both the debate on pluralism and the Egypt Party and then was one of the leaders of the SLP until it got too critical, is a symbol as well as an example of roles and their limits.

Others played their roles more wholeheartedly, both providing a home for opponents of the regime and expressing their own opposition across the board. The SLP and the New Wafd are the best examples of vocal opposition, although their expectations differ. SLP was an active 'pressure party' (Hinnebusch, 1985), seeking to affect government policy and limit some of the directions which it criticised. It understood and operated within government's procedural limitations, and in return sought to impose substantive limitations of government policy. There is no evidence that it was specifically effective on any policy measure, and that may have led it into broader criticism of the government in press and parliament after 1980. Nor is there any evidence that the party had any illusions about its ability to join in, let alone form, a government. It was not only a 'corrective opposition'; it was also a permanent opposition. It must have been satisfied with that role (had it been allowed to play it fully), since from the very outset it could not have expected anything else. Indeed, both the Wafd and the SLP were torn apart (in 1984 and 1980, respectively) over whether to accept appointed seats to parliament, lest they be compromised by that much dependence on the government.

The New Wafd just as clearly has wider aspirations. If it seems unlikely that they be fulfilled, one must remember that the 65-year history of the Wafd is not only one of unfulfilled expectations but, more deeply, of role imbalance, in which the three main actors of the system — crown, coloniser and party — pulled in different directions and eventually destroyed the polity by 1952 (Deeb, 1979; Colombe, 1951). The Wafd seeks to be the government party. Curiously, as long as it maintains that optimism, it implicitly redefines the political system as one of two potential governing parties and adds to its legitimacy. The fact that it makes its demands as an aspirant to power, not just a constructive and permanent opposition, is a support for the system. Other role complementarities are not evident as yet: the Wafd has neither served as a limitation nor a source of ideas, nor has it drawn off a dissident part of the government's social support group and left it with a more coherent social base (Hinnebusch, 1984a) — all roles it could potentially play as the future unfolds.

Is there some mechanism that can bring roles and role expectations into balance, so that the Wafd only does and aspires to do what serves the government's purposes at the same time as it serves its own, and the same for government? Conceivably so, and it would be accomplished by conditioning or on-the-job socialisation, as has happened to some degree with the USFP in Morocco and also to some degree with the old Wafd. Neither of these cases is an exact parallel, though, nor is the SLP, which became more vocal as it became learner. Present divergences of views on the proper role for the New Wafd suggest that unless one or the other or both sides adjust their roles and expectations to fit the other's (as seems unlikely), there is likely to be continued conflict that will point up the incapacities of the authorised system and drive people to play their politics on its unauthorised fringes.

Corporate opposition groups in Egypt are in a different position. Their primary interest is in representing their members' interests, not in opposing government, and their members' interests are relatively homogeneous. Egypt has a more active corporatist structure than many Arab countries. If its labour unions have been dominated by a long association with the ASU, its professional syndicates are vigorous defenders of their own interests and autonomy, and hence of a liberal pluralism that includes opposition. Besides the press, which operates in competition with one another rather than as a syndicalised corps, the most independent profession

237

is the lawyers. Another non-opposition professional group are engineers. Sadat in 1981 and Mubarak in 1983 tangled with the Lawyer's Syndicate, with a little help from parliament and then the constitutional court. In the end, the presidential measures of control of 1981 were declared illegal and the lawyers' leadership restored to office. Sadat's umbrage was originally roused by the syndicate's critical statements on Egyptian relations with Israel, statements which stopped after the leadership was changed. By the time the leadership was restored, it was the presidency which had changed, and a *modus vivendi* was reached by which the syndicate's oppositional activity would be reduced. Functional groups can function without being an opposition, if the government will let them do so. If they do take on an oppositional role, it is either because opposition has become widespread or because no one else can play the role effectively. In neither case is there any complementarity of roles for government.

The Egyptian case brings out the fact that roles are not necessarily complementary by definition, and that systems are not necessarily in equilibrium. Some people are not content with the limits government places on their activity and government does not feel served by the form their behaviour takes. The resulting conflict may occur within the polity (as in the case of the Wafd) but it may also serve to drive the opposition outside the polity and into unauthorised activity. Examples of this effect include borderline groups such as Dawa, the National Coalition, and eventually the victims of the September (1981) round up, but also out-and-out out groups such as *Takfir wa al-Hijra*. The latter justify their righteous opposition by entering into conflict with the government, since the source of the evils they perceive is blatant and close at hand. The government justifies their existence but the reverse is not true; they have been too far from the frontiers of authorised activity to be useful to government as a frontier marker or even as an example. As true believers, they find persecution of their comrades only an encouragement in their defence of high stakes and noble purposes, not a deterrent.

The most interesting cases are the undecided or borderline groups. Al-Dawa and its leader Omar Tilimsani were brought into the polity by Sadat, to strengthen his position on the religious right. That served the purpose of the Dawa group well enough but it also legitimised the general platform of the extremists and aroused, if not alienated, the Copts. Al-Dawa and the government served each other's purposes while serving their own, but in the process they helped strengthen the very opposition they sought to undermine. In the discussion thus far, a frequent conclusion has been that it is better to authorise opposition than to force it outside the policy; yet in the case of religious opposition, there are advantages to both courses.[3] The attempt to co-opt a part of the religious opposition was not effective in taming the rest, even in the presence of a complementarity of roles. At this point, it is not yet clear whether the case stands as an exception or a conclusion.

The remaining groups of undecided include the National Coalition, which issued a number of proclamations against Sadat's policy in the spring of 1980, and the large number of people (including some of the National Coalition's signatories) who were arrested in September 1981 and only gradually released by Mubarak in the following year, who are evidence of shrinking consensus. The opponents' action served two of their interests — that of conscience, and that of enlarging the area of debate. They ran into the government's intention to do just the opposite. It was no doubt the massive scale of the arrests that caused or confirmed the climate of opinion within which Sadat's assassins and their support group operated.

In general, the Egypt of Sadat and Mubarak supports the analytical notion of system stability through role complementarity. For the most part, government opposition has followed its own interests, accepting both the position of the other party in the state and its own, and using the other for its own purposes. To the extent that this complementarity worked, the stability of the system was maintained. But Sadat's message of liberalism fuelled greater expectations than he was ready to fulfill, particularly as time went on. Some opposition groups were content to play a limited official or tame role, as seen, but others were not, and their members increased along with the limitations on their activity. This misfit provided the setting that permitted, if not legitimised, the assassination. It should be noted that nothing in this imbalance or in any other analysis that is essentially structural will explain the assassination itself. Assassination is a haphazard, individual act, and its chances of success are random, not a barometer of the stability of the regime or the strength of the opposition.

After the assassination and succession, relations between government and opposition returned to stalemate until the 1984 elections. Even then, the opposition parties seemed to be as confirmed in their various roles as the government in its own. Expectations have not yet crystallised: the Wafd has to grow used to its new role and government to its new opposition, and above all the polity has to

239

decide whether it considers a president who in five years has crossed no canals, corrected no revolutions, and created no openings to be a welcome relief or a bore. Only then can roles be assigned and complementarities assayed, although in the interim stability is maintained, *faute de pire*.

EMERGING PLURALISM: TUNISIA

Tunisia is a presidential monarchy, dominated for its three decades of independence by the father figure of the Supreme Combattant, Habib Bourguiba, and by his companions in arms, the Socialist Constitutional (or Destourian) Party (PSD). Power is centralised at the top but the base of the political pyramid is small, since the country has a small and homogenous population with concentrated distribution over a small territory. Nonetheless, Tunisia has had repeated experiences with pluralism. Immediately after independence, Bourguiba not only had to eradicate fundamental opposition within his own party as he consolidated his power but also had to undo the pretensions of the General Union of Tunisian Workers (UGTT) to organise a socialist opposition party from scratch. By the end of the 1950s, the dangers of opposition has been eliminated and an open party co-opting new elites as they arose was established under the benevolent aegis of the president. He placed and replaced his lieutenants at will, for though they might represent different currents of opinion, none had any independent source of power that escaped his control.

Although the 1960s might be termed the socialist decade of Ahmed ben Salah, the former UGTT leader and economic czar lost his position because he was busily building an independent source of power. The 1970s became the liberal decade of Hedi Nouira, the prime minister. A more important watershed in the latter period however was 1974, when young, liberal, pluralist elites were evicted from the party leadership. The PSD closed its ranks and became a bureaucracy, just at the moment when pluralism began to emerge in Tunisian society as a result of the successful economic management of Nouira's administration. Heretofore, opposition had been a matter of individuals, who could be sent into private life for a while to cool their heels before being recalled to service by the president. After the mid-1970s, opposition began to find a social base, and since it was no longer accommodated within the nation-party it began to look for organised expression of its own. The Nouira era had the liberal option, actually made pluralism and civil rights its platform and found supporters among the middle class and scattered disaffected regions. Ahmed ben Salah's Popular Unity Movement (MUP), representing the socialist option, had first to be separated from its exiled leader, but the MUP II was acceptable and also tapped middle-class dissatisfaction. The Tunisian Communist Party (PCT) should probably also be included in this list, since it was the first party to be authorised in the 1980s, and was a companion of the Destourian movement in the nationalist struggle, even if not a branch. Like the others, the PCT is a movement of professionals and intellectuals, a safety valve for dissatisfaction rather than a mass challenge to PSD. The government party looks on these movements with some scorn or with patronising camaraderie, since the leaders are former colleagues and the parties pose no real threat.

The Islamic Tendency movement is another matter, being neither a Destourian offshoot nor a negligible safety valve. Hence it is not authorised. Until 1983, there was not the slightest indication that the government found any value in the MTI. The only usefulness of the movement was to facilitate the identification of hostile opposition leaders, who were in fact tried and sentenced to jail in 1981. In 1985, during the Tunisian-American crisis over the Israeli bombing of Hammamet, Prime Minister Mzali received an MTI leader, as a move to signal his foreign policy dissatisfaction and his domestic policy to pass before the polity could react to these developments but in the pluralist 1980s of Mohammad Mzali, the new prime minister, a number of responses emerged. The first was a reinvigoration of the party itself, reopening the leadership of party auxiliaries to new voices and recalling liberals back to the party fold. The second was the opening of elections to multiple candidacies under the single party in 1980. And the third was the cautious tolerance and finally authorisation of opposition parties, first as movements and newspaper publishers, then as contenders in the 1981 parliamentary elections (which were then rigged to prevent the true size of the opposition being known), and finally as authorised parties.

Observers have long felt that the inevitable evolution of Destourian politics was towards a multi-party system. As socioeconomic pluralism developed as a result of the impressive Tunisian growth, political pluralism pressed for recognition within the party. Acceptable at first, it became too broad in the mid-1970s, just at the same time as internal pressures within the leadership called for a narrowing of political positions. Thus, most of the opposition movements were spin-offs from the single party, and they were welcomed

241

by the government to the extent that they removed the tendency to form factions from within the PSD and took it outside, where it would attract a minimum of followers. Opposition parties became the functional equivalent of the temporary political banishment of individuals of the 1960s. Ahmed Mestiri's Socialist Democratic Party (PDS) represented breadth, but the MTI was in general of little use to the government.

The most serious challenge to the government has been the UGTT. The nationalist trade union, both partner and member of the Destourian nationalist movement, has long had a dual nature, as single overarching labour union and as potential opposition party. It made its bid for party status in 1956 and was denied; eight years later it was back in an opposition role over economic (devaluation) and social (wage freeze) policies, and in the late 1970s — beginning in 1976 — it was in open conflict with the government. The next year the government repeated its tactic of 20 years earlier and broke labour unity by creating its own Destourian labour movement, the National Union of Tunisian Workers (UNTT), but the UGTT only pushed its own opposition further to the point of precipitating the bloody riots of January 1978. The government gave strength to this ticket and prestige to the UGTT claim of being a party when it ran a successful joint slate of PSD-UGTT candidates in 1981, but that did not prevent continuing conflict and finally arrest of the UGTT leadership. Certainly the conflict after 1968 was closely tied to the personality of the UGTT leader, Habib Achour, but he was broadly supported by the union membership. When Tunisia finally becomes a multi-party system, a socialist labour party based on the UGTT will be the PSD's main opposition.

It was the long-term hope of alternance that kept up the faith of the various opposition groups, coupled in varying measures with belief in the rightness of their cause. Thus, the Tunisian oppositions were closer in their reasoning to the Wafd than to the other Egyptian or Moroccan parties. Nothing in the government's behaviour confirmed the parties' long-term hopes, but all of them read the multi-party prospects of the political system and the pluralist evolution of the society and economy as foundations for their fortunes. Like the Wafd, they have not yet faced the test of their faith, but unlike the Egyptian situation, the slowly evolving nature of a Tunisian multi-party system can keep their hopes alive for a longer time without being satisfied than the already proclaimed doctrines of pluralism in Egypt. Thus the Tunisian opposition parties have also been inspired by a certain notion of patriotism, that justifies their role in bringing about political pluralism for the good of the country and in accordance with various waves of history (liberal, socialist, Islamic), even if the government does not recognise that such actions are in Tunisia's best interest. In sum, it is largely supported by the perceived evolution of the country towards a functioning multi-party system and eventually toward party alternance in government.

Similarly, role complementarity is limited on the government side. The official single party is both scared and scornful of the opposition. It is still operating under the mystique (*fassabiya*, as it is called) of nationalist-movement-cum-single-party unity, and is fearful of the threat to omnipotence, predominance and employment that new parties might bring. Above all, the PSD is fearful that new parties might call into question the gains and accomplishments of the Bourguiba era, to the point where legislation authorising opposition parties requires them to pledge not to challenge or undo the measures of independence to date. To many Tunisians, this wariness and suspicion of opposition to the point of falsifying electoral returns that were only a small challenge to the PSD monopoly and none to its predominance, is unwise and unnecessary, but in Tunisia such decisions are made at the highest level by one or two persons (in this case, Bourguiba, Mzali and Interior Minister Driss Guiga in 1981).

On the positive side, the government can see two values in opposition. It can be a safety valve or lightening rod, which gives vent to criticism and indeed is happy to do so, but without being strong enough to challenge the PSD. It can also be a tamer and more easily controlled alternative to restive opposition imprisoned within the government party itself. Internal opposition would be more dangerous to single party unity, even if not successful, and would be more threatening to current directions of the party if it ever were actually to succeed in winning control of the PSD.

CONCLUSION

The argument of this analysis has been that the stability of contemporary Arab regimes can be partly explained by a complementarity of roles, expectations and activities between government and oppositions which provides support for the polity. The different types of polity in the countries studied support the analysis. But the analysis has left some important questions unanswered. Under what conditions (since the cases show that the answer must be conditional, not absolute) is stability served by bringing the opposition into the polity or by forcing upon it unauthorised status? What determines the opponents' decision to adopt one sort of role or another, or to work within the polity or outside it? The analysis has dealt with the perplexing question of explaining the opposition's acceptance of its seemingly hopeless position, by pointing out satisfactions in limited or even broader activity, but it has only noted these satisfactions, not explained them.

Attempts at a broader explanation can only be partial. Going back to the social basis of government and opposition, one might assert that if social (or class) demands are not met, dissatisfaction grows and opposition becomes too large for the polity to absorb, forcing it to move outside. When opposition is small or specific, it is better to keep it in the polity under control; when it becomes too large, it is a danger to government, whether in the polity or outside. But not all opposition is socially- or class-based, and not all dissatisfaction becomes opposition.

Another explanation can be traced back to conscience, asserting that there are objective levels or thresholds of discontent which correspond to and therefore explain various roles and expectations within the opposition. But conscience is subjective, not objective, and does not provide an independent measure of opposition (Moore, 1966, Appendix). Even if these thresholds are not fixed, however, conscience does offer an important ingredient in explaining satisfaction in opposition roles. Individuals can remain active, concerned participants in the polity but enjoy freedom from the constraints of a government party by joining an opposition party, preferring ineffectiveness with freedom to ineffectiveness without it. Government interest in this unusual mixture of 'exit, voice and loyalty' is more obvious.[7]

In the last analysis, the argument of role complementarity is a historical argument. It has served to explain stability in particular places at particular times, but its effectiveness depends finally on its acceptance. At a particular time, governments see opposition that is kept within bounds as useful and acceptable; and at a particular time, oppositions too are willing to fill a limited role, where their sense of purpose can be met without conflicting with the government's sense of purpose. This complementarity can even cover extended times of unfulfilled hopes of alternance — a revision of the initial hypothesis — as well as times when neither side has any prospect of alternance in mind. In such cases something must happen at some point to those unrequited aspirations: either they are finally realised, or they become mythicised and millenial, or they are dropped, or stability disappears. In the Middle East, the first occurred in Israel with Likud, the second has been the fate of most Communist parties, the third is the story of the parties of the Moroccan nationalist movement, and the fourth is the history of Egypt in its first 30 years of independence.

That historical period also has longer term implications. The choice among the four eventualities is part of the larger process of establishing myths of government, a large and elusive selection of interpretations. Some systems will never regard government and opposition as complementary in any form. At the end of the twentieth century, Algeria, Libya, Iraq and possibly Syria are in that category, and thus are not covered in this chapter since the explanation given does not cover their cases. Others accept a permanently subordinate opposition, where opponents 'know their place' and are satisfied to be there, content to provide policy suggestions and small but autonomous political organisations without hope of achieving power. Still others will only be satisfied with alternance, and role complementarity can only be an explanation over a transitional period. Thus, the explanation, while accurate, calls for a further explanation on a higher level where it cannot rationally be provided. Ultimately, there is no answer (as yet) to the question whether one or another type of political myth will obtain. Part of the explanation lies somewhere in the conditions of transition and the stability under which role-complementarity is effected. Contemporary Arab polities are still developing political systems, which means that political myths are still being set up. Once in place they undergo challenges and changes, to be sure, but that is a different period of evolution to the time of their actual creation. Creation means not only invention but also testing under use and over time. Role complementarity found in the supportive position of the opposition is, then, a temporary explanation of stability, but the extent to which it contributes to stability in the longer run — the next 15 years of the century — depends on the success with which it either becomes part of the political culture or serves to hold things still while institutions of democractic alternance are being prepared.

NOTES

1. It has been suggested that the PLO would also make a useful case study. On the other hand, it is worth noting that the oil windfall states of the Gulf and the Mediterranean would not.

2. A similarly 'symbiotic', but more positive, relation exists between king and *ulema*, and is examined by Donna Lee Bowen, (1985) 'The paradoxical linkage of the ulema and monarchy in Morocco', *Maghreb Review*, *vol. 1 no. 3*, p. 8.

3. Vatin (1982) suggests a more complex and convincing explanation: that religious language and locations are used to express opposition because other ways are blocked or restricted. The implication would be that secular oppositions should be allowed to perform, so as not to force disaffected elements to take refuge in the mosques, where they are harder to combat.

4. 'But there are many other cases where competition does not restrain monopoly as it is supposed to, but *comforts and bolsers* it by unburdening it of its more troublesome customers . . . Those who hold power in the lazy monopoly may actually have an interest in *creating* some limited opportunities for exit on the part of those whose voice might be uncomfortable,' Hirschman, 1970, *Exit, voice and loyalty*, Harvard University Press, Cambridge, (Massachusetts) p. 59, also 115f.

10

Notions of the State in Contemporary Arab–Islamic Writings

Fahmi Jadaane

In 1922, following the revolution of Mustapha Kamal, the National Turkish Assembly issued an edict requiring the separation of the sultanate from the Caliphate. This edict was accompanied by a manifesto entitled 'The Caliphate and the People's Power', published in both Arabic and Turkish. The manifesto acknowledged the legal basis for the principle of succession in Islam, but insisted that its actual conditions were not met except in the orthodox Caliphs. The other Caliphs who emerged later were nothing but 'heads of the Muslim community', with their rule having administrative but not spiritual significance.

The manifesto distinguished between a genuine and non-genuine Caliphate on the ground that the former satisfies all the conditions that are necessary for the official instatement of the Caliph, and specifically that the Caliph is voted into office by the nation; whereas the latter lacks these conditions, as the Caliph is brought to office by conquest and use of power. The rule of the latter is a reign but not a Caliphate. This conclusion applied to Umayyad rule — except for 'Umar ibn 'Abd al-'Aziz, and to Abbasid rule in general.

The authors of the manifesto used a quotation from the Azharite al-Iji, author of *al-Mawaqif*, in which he states 'the necessity of installing an *imam* over the Muslims when a person is found to qualify for the conditions of an imam and not otherwise'. They took this to mean 'that a government could be established and a person inaugurated without the former being called a Caliphate, nor its head a Caliph, and without any harm coming to the Islamic nation from that' ('Abd al-Ghani Sani Bey, 1924: 22). The manifesto concluded that a genuine Caliphate cannot be restricted, because it is one of prophecy, but a

247

nominal Caliphate may be. Since the Caliphate has become synonymous with authority and reign, i.e. it has become a purely political matter conducted in an arbitrary manner, it is imperative, in these 'later times', to restrict it so that power will be placed in the hands of the nation, its true owner (ibid.: 66).

This formulation, in fact, was a preparation for the radical edict that was issued in March 1924 officially abolishing the Caliphate and instituting a 'civilian' rule and a secular state. In Islamic circles throughout the Muslim world, and particularly in Egypt, strong protests and violent reactions were generated by that edict. Some thinkers, however, received it positively and publicly supported it, setting off a controversy that pushed the issue of 'state religion' to the forefront in the writing of the constitutions of modern Islamic states that were achieving independence or forming between the two world wars and thereafter. The issue that was raised is: what is the place that religion ought to occupy within the general political structure of the state? Naturally this issue is not considered problematic by contemporary Arab thinkers who follow a liberal, secular or positivistic line. It is resolved by them *a priori* in the process of a decisive separation between the religious and the political or the worldly spheres. The former encompasses the personal spiritual life of the individual and the latter is the basis for the modern state and the means by which it organises its affairs and the societies that depend upon it.

Matters are not so simple for Muslim Arab thinkers who believe that Islam loses its basic significance if it is deprived of its social dimension or political connotations. The great phenomenon of modern 'civilisation' and the backwardness of the Islamic world, the receding of its culture and the weakness of its states, are evident. Today's Muslim is thus unlikely to be trustful of the dogmatism of traditionalist writers who reject political and social changes. And yet, eliminating the problem simply by abolishing the political and social role of Islam is not the solution. Muslim Arab thinkers have debated this matter since 1924. Their experiences diverge sometimes and converge at other times to the extent that it can be said that, in spite of their undoubted common adherence to Islam, these thinkers represent a vast range of ideas, with some at the limits of 'radical temporal thought' and others at the limits of 'radical religious', or, one might say, 'theocratic thought' and numerous currents in between.

'ALI 'ABD AL-RAZIQ: THE BOOK AND THE WAVES

The first radical expression in the Arab countries following Kamal's overthrow of the Ottoman Government was shaykh 'Ali 'Abd al-Raziq's book on the Caliphate. In 1925, this Egyptian Azhari judge published a book entitled *al-Islam wa 'Usul al-Hukh* (Islam and the Principles of Government) in which he developed a new doctrine of Islam. Is the Caliphate necessary, he asked, or required by Islamic law? Is there a specific Islamic system of rule? His answer is that the Caliphate is not an integral part of Islam, for neither the Quran nor the *Hadith* refer to it, nor is there consensus on it. Its historical existence does not imply the necessity of its continuation. Moreover, the presence of a Caliph is not necessary for worship nor the realisation of the common good. He sums up by saying:

> Islam has nothing to do with the kind of Caliphate known to Muslims, with the desire, awe, glory and power with which they surround it, with any legal system or any other function of government, or state positions. All of these are purely political schemes which have nothing to do with religion. Religion neither acknowledges nor denies them, neither stipulates nor prohibits them. It left them for us to tackle by resorting to rational principles, the experiences of nations and the rules of politics. The falsehood that has been spreading among people, concerning the Caliphate being a part of religion and of 'monotheistic beliefs', is the fabrication of kings and sultans who used it to defend their interests and thrones. There have been dire consequences of this for the Muslims. Thus, there is nothing in religion to prevent Muslims from competing with other nations in all social and political spheres, and from destroying the old system to which they submitted and through which they became degraded, establishing the rules of their reign and the system of their government on the basis of modern reasoning and the most solid aspects of what the experience of nations have shown to be the best rules of government.

This view was so daring that it led the council of learned elders of al-Azhar to attack the book and bring its author to trial. This ultimately led to his name being struck from the register of learned men of al-Azhar and to his being deprived of all

249

legal and administrative positions.

A wider circle of critics, both in and outside Egypt, responded to and attacked 'Abd al-Raziq's thesis, because it justifies the idea of a secular state *à la* Ataturk.

For a long time, 'Abd al-Raziq did not respond at all, although he remained convinced that his stand did Islam a great service, opening its eyes to the evil of the exploitation of dictators and the folly of those to whom affairs were entrusted, but who were concerned only with their own interests. It is probable that he knew that a thesis like his could never be well-received in a traditionalist Islamic environment, and, indeed, it did not evoke any positive response among the learned men of religion and religious law.

The other case that deserves mention is very similar to 'Abd al-Raziq's, and is that of another Azhari, Khalid Muhammad Khalid who, a quarter of a century later, published a book entitled *Min Huna Nabda'* (From Here we Start) in which he showed complete agreement with the political opinions of 'Abd al-Raziq and attacked those he called the 'men of the priesthood', calling on governments and societies with respect and concern for their religion to take all possible initiatives to 'isolate the wicked priesthood and purify religion of its defects' (Khalid, 1950: 47). In his opinion, religious government is nothing but an instrument of dictatorship creating only disasters and suffering for humanity. The renaissance of society as well as the survival of religion itself are not possible without limiting the power of the priesthood and separating civilian from religious power. In this way, religion can achieve the ends for which it was revealed: love, the glorification of God, and the unification of people.

Khalid acknowledged that the Prophet engaged in negotiations, contracted treaties and was involved in many aspects of political power, but he only did this for necessary social reasons beyond his control. Had it not been for these reasons, he would have preferred to devote himself to spiritual affairs alone. It was he who said to 'Umar: 'Easy, 'Umar! Do you think it is Xerxesian? It is a prophecy and not a rule.' He said to his companions: 'You know more about your earthly affairs', indicating by this that it is for the people to manage their worldly affairs.

Furthermore, in Khalid's opinion, combining religious with worldly power endangers the existence of religion itself, for religion represents eternal spiritual truths not subject to variation, whereas the opposite holds true of political aims and means. Thus, if no separation is effected between religion and the state, then religious truths become subject to change and their destiny becomes intertwined with that of the state and its constantly varying political means (ibid.: 47). This damages religion, although it is meant to benefit it.

We could place shaykh 'Abd al-Hamid ibn Badis' position in line with that of 'Ali 'Abd al-Raziq concerning the Caliphate. His untimely death in 1940, while his country suffered under French colonialism, made it impossible for him — the founder of the Association of Algerian Learned Muslims — to follow 'Abd al-Raziq more than halfway (Jadaane, 1981: 334–48).

Ibn Badis openly decried the state in which the Ottoman Caliphate ended and the call of some Azharis for the Caliphate to be turned over to the king of Egypt. In this he showed agreement with 'Abd al-Raziq, for whom this issue constituted one of the driving forces behind his writing *al-Islam wa 'Usul al-Hukm*. Ibn Badis, in tracing the development of the Caliphate system, said:

> The Caliphate is the highest Islamic position designed for the execution of Islamic law and its protection through knowledgeable, experienced and insightful councillors who have wide powers, and through the force of soldiers, commanders and other means of defence. One person occupied this position at the start of Islam and, despite some disagreement, for some time thereafter. But then it became necessary to have more than one position in the East and West and ultimately it was stripped of its original meaning and reduced to a superficial, sanctifying symbol that had nothing to do with the realities of Islam. The day the Turks abolished the Caliphate — and we are not justifying all of their actions — they did not abolish the Islamic Caliphate in its Islamic meaning, but abolished a system of government peculiar to them and removed a fictitious symbol that needlessly captivated the Muslims and turned against them fanatical Western states frightened by the spectre of Islam (Ibn Badis, 1968: Vol. 2, 410–12).

Ibn Badis observed that some colonial powers, especially Britain, — knowing the Muslim fascination with the name Caliph — wanted instrumentally to restore the idea. He strongly warned against this and cried: 'Islamic nation today, stop being vain and deceived and enslaved by these scare-tactics, even if they do emanate from under cloaks and turbans!' The reference here is to the claim of the Azharis with regard to the Caliphate of the king of Egypt.

Ibn Badis did not hesitate to say 'that the Caliphate is a dream that won't come true. Muslims — God willing — will some day come to this opinion.' This might suggest to some that Ibn Badis totally adopted 'Abd al-Raziq's doctrine in depriving Islam of its political aspect. But what he, in fact, intended was to insinuate that the Association of Learned Muslims, because it operated under the shadow of French colonialism, should not interfere in political affairs to avoid any harm being done to its members at colonial hands. And when, given the transitional conditions of the times, he called for replacing the power of the Caliphate with a Muslim group — a group composed of know-ledgeable and experienced persons — he was primarily interested in keeping the hands of the occupiers away from the religious and educational administrative bodies of Algeria, so that the latter could preserve its Algerian–Arab–Islamic character. Thus, the Algerians, and not the French, would maintain control over their own affairs.

Otherwise, Ibn Badis maintained openly that 'there are two aspects to the Muslims, as there are to other peoples belonging to different nations: a political aspect connected with state affairs, and a social-educational aspect'. If they have no say on the political aspect, it is because political guidance is a matter for independent Muslim nations, whereas religious and educational guidance is a matter for both independent and dependent nations.

Nevertheless, careful examination of the thirteen rules he set for a political system in Islam, taking as his point of departure Abu Bakr as-Siddiq's famous scheme when he was inaugurated Caliph, clearly denotes that Ibn Badis saw the nation as the source of all power. For him, no nation should be ruled except in accordance with the law that it chooses for itself, and to the execution of which it commits its rulers. That responsibility should be shared by the state and the citizens, within the limits of the law (*ash-Shihab*, January 1938: 468–71). More import-antly, he believed that the conditions for an advanced and progressive life are equally available to the entire human race and that whoever avails himself of such conditions achieves the desired results, whether pious or not, believer or otherwise.

When the Muslims took to urbanisation in accordance with the dictates of their religion, they prevailed in the world and raised the banner of genuine civilisation with their science and industry. When they neglected the conditions of urbanisation, they fell behind:

> to the extent of almost coming behind all other nations . . . They, as a result, lost their worldly goods, having gone against God's will, and were condemned to the low and degraded state they are in. The best medicine for the backward Muslim's fascination with the advanced non-Muslim is to realise that his being a Muslim is not the cause of his backwardness. The non-Muslim does not progress because of not being a Muslim. The cause for progress or backwardness lies in whether or not one satisfies the proper conditions (Ibn Badis, 1964: 78).

One can therefore say that Ibn Badis, in agreement with 'Ali 'Abd al-Raziq in rejecting the altered or distorted Caliphate system, did not go along with him in ascribing religion to the purely spiritual. What appears to be the case is that, for practical reasons, he set aside the political role of religion, pending the stage of independence. But the fact that he tied the political system to the power of the nation and the rule of law, and his belief that progress and backwardness are a matter of adhering to or neglecting worldly conditions, bring him decisively closer to the main issue that 'Abd al-Raziq defended and made dominant in his book.

THE 'RADICAL RELIGIOUS' CURRENT

The effect left by 'Abd al-Raziq's argument was felt in the crystallisation of new Islamic political ideas around questions of rule, power, state and nation. Yet, it would indeed be a gross exaggeration to believe that these new ideas were a response to one single stimulus, namely the provocative work of 'Abd al-Raziq. In addition to it, various Muslim countries were being Westernised, owing to the control by colonial powers over them. There were also modern political institutions based on Western rationalism, which the Muslim learned and intellectuals could no longer completely and unconditionally reject without falling into curious paradoxes.

Thus we find that the strongest voice opposed to 'Abd al-Raziq's theses, namely that of shaykh Muhammad Bakhit al-Muti'i, ultimately set aside the idea that the power of the Caliph is directly derived from God, arguing that the nation is the source of the Caliph's power and that Islamic rule is democratic, free, and consultative, with the Quran and tradition acting as its constitution. This stance made it appear possible to reconcile Islamic with modern concepts.

Viewed from a different perspective, however, it did not represent a retreat with regard to the question of the separation of religion and the state. A strong current against this separation began to make headway and gain support, calling for the re-establishment of the Islamic state and Islamic society under the umbrella of Islamic law. One consequence of the influence of this current was the fact that modern Islamic states introduced into their constitutions a provision to the effect that Islam is the religion of the state or that Islamic law is one basic source of legislation in the state, if not the main source. But these constitutional details are, on the whole, formal and did not suffice in the eyes of some religious movements to force them to swerve from their solitary and radical demands and struggle for the establishment of an Islamic political system and state, as well as for the re-establishment of a Caliphate.

HASAN AL-BANNA AND THE MUSLIM BROTHERS

The new movement born in response to 'Ali 'Abd al-Raziq's provocative claims, goes back to shaykh Muhammad Rashid Rida (d. 1935), who was among the great advocates of traditionalism (*as-salafiyyah*). He himself described al-Raziq's book as one that constitutes 'a last attempt on the part of the enemies of Islam to weaken this religion and divide it from within'. He affirmed, with shaykh Bakhit al-Muti'i, (al-Muti'i, 1344; Ibn 'Ashur, 1344) that Islamic law requires power to maintain and apply it and that it is not possible to reform Islamic law without re-establishing that Islamic state and instating a Caliph endowed with the power to interpret the law (through *ijtihad*). 'The Caliph should see to it that the law is observed and that the government is based on *shura* and should seek to revive Islamic civilisation and strengthen it with the knowledge and technological skill necessary for a strong structure and impregnable progress.'

It was Hasan al-Banna who headed this new movement, inspired by the traditionalism of Rashid Rida and contemporary events. The Muslim Brotherhood, which he began to form in Isma'iliya in 1928, was the most outstanding contemporary Arab–Islamic movement among those who sought to manifest Islam in a society ruled by an openly Islamic authority. But it must be emphasised here that no final crystallisation of the elements of the Brotherhood's understanding of Islam as a political system can be seen. The ideas of Hasan al-Banna and 'Abd al-Qadir 'Awdah represent the primary sources for this understanding; very little has been contributed by writers in the following twenty years. The novelty that might be encountered in an intellectual belonging to the Brotherhood, like Sayyid Qutb or Yusuf al-Qardawi, reflects a practical radicalism related to the application of principles more than to innovation in theoretical concepts.

As for Hasan al-Banna, his thought must be related to the prevailing climate in Egypt in the 1930s and 1940s, charged with political enmities, warring parties, British occupation and the strong current of Westernisation. In the speech which he addressed to the king of Egypt and the rulers of other Muslim countries in 1366 AH, the General Guide of the Muslim Brothers spoke of a dual task:

> The first is that of freeing the nation from its political shackles in order to attain its freedom and regain its lost independence and sovereignty, and the second is that of rebuilding it so that it can advance alongside other nations and rival them in the field of social perfections.

When he called on his audience to determine the path which they must take, he could envisage for them only two alternatives: 'The first is that of Islam, its principles, rules, culture and civilisation; the second is that of the West, its modes of life, its systems and styles.' Naturally, for him, 'the way of Islam and its rules and principles, is the only way we must take and to which we must guide the whole nation, now and in the future' (al-Banna, 1981: 274). He saw Islam as

a comprehensive system embracing all aspects of life: it is a state and a country, a government and a nation: it is morality, power, mercy and justice; it is culture, law, knowledge and legislation; it is material good, wealth, profit and richness; it is a struggle, a message for an army and an idea; in as much as it is a true doctrine and religion (ibid.: 256).

Islam alone is capable of rebuilding the unity of a nation shaken by a system of political party pluralism and infighting. In spite of the fact that al-Banna called for strengthening the relations between all Islamic countries, especially Arab ones, in preparation for serious and practical thinking about the issue of the lost Caliphate (ibid.: 290), he did not argue for the latter system. What really preoccupied him was the establishment of a genuine Islamic government. Islam does not accept chaos and does not permit the Islamic group to remain without a leader (imam). Anybody 'who thinks that religion, or more accurately, Islam, does not deal with politics or that politics is not of its concerns does injustice to himself and to his knowledge of Islam'. The Islamic state has a message that does not depend on the establishment of a static, dispirited administration or government, but on a state apparatus that 'protects, spreads, conveys and strengthens it'. The greatest mistake Muslims committed, lies in the fact that they forgot this foundation and separated religion from politics, although admitting the close connection between the two.

Al-Banna then turns to Egypt where the Constitution explicitly states that Islam is the state religion. But in his eyes this did not prevent politicians and leaders of political bodies from corrupting Muslim ideas, sensibilities, and tastes, by trying to drive a wedge between the instruction of religion and the requirements of politics. And this was the beginning of weakness and the source of corruption.

The solution lies in the establishment of an Islamic government based on the following foundations: responsibility of the ruler, social and spiritual unity of the nation within a fraternal framework, and respect for the nation's will and commitment to its opinion. A sound application of these rules creates a balanced society, and the function of the representative body of the nation is the observation and maintenance of these rules. This does not necessarily mean resorting to parties to operate this representation. For although parties are one of the bases of the parliamentary system, it is possible to bring about such a

THE STATE IN ARAB-ISLAMIC WRITINGS

system without parties, that is, through a limited representative electoral system where those who are elected and become the holders of real power are qualified persons, free from any pressure or control dictated by an external force, whose campaign claims are subject to moral criteria and restrictions, and where violators do not go unpunished (ibid.: 317–33).

Thus, Hasan al Banna comes conspicuously closer to the Western concept of democracy, so much so that he himself declares that there is nothing in the parliamentary system that contradicts the rules of the Islamic system of government. In that respect 'it is neither far from the Islamic system nor extraneous to it' (ibid.: 322). Even with regard to the question of the responsibility of the ruler, in al-Banna's opinion the element of Islam's doctrine that states that the head of state is responsible and, as al-Mawardi showed in *al-Ahkam as-Sultaniyyah*, can delegate power to others, has a counterpart in modern constitutions, especially in that of the United States.

Al Banna, however, contented himself with these few principles which later became the guide for the Muslim Brotherhood's political writers, at the forefront of which is 'Abd al-Qadir 'Awdah. Considered the greatest political theoretician of the Brotherhood, he was the first to dedicate a whole book to the political question, dealing with the matter of an Islamic government, its functions and characteristics; the Caliphate and its conditions; the consultative bodies (al-shura) and powers in the Islamic state (Jadaane, 1981: 363–72).

Who rules? This is the central question for 'Abd al-Qadir 'Awdah. The answer to it is not difficult: 'God rules and commands' and human beings, whom God has delegated, have no choice but to obey His command, refrain from what He prohibits, and resolve differences by reference to what He revealed, for their being delegated is subject to their abiding by the law of God. The Quran, which was revealed to His Prophet, was revealed to become the ultimate law of mankind, and whoever refrains from judging by what God revealed is an 'infidel', is 'unjust' or is disobedient to God ('Awdah, 1951: 55–9).

Rule is the unifying origin and it is supported in Islam, for Islam is not merely a doctrine but also a system, and it is not merely a religion but also a state. Every order in the Quran and the *Sunnah* requires, for its execution, the establishment of Islamic rule and an Islamic state. For Islam to become

257

established within the limits set by God and shown by the Messenger, it is required that an Islamic state be established that founds Islam within its set limits.

The application of most of the practical principles of Islam is not a matter for individuals but for governments, and this alone decisively shows that to rule is in the nature of Islam and its requirements and that Islam is a religion and a state. The ideal state in Islam is the state which subjects the worldly to the religious, 'Where religion cannot exist without the state, nor can the state be sound without religion' (ibid.: 68).

If governments originally arise for necessary social reasons, then it is imperative that they be Islamic. This does not mean that the rulers must be Muslims but they should refer to Islam and take the Quran as the 'constitution for rulers and ruled'. For the function of a government is 'to do what God commands' and to judge by what He revealed. It is obligatory for the ruled to obey their governments and those in charge as long as the latter obey God. If that is not the case, the ruled may renounce obedience to the government.

An Islamic government is unique and distinct with respect to three characteristics. The first is that it is a Quranic government, i.e. the Quran — the revealed Word of God — is its ultimate law. The second is that it is a government of shura limited by Islamic law. The third is that it is a Caliphate or imam government, in a sense which 'indicates a specific type of government', since the Caliphate, imamate and great imamate are synonyms denoting one thing, namely the higher presidency of the state and nothing more (ibid.: 72–7).

The government 'represents the community to bring it under God's law and to supervise its interests'. The Caliph or imam is 'the representative of the first government', thus, he represents the entire community in his capacity as Caliph and is instated by the community in order to represent it. 'His power is and always will be derived exclusively from his position as a representative of the community which instated him and has the right to check him and prevent him from stepping outside the limits of his representative position' (ibid.: 81).

The government of a Caliph is not complete unless chosen by the community, not only because choice is a logical or social necessity but also because the Quran imposed on Muslims to manage their affairs by consultation (shura).

Choosing a Caliph in this manner confirms that the Caliphate is no more than a representative contract ('*aqd niabah*) between the community and the Caliph, whereby the community entrusts the Caliph with transacting what God commands and managing its affairs within the limits of what God revealed. The Caliph, in turn, accepts to carry out such an assignment in accordance with God's commandments. So long as the Caliph does what God commands, he may remain in office indefinitely. If, however, he deviates from what God commands or develops some trait that requires deposition, then the community should be able to depose him from office and instate another in his place. When he dies, his reign ends with his death (ibid.: 81–2).

An Islamic government is therefore not an 'absolute dictatorship', because it is limited by the Quran as a constitution. Nor is it a 'legally-based government', that is, subject to human laws, for its edicts originate from God, are fixed and permanent and cater neither to the whims of the rulers nor to those of the ruled.

Although parliamentary governments in the world are based on some form of shura, it remains the case that shura in Islamic government is not similar to the one on which parliamentary governments are based (ibid.: 83).

And in spite of the fact that one of the functions of an Islamic government is to uphold religion,

it is not to be considered the kind of religious government that constitutional law calls theocratic. For an Islamic government does not derive its power from God but from the community. It does not achieve power or resign it without the community's decision. It is limited in all its actions by public opinion. This is so since Islam does not deprive people of their freedom of action nor does it reign over all their affairs. It leaves it to them to organize themselves and look after their private and general interests. The Quranic texts yield comprehensive judgements and general outlines for the way to govern and administer and leave what ranks below this to the men of power to organize in accordance with the laws they set (ibid.: 82–3).

Furthermore, the Islamic system of government differs from democracy in that 'it does not leave it to human beings to set the criteria determining the limits to justice, equality and the rest of human virtues', for Islam itself sets these higher criteria for human life. Even though the Islamic system is similar to the republican one with regard to the way the president of the republic is chosen, it differs from the latter in allowing a mandate for life. But it also differs from a monarchy in leaving it to the community to choose as ruler whoever they deem best and most able.

The Islamic system is therefore unique. Muslims did not put the Islamic system into effect after the death of the Prophet except during the era of the orthodox Caliphs, after which the system was transformed by individual whim into a formidable reign that did not hesitate to obstruct the application of Islamic rules. The state was, however, built on a sound basis during the era of the Prophet himself. Material power was built on spiritual power and the state was founded on the four basic pillars: people, political independence, land and sovereignty. Thus the existence of a state is not to be doubted even if we grant, for argument's sake, the absence in that state of internal procedures such as the appointment of judges and rulers, the existence of accounting offices and a proper budget, as well as the absence of any talk about the system of rule and the grounds for shura — to which some (and the reference is to 'Ali 'Abd al-Raziq) appealed to raise doubts about the existence of an Islamic state during the Messenger's time (ibid.: 97).

Following this, 'Abd al-Qadir 'Awdah gives a detailed and complete picture of the Islamic state through a discussion of the following three issues: the Caliphate or great imamhood, shura and the people's power, and the distribution of powers in the Islamic state.

On the Caliphate, his opinions do not, on the whole, deviate from what was determined by legal experts, Ibn Khaldun and the author of *al-Ahkam as-Sultaniyyah*. The function of the Caliphate is 'to uphold Islam', i.e. to uphold religious and state matters within the limits drawn by Islam, for the Caliphate 'as a presidential office, has wide powers ranging from the management of religious to worldly matters in the name of the Prophet'. Upholding it is a duty, neglecting it is a sin. It is 'rationally obligatory', as al-Iji claimed in *al-Mawaqif*. The conditions that must be met by a Caliph or an imam are: being a

Muslim, male, responsible, knowledgeable, just, competent, sound and a descendant of Quraysh. The last condition is controversial, 'Nothing, of course, can prevent the setting of other conditions if required by the general good', or 'the circumstances of life which vary with time'.

For the instatement of an imam in office, the only legitimate way is through choice by key powerful figures and the candidate's acceptance of the office. This amounts to a contract that takes the form of readiness and acceptance: readiness of the men of shura to choose a Caliph, and acceptance by the latter to serve in the office for which he has been chosen. 'Imama based on conquest, though approved by some Muslim legal theoreticians, has led to the worst kind of wrongs and to the division of the Muslims, weakening them and destroying the bases of Islam. Had those legal theoreticians foreseen these consequences, they would not have licensed it for a single moment'.

The same applies to acquiescence in the idea of regency as formulated by Mu'awiyah after the fashion of *istikhlaf* utilised by Abu Bakr to prepare the way for 'Umar to succeed him. Istikhlaf is nothing but an 'act of nomination' performed by the key powerful figures. The idea of regency, however, betrays the interests of the Islamic nation and deprives it of its right to choose rulers or remove them from office. To acquiesce in it is to acquiesce in a falsehood and to disobey God ('Awdah, 1951: 138).

The Caliph is an individual representing the nation. His power is derived from the fact that he represents the Islamic nation. His government is considered representative of the community and it is up to the people to widen or narrow the scope of the Caliph's power. If he deviates from majority opinion, then they no longer owe him obedience. It is in the Caliph's or great imam's power to ask the help of others to deal with the affairs of state in their capacity as ministers, directors, judges and officials of all kinds. Legally, they are considered empowered to speak for the nation and are not to be removed if the Caliph is removed from office or if he dies, as long as they do their job properly. The Caliph should not be treated as sacred, nor should he receive any special treatment. If he makes an error, there is nothing to absolve him from responsibility and thus he is subject to punishment like everybody else. His representation of the people in upholding Islamic law is not limited in time, and may last as long as he lives and is able to do his work and does nothing that requires his removal from office. That is, as long as he does nothing that could 'change his condition' in a way that reflects a loss of some of the traits which constituted the basis for his being chosen for the Caliphate. For example, if 'his justice is tarnished' or his 'body maimed' through the loss of senses or limbs, or if his behaviour is so affected that he loses control over things and becomes subject to others or subdued by an enemy with no chance of escape, his replacement could be considered.

Shura is a central pillar, not only of faith, but of Islamic rule in particular, and it is obligatory for the rulers and ruled. Legal experts have determined that it is one of the principles of Islamic law, and any ruler who rejects it ought to be removed from office. Shura, however, is not absolute, but limited by the provisions and spirit of Islamic legislation. It is to be applied only in cases where provisions are lacking and should not go beyond the limits of Islam. It is subject to certain rules: it is a determined right for the rulers and the ruled; it is one of the duties of the rulers but not one of their rights; it should be based on sincerity to God and a desire to elevate Islam; the opinion of the majority of consultants only and not a unanimity is required; the minority should follow the opinion of the majority. Thus, if shura were applied soundly, it would lead to the good of the world, and would help to avoid the failure that has afflicted democracies and dictatorships alike.

But, who, in fact, are the men of shura? They are figures of power and councillors of the Islamic nation, chosen from among those who are 'familiar with Islamic law, with the branches of knowledge, arts, crafts and other affairs pertaining to the interests of the nation'. The determination of their number and way of choosing them depends on circumstances, but they must satisfy requirements such as justice, knowledge in its widest sense, ability and wisdom. Their power is the power of the people themselves, because they in fact speak for the people and are the men of opinion and influence in the nation and the representatives of the nation's will. Rulers 'are committed to executing what is yielded by shura and to upholding it in the manner approved byt he representatives of the nation. The nation in this case is the source of their power' ('Awdah, 1951: 17).

There are five powers in the Islamic state (i) the executive power, at the top of which comes the head of state, i.e. the imam who holds it alone with those who assist him such as ministers and rulers, etc.; (ii) the legislative power which is held by those who have the ultimate say among the people, i.e. the imam and the councillors; (iii) the judiciary power which is represented by judges who are appointed by the imam in his capacity as a representative of the people; (iv) the financial power whose administrators are appointed, removed from office and supervised by the imam; (v) the power of observation and evaluation which is held by the people as a whole and involves observing and evaluating the rulers. Councillors, learned men and jurists represent the nation in this task.

FROM AL-BANNA TO AN-NABHANI

Several writers followed the line originally stated by Hasan al-Banna: writers like 'Abd al-Karim al-Khatib, Taha 'Abd al-Baqi Surur, Muhammad Yusuf Musa, Muhammad al-Mubarak and Yusuf al-Qardawi. These writers openly state that Islam is a religion and a state, that it is obligatory for a Caliph or imam to execute Islamic law, that the nation is the source of state power and sovereignty, that the function of an Islamic state is to act as the guardian of the faith and administrator of worldly policy, and that the Islamic system is unique: it is neither theocratic nor monarchic, it is merely Islamic (al-Khatib, 1963; Musa, 1964). Though these writers often come close to the democratic concept of the state, they are careful to renounce it in favour of the concept of a distinct system which constitutes a unique synthesis between the religious and the worldly. For this reason they do not hide their preference for the term Caliphate or imama in spite of their emphasis that what is intended is merely the presidency and politics conducted in accordance with the rules of Islamic law.

Muhammad al-Mubarak presents us with the final aspect of the Islamic system of government as seen by this group of theoreticians, an understanding that reaches its zenith in the writings of Abu al-A'la al-Mawdudi (al-Mawdudi, 1967). Muhammad al-Mubarak's central question is: does Islam itself, in what it basically teaches and requires, impose on its believers the task of establishing a state based on it? The answer is undoubtedly in the affirmative. All contexts indicate the necessity of such a state: the Quran contains rulings whose applications cannot be conceived without a state or political power adopting them — rulings covering matters such as restrictions, inheritance, *zakat*, the call to *jihad*, as well as rulings pertaining to the ruler himself and his subjects. Secondly, the general conception of existence in the Quran must find expression in a social and vital frame of reference that can safeguard and nourish it. This can only be achieved within the context of an Islamic state. Thirdly, there are many instances in *Hadith* that commit us to establishing rule; and, finally, the Prophet himself established a state, the preservation and continuity of which the Muslims have ensured, generation after generation (al-Mubarak, 1981: 12–18).

The purpose of establishing an Islamic state is 'the safeguarding of the principles of Islam, especially the doctrine of monotheism which is the positive way for liberating mankind and putting into effect Islamic laws to establish human society on a foundation of justice, cooperation, integration and higher moral ideals' (ibid.: 23).

The state of Islam is a doctrinal or ideological state, i.e. it has ideological concepts and principles forming its basic and ensuring the application of its fundamental norms pertaining to human dignity, equality the observance of Islamic legal edicts, the safeguarding of the principle of 'succession on earth' (*Istikhlaf fi al-Ard*) and fraternity in doctrine and faith (ibid.: 24–8).

Islam, however, does not impose a form of government that is well-defined and detailed. Rather, it represents 'general principles' and rules which constitute ideal goals that mankind aspires to achieve, leaving the details and practical applications that lie supported by these principles and rules for peoples' interpretation according to their various states, environments and circumstances (ibid.: 29, 52). The most prominent of these principles is the reference to the nation's opinion when instating a ruler or a head of state. It is for the people to determine the latter through a choice based on: a contract between them and the ruler; his acknowledgement of this; the commitment to the rules of Islamic law in matters where there are provisions and to interpretation ruled by shura where there is no provision; the principle of shura; the principle holding the ruler responsible before God and the people's right to judge, watch and criticise him; the principle of equality among people; justice; the rights of man, such as the right to protect oneself, one's honour, mind, possessions, morality and religion; the principle of mutual social responsibility; obedience to the ruler in exchange for his abiding by Islamic law and by whatever is of interest to the Muslims (ibid.: 29–50). Al-Mubarak's use of the term 'Caliphate system' to refer to the Islamic system of government should not be understood to mean more than a reference to the presidency of the state along Islamic lines, i.e. 'basic principles found in Islam in its two main sources: the Quran and Sunnah and whatever the learned Muslims in every age have deduced in the field of government and the state' (ibid.: 50).

Al-Mubarak mentions three component parts of the state: the authority or governmental apparatus over which the head of state presides; the people governed by this authority; and the territory within which the rule of this authority prevails. In dealing with the tasks of the head of state and the conditions for choosing him, he follows al-Mawardi as referred to by 'Abd al-Qadir 'Awdah. He adopts the modern distinction between the legislative, the judiciary, and the executive power (ibid.: 79–85). Then he follows Ibn Hanbal and Ibn Taymiyyah with regard to the question of the function of the state. He confines that function to 'ensuring internal security and external defence, establishing legal justice, achieving financial and economic sufficiency for the individual and society; spreading the doctrine of Islam through jihad and safeguarding it against any deviant behaviour' — that is what he calls 'the doctrinal-ethical' function — and installing men to run the affairs of the state who are characterised by ability and loyalty.

For al-Mubarak the nation, in the Islamic sense, is 'a human society based on common beliefs' (ibid.: 100). He affirms that this involves a 'humanistic concept' in contrast with the 'backward', 'static', nationalistic concept of a nation, one that perfectly agrees with the prevalent tendency in today's world to renounce nationalistic groupings in favour of ones based on ideas and ideological systems. Now, the nation as a basis for the state has rights protected by the state, for rulers simply 'speak for' or 'represent' the nation. And the nation, i.e. the people, holds the power, although it is not a legislative power except with regard to matters of opinion and *ijtihad* not determined by the original sources of Islamic law. As far as the individual is concerned, the state offers him the right to life and self-preservation, the right to own and profit, the right to equality, to personal freedom of belief, thought, opinion, criticism and to political freedom (ibid.: 115–24). These types of freedom remain limited for him by the principle prohibiting deviation from the ideology of the state or advocacy of a different and opposite ideology, for this would amount to an act of civil disobedience against the state and a call to rise against it and remove its Islamic character. Those who renounce Islam, its ideology and its law have no choice but to refrain from identifying with a state based on it and a society that believes in it and grounds its solidarity in it, and must identify instead with a different state and a different society (ibid.: 117). Any freedom practised in the Islamic state should not deviate from the criteria set by Islam nor should it conflict with the basic teaching which the state is entrusted with upholding, namely that of advocating Islam in all areas of social life.

With regard to the state territory, which is the third component of the state, al-Mubarak adopts the old distinction between *Dar al-Islam* and *Dar al-Kufr*, namely 'the home of Islam' and 'the home of disbelief' and considers the two mutually exclusive. People belonging to the latter are either in a 'state of truce or peace' with the Muslims because of some treaty they concluded with them, or in a 'state of war', thereby making their Dar al-Kufr *Dar-Harb*, namely 'the home of war'. Acquisition of territory by the Islamic state is effected by two means: either the people of that territory convert to Islam, while remaining on it and thus transform the territory to Dar-Islam, or the territory is conquered by the Muslims and subjected to Islamic rule. The state and individuals have to protect the borders of this Dar by force, and Muslims have a duty to live within its boundaries and not to live in Dar al-Kufr except for accidental reasons (ibid.: 135–6).

Al-Mubarak concludes that the Islamic state has the following defining characteristics: the state in Islam is an ideology, as well as a system of laws emanating from the latter. The Islamic state is not to be described as either religious or civil, but could be 'described as jointly religious and civil' or neither, since it is a unique system. The Islamic state is also a humanistic and moral state that does not aim to prevail over others or to accumulate wealth or military glory, but at liberating man from all forms of enslavement and binding him by a higher bond, namely 'submission to God alone and the upholding of justice for all people'. The Islamic state is, furthermore, a state of culture, engaging in various activities, of an educational, practical, material, intellectual and psychological nature. It is a humanistic and worldly state. Finally, it is a state with solid foundations and forms that evolve with the evolution of social and cultural conditions (ibid.: 137–44). One can, in fact, hardly distinguish between the position of 'political advocates' and that of the learned men of religion (Ghoshah, 1971).

The picture of religious radicalism we have been presenting would not be complete without considering the basic contributions made by an active Palestinian intellectual in Jerusalem in the early 1950s. This is Taqi ad-Din an-Nabhani, who founded a political party in the true sense of the word, aiming openly at establishing an Islamic state, restoring the Caliphate and declaring unrelenting war against all established political systems in the Arab world. The party he established is the Islamic Liberation Party (Hizb at-Tahrir al-Islami) which is, practically and theoretically, the counterpart of the Muslim Brotherhood.

Nabhani's early writings and pamphlets go back to 1952. His first book was entitled *ad-Dawlah al-Islamiyyah*, and was published one year after 'Awdah's book *al-Islam wa Awda'una as-Siasiyyah*. In it, Nabhani presented a preliminary and general outline for an Islamic system of government. The same year he published another book entitled *Nizam al-Hukm fi al-Islam*, in which he defined in complete detail the nature of this system in all its organisational aspects. No sooner had the latter appeared than he presented us with another, *Nizam al-Islam*, in which he went further by including a chapter devoted mainly to detailing the system's prospective constitution. This constitution contains ninety-nine articles, the first fourteen of which are general rules. The book in its entirety represents the first complete scheme for a state and its system, i.e. the first to appear in contemporary Islamic thought. It is one that agrees with most of 'Awdah's ideas, but it is better defined, more concise, clear, complete and radical. Besides the fact that an-Nabhani's ideas have, since the 1950s, been the distinguishing ideas of the propagandists of his party which spread widely in the Arab Near East (Palestine, Jordan, Syria, Lebanon and Iraq), it is certain that these ideas also had a clear influence on a number of Muslim Brotherhood thinkers like Sayyid Qutb, al-Mubarak and others. This was so in spite of the differences between these two movements with regard to their methods. Whereas one sees the starting point for achievement of a

267

renaissance in the transformation of thought and concepts through the establishment of a state, the other sees that starting point in a process of comprehensive moral, educational and religious transformation, i.e. in a behavioural transformation of the individual.

An-Nabhani affirms that Islam brought the world new concepts about the universe, man, life, and values which completely overturned old concepts. It imposed on Muslims not only the necessity of committing themselves to new concepts, but also of changing the old concepts of the rest of the people through the spreading of the doctrine of Islam. The primary task of Muslims, in fact, is the advocacy and furthering of the message of Islam, and the highest ideal is God's approval of their work. This approval can be obtained only if their work is directed at 'guiding the whole of humanity to Islam'. But that can be done only through domination or power based on it, and this power is the Islamic state. That is what

> the task of the Islamic state has been from the first moment of its inception and will be until the day of Judgement: applying Islam and conveying its message to the world until it is universally accepted. It is this that makes Muslims the leaders of the world and the Islamic state, through Islam's fulfilment of the necessary requirements for worship and happiness, one which leads the world to good and happiness (an-Nabhani, 1952: 36).

The states that rule the world today, according to an-Nabhani, whether capitalist or socialist, are grounded in a purely materialistic mentality, making it possible for the culture of materialism to dominate mankind. Because of this, mankind has undergone 'spiritual crises' that have caused destructive psychological misery and evil to spread everywhere. 'For this reason it is necessary, in order to save the world, to have a state established on a spiritual basis' combining spirit with matter, making it possible for the culture of spiritualism to dominate life. The Islamic state is the only way to achieve this great accomplishment, and herein lies the necessity of its establishment.

Moreover, Muslims today are in a state of backwardness, degradation and remoteness from the teachings of Islam, and they are 'subject to the system of Kufr in their own country.

They are subject to its rulings, are controlled by the culture of materialism, and their Dar (home), from the perspective of Islamic law, is Dar Kufr and not Dar Islam.' Thus, it is 'imperative for them to bring about the Islamic state, to be subjected to the rulings of Islam' and to instate a Caliph as the head of state to fulfil what is required by Islamic law and reason.

> What has to be done in the way of setting limits and filling gaps cannot be done without the Caliph. Governing in accordance with the requirements of revelation as well as bringing what is beneficial to the people and warding off what is unbeneficial cannot be done without him (ibid.: 152).

Muslims are all sinners until they establish the Islamic state and officially inaugurate its head. What is meant here is not an Islamic state in name or in abstract, but one that applies the rulings of Islam in so far as it is a system emanating from the Islamic ideology and saturated with the Isalmic idea, the Islamic spirit and the Islamic mentality. With this,

> life's motivating forces will be reborn from inside the soul, and a mental, psychological and social environment that can guarantee Islamic legislation and laws will exist and effect a total and not a gradual transformation towards a perfect Islamic existence (ibid.: 156).

Nobody can deny that Islam is a religion requiring a state or claim that the Islamic state is a purely spiritual one or that religion in Islam is something other than the state. Islamic law openly calls for the necessity of establishing a rule and a dominion. The verses of the Quran constitute straightforward evidence that Islam should lead to a state and that government ought to be in accordance with God's revelation. Further, the Quran has legislated matters pertaining to wars, politics, criminal behaviour and social and civil activities.

Islamic rule, in an-Nabhani's opinion, rests on four bases: the first is the predominance of Islamic law; the second, that government should be by the people; the third, that instating one Caliph for all Muslims, to represent the people in government, is an obligation of the people; the fourth, that the people have the right to ijtihad and to propose the legal rulings required to deal with the problems of life. But the right to legis-

269

late belongs to the Caliph and not to the people, for it is up to him 'to choose what legal rulings from among the statements of the practitioners of ijtihad should be binding on judges and rulers; it is up to him to deduce rulings through a correct ijtihad and make them binding on his followers' (ibid.: 83).

At any rate, shura is a right that the Caliph owes to all Muslims. He owes it to them to turn to them whenever consultation is necessary in matters concerning them (ibid.: 16). Given the extreme importance of shura, an-Nabhani considers the Council of Councillors (*Majlis ash-shura*) to which the Caliph refers concerning national matters, the first of the seven pillars of the state. The rest are: the head of state, the executive body (the assistants), the administrative appratus, the rulers (*wulat*), the judiciary and the army. All of these, he asserts, were established by the Prophet himself as a part of his organisational structure of the Islamic state.

What attracts attention in this structure is that the members of the Council of shura should be elected and not appointed, for they 'speak for the people and represent individuals and groups in their countries and areas. Every citizen of the state, whether man or woman, Muslim or non-Muslim, may become a member of the Council of shura' (ibid.: 20). The functions of this council are: giving an opinion on legislation; acting as a check on the government, the rulers and the Caliph's assistants; discussing matters of government with the Caliph and judging the way he conducts these matters. The Muslim Council members have the power to nominate the Caliph whom the nation elects and instates. The head of state is the one

> who rules and executes the law on behalf of the people. He is the one who puts legal rulings into effect, that is, makes them law. He is the one who runs and conducts the affairs of the nation. But he is neither the symbol of the latter nor the source of its powers; he is simply the executor of God's law. His presidency is not to be recognised unless it is conferred on him by the nation. He ought to be obeyed only within the limits of the law (ibid.: 29).

The head of state has wide powers within the limits of the law: he is the one who appoints the members of the executive branch and all branches of government except the shura Council. He also renders legal rulings binding by adopting them. He prepares the state budget, and declares war, makes peace, concludes treaties and conducts all matters pertaining to foreign policy.

> To give the head of state all these wide powers does not at all mean that he is sacred or has a divine right, for he does not rule on behalf of God but on behalf of the people, and all of the people have the right to judge him. To be a Caliph does not mean to be either a dictator or a saint (ibid.: 38–9).

His term of office is indefinite. He can, in fact, stay in office as long as he works at executing the law and does not violate it, otherwise he ought to be deposed. 'He can be deposed through a legal ruling issued by a legal body, namely the court dealing with injustices.' This court can rule on the question of whether or not he has adhered to Islam and can determine what is a sufficient basis for deposing him.

> If he were not to submit to the ruling of this court, he would be considered disobedient to God and the Muslims would be required to depose him because their original approval of his instatement in office would no longer be binding on them (ibid.: 41).

An-Nabhani feels that the system of regency adopted by Mu'awiyah is contrary to Islam. Abu Bakr did not confer regency on 'Umar. The latter was elected by the people while the head of state was still alive and was then officially instated in office (ibid.: 115).

In dealing in detail with all important aspects of the state, an-Nabhani always draws inspiration from the Age of the Prophet and from *al-Ahkam as-Sultaniyyah*, and he uses some modern legal terms in the manner of 'Abd al-Qadir 'Awdah. His ideas on the state are crystallised in a proposal for a constitution whose articles are relative to the nature of the system of government and seven essential bases (articles 15–99); the social system of the state (articles 100–10); the economic system (articles 111–57); educational policy (articles 158–69); and foreign policy (articles 170–82) (ibid.: 80–113). He winds up by repeating that the system is founded on a spiritual basis: the Islamic ideology. Morals, then, are not the basis of society but

271

the effects of the application of the system and Islam in general (ibid.: 114–15).

But how is the Islamic state to be established? The only way to resume the Islamic way of life, in his opinion, and to establish the Islamic state, is 'to transmit Islamic teachings' to all areas and societies, to educate societies in the right Islamic concepts and to have the advocates of Islam interact with their societies to create a general awareness of Islam among public opinion. This interaction can thus be transformed into a 'militant movement' aimed at establishing an Islamic state, exactly in the way the Messenger went about it when he established the first Islamic state. This means looking for a territory that can be used as a starting point from which to spread the doctrine to other Islamic areas and to develop the great Islamic state that is to convey the message of Islam to the world (ibid.: 162). Conveying this message requires bringing up an Islamic intellectual leadership that is at once strong, straightforward and daring, ready to challenge any situation or concept opposing Islam and relentlessly to apply Islam to the letter, with no sign of neglect or slackening or tendency to compromise with anybody on any matter pertaining to Islamic teachings (ibid.: 56).

The nation, which constitutes the practical means on earth of putting Islam into effect, by checking on and judging the ruler, needs to have a smaller group exhibiting a profound understanding of Islam and a strong fear of God, one that will work at providing the people with an intensive Islamic education aimed at building the Islamic character of the nation. This group is the 'party of principles' that arises on the basis of Islam, making advocacy its only task. Thus the real guarantee for the application of Islam and its advocacy and application is an Islamic political party (ibid.: 122). This leading party of the nation acts as a monitor to the state and as the advocate of Islamic principles, for the way to advocate the latter is through politics (ibid.: 121).

To achieve such a goal, the Islamic Liberation Party was established in 1952 and followed a radical line in its political advocacy of the re-establishment of the Islamic state. In its merciless criticism of the Arab political establishment, it brought on itself equally merciless harassment. Together with other reasons that cannot be detailed here, the party gradually weakened but did not totally disappear.

An-Nabhani's ideas had a substantial effect on the thought of a very prominent intellectual of the Brotherhood, namely Sayyid Qutb. Qutb began his career, after his initiation into the Brotherhood, by concerning himself with the question of social justice in Islam. He soon hit upon the role of the elite in bringing about the process of change. He also discovered that the principle of God's rule, on which the entire Islamic system is based, cannot be realised merely by upholding the creed and practising worship within 'the organic existence of the dynamic association of a pre-Islamic nature that in fact exists' (Qutb, n.d.: 65). What is required for its realisation is the actual existence of Islam. And this does not come about through individuals who are Muslims only in theory, but through 'the representation of the theoretical base of Islam, i.e. the creed, in a dynamic, organic association that is from the first moment . . . separate and independent from the dynamic pre-Islamic organic association that Islam aims at abolishing'. The new association should be centered around a new leadership that will turn people to the divinity of God alone, to the fact that he is 'the Lord, the Prince, the Ruler, the Possessor of power and the Law-giver' and confine their loyalty to the new Islamic dynamic, organic association (ibid.: 65–7). The aim of this Muslim leadership is to put an end to any attempt at reconciliation with the pre-Islamic concepts prevalent on earth and the pre-Islamic countries existent everywhere and 'to move people from *jahiliyya* to Islam. The choice is between Islam or jahiliyyah, the rule of God or the rule of jahiliyyah.' However well-intentioned they may be, pre-Islamic societies cannot pursue solutions to their problems through Islamic law, because their society is not ruled by Islam.

Besides giving signs of the dissent within the Brotherhood as to how its advocacy should be carried out, a split also manifested by the *Jama'at al-Muslimin* group was unveiled in Egypt in 1980. Its ideas constitute a straightforward rejection of any 'moderate, middle ground' position, such as accepting the principles of Islamic law as a main source of legislation or the constitution. This is expressed by another radical writer, namely Yusuf al-Qardawi, when he states that the 'Islamic solution' aspired to specifically means the establishment of an Islamic state or purely Islamic rule which has in Islamic legislation its 'one and only guide' and 'reference' for all its rulings (al-Qardawi, 1974: 82). The Islamic solution is one 'that adapts all conditions and systems to the rulings of Islam and not one that adapts the rulings of Islam to conditions and systems' (ibid.: 95).

BETWEEN 'ABD AL-RAZIQ AND TWENTIETH-CENTURY *SALAFIYYA* IS A SYNTHESIS POSSIBLE?

From a dialectical perspective, thesis and antithesis cannot endure radical opposition for long. There must be a fresh starting point in which the two extremes are blended and possibly transcend their mutual contradiction. On the one hand then, there was the thesis of 'Ali 'Abd al-Raziq which reduced religion to the realm of spirit, pushing politics away from its domain. On the other hand, the opposite thesis conjoined politics with spirituality and went on to consider the restoration of the Islamic state and the Caliphate as necessary maxims not subject to compromise. A mediating synthesis inevitably emerged to overcome this opposition. It took two main lines, of which I call the first legislative and the other humanistic.

The seed of the legislative attitude goes back to 'Ali Abu al-Futuh who argued in 1905 that the established principles of Islamic shari'ah are appropriate for modern times, marked by civilisation and development. He held that the norms and precepts of modern secular law have counterparts in the fundamentals of Islam (al-Futuh, 1905: 5–6). 'Abd al-'Aziz Jawish laid emphasis on the same notion and professed, perhaps for the first time, that Islam is valid for every time and place (Jawish, n.d.: 45). This attitude matured in the hands of the famous professor of law, 'Abd al-Razzaq as-Sanhuri and appeared, in one respect, at odds with the radical theory of 'Ali 'Abd al-Raziq. One year after the 1936 treaty between Egypt and Britain, as-Sanburi called for recourse to Islamic law in order to modify previous Egyptian legislation. The former was to be considered a source and should not be abandoned as had been the case a century earlier. He also stressed the fact that a number of precepts in Islamic shari'ah go beyond Western laws. Professor as-Sanhuri seems to have no doubts that Islam is both religion and state and that the state must have a kind of jurisprudence upon which to depend in forging its own laws. He refers in this connection to Muslim *fiqh* which considers the Quran and prophetic tradition its higher sources. The cardinal principle chosen by as-Sanhuri for this proposed law is that it should be based on the fiqh in such a way that it accords with civilisation and the spirit of the age.

It must be purely Islamic jurisprudence with regard to its logic, form and style, and not a mere imitation of Western law. It should not deviate from the shari'ah principles, assuming that evolution entails this departure. Hence, shari'ah being dependent upon ijtihad and consensus (*ijma'*), is fertile to the degree that it can meet all factors of evolution (Jadaane, 1981: 355–6).

In 1939, the lawyer Ahmed Husayn also called for the re-vision of constitutional laws in the light of Islamic shari'ah, maintaining that Islam is the source of legislation. Along this line, in 1940 the Iraqi 'Abd al-Rahman al-Bazzaz condemned those who disown shari'ah from the constitution of their country and confirmed the doctrine that Islamic legislation copes with evolution and does not deny canonical change. It is distinct from other modern laws and goes beyond them, thanks to its intrinsic merits. The way to overcome the inferiority afflicting the Arab–Muslim nation is by establishing a strong modern state that believes in Islamic morals: a Muslim state without priesthood; a socialist state without extremisms, like communism. It should be a consultative state, free of the hypocrisy of democratism and immune to anarchy (Jadaane, 1981: 361–2). Al-Bazzaz recognised that establishing such unity was difficult and that the position of the Caliph could possibly become simi-lar to that of the Pope in Catholic Christianity, which would be unacceptable to the Muslim community. In addition, the Caliphate, despite its deep roots as an Islamic system, is among the precepts of religion which are liable to change and replace-ment by another system when agreed upon by the nation, for shura and the consensus of the nation form the basis in this question (ibid.: 363).

'Allal al-Fasi, the historic leader of the Istiqlal Party in Morocco, agrees in general terms with the thesis of al-Bazzaz. He condemns what he stigmatises as the new *Isra'iliyyat* which appeared when 'ali 'Abd al-Raziq called for the isolation of the state from religion. Al-Fasi stresses that religion cannot be put outside the domain of socio-political life, for such a separation would imply the estrangement of 'the highest ideal which Islamic shari'ah lays down for people', and that is 'the realization of the divine will to build life on this earth and achieve justice among people' (al-Fasi, n.d. 157). This means that legislation in the state necessarily stems from the spirit of Islamic shari'ah and its rules. In other words, the Muslim must produce the laws which he is to obey, making use, in particular, of the general rules of *istihsan* and *masalih mursalah* which open the door to legislative progress (ibid. 159).

The serious role in legislation assigned by al-Fasi to the Muslim individual is a counterpart to another role, no less serious, in the relationship between the state and nation. For if God enjoys the ultimate sovereignty and order in the ruling system, then it is equally true that political and practical sovereignty is left to the people who are entitled to elect and dismiss legislators and members of the government. In a word, ordinance is for God, power is for the nation. The constitution of the state must be in accordance with the principles and rules of the shari'ah (ibid.: 38, 315–16).

The state is Islamic when its laws conform to the shari'ah or when they derive, partially or totally, from its maxims and rules. This point was well discussed by 'Abd al-Hamid Mutawalli, a professor of constitutional law, when he confronted a controversial item in the Egyptian Constitution, namely whether 'the basic rules of the Islamic shari'ah are the only source of legislation' or 'are just a source among others' (Mutawalli, 1977).

Professor Mutawalli naturally addressed two other questions first, namely, is Islam a religion and a state as well, and is there a system of government in Islam: Caliphate or otherwise? His answer to the first question is a compromise between the two well-known contrasting opinions: firstly, that of 'Ali 'Abd al-Raziq holding that Islam is only a religion, and secondly, the doctrine which maintains that Islam is both a religion and a state. Mutawalli finds that both doctrines tend to exaggeration and inaccuracy. To put the question in the form, is Islam a religion and a state, is erroneous. To answer it negatively would lead to a fallacy and the denial of historical facts, whereas to give an affirmative answer would encourage the belief that Islam came with a complete ruling system and this is, in fact, uncertain. A valid question would be whether Islam contains the general basis for a ruling system in the state. There can be no dispute about this. The Quran professed shura, freedom, equality, justice and other principles pertaining to government. Such principles are valid for all humanity, irrespective of time and place. The Quran introduces them in general terms, i.e. they are pliable in form and content, susceptible to modifications according to the sort of milieu and age in which they are to be applied. In this connection, the Quran does not disclose details nor particular facts; there is no mention in it of the forms of principles, which could vary with time and place (ibid.: 104 5).

Thus, the final answer given by Mutawalli is that Islam is a religion and a state, not based on a specific system of government, but on general principles of government, applicable in various times and places. The Caliphate system is not a principle of government in Islam, but only one form, and particularly a form providing a head of state (ibid.: 153). Its concern is not with faith, but with temporal jurisprudence (ibid.: 152). The instatement of a Caliphate (in the form visualised by Islamic jurisprudence experts) is considered to be in our time, like consensus, a virtual impossibility. Moreover, the establishment of such a system in our day and age would lead to an embarrassment which Islam would rather see the Muslims spared (ibid.: 163).

But coming back to the question which aroused a good deal of argument, namely, whether the principles of shari'ah form 'the main source of legislation' or only 'one main source', Mutawalli finds that these principles are capable of development and can meet the needs of people and of sound government under varied temporal and geographical conditions. As sublime principles, capable of building up a great civilisation and of filling the needs of legislation and culture, they demand adoption as the basis for the constitution (ibid.: 245). Mutawalli finds that this formula leaves room for reference to other legal sources in planning legislation for the modern state. In my opinion, it is an inclination towards the legislative tendency which is an attempt to follow a middle course between the two sides in dispute: Islam as a religion and Islam as a religion and a state.

The other aspect of the thesis and the antithesis is what I call the humanistic aspect. This is represented by Muhammad Ahmad Khalafallah in a book published (in Arabic) in 1973 entitled *The Quran and the State*, and by Muhammad 'Amarah in his *Islam and Religious Power*. Both men are of the opinion that Islam does not carry a specific political system. The former believes that questions of government are left by God's authorisation to man and his commitment to public good. The latter calls for a distinction, not a separation, between religion and state in Islam and the feels government should be left in the hands of man. Both opinions lead to the view that the state is national in nature, committed to the rulings of shari'ah, but that, in the human field, legislation is effected through the will and power of the community.

On the question of 'the Quranic state', Muhammad Ahmad Khalafallah has this to say:

Concerning the formation of the nation and the establishment of the state, the Holy Quran draws only broad guidelines which safeguard against error and guide along the right path, the path of right, justice and public good. The Holy Quran has left to man the details and things affected by time and place (Khalafallah, 1973: 3–4).

The root of this opinion is that Islam is based on two major elements: religious faith and actual practice. The former is concerned with belief in one God, his Angels, Books, Messengers and the Day of Judgement. It is a permanent state of belief, not liable to change. Actual practice has two aspects: a religious life represented by acts of worship, performed in accordance with what God demanded of man after some deleterious aspects of earlier religions were abolished and the sound ones endorsed by Islam; and a civil life represented by matters that are changeable because they are connected with man who is not eternal or everlasting, but changeable (ibid.: 33).

The aim of Islam is to purify souls and rid minds of superstition, to liberate man from man, clearing the hearts of people to help them behave well in life and achieve perfection and happiness, so that the nation will be 'the best nation among mankind'. This depends on its ability to order the doing of good and the prevention of evil, i.e. the realisation of public good or the good of humanity.

Khalafallah asserts that the legislative institution set up by the Prophet was fully committed to the system of shura defined by the Quran ('and consult them in matters'). He also points out that

in the time of the Prophet, there were two powers of legislation: that of the Creator, and that of the Prophet and the aldermen of Islam. Each of these powers had its own field of action. That of divine power was in portraying divinity, explaining religious beliefs and marking what is religiously taboo or otherwise; the field of human power, in the hands of the Prophet and his aldermen, dealt with questions of religion, politics, economics, administration, security and war (ibid.: 58).

Religious questions are a divine affair in which human beings have no say. Worldly questions, on the other hand, such as the policies of the nation, are delegated by God to Muslims on the basis of a consultative government committed to realising the public good in a framework of justice, equality and common interest: the shura system. By delegating this system to them, 'He has given us full freedom and independence in our worldly affairs and social interests' (ibid.: 68).

Legislative power lies with the councillors and aldermen, that is, the legislative body which the nation freely chooses on the basis of general elections, in which some members represent constituencies while others are chosen by technical and professional institutions. These free individuals, chosen by the nation, form a People's Council which ought to be obeyed in matters of common interest. Its authority is limited to worldly affairs. As for questions of worship and religious beliefs, these matters concern God and his Messenger alone (ibid.: 75).

The question of choosing the head of state is left to the Muslim community to decide according to circumstances. That is to say, it is a question of ijtihad (ibid.: 134), which divine will does not touch. To Khalafallah's mind, the way of reaching the position of head of state is by election or choice, not appointment or regency in the manner of the Umayyads. The selection of the head of state by the majority of citizens in a public election is the best way to ensure stability of government. This would make revolt by the minority an unlikely event. To name the head of state Caliph or imam is a temporal consideration. It is our right to give the head of state whatever name we see fit in accordance with our own stage of civilisation. This is acceptable in religion, as it does not violate any text.

The Quranic state is a welfare state, concerned with directing the life of every member in the human community towards the achievement of public good, irrespective of sex, race, language or religion.

This is realised through land development and the use of its products to help the people. By changing the world and using it for the benefit of the people, it is possible to achieve a religious tie between God and man, represented from the beginning by the principle of Caliph delegation.

To say that the Quranic state is a welfare state also means it is a state based on equality, 'realising a large integration in the Islamic community at the expense of the rich for the benefit of the poor and needy' (ibid.: 173) and using the human mind and its readiness to build sovereignty and civilisation.

In the final analysis, how does Khalafallah's attitude differ from that of 'Ali 'Abd al-Raziq? Does he really make an attempt to mediate between 'Abd al-Raziq's thesis and its antithesis? It seems to me that there is a difference between the two which does not lie only in the peaceful, pious method of presentation which Khalafallah chooses, quite different from 'Abd al-Raziq's provocative method. The main difference lies in the face that Khalafallah recognises that the Quran laid out the guidelines of a government system and that God delegated to man the working out of the details. This is a new and novel idea, which cannot be found outside Khalafallah's thought. In all cases, it means that the rulings of the People's or Nation's Council, which represents the majority, are divine rulings and that the legislative body, whether we like it or not, speaks in the name of God. Perhaps this is the conciliatory point in Khalafallah's writings.

It is obvious that Muhammad Ahmad Khalafallah, in his *Quran and the State*, tried to avoid the pitfalls of 'Ali 'Abd al-Raziq's theory and did his best to get round them. Moreover, a close look at a later article by him, published in the *al-'Arabi* monthly, seems to indicate that he is aiming an answer at the new radical Islamic groups which demand a Caliphate system. This makes it difficult to see a real difference of opinion between the two men. In this article, Khalafallah frankly distinguishes between the system of prophethood and that of Caliphate. It is the same distinction previously made by Ibn Khaldun between Caliphate and kingship. Khalafallah considers prophethood a religious system, and asserts that it cannot in any way be a system of government: Muhammad the son of 'Abdullah was a prophet and a messenger of God and not a king or a head of state (an idea already presented by 'Ali 'Abd al-Raziq).

The Caliphate is a system of government which can take forms that are suitable for modern times. But the Caliphate system cannot be a religious system since there is no text to support it. Its source is ijtihad, which means that the human mind is the author of the Caliphate system. If the government system in Islam has its source in ijtihad and not in a text, then the system is open to new ijtihad, since, as purely human reasoning, it is always liable to reconsideration. Therefore, religious groups should abandon the idea that the Caliphate is a religious system of government, and accept that the system of government in Islam is liable to new interpretations and ijtihad (Khalafallah, 1984: 41–5).

Turning to Muhammad 'Amarah, we find that he is not far in his reasoning on this question from the ideas of Khalafallah. His main concern is to separate political power from religious aspects ('Amarah, 1980), to strip the ruler of the sanctity and infallibility implied in endorsing religious power (or the supremacy of the fiqh after the Shi'i style), and to emphasise the principle that power belongs to the nation only. He is adamant that the Islamic political heritage should distinguish between politics and religion, between a political group and a group of believers (ibid.: 111–12) and that anything beyond spreading the religious message is no longer religion but a form of politics, subject to reason, meditation and interpretation (ibid.: 131). He feels that Imam Qarafi decided upon this question by fully describing the distinction between the worldly and the religious, the judicial and the political.

He asserts that the theory of religious power is alien to Islam and that it penetrated Shi'i Islamic thought through the Persian Xerxian heritage (ibid.: 133). The new advocates of religious power among contemporary Muslims want the Islamic nation to inherit the backwardness, the despotism and the darkness which the Persians, the Byzantines and the Europeans suffered throughout the Middle Ages. Muhammad 'Amarah attacks the motto: rule is God's alone, saying that it deprives the nation of its political sovereignty (ibid.: 40) and Muslims of their human will. By offering rulers a divine right over them, it sets up a theocratic government, as desired by al-Mawdudi (ibid.: 46), and gives undue credence to the Shi'i vision of politics.

The real Islamic attitude, in 'Amarah's opinion, is that a separation of religion from the state in as much to be rejected as a union between religious and political powers. To draw a distinction between the two is a sound attitude. Islam, as a religion, has not specified a definite system of government for the Muslims, because that is left to be developed according to public interests and in the general frame of reference of the comprehensive rules set up by this religion (ibid.: 82). For him, the Islamic attitude boils down to two principles: the first is religion, revealed to us in the Quran, which we have to receive in a spirit of faith, with the help of the prophetic tradition and our own reason (which is God's agent in man); the second is what is worldly, judicial and political. These principles have to be dealt with through interpretation (ijtihad) and reasoning, provided the criterion and aim are the interests of the entire nation and the avoidance of possible harm, within the framework of the general directives and comprehensive rules prescribed by the Quran (ibid.: 17–18) and in the light of supreme human rules and ideals which may bring the Muslims closer to the achievement of the community they desire (ibid.: 18 and 83).

It is quite obvious that a rational human tendency influences 'Amarah's thought and that a preoccupation with the New Islam advocates who follow Khumayni and the Iranian Islamic revolution lurks behind his critique of religious power and his effort to disentangle Islam from any attempt to impose a uniquely radical religious character on its social and political systems and institutions. His view that reason is God's agent in man is comparable to Khalafallah's theory that God authorises man to implement worldly laws and systems.

In any case, one can finally say that the third alternative, generally speaking, is more acceptable to enlightened Muslims in modern times. It is an attitude which avoids the extremes of temporal radicalism, on the one hand, and saves Islam from slipping into the labyrinth of adventurous experiments on the other. It is also a natural attitude for states based on Islamic communities that cherish an Islamic heritage. Undoubtedly, radical Muslims may see in this attitude a type of leniency which should not be allowed. But the fact is that this question will always remain open to discussion and interpretation, especially when viewed in its highly complex framework, and when the paths of action taken are strewn with fatal dangers. I may finally add that what is more important than forming an Islamic state and what should come prior to any consideration is to provide the educational, spiritual, intellectual, economic and social conditions needed to implement the terms of humanistic Islamic life. The road to that objective is undoubtedly long, but to take a short cut preferred by our ideal desires may not be the best way to reach 'the cursed tree' and climb it. A union between the formula of 'no salvation except through the Islamic state' and the other formula of 'no salvation except through Islam' is, undoubtedly, a dangerous indication of impatience rather than a response to the real requirements of Islamic revelation.

11

Arab Regimes: Legitimacy and Foreign Policy

Adeed Dawisha

When a regime embarks on foreign activity, the analyst can usually uncover a variety of motivating factors. In this, the analysis of Arab politics is no different from the analysis of politics in any other international regime. One can list a number of political, ideological, economic and geo-strategic reasons for Syria's decision to intervene in Lebanon and for its consciously anti-American policies, for Iraq's invasion of Iran in September 1980, for the support accorded to revolutionary groups such as the Palestinians and Eritreans by the conservative regime of Saudi Arabia, for Morocco's active pursuit of its claims on the Western Sahara, and for Libya's interventionist activities in Africa and the Middle East. However, one factor which has always been, and continues to be a potent motivating force of foreign policy in Arab politics is the effort by Arab regimes to legitimise their rule by undertaking foreign ventures. It is no exaggeration to argue that in all the above examples, the efforts by regimes at domestic legitimisation constituted a primary, if not the only, motivating factor.

This is not to suggest that the search for legitimacy necessarily motivates Arab leaders to embark on foreign ventures. However, given the environment in which Arab politics operate, it is easy to see why there is such a strong correlation between foreign policy and domestic legitimacy. Conflict in the area is endemic: there is the perennial Arab-Israel struggle; there is the constant conflict over territorial issues born out of the colonial legacy and in some cases still not satisfactorily resolved; there are the immense number of sectarian and ethnic divisions that cut across state boundaries, causing not only intra-state, but also inter-state, conflict; and finally there is the identification by the citizens of the various Arab states with the universalist values of Arabism and Islam. Not only do these two ideological forces tend to weaken people's identification with their own states, Arabism and Islam also are regularly used by Arab leaders to appeal to the loyalty of the citizens of other Arab states, thus undermining the legitimacy and stability of their regimes.

Aware of the potential for conflict in their area, Arab states have tried to limit the opportunities and regulate their relations through regional institutions and practices such as the League of Arab States and the summits of the Arab Heads of State. The Arab political environment, whether conflictual or cooperative (or both), is characterised by an intense level of inter-state activity. It is this kind of environment that makes foreign policy such a convenient vehicle for regime stability and legitimacy.

The concept of legitimacy has been explored by many different theorists, and whereas the thrust of their analyses may differ, they all tend to agree that, in the final analysis, only uncoerced acceptance by the citizens of the state makes a government legitimate. According to David Easton 'what differentiates political interactions from all other kinds of social interactions is that they are predominantly oriented toward the authoritative allocation of values for society. . . . An allocation is authoritative when the persons oriented to it consider that they are bound by it' (Easton, 1965, p. 50). Similarly, Max Weber, identifies three types of legitimacy: the traditional, the charismatic and the legal-rational. In the first and second types, obligations and loyalty are to a person, the traditional chieftan or the heroic or messianic leader; in the third type, obligation is to the legally established impersonal network of institutions (Weber, 1947, pp. 325–8). In all three types, however, legitimacy is defined in the context of people's acceptance of their governments and of their leaders. Thus, in discussing the second type of legitimacy, that of a charismatic leader, Weber posits this as a relationship in which the people perceive qualities in an individual which impel them to follow him, and as such, 'it is the duty of those to whom he addresses his mission to realise him as their legitimate and charismatically qualified leader' (Gerth and Wright Mills, 1970, p. 247). Again, the definition refers to a relationship between governors and governed, in which the latter enter uncoerced into the relationship. Herbert C. Kelman puts it succinctly. He defines a government as legitimate:

When it is perceived as having the right to exercise authority in a given domain and within specified limits. Thus, when the administration of a legitimate political system makes certain

285

demands, citizens accept them, whether or not they like them. An individual citizen may or may not be convinced of the value of the action he is asked to take; he may or may not be enthusiastic about carrying it out; and he may, in fact, be very unhappy about it. If it is within the limits of legitimacy, however, he willingly meets the demand without feeling coerced, and considers it his duty to do so (Kelman, 1969, p. 279).

This relationship is institutionalised in Western political thought and practice through the creation of political institutions. By facilitating the participation of the citizen in the body politic, these institutions become the symbols of system legitimacy, and the means by which citizens show their acceptance of the political system. The seventeenth century English philosopher John Locke argued (Locke, 1960) for a legislative power to run alongside, and independently of, executive power. Moreover, he contended that the legislative power should be superior to the executive, and that legislative institutions would be the means by which people participated actively, through representation, in the affairs of the state. As an example, he said that people's properties should not be taxed or taken from them except by their own consent or that of their representatives.

It is this tradition of representative democracy which underpins the whole notion of legitimacy in Western societies. Legitimacy in this sense is invested not in the ruler but in the political system as a whole. In North America, Europe and Japan, it is the parliamentary system of government that is legitimate, and government officials, elected through the institutions of this system of government, acquire their own legitimacy from the legitimacy of the system.

Lacking legitimacy based on mass participation through political representation, and realising how crucial legitimacy is for the stability of the political order, political leaders in the Arab world constantly endeavour to win the acceptance of their population, or at least their acquiescence in their leadership. This is usually done through the leader's efforts to create in the minds of his people an image of himself as a meritorious and successful leader. This is a difficult and uncertain process; indeed, it is like a journey on a Cairo bus: not only will one get a bumpy ride, but one may never arrive at the final destination. However, when an Arab leader embarks on the hazardous mission of acquiring legitimacy through success and achievements, he starts with some favourable omens that relate to the apparent susceptibility of Arab populations to the notion of centralised and authoritarian regimes.

Prior to the birth of the modern Arab state, the core societal units in the Arab world were (many would argue continue to be) the tribe, the village and the extended family. For centuries, the pattern of political loyalty in the tribal and village communities was hierarchical, with authority focused on the Sheikh or Rais. Although he was bound by tribal and village laws and customs, the Sheikh or the Rais, assisted by elders and religious personages, acted as the central authority, the final arbiter of power and the ultimate dispenser of justice. Similarly, the extended family has traditionally been hierarchically structured with authority resting in the hands of the oldest member. Deference to, and respect for, family elders creates a far greater conformity within an Arab family than is usually the case in a Western family, where intra-family relationships are less hierarchical. Transferred to the national milieu, therefore, the respectful and ready acceptance, in a tribal, village or family context, of a hierarchical social structure with a clearly identifiable authoritative personage at the top tends obviously to lessen rebellious tendencies among the populations against authoritarian regimes.

Even more crucial in this context is the role of Islam. As the religion of the overwhelming majority of the Arab people, Islam tends to pervade social custom and to dominate cultural and political attitudes. To this day, many of the values, norms of behaviour and attitudes of the Arab populations emanate from the inspiration and moral teachings of Islam. Accepting no separation between state and religion, Islam represents for the Muslim Arab much more than a system of spiritual guidance; it is accepted as a comprehensive social, political, legal and cultural system, and as such, even after years of 'modernisation' and 'secularisation', Islam remains a powerful and pervasive force in the Arab world.

Islam tends to bestow legitimacy on the centralised structure of political authority in the Arab world. The first major decision that the first Muslim community had to make was the election of the first Khalifa (successor) on the death of the prophet Mohammad. The Khalifa was given religious and political authority, a decision based on the Sunna (the traditions of the prophet) that religious and temporal power are inseparable. Moreover, the centralisation of authority is embodied in Islamic political heritage through the pronouncements of renowned Muslim jurists, theologians and philosophers in the centuries following the death of the prophet. Thus, according to the fourteenth century philosopher of history Ibn Khaldun, 'It is in the nature of states that authority becomes concentrated in one person' (Issawi, 1950, p. 114).

287

These same jurists prescribed almost total obedience to the ruler by fostering the belief that 'rebellion was the most heinous of crimes'; a doctrine which was consecrated in the juristic maxim, 'sixty years of tyranny are better than one hour of civil strife' (Gibb, 1955, p. 15). The famous eleventh century theologian al-Ghazali teaches that, 'An unjust ruler should not be deposed if strife would follow' (Hourani, 1962, p. 14). It is true that theologians, such as al-Mawardi (d. 1058), had argued that if the ruler did not fulfill his function, he should be removed from power, but none could indicate how this could be done legally or constitutionally. On the other hand, jurists such as al-Ash'ari (d. 935), 'Not only denied any right of popular revolution, but also emphasised the Caliph's full claim to obedience even if he had disregarded or violated his duties' (Khadduri, 1955, p. 12). This school of thought was extended some centuries later by the constitutional theorist Ibn Jama'a (d. 1333), who argued that, 'Self-investiture by armed force is lawful, and obedience is due to such a ruler' (Rosenthal, 1958, p. 45). The fact that Ibn Jama'a wrote under the militaristic rule of the Mamluks may explain his point of view. Nevertheless, his views, and the views of the other theologians, constitute prescriptive knowledge embodied in the culture and heritage of the Arab/Muslim people, and as such must have an impact on the way contemporary Arab populations have reacted to authority.

This may explain in part the endurance of authoritarian rule in the Arab world. In every Arab state (apart from Lebanon), the centralisation of power in the hands of one man has been the dominant feature of Arab politics over the last four decades. Opposition parties and groups hardly exist except in clandestine forms, and with the notable exception Kuwait, where opposition officially exists, they are blatantly manipulated by the regime. Institutions, such as parliaments and assemblies are sometimes created by the regimes to act as rubber stamps for government policies. And when assemblies, parties and mass organisations outgrow their original purpose or begin to act independently, they are ruthlessly cast aside by the ruling group. President Gamal Abd al-Nasser created three successive mass parties between 1953 and 1962. Nor did he feel himself to be necessarily bound by the decisions of his cabinet. Professor Boutros Boutros-Ghali, in analysing the working of Egyptian foreign policy under Nasser, states that 'The formulation of foreign policy . . . is strictly the prerogative and sole responsibility of the chief executive. The extent to which the executive is guided by the counsel of his principal associates, including the minister of foreign affairs, is a matter of personal choice' (Boutros-Ghali, 1963, p. 320). Professor Ghali, who later became Minister of State for Foreign Affairs under Nasser's successor, Anwar Sadat, must have congratulated himself many times on how true his analysis was. Similarly, the dazzling array of Libyan institutions of supposedly mass participation, from the Arab Socialist Union to the various popular committees, are the product not so much of Libya's democratic traditions, which itself is a contradiction in terms, but of the restless soul of Libya's sole ruler, Muammar Qadhafi.

Naturally, some Arab countries can point to political institutions that participate fully in the decision-making process. The Neo-Destour party in Tunisia, the FLN in Algeria, the NLF in South Yemen and the Baath in Syria and Iraq are all long-standing organisations that are capable of setting limitations on the chief executive's freedom. Even in these cases, however, power, in the final analysis, resides with the chief executive, for to set limitations is not for formulate or reverse policies, and to argue a point is not to make the argument stick. To generalise from the Syrian case, the late Ahmad Iskander, Syria's Minister of Information until his death in 1983, confirmed in an interview that in meetings with the top membership of the Baath Party, the President was the dominant personality, and the final decision on any policy was always the President's responsibility (Dawisha, 1980, pp. 102–3). Whatever the regime, therefore, the power to make decisions and enact policies in the Arab world continues to reside with the man at the top, and it is he who dominates the decision-making process and who determines the country's policy orientations. Unlike the pluralistic models of political behaviour, therefore, in which the chief executive derives his authority (defined as the legitimate exercise of power) from the legitimacy of the political system, political theory and practice in the Arab world have tended to elevate the ruler to a position of dominance over the legal-institutional structure, thus making the legitimacy of the political system dependent on the authority of the ruler.

Authoritarian leaders, however, cannot trust the survival of their political orders to the force of history alone. Conspirators as the majority of them are, they need more than the assurances of the past to make them sleep comfortably at night. They know that the attitudes of nations are shaped not only by the memories of the past, but also by the experiences of the present. The past influences people's perceptions of the present; but the present provides an ever-changing environment that constantly expands the limits of human and intellectual horizons. This in turn modifies the people's memory of their past.

The curse of the present for the Arab authoritarian rulers is the impact of the process of modernisation on their traditional societies. With increasing urbanisation, accelerated education and creeping Westernisation, traditional values and attitudes, which could be relied upon to underpin the stability of the Arab regimes, were bound to be questioned. Tribal values were being gradually eroded by urban living, the expansion of economic life began to dissipate the physical unity and inner coherence of the family, and Islam was confronted by Western secularism. In short, the Arabs of the second half of the twentieth century were demanding more of their rulers than their forefathers ever did. The traditional values of their political culture still held sway over the minds of the Arabs, but increasingly, as their eyes opened to new social and political realities in the world around them, they began to demand changes to their own political situation.

Just as the process of modernisation proved to be curse for the rulers, it ended as a curse for the ruled as well. For with modernisation came technological advancement, and that placed in the hands of the rulers methods of social and coercive suppression that made earlier means of population control pale into insignificance. However, the rulers knew only too well that more was needed to ensure the stability of their regimes, so a two-pronged maxim was followed: put fear in people's hearts, but also try to win their support, no matter how grudgingly given. On the other side of the fence, the ruled realised very quickly through bitter experience the futility of demanding genuine and full political participation; at least, however, they could demand intelligent and worthy leaders. Once the needs of the rulers and the demands of the ruled converged, achievements in foreign policy, magnified and exaggerated by the states' propaganda machines into great heroic acts, became, from the 1950s onwards, a central legitimising agent for Arab leadership.

The process began with Gamal Abd al-Nasser in the mid-1950s. His defiance of the West in a number of dramatic political acts ranging from his attacks on the Baghdad Pact, through the purchase of Soviet weapons, to the momentous decision to nationalise the Suez Canal company in 1956 won much support among the Egyptian population, humiliated as it was by almost a century of British presence on its soil. And when the Suez expedition, mounted by Britain and France in alliance with Israel, failed to wrest the Suez Canal from Egyptian control, the process of the domestic legitimisation of Nasser's regime was complete. According to a commentator, who hardly counts as an admirer of Nasser, Suez gave the Egyptian president 'almost unlimited credit in his own country and throughout the Arab world' (Laqueuer, 1968, p. 36). Through skillful and effective use of his propaganda machine, Nasser created in the minds of his people an image of himself as the first genuinely local hero who not only had dared to defy the might of the West, but had actually won. From then on, Nasser's legitimacy as Egypt's president, and the legitimacy of the political order which he had created were not to be questioned, until the 1967 war with Israel, which, as an episode of Nasser's controversial history, was the complete antithesis of Suez. We shall come back to the 1967 war below.

The man to succeed Nasser as president of Egypt in 1970 was Anwar Sadat, a man who had spent all his political life under the towering shadow of his predecessor. Indeed, Nasser himself used to refer to Sadat as *Bikbashi Aywa* — Colonel Yes-man. When, by virtue of his being Vice-President (a largely ceremonial and inconsequential role) at the time of Nasser's death, Sadat ascended to the presidency, his credibility, to say nothing of his legitimacy, was very low indeed. Yet the new, and allegedly makeshift president had learned well from his predecessor, and a series of bold foreign policy measures that surpassed even the exploits of Nasser, had, within a few years of his ascension to power, established him as the undisputed leader of his country.

The process began in 1972 when, in a bold move, he expelled over 21,000 Soviet personnel from Egypt. Given that most observers had by that time concluded that Egypt had become a political and military satellite of the Soviet Union, Sadat's dramatic act increased his prestige immeasurably both inside Egypt and in the Arab world. This was followed by the greatest 'achievement' of his eleven years as president — the launching of the October 1973 war against Israel and the successful military crossing of the Suez Canal. Until it happened, no one had thought it possible, not even the renowned experts of Western intelligence. And when it happened, and when everyone knew that it was Sadat who made it happen, the man finally emerged from the shadow of Nasser. In the words of Fouad Ajami, 'The war provided Sadat with his great act. The crossing of the Suez Canal became the mandate to create his kind of Egypt' (Ajami, 1981, pp. 95–6). The propagandists lost no time in making the October war not only the foundation upon which the legitimacy of Sadat's Egypt rested, but also a sort of moral dividing line between an old defeated and oppressive Egypt under Nasser and a new, heroic and invigorated Egypt of Sadat. The term *al-'Ubur* (the crossing) became the symbol of the new legitimacy; it became 'the crossing from defeat to victory, division to unity, shame to dignity, oppression to justice, terror to security' (Ajami, 1981, p. 96). Sadat had arrived; at last, he was his own man, needing no patron, memories of the past. He had became *al-Rais* in his own right. A major foreign policy 'success' had established Sadat as the unchallenged leader of his country.

For a while, he tried to sustain his authority with domestic achievements. The crossing of the Canal was supposed to be followed by the 'economic crossing' and the 'political crossing' in Egypt. Liberalisation of the socialist economic order and democratisation of the authoritarian political system were to follow now that Egypt had overcome the 'cycle of shame' and Sadat had established his legitimacy. Sadat, who three to four years earlier had been the brunt of the Egyptians' famed sardonic humour, was single-handedly transforming Egypt: from a socialist to a capitalist economy, from a pro-Soviet to a pro-American country, and from an authoritarian to a democratic state.

All this, however, met with little internal applause. Economic liberalisation (*infitah*) did no more than stir the lethargic Egyptian economy, creating hardly the promised land that Sadat and his propagandists confidently predicted. But it did create a rich class of people, seemingly dedicated to conspicuous consumption, whose antics and excesses fuelled the resentments of those, the majority of Egyptians, whose own economic situation not only did not improve, but in relative terms actually worsened. And while the shift from pro-Soviet to a pro-American orientation was met at first by almost universal approval, America's image was gradually eroded by the regime's conscious effort to equate Egypt's promised economic revival with America's help and encouragement. So, as the infitah began to falter, the blame was being increasingly directed not only at the regime, but also at the outside power which encouraged and, in the eyes of many Egyptians, actually planned the economic strategy.

Most disappointing was the failure of the political liberalisation of Egypt. Sadat would talk incessantly about democracy in Egypt; his propagandists would paint a glowing picture of genuine political representation, and of a free and dynamic electorate filled with the kind of affection and admiration for their president that persuaded no less than 98 per cent of them consistently to vote for him and for all his policies. Of course, as usually happens in the Arab world, the reality did not correspond to the regime's claims. The people, whose perception and intelligence more often than not have been grossly underestimated by Arab regimes, could see Sadat's democracy for the sham that it actually was. Sadat was allowed, in the wake of October 1973, to experience the seductions of absolute power, and like all addicts, it was too much to ask the man to share his 'high' with someone else. For all the protestations of the president and his men, and for all the cosmetic changes that they tried to affect in the political institutions of the country, Egypt remained an authoritarian political system, dependent for its *raison d'être* on the legitimacy of 'the man at the top'.

It was no coincidence, therefore, that Sadat's 'historic' trip to Jerusalem came when it came. By 1977, the glow of al-'Ubur was beginning to markedly recede; nothing much had come out of the other crossing — Egypt's political and economic liberalisation; and generally the universal optimism of the immediate post-1973 era was giving way to mounting scepticism and cynicism directed towards the regime, its policies, its rhetoric and its promises. It was therefore time for yet another 'heroic' foreign policy act — the dramatic trip to Jerusalem at the end of 1977. Of course, the Jerusalem trip was dictated by a number of factors, many of which were of an ideological and strategic nature. But there can be little doubt that the initiative, in its announcement and its execution, in the publicity that surrounded it, and in the manner by which the Egyptian propaganda machine used it to resurrect the tarnished image of the president, was also meant to achieve what the October war and the expulsion of the Russians had once achieved for the domestic legitimacy and stability of the Sadat regime.

The evidence is still not conclusive, but it looks as though this last of Sadat's heroic acts was not the domestic success that he had anticipated. The Egyptians did not want war with Israel but neither, it seems, were they ready for fully-fledged peace, and as such the Jerusalem trip and the subsequent Camp David accords, which made Sadat an American superstar, did little to allay the alienation of the mass of Egyptians from the unpopular domestic policies of his regime. Sadat's assassination, and the sheer nonchalance with which the ordinary Egyptian reacted to his death was testimony to that.

In contrast, Syria's risky foreign policy activities in the wake of Israel's invasion of Lebanon in 1982 seemed to go a long way towards cementing the authority and stability of President Assad. This was especially crucial to the Syrian president, as he and a number of key members of Syria's leadership belong to the minority Alawi community. The Sunni Muslims, who constitute the vast majority of the Syrian population, have had a long-standing antipathy towards the Alawis. The orthodox Sunnis have long considered the Alawi sect, which is an esoteric offshoot of Ismaili Shi'ism that seems to have absorbed animistic and Christian beliefs, as bordering on the heretical. Moreover, the contrast between the Alawis' recent political ascendency and their traditional inferior social and material status was bound to fuel the resentment of the Sunni Syrian population.

Sensitive to this underlying tension, President Assad endeavoured throughout the 1970s, to make the Baath Party the main ideological base and political arm of his regime. This tended to blur the regime's dependence on the Alawi community for its security. The situation changed dramatically with the onset of the 1980s. The growing opposition of the well-organised and highly fanatical Muslim Brotherhood to the Assad political order led to a number of bloody encounters, culminating in the uprising in the predominantly Sunni city of Hama in February 1982. During three weeks of seemingly limitless brutality, thousands of Muslim Brothers and innocent civilians were killed and almost half the city was razed to the ground primarily by the units of Siraya al-Difa, a crack, impeccably-trained military force made up entirely of Alawis and commanded by the President's brother, Rifat al-Assad. During this period, in terms of legitimacy, the Assad regime went through probably its weakest period. It was perceived by the Sunni majority population as a blatantly sectarian regime, wholly dependent on coercion that was ruthlessly perpetrated by members of its minority sect.

Paradoxically, it was Israel's invasion of Lebanon in June 1982 that restored to the Assad regime the credibility which it had almost completely lost after the Hama incident. By projecting Syria as the only Arab country that dared to confront Israel militarily, the Damascus government put itself forward as the champion of the 'Arab nation' (Khaddam al-Halim, 1983, p. 15). What is more, the Syrian leadership's obstinate stand, in the face of seemingly overwhelming odds, against the Israeli-Lebanese 17 May agreement, and later against the might of America's military power, brought Hafez al-Assad and his colleagues immense credit in Syria and in the Arab world. When the Americans ignominiously withdrew and the Israeli-Lebanese agreement was abrogated, Assad's prestige soared.

This series of foreign policy 'achievements', regained for President Assad the legitimacy he had lost after Hama in early 1982. The

Syrian president had no doubt hoped that his vigorous portrayal of Syria's 'steadfastness' as a heroic defender of Arab rights would create in the country an image of the Assad regime that was more 'Arab' and less 'Alawi'. Whatever the sectarian characteristics of his regime, therefore, President Assad would be embraced by the virulently Arabist Syrian population as a true and committed Arab leader, for he knew that to project himself as fighting on behalf of the 'Arab nations' was probably the best way to erase from the people's perceptions the regime's Alawi affiliations.

Assad's endeavours were risky, for a possible defeat at the hands of the Americans or the Israelis could have had the opposite effect on the Syrian population; he would not have been the successful and courageous defender of Arab rights, but the reckless adventurer who brought shame and despair on his country. I return here to a point I made earlier: the path towards legitimacy through foreign policy acts has been a risky, even hazardous, practice for Arab leaders. In the case of President Assad, he had emerged 'victorious' by the spring of 1984, and as a result, his legitimacy was seemingly restored and his position consolidated. But there have also been failures — cases when leaders went too far, miscalculated and lost.

The most obvious example was the June war of 1967. The prestige of President Nasser in the mid-sixties had been undermined by an almost continuous economic crisis, which itself was exacerbated by Egypt's morale-sapping and financially-ruinous military intervention in Yemen. Moreover, the acclaimed leader of Arab nationalism's cautious policy towards Israel, which was in stark contrast to his fiery rhetoric, put his credibility in question among many Egyptians as well as Arabs. When in the spring of 1967, therefore, tension on the Syrian-Israeli borders abruptly increased with Israeli leaders making veiled threats about the Syrian regime and with rumours circulating about Israeli massing of troops on the Syrian border, the chance for Nasser to seize the moment to re-establish his prestige was too good to be missed. In May 1967, he decided to ask the United Nations to pull its peace-keeping forces out of Sinai, to assert Egyptian sovereignty over the port of Sharm al-Sheikh and to close the straits of Tiran to Israeli shipping. Once the implementation of these decisions achieved his political objectives of restoring his regime's credibility Nasser, who did not particularly want to fight Israel, began to wind down the crisis through super-power diplomacy. He obviously hoped that the superpowers, fearful of being drawn into the conflict, would compel Israel to accept the newly created situation, leaving him with a great political victory that would silence his critics and erase from their minds Egypt's economic ills and its disastrous intervention in the Yemen. It almost worked, except that nobody had calculated for the presence in Israel of leaders who were just as adept at the game of risk-taking.

Nasser was to rule Egypt until his death in 1970, but the end of his charisma, and of his almost mystical hold on the masses were signalled by the June 1967 defeat. 'He would stay in power' Ajami writes, 'not as a confident, vibrant hero, but as a tragic figure, a symbol of better days, an indication of the will to resist' (Ajami, 1981, p. 85). The people stayed with Nasser; but they were no longer bound to him.

A more recent example of an Arab leader who used foreign policy to broaden his mass support, until he over-reached himself, is President Saddam Hussein of Iraq. In Hussein's case, however, the initial efforts at legitimisation were carried through by domestic reforms. Using Iraq's immense oil wealth, Hussein embarked in the mid and late 1970s on massive development and social welfare programmes which were aimed at broadening his support in the country. With an eye towards bridging the gap between rich and poor, he vigorously pursued policies that included rapid improvements in housing, education and medical services, and enacted legislation on social security, minimum wages and pension rights.

By 1979, foreign policy was beginning to supplant domestic reform as the main vehicle for Hussein's legitimisation. Seizing the opportunity left by Egypt's withdrawal from Arab politics because of Camp David, the Iraqi President embarked on diplomatic activity during 1979 and 1980 aimed at establishing Baghdad as the core of Arab political action and himself as the central figure among Arab leaders. In a speech in April 1980, Hussein declared that Iraq had 'always had a unique historical position within the Arab nation' and that 'the Iraqi army will remain strong to defend the honour of all Arabs fighting foreign forces' (Al-Thawra, 17 April 1980). Two months earlier, the President in a much trumpeted proclamation had enunciated his Arab National Charter which set out and communicated to other leaders in the area Hussein's ideas on future Arab political action.

Beyond the Arab world, President Hussein lobbied hard to bring the conference of the leaders of the non-aligned world to Baghdad in September 1982, a move that would have given Hussein the opportunity to assume the mantle of leadership of the non-aligned world. In order to pave the way, throughout 1980 the Iraqi received more than 30 Third World heads of state and prime ministers. All this activity certainly had the desired effect. By the end of 1980, Hussein had successfully changed his image from that of a ruthless but anonymous party-man in the early 1970s to one of a meritorious and substantial popular leader. With his domestic legitimacy seemingly guaranteed, President Hussein set out to make the 1980s the decade in which he would fill the void of Arab charismatic leadership vacated by Nasser after the 1967 defeat. And the young, ambitious Iraqi president might have succeeded had it not been for the intervention of the old and frail, but ruthlessly committed, Ayatollah Khomeini.

The entry of Iraq's armed forces into Iran in September 1980 was motivated by a number of reasons, not least by Khomeini's obstinate insistence on imposing his brand of revolutionary Islam on Iraq. It is true that the Iraqi leaders were concerned about the new Muslim Iranian regime 'trying to instigate fanaticism, resentment and division among the peoples of the area', (Al-Thawra, 18 September 1980) and it is also true that the new Tehran leaders resolutely dismissed all Iraq's overtures for neighbourly relations, preferring instead to mount increasingly hostile verbal onslaughts against Hussein and the Baath Party. Nevertheless, there seems to have been more that mere defensiveness in the Iraqi decision to invade Iran in 1980.

The reports coming from Iran had painted a picture of the political order as one of utter chaos, with a number of competing centres of power that were more interested in fighting each other than building a viable political structure. The news about the economy was hardly any better. Oil production had fallen sharply; there was a foreign currency reserve crisis, and food and consumer shortages were rampant. Most crucially, after the collapse of the Shah's army, Iran's fighting capability was thought to be almost negligible; most of Iran's officer corps had fled, been executed or put in prison, and the equipment, lacking spare parts, was becoming nearly unusable. What is more, the Iranian clergy had succeeded in alienating almost the entire international community. In short, the aggressively expansionist revolutionary Iran of September 1980 was, by all accounts, an easy target for a bold military operation by the Iraqi leader, frustrated as he was by Iran's seemingly limitless hostility towards him and his regime.

Once he had convinced himself that a military operation against Iran would not be costly and would be successful, Hussein could immediately see the benefits that would accrue to him in Iraq and the Arab world generally, once this 'bold' feat was achieved. He would go to the Arab summit conference scheduled in Amman two months later as the first Arab leader since independence who had been able to defeat a foreign enemy. And if he could do it in less than the six days it took Israel to defeat Nasser, then all the better. He would immediately and without question be raised to a level above that of his Arab competitors like Syria's Assad, King Hussein of Jordan and King Khalid of Saudi Arabia. How could anyone ever again challenge the status of the dynamic young leader who had transformed his country economically and socially, had become a major figure internationally, and had inflicted a humiliating defeat on a major power that could have become a main threat to the stability of many Arab regimes? In the exuberant days of 1980, when everything seemed to go well for Iraq, Saddam Hussein probably could almost hear the late President Nasser declaring the young leader of Iraq the natural heir to the mantle of Arab leadership. With all this, his legitimacy inside Iraq, as the leader who had achieved the ultimate in success, would probably be guaranteed for life.

It is said that dreamers eventually come down to earth with a painful thud; and Hussein's dreams were to shatter against the rock of religious commitment and revolutionary enthusiasm. The hopes for swift and famous victory never materialised; the conflict became a war of attrition that cost Iraq dearly. Economic development was arrested and reversed, social cohesion began to show signs of strain, and as more and more of Iraq's youth sacrificed their lives in this senseless war, the people's morale sank deeper into despair. In this mood of hopelessness, they could hardly be expected to applaud the leader who plunged them into this seemingly unending abyss. It was not that Hussein had completely lost his support, since he still had much good will from earlier days, and in any case, Iraqis resented Tehran's insistence on the removal of Hussein as a condition for the cessation of fighting, for people do not, as a rule, take kindly to foreign powers interfering in their domestic affairs. But the halo of merit and success, which had underpinned Hussein's legitimacy, had deserted him, and he was left to pick up the pieces and somehow try to start the whole process of establishing legitimacy all over again.

Whether the leader is successful or not, the way in which he acquires legitimacy in the Arab world must make his tenure, by the very nature of the process, a transient phenomenon. Success in a particular foreign policy venture will fuel people's enthusiasm — but only for a while. Sooner of later, the enthusiasm will wane, and the leader will have to provide the population with yet another dose of visible and applaudable achievements. The Arab leader has to have a career portfolio of successive 'success stories' in order to maintain his credibility, his legitimacy and ultimately the stability of his political order. It is only through genuine participation in the political process by the people that the unshakable and permanent legitimacy of the political order is guaranteed. There is, however, no sign that the Arab leaders are ready for such a fundamental departure from the present order of things, and as such, foreign policy seems destined to continue to play a central role in the legitimisation of Arab leaders and their political orders.

12

The Impact of Palestine on Arab Politics

Walid Kazziha

The relationship between the Arab regimes and the Palestine question has, since the First World War, been a continuous theme in Arab politics. Most of the literature on the subject addresses itself to that aspect of the relationship which deals with the impact of the Arab political order on the Palestine issue. However, very little serious attention has been devoted to examining the effects of the Palestine problem on the evolution and development of the Arab regimes. Perhaps the most important reason for such an uneven interest is the obvious and direct way in which the Arab governments exert their influence on the fate and future of the Palestinians, while the reverse is not so clear except in certain instances. It is the objective of this chapter to examine that latter aspect of the relationship, and study the extent to which the Palestine cause as an issue, and more recently as a political movement, has affected the structure of some Arab political systems and influenced the internal unity of Arab societies, and pro-Arab solidarity. In this respect, a word of warning is in place. The importance of the subject should not be exaggerated. Barry Rubin once claimed (1981: 22) that, 'From 1918 to 1948, and from 1948 to the present, the Palestine conflict decisively shaped the political and intellectual structures of all the Arab countries.' A sweeping generalisation such as this is misleading. A more accurate understanding of the situation would reveal that more often the policies of the Arab regimes and Israel towards one another have shaped the nature of the conflict and the fate of the Palestinian people (Kazziha, 1979).

Before 1948, many Arab countries, especially those of the Arab East and Egypt were influenced by the developments in Palestine. The armed clashes between the Arabs of Palestine on the one hand, and the British authorities and Zionist settlers on the other, provoked

300

a strong Arab sentiment among the peoples of the region. The events of 1936–39 in Palestine had a tremendous impact on the political views and opinions of the Arab youth and the attitude of some Arab governments. It contributed to the political consciousness of that generation of Arab officers who by the early 1950s began to play a decisive role in the political fortunes of the Arab countries around Palestine. Some of the leading Syrian officers, whose names were later associated with a series of military *coups*, had their first political experience in supporting their Arab brethren in Palestine. Similarly, some of the Iraqi officers who came to power in 1936, had on a number of occasions assisted the Palestinian rebels during the 1936–39 uprising.

Nasser in his little book, *The Philosophy of the Revolution* (1954), describes his early attachment to the Palestinian cause and how he found it a first element of his Arab consciousness. He wrote:

When I asked myself at that time why I left school so enthusiastically (to protest against the Balfour Declaration) and why I was angry for this land which I never saw, I could not find an answer except the echoes of sentiment.

Later, when he was at the military school studying Mediterranean defence problems, he began to see more clearly that 'When the Palestine crisis loomed on the horizon I was firmly convinced that the fighting in Palestine was not fighting on foreign territory. Nor was it inspired by sentiment. It was a duty imposed by self-defence.' He concluded that,

As long as the region is one, and its conditions, its problems and its future, and even the enemy are the same however different are the masks that the enemy covers its face with, why should we dissipate our efforts? (Seale, 1966: 192–3)

By 1948, Palestine had become not only a part of Arab politics on the official level, but also an essential element in the political consciousness of the Arab youth and army officers, who came to power in some of the countries of the Arab core during the 1950s.[1] It contributed to the final collapse of the old regimes in Syria, Egypt and Iraq, and threatened on a number of occasions to bring about the final demise of the monarchy in Jordan.

The Palestine war of 1948, and the defeat of the Arab armies in that war, had a direct impact on the relations of power within some

Arab societies. It undoubtedly discredited and weakened the position of the ruling elites in the Arab world, who were accused of negligence, unpreparedness and even outright treachery. The defeat paved the way for the army to step in and take the reins of power into their own hands. Palestine was one of the most important factors in bringing about such a drastic change after 1948.

In Egypt, the army took over power and dissolved the monarchy. The Free Officers in their first statement legitimising their move declared:

> Egypt has undergone a most critical period of bribery, corruption, and government instability in her recent history. These factors had a great influence on the Army. People who received bribes and those with ulterior motives contributed to our defeat in the Palestine war. After the war, corrupt elements increased, and traitors plotted against the Army . . . This was in order that Egypt would be without a strong Army to protect her. (Sharabi, 1966: 162–3)

In Iraq, the Palestine war had a latent but similar effect. According to Khadduri,

> The events which prompted the officers to contemplate intervention in domestic policies probably go back to 1949, after some of them had returned from the Palestine war believing that instructions had been given by higher authorities which prevented their full participation in military operations. (Khadduri, 1969: 20)

The new Arab regimes which emerged after the Palestine war were characterised by the shift of political power and social influence from the hands of the old landowning-merchant classes to the middle classes, with a special and significant role for the army (Halpern, 1970: 51–78). The new state structures which were established in Syria, Iraq and Egypt were diametrically opposed to any liberal or democratic tendencies in society, and sought to consolidate the authoritarian rule of the army officers and their allies. Ultimately, the Palestine issue provided the new rulers with a pretext to exercise full control over society in the name of preparing for 'the battle of destiny'. Consequently, the political, economic and social life of society was monopolised and the state came to rule supreme over individuals and the community as a whole. Perhaps at no time in the modern history of the Arab world was the impact of

Palestine on the Arab state structure more evident and direct than it was in the decade which followed the Arab defeat in 1948. During that time, Palestine acted as the focus of political solidarity in some Arab societies, and tended to minimise the influence of the elements of dissension within each of them. On a pan-Arab level, it provided the movement for Arab unity with added vigour, which further threatened the *status quo* of the majority of Arab regimes.

However, the consequences of the war in Palestine were not limited to a change in the structures of some Arab states, but extended to include a change in the policies of the Arab regimes towards each other and towards the world around them. In this respect, the effects of the Palestine issue might have been less direct and obvious.

In the years following the war, the old rift between the Hashemite camp in the Arab world on one side and the Saudi–Egyptian alliance on the other began gradually to give way to a more intensive inter-Arab conflict between 'the reactionary regimes' and 'the progressive regimes'. Undoubtedly, the unity between Syria and Egypt in February 1958 and the collapse of the Hashemite monarchy in Baghdad in July of the same year enhanced Nasser's role in the region. The Saudi monarchy, however, felt that the growing power and the long arm of Egypt were threatening it and other traditional regimes in the Arab world. It therefore decided to lead the anti-Egyptian camp. The Arab world was thus split between two kinds of regimes: those who championed the cause of radical change and those who opted for maintaining the *status quo*. Each of the two blocs projected a self-image; a self-image of which Palestine was an integral part. The Saudis argued for moderation and caution and seemed to assign the Palestine issue a secondary position in their list of priorities, while giving the Nasserite and Soviet threats their maximum attention. On the other hand, Nasser and the Syrians were becoming increasingly the prisoners of their own self-image as the champions of the Palestine cause. The radical bloc, however, was suffering from divisions within its ranks. First 'Abd al-Karim Qasim of Iraq led his country away from a union with the UAR, and thus precipitated a conflict between Baghdad and Cairo. The split in the revolutionary camp reached its climax in the secession of Syria from its unity with Egypt in September 1961. As a result of these events, the radical regimes in the Arab world were now more than ever involved in a process of outbidding each other over the Palestine question. 'Abd al-Karim Qasim repeatedly declared that he had prepared a plan for the liberation of Palestine. He claimed that he was organising an army of Palestinians to execute that plan. He even went so far as to distribute among some of the members of the Palestinian force he enlisted a medal called 'the Return'. The secessionist and later the Ba'th regimes in Syria accused Nasser of betraying the cause, because he allowed UN troops to be stationed as a buffer between his forces and the Israeli army in the Sinai (Kadi, 1966: 92–3). The more the internal and external pressure mounted against the radical regimes, the more they were eager to project an image of themselves as worthy of the expectations of the Arab masses.

Egypt, as the most powerful radical Arab country, and Nasser, as the most charismatic Arab leader, were under tremendous pressure to pose as the chief guardians of Arab rights in Palestine. Had this self-image been confined to the realm of Arab politics and inter-Arab conflicts, no serious repercussions would have ensued. Unfortunately, however, the US chose to take that image at its face value and proceeded to counter Nasser's influence in the Arab world by throwing its full weight behind his Saudi adversary. Similarly, Israel found in that projected image a convenient pretext to cut Egypt down to size when the opportunity presented itself in June 1967.

The Palestine cause as an issue in inter-Arab conflicts had little direct bearing on the development of the Arab political systems. However, the Palestine cause as an element in the Arab–Israeli conflict conveniently served Israel the opportunity to deliver a devastating blow to the political and military structures of the Arab regimes around Palestine. The Arab concern for Palestine proved to be less serious than expected. While the Arab governments were carelessly toying with the Palestine issue in their summit meetings and in public, Israel was taking their threats more literally and was preparing for a final showdown.

Another important consequence of the Palestine war in 1948 was the introduction of the Soviet Union as a power in the politics of the region. Until the late 1940s, the Arab world in its entirety was considered to be part of the Western sphere of influence, despite the fact that by that time some of the Arab countries had gained their political independence. However, the emergence of Israel, and the unhesitating Western support for it, alienated the majority of Arabs. Some of the Arab regimes, notably Iraq under the Hashemites, nevertheless continued to pin their hopes on the West: 'General Nuri (as-Sa'id) counted on an ultimate solution for the Palestinian question in favour of the Arabs through co-operation with, rather than by opposition to, the West' (Khadduri, 1969: 53).

The radical regimes, on the other hand, realised that relying on the West for a favourable solution to the problem was hopeless.

Israel's repeated attacks on the Arab territories around it, which culminated in 1954 in the famous raid on Gaza, prompted Nasser and the Syrians to turn to the Soviet Union for military aid. The tripartite aggression against Egypt in 1956 only helped to cement that relationship. As the Israeli military threat against the Arab countries increased, the radical regimes tended to draw closer and closer to the Soviet Union. The relationship with the Soviet Union was not limited to the political and military aspects, but was soon extended to economic fields to include trade, financial aid and the transfer of technology in the industrial and agricultural sectors.

A great deal of academic effort has been expended on examining the nature of the relationship between the two superpowers and their Arab allies. One aspect which has not been sufficiently emphasised is the impact of that relationship on the structures of the Arab states. The Americans seemed to have a tendency to forge a multiplicity of links with a wide range of elements inside an Arab country. For example, in the case of Egypt during the post-Nasser era, the American government, businessmen, intellectuals and experts all contributed to the formation of a network of links between Egypt and the US. These links were established on a number of levels, including the official and non-official, private and public, local and national. They affected the lives and welfare of a variety of Egyptian social classes and individuals, who became part of the network. The pressures which this type of relationship generated on the state structure undermined its monopolistic tendencies, especially in the economic and cultural fields. Some of the earlier functions of the state were reluctantly conceded to the private sector and to the emerging bourgeoisie of the open-door policy.

On the other hand, the relationship between the Soviet Union and Egypt in the past has produced a contrary effect. The Soviet Union was and still is heavily dependent on bureaucracy. And as a bureaucracy it showed a clear preference for dealing with another government bureaucracy in the Arab world. Its influence was thus limited to forging links with the state apparatus and not with independent groups within society. The nature of such a relationship tended to reinforce the monopolistic impulses of some Arab states.

To sum up, the choice of a superpower ally, namely the Soviet Union by the radical regimes in the Arab world was determined by their own perception of how to deal with the aftermath of the Palestine war. However, once that choice was made, the type of relationship which evolved enhanced the process of concentrating enormous power in the hands of the radical Arab states. On the whole, superpower intervention tended to reinforce the political divisions in the Arab world and led to the emergence of some social and economic systems which were diametrically opposed to each other. As a consequence the cause of Arab unity was weakened.

Underlying the importance of the Palestine question, whether viewed in the context of the evolution of radical regimes, as a factor in inter-Arab political conflicts, or as an issue in the relationship with a superpower, is the simple fact that since 1948 Palestine has become a legitimising resource for Arab governments. Michael Hudson wrote:

> It is difficult to emphasize sufficiently the importance of the Palestine issue for the politics of legitimacy in the Arab world. Today Palestine is as much, if not even more, of an issue . . . than it was in 1917; for not only is Palestine rich in national and religious symbolism for all Arabs, it is also a crucial geographical linkage between the eastern and western Arab world. (Hudson, 1980: 118)

The defeat of the Arab armies around Israel in June 1967, however, modified the stand of some Arab governments. The emphasis of Egypt, Jordan and to a lesser extent Syria, shifted after 1967 from the idea of liberating Palestine to the idea of regaining the Arab territories lost in the war. In July 1970, Nasser accepted the Rogers Plan, and three days later the Jordanian government followed suit. The plan offered no specific solution to the Palestinian problem but it proposed a settlement between Israel and the Arab countries based on the return of Arab territories occupied during the war in exchange for formal Arab recognition of Israel. The government of national unity in Israel at that time rejected the scheme. On the other hand, the Jordanian monarchy, who for a number of years had taken pride in sponsoring the notion of a unified Palestinian and East Jordanian family, was willing to settle for the return of the West Bank, foregoing the rest of Palestine. The Syrians too after 1967 seemed to be more interested in the liberation of the Golan Heights than Palestine proper.

Undoubtedly the defeat of 1967 relegated Palestine, as a source of legitimacy for the Arab governments around Israel to a secondary position. The occupied territories now gained precedence over everything else. While a shift away from Palestine was taking place among some countries of the Arab core, a shift in the opposite direction was being noticed among some countries of the periphery. Soon after the June war, Saudi Arabia and the Arab states in the Gulf began to take an increasing interest in the Palestine question. The growing involvement of the moderate regimes in the Palestine cause was motivated by a number of considerations. Chief among these was the decline of Egypt as a regional power and leader of the Arab radical camp. Among other things, the June war discredited Nasser and the Ba'th on all levels. The regional balance of power tilted heavily in favour of the moderate and conservative forces in the region. The death of Nasser, in September 1970, left King Faisal of Saudi Arabia as the most influential Arab leader until his assassination in 1975. Sadat inherited a weak and defeated Egypt; he tended to keep a low profile in Arab politics, in view of his need for Saudi financial and political support. His relative success in the 1973 war did not regain for him the position among the Arabs which Nasser held in the past. In any case, under Sadat, Egypt rapidly moved towards a settlement with Israel, in spite of the objections of the other Arabs. Thus the role of political leadership in the Arab world finally fell to Saudi Arabia. And with that role, Saudi Arabia inherited the responsibilities of meeting the challenges which were facing the Arab world. First among these challenges was the Palestine cause. In short, Saudi Arabia had to give the Palestine question top priority by virtue of its new role as the leader of the Arab world.

Another factor favouring Saudi concern was its growing fear of Israel's military might in the region. After Camp David Israel seemed more inclined, and even eager, to use military force in its efforts to achieve its political objectives. The Israeli raid on the nuclear reactor in Baghdad in 1981 did not go unnoticed. The Israeli bombers, in carrying out their mission, flew over Saudi air space. The vulnerability of Saudi national security was clearly demonstrated. Soon after the raid, Israeli jets violated Saudi air space, causing the government of Saudi Arabia to launch a number of strong complaints to the US government. The Israeli invasion of Lebanon in the summer of 1982 went a step further in showing the Saudis how much of a regional superpower Israel had become. Similarly, while keeping an eye on the Iranian threat in the east, the Arab Gulf states showed a growing concern for the Palestine question in the west. In September 1981, the Gulf Co-operation Council at Taif affirmed in a communiqué the primacy of the Palestine question, as if that primacy formed an integral part of the Gulf's security. Likewise, the Fahd Plan of August 1981 was a striking example of the gradual advance of the Gulf towards the centre of the

Arab scene on the issue of the Arab–Israeli conflict. Since 1967, and even more so since the conclusion of the Camp David Agreement, Israel not only posed a threat to the sovereignty of the Arab countries around it, but also to countries of the Arab periphery. Statements made by Israel's Defence Minister during the invasion of Lebanon concerning the extension of his country's strategic interests to Pakistan seemed to confirm the worst fears of the Arabs.

A third important consideration in the growing involvement in the Palestine question on the part of Saudi Arabia and the Gulf states, was the nature of the Palestinian presence in these countries and Israel's reaction to that presence.

With the exception of Egypt, the rest of the Arab countries around Israel had a sizeable Palestinian population. In the case of Jordan, they formed a majority, while in Lebanon and Syria, though a minority, the Palestinians had considerable political influence (Dajani, 1978). On many occasions the Palestinians acted as a destabilising force in these countries. A case in point was Jordan in 1970, and Lebanon until very recently. The political and social dissatisfaction of the majority of Palestinians, who lived in refugee camps in the Arab countries around Israel, very often added to the instability of these regimes (Sayigh, n.d.: 102). Until 1967, the Arab governments were able to contain the political influence of the Palestinians, however, after that, the newly emerging militant groups acquired some measure of autonomy, especially in Jordan and Lebanon. The difficulties of the Arab regimes were further exacerbated by Israel's policy of massive reprisals against the territory of the host Arab country whenever the Palestinian commandos attacked Israeli targets. The Arab regimes faced the dilemma of either tolerating the Israeli reprisals or suppressing the Palestinians. In the final analysis, the Jordanian monarch and the Lebanese government chose the latter option. In Jordan, King Hussein succeeded, but in Lebanon, a civil war ensued and engulfed the whole country. Consequently, the authority of the central government rapidly disintegrated. Syria, however, did not face such a dilemma. The successive regimes in Damascus kept a tight control over the activities of the Palestinians. At the same time, the resistance movement refrained from using Syrian territory to launch its attacks against Israel. The Fedayeen appeared to be 'conscious of the vital need to maintain good relations with at least one of the countries on Israel's eastern periphery' (Jabber, 1973: 101).

On the whole, the Arab regimes on Israel's borders had, since 1967, realised the importance of containing the disruptive influence of the resistance movement in order to avoid any further Israeli threats to their territorial sovereignty. In the process of reaching this conclusion, the centrality of the Palestine issue in the policies of these countries was gradually undermined. Egypt satisfied itself with what in effect was a bilateral settlement with Israel, while Jordan aspired to achieve a similar arrangement without any success. Syria seemed to opt for a different policy; however, its continued antagonism to the PLO's legitimate leadership made for doubts as to its real intentions. The question remained whether Syria was at all interested in reaching a satisfactory solution to the Palestine question, or was more concerned with regaining its sovereignty over the Golan Heights.

The Palestinian presence in Saudi Arabia and the Gulf states did not produce the same effects as it did in the countries directly bordering Israel. For one thing the Palestinian communities which settled in the Arab Gulf states generally refrained from involvement in the internal politics of these countries. For another, the Palestinians in the Gulf did not pose a direct threat to Israel's security, and therefore did not provoke Israeli retaliation. The Palestinians in Kuwait:

despite their negative and repressed feelings due to their being denied certain political privileges, nevertheless do not pose any direct threat to the *status quo* in the Gulf because of the freedom they enjoy to organise themselves vis-à-vis the outside world, and their relative economic comfort. (Al-Rumayhi, 1982: 98–9)

However al-Rumayhi also points to the fact that 'there is also a Palestinian middle class which is perfectly satisfied with its material status and shuns any Palestinian political activity if it conflicts with current policies' (Al-Ramayhi, 1982: 98–9).

His expectations for the 1980s in the Gulf were that the Palestinians were not likely to have

a direct role to play in socio-economic transformation. Most of the social groups of the Palestinian community seek, above all, to preserve their source of livelihood, and are therefore not prepared to be engaged as a party in any internal political conflict. (Al-Rumayhi, 1982: 106)

The Palestinians in the Gulf differed from those who lived in the refugee camps in Lebanon, Jordan and Syria. They were politically

309

less excitable and showed a greater degree of satisfaction with the social and economic conditions under which they lived. Furthermore, with the exception of the raid on Baghdad in 1981, the Gulf states had been spared massive Israeli reprisals. Israel's self-restraint could be a result of the logistic and operational difficulties involved in carrying out such missions against distant targets, or an outcome of various political considerations.

Whatever the reasons were for Israel refraining from attacking the Gulf countries, the truth remained that the Palestine item had been put at the top of the political agenda of the Gulf states and Saudi Arabia. The new position was cautiously adopted without paying the price that Arab countries adjacent to Israel had paid in the past. The benefits of supporting the Palestinian cause were many. It enhanced the Saudi image among the Arabs. More importantly, it gained Saudi Arabia and the Arab Gulf states the local support of their own people, at a time when such support was desperately needed to maintain internal unity.

> The tensions born from extremely rapid social change, the need for a foreign and Arab labour force (Mashreqi and Egyptian), the over-conspicuous alliance with the US, all worked together to destroy the old consensus and reveal the anachronism of state structures. In order to legitimise their hold on power, the Gulf countries seem to be forced to prove the positive use of their power, in other words to work for tangible results in Palestine (Al-Rumayhi, 1982: 331–2).

In the Gulf area, the Palestine question appeared to act as a rallying point for domestic and regional unity.

The October war in 1973 seemed to reinforce the shift in the positions of the countries of the Arab core and the periphery towards the Palestine question. Egypt and Syria regained some of the credibility they had lost in 1967. Consequently, they were able to pursue their policies regardless of Palestinian objections or antagonism. On the other hand, Saudi Arabia and its Arab neighbours were enabled by the enormous increase in their oil revenue after the war to subsidise the Palestine issue on every possible level: the Palestinian, the Arab, the Islamic, the African and the international.

Until 1967, the impact of the Palestine question on the policies and structures of the Arab states was basically determined by the strength of the moral and political commitment of the Arab peoples to it. In many parts of the Arab world, the issue inspired the greatest sympathy and dedication. Its appeal extended to all parts of the Arab world including the Arab North African countries. The participation of a Moroccan unit in combat on the Syrian front during the October war, was perhaps one of King Hassan's most popular acts after he came to power. Similarly, the despatch of Algerian troops to Egypt in 1967,

> may have been the first major issue in which the Boumedienne government acted with considerable mass support. The Algerian revolution touched the lives of all Algerians and gave them a particular world view. The Arab–Israeli conflict brings that world view into focus and revitalises Algeria's revolutionary self-conception. (Roughton, 1969: 444)

After 1967, a new dimension of the Palestine question emerged. The rise of a national movement to lead the struggle of the Palestinian people had a distinct impact on the political developments in some countries of the Arab East. In its formative stage which extended from the late 1950s until 1967, the movement gradually succeeded in separating the Palestine issue from other Arab issues. In itself this was an important achievement on both the theoretical and political levels. For a long time before the 1960s, the Palestinians had subordinated their national outlook to the wider struggle for Arab unity. For them, Arab unity was the road to Palestine. On a practical level, the distinction made between their own cause and that of the other Arabs led to the gradual dissociation of the Palestinian communities from the political concerns of the pan-Arab parties. Fewer and fewer Palestinians were now willing to participate actively in the ranks of the Ba'th Party; instead they opted for Fatah and other Palestinian organisations. Equally important in this respect was the formation of the Palestinian Liberation Organisation (PLO), in 1964. Yet the establishment of the PLO under a wide official Arab umbrella saved it from becoming entirely controlled by one Arab state or another. It provided its leadership with limited room for political manoeuverability and survival, which proved to be of utmost importance in later years. At this stage, the Palestine question was reformulated by the different organised groups of Palestinians, who later on joined the ranks of the PLO (Quandt, 1974). Palestinians concerned with the political fate of their own people were trying to find answers to some crucial questions addressed to them by their compatriots and others. What was the specific role of the Palestinians in the struggle for Palestine? How did that struggle relate to the wider Arab struggle? What kind of Palestine did they want to achieve? What was the nature of Zionism and how did it differ from Judaism? What was the relationship between Zionism and imperialism? Questions of strategy were also discussed and a general consensus emerged among the various groups of the movement by the mid-1960s, recognising armed struggle, with the Palestinians as its vanguard, as the most effective way of achieving their political aims.

During this formative period of the rise of the resistance movement, the Arab governments 'were always able to confine Palestinian radicalism within easily manageable limits' (Cobban, 1984: 197). However, this did not prevent the efforts of the movement from bearing some important fruits. By 1967, the movement had succeeded in persuading the majority of Palestinians to view their struggle as most vital, requiring their full commitment. It created a general disposition among the Palestinian communities in the diaspora, more receptive to the notion of Palestine-first. In 1966, the Jordanian monarch became so distressed by the growing popularity of the PLO among his Palestinian subjects that he ordered the closure of its offices and arrested some of its leading elements, despite the objections of some Arab governments.

In the early stages of its evolution, the PLO was able to win the support of Egypt, Syria and Iraq to form conventional military units under the leadership of Ahmed al-Shuqairy, head of the PLO. At the same time, Yasser Arafat, leader of the largest clandestine organisation, Fatah, not yet a member of the PLO, managed to gain the political and military assistance of Syria and Algeria. Since 1962, the Algerians had lent their support to Fatah and introduced some of its leaders to Chinese, North Korean and Vietcong officials. In 1965, Boumedienne sent Fatah a first arms shipment (Cobban, 1984: 31–2). Furthermore, the emergence of the PLO in 1964 with the reluctant consensus of the Arab governments and the establishment of its offices in several Arab capitals encouraged the Palestinians to associate themselves, for the first time since 1948, with a recognised and popular Palestinian authority.

Up until 1967, it would seem that the impact of the resistance movement on Arab policies and structures were mainly moral and intellectual and, whenever inter-Arab conflicts allowed, also political. But once they had given their approval to the formation of the PLO, no matter how fragile it was intended to be, and once they had committed themselves to the idea of a separate Palestinian entity, the Arab states found it extremely difficult to withdraw from that position. Whenever they attempted to do so, they had to face pressures from their own people, the Palestinian communities, other Arab governments and even some international forces. The Palestinians managed to gain a tentative foothold *vis-à-vis* the Arab regimes. The search, after 1967, was for a more stable and permanent position in the midst of a changeable and treacherous Arab environment.

The Arab defeat in 1967 offered the resistance movement the opportunity to consolidate its position. Many factors contributed to the growth of the political and military powers of the movement. Chief among them was the temporary set-back suffered by the Arab armies around Israel. Another was the massive popular support for the resistance movement, especially after the Karameh battle in Jordan in March 1968, as a symbol of Arab defiance of Israel's power. A third was the ability of the leadership of the movement to exploit Arab differences to its own advantage. In 1968, Fatah took over the PLO and gained official Arab recognition. A year later, Yasser Arafat became chairman of the executive committee of the PLO. Whatever the reasons were for the growth of Palestinian power after 1967, one of the most distinctive features of that power was the military impact of the PLO on the political structure of some Arab countries. A direct impact which, in the case of Jordan, seriously threatened to transform the whole political fabric of society, and in the case of Lebanon, eventually contributed to its end. The general climate of public opinion among the Arabs after 1967 was highly conducive to the notion of armed resistance. Defeat, in its most direct and conspicuous form, was basically a military defeat; its scope and scale had not been anticipated. It left the Arabs, governments and peoples, with a deep feeling of shame and humiliation; a feeling which could not be redressed without some military success. If that success was to be achieved at the hands of the Palestinian fighters, then no effort was to be spared to provide them with whatever assistance they needed. For a short while, the whole Arab world seemed to stand behind the Fedayeen. It was at this point that the resistance movement sought to consolidate its military position in Jordan, Lebanon and Syria. Unfortunately, the honeymoon between the Arab governments and the PLO was short-lived. Less than a year after the June war, armed confrontations between the resistance movement and the host Arab governments ensued, with the aim of eliminating the PLO's military presence and subduing its political influence. In Syria, the independent military presence of the movement was short-lived and manageable. In May

1968 the Syrian regime sponsored the creation of the Saiqa organisation in an attempt to counter the influence of Fatah. The new organisation grew very rapidly and backed Salah Jadid, the leader of the left-wing faction of the ruling Ba'th party, against the military wing led by Hafez Assad.

In 1970, Assad took control and once and for all brought the Saiqa entirely under his authority (Quandt, 1974: 65). To all intents and purposes, the resistance movement in Syria was now cut down to size and lost any practical leverage *vis-à-vis* the Syrian regime.

In Jordan the independent military presence of the resistance movement lasted for three years before it was brought to a bloody end in September 1970. During those years the movement succeeded in creating a dual power situation in the country. Palestinian institutions parallel to those of the Jordanian government were gradually established. The PLO in Jordan posed a direct threat to the traditional power structure in that society, and almost brought about its downfall. It would seem, however, that the military capabilities of the resistance movement were not strong enough to stand up against the forces of the monarch. The movement also failed to gain the support of the East Jordanians who, by and large, remained firmly loyal to their king (Al-'Azm, 1973: 148–55). Above all the leadership of the PLO and especially Fatah did not have the political vision or determination to resolve that dual power situation in its own favour. Furthermore, by the end of July 1970, the movement's relations with one of its main Arab protectors, namely Nasser, had become extremely strained, due to the latter's acceptance of the Rogers Plan. Eventually, when a final showdown occurred, the PLO was relatively isolated, its leadership hesitant and its forces in no way a match to government troops.[2]

Once the PLO was defeated in Amman, its forces took refuge in Lebanon. By 1969, the movement had reached an agreement with the Lebanese government, guaranteed by Egypt and other Arab governments, which allowed its fighters relative freedom of movement to operate against the Israelis in the south and provided protection for its own people in the refugee camps. Soon, however, the Palestinian forces were sucked into the quagmire of the Lebanese civil war, of which they were a minor cause and a major victim. In spite of their reluctance to get involved in any important way in the conflict beween Christians and Muslims, they were unable to maintain that position, especially when their own refugee camps (Dbayyieh, Jisr al-Basha and Tall az-Za'tar) were stormed and levelled to the ground by the Pahalangist forces (Cobban, 1984: 68).

The PLO exercised its political and military influence in Lebanon with the hope of achieving one primary objective. It sought to establish for itself a safe base which would enable it to organise and build its own political and social institutions among the dispersed Palestinian communities, and furthermore, allow it to pursue its military activities against Israel.

In its attempt to secure for itself that safe base, the PLO had to rely on the support of the Muslim and radical political forces in Lebanon. In return, it had to offer its allies some measure of military backing against their age-old adversaries, the Maronites. The involvement of the Syrians and Israelis in the conflict further complicated the position of the PLO which found itself torn between the need for a base in Lebanon, and the enormous price it had to pay for being drawn into the conflict. Finally, the invasion of Lebanon by Israel in the summer of 1982 led to the departure of the Palestinian forces from Beirut and, towards the end of 1983, Syria terminated the political and military presence of Arafat and his men in Lebanon. However, before their withdrawal from Lebanon, the PLO forces had contributed in no small way to the gradual disintegration of the Lebanese political structure.

To conclude, the military impact of the resistance movement on some of the Arab regimes around Israel was not uniform. In the case of Syria, it was brief and negligible, and confined to a limited and unsuccessful role during the struggle for power between the competing wings of the ruling Ba'th Party. In Jordan, the PLO temporarily managed seriously to undermine the very basis of the existing system of government; but the monarchy soon recovered and successfully took the initiative against the PLO. In Lebanon, the PLO, along with other internal and external forces, brought about the collapse of the Lebanese state. On the whole, the influence of the PLO in these Arab countries seemed to act against domestic or regional unity. Generally speaking, as a movement with a military presence in some Arab countries, the PLO had the potential of disrupting the *status quo* and the whole fabric of state and society.

The influence of the PLO on its surrounding Arab environment was by no means limited to its military presence, however. Some political movements in the Middle East and the Arab world viewed the PLO as a model for national struggle. Many of the Iranian groups which took part in the Iranian revolution were closely associated with the PLO, and some received their political and military training in the refugee camps in Jordan and Lebanon (Al-Rumaihi, 1982: 89). In 1968, a small group of rebels in Dhofar,

315

influenced by the radical factions of the PLO, formed the Popular Front for the Liberation of the Occupied Arab Gulf (Kazziha, 1975: 93). Similarly, around the same period, a splinter group from the Communist Party of Iraq organised a 'people's army' and advocated armed struggle against the regime, but failed to make any headway (Kelidar, 1979: 192). On the whole, the resistance movement after 1967 inspired a new pattern of political activity in the region, characterised by the adoption of violent means to alter the *status quo*.

However, the greatest success of the PLO was not in its military endeavours, nor in being a revolutionary model for others to emulate. The greatest achievement of the PLO was in the political realm, in the ability of its leadership to create among its people a keen sense of commitment to its own national cause. A new feeling of national solidarity and national identity emerged among the members of the Palestinian communities. The PLO was the underlying structure which gave form and direction to the rising sentiment of Palestinian nationalism. The long, trying years of sweat and blood in Jordan and Lebanon had not been wasted. These years were necessary for building up a national movement capable of surviving on the national soil of others. Jordan and Lebanon had a great importance for the PLO, not as military bases for launching significant offensives against Israel, but as a refuge against outsiders, whether Arab or Israeli. Beirut, where the movement spent a decade and half of its life, was a sanctuary, but more important, it gave the PLO ample time to set up its links with the Palestinian communities in the diaspora. It served to provide training grounds for the movement's political cadres. In Beirut, the PLO was able to build the necessary structures capable of pooling the human and material resources of the Palestinian people. The political, economic, social, cultural and military structures which were built up around the PLO were decentralised in order to meet the needs of a dispersed nation. In that respect, Beirut served as a co-ordinating centre for the activities of all these institutions, and when the PLO finally left Lebanon, it lost its co-ordinating centre. However, by then the PLO had established its position as the effective representative of the Palestinian people. In 1974, the Arab governments recognised the PLO as the sole representative of the Palestinians. Soon afterwards, Arafat made his appearance at the UN and his organisation gained the status of observer.

A strong expectation after the withdrawal of Arafat and his men from Lebanon was that the PLO would now be at the mercy of the

Arab governments. Deprived of its co-ordinating centre, its sanctuary and its military base, it was now entirely dependent on the Arab regimes. On the political level, this expectation proved inaccurate. The resistance movement seemed to be more viable than expected, for specific Palestinian and Arab reasons.

Throughout the 1970s, the Palestinian communities in different parts of the Arab world showed a growing sense of political solidarity, not to be compared with that of two decades earlier. Attempts made by Arab and non-Arab parties to divert the attention of these communities from their national cause failed miserably.[3]

It would seem that the decentralised structure of the PLO had eluded any attempt on the part of the Arab regimes or Israel to destroy it. The fact that its political institutions, social welfare apparatuses and propaganda machines were spread over a number of locations in the Arab world and abroad prevented its total defeat. The organisational flexibility of the PLO enabled it to withstand and survive the mounting pressures of the Arab regimes against it, and the successive Israeli attempts to liquidate it politically and militarily. Moreover, since its inception in 1964 the PLO had experienced its fair share of Arab politics. Its political leadership was exposed to a wide range of Arab intrigues and continuous manipulations. Arafat became one of the most skilful of Arab leaders. He developed a sense of survival sharper than anyone else. Without exaggeration, he became a master in the game of checks and balances in the region. Within his own organisation, Fatah, he kept a close rein on his colleagues and followers, despite many Arab attempts to split his ranks. As a charismatic leader he used his powers of persuasion to reconcile a variety of different ideological positions held by his followers. On the level of the PLO as a whole, he maintained a balance between those different factions and, in the Arab context, he successfully played off one or more Arab regimes against each other. More recently his sense of political survival has brought him closer to Egypt and Iraq in order to balance the Syrian pressure against him. Under Arafat's leadership the PLO has consistently exploited the lack of Arab consensus to its own advantage.

It is a fact that since 1967, the Arab world has witnessed the gradual but determined rise of a new national entity in the Middle East, namely the Palestinian entity.

To sum up, since the establishment of the state of Israel, the Palestine question has had a tremendous impact on three major areas in Arab politics. First, it paved the way in some Arab countries for the advent of the army to power. Throughout the 1950s, Palestine was a code name for political change and army take-overs in the Arab world. Very often, the domestic credibility of the political regimes, especially those of the Arab core, rested on the level of their commitment to the Palestine cause. Second, Palestine acted as a rallying point for internal solidarity in many Arab societies. It was continuously utilised by the Arab regimes or by the opposition political groups and parties to achieve total or partial consensus. The Palestine issue was regularly invoked by the Arab rulers at times of internal crises to buttress the internal unity of their societies. Palestine continues today to be employed as an important factor in promoting the domestic political cohesion of the countries of the Arab Gulf and North Africa. Finally, since 1948, the Palestine issue has been instrumental in the process of achieving a certain measure of political and military co-operation between the Arab countries. In this respect the Arab countries have, on occasion, shown some willingness to act collectively on issues concerning the international recognition of the PLO and the rights of the Arab countries over the territories occupied by Israel in June 1967. However, these moments of joint effort have not, at any point, reached a level of co-operation in any way approaching political or military integration, nor have they ever lasted. Palestine may have contributed, at times, to a general form of pan-Arab solidarity, but on its own, it has not provided a basis for Arab political unity.

NOTES

1. Countries of the Arab core include Egypt and the Arab East, while those of the Arab periphery include Saudi Arabia and the Gulf states.
2. The Iraqi troops stationed in Jordan stood aloof, while the Syrian military intervention during the fighting was only half-hearted and ineffective, due to an internal struggle for power within the ranks of the Syrian leadership.
3. A case in point was the attempt of the Israeli authorities to form the Village Leagues in the West Bank. Similarly, the efforts of King Hussein to provide a substitute leadership for that of the PLO did not have any significant success.

13

Economic Interdependence and National Sovereignty

Samir Makdisi

INTRODUCTION

This chapter has three main objectives: the first is to examine the nature and manifestations of economic interdependence and the factors which influence it with special emphasis on policy interdependence; the second is to discuss the Arab countries' economic interdependence — at the structural and policy levels, and in both the global and the regional dimensions; the third is to attempt an assessment of the relationships between economic interdependence and national sovereignty as revealed by the case of the Arab states.

The chapter is divided into four main sections: (1) economic interdependence: nature, manifestations and underlying factors, (2) economic policy in an interdependent world, (3) the Arab economies: links with the world economy, regional links: dependent, interdependent and autonomous policies and (4) economic interdependence and sovereignty with special reference to the Arab states.

ECONOMIC INTERDEPENDENCE: NATURE, MANIFESTATIONS AND UNDERLYING FACTORS

The economic and financial links between the national and international economies are multifaceted and so are the manifestations of economic interdependence. In what follows we explore (1) the nature and manifestations of economic interdependence and (2) some of the factors which appear to govern the degree of interdependence between national and world economies.

Nature and manifestation of economic interdependence

Economic interdependence arises at all levels of international economic relations, specifically: (i) in trade, (ii) in capital movements, (iii) because of factor movements and (iv) in technology.[1] The degree of interdependence in each of these categories may differ widely from country to country. For some, the major link may be trade relations, for others, trade and capital movements may be equally important and for still others trade and the transfer of technology may constitute the most important links with the outside world. Finally, there are countries for which trade, capital and factor movements are all important ties with the outside (this being the case for the Arab oil exporting countries).

Historically, trade movements have been the most important link between national economies, followed by capital movements. In more recent years, factor movements and technological ties have come to assume a growing role in determining the nature and extent of economic interdependence among sovereign nations.

Interdependence implies a two-way or mutual dependence between national economies. For small countries this generally translates into dependence upon the larger countries, though the latter may in turn heavily depend on certain smaller countries for specific strategic imports. Among larger industrialised economies, the issue of mutual interdependence becomes more meaningful, though here again some countries are more 'dependent' than others.[2]

Given the various links between an individual economy and the world economy, three dimensions of interdependence need to be identified. The first is structural dependence, i.e., the extent to which the welfare of a given country is dependent upon world markets, whether on the demand or supply side, because of the structure of natural endowments and of the productive system existing in the country. This refers to a major aspect of integration with the world economy. Countries which depend upon exports of few raw materials are, for example, highly dependent upon demand abroad for these products and their economic welfare is therefore linked in a major way to the level of this demand. Countries with more diversified economies may not be less dependent on the world economy but may be able to better withstand the impact of external fluctuations and have more freedom in terms of adjustment policies. Generally the more integrated national economies are via the goods and financial markets, the more closely the goods and assets of one country will act as substitutes for the goods and assets of another and the greater the degree of interdependence will be.

This brings us to the second dimension which relates to policy interdependence, i.e. the impact of policy measures in an economically interdependent world. Policy actions taken in one major country are bound to affect the domestic economies of other countries. Adjustment mechanisms which operate or are permitted to operate in response to policy actions taken abroad have a direct bearing on the degree of interdependence countries care to tolerate. Exchange rate and interest rate policies, inflation rates and money stocks are all major issues pertaining to policy interdependence among countries (Swoboda, 1983: 76). They are of paramount importance to the larger countries and to countries participating in regional groupings: hence the emphasis laid by such groupings on the need for policy co-ordination (Hamada, 1979: 294). The more integrated national economies are, the greater is the need for policy co-ordination.

The third dimension has to do with the political implications of interdependence. Some countries are more willing than others to be integrated in the world economy or in a regional economy, and to accept the limitations on independent economic action which this integration may require. Two structurally similar economies may pursue different policies with regard to economic and financial interactions with the outside world. One may choose to be highly open while the other may attempt to insulate its economy via restrictive policies. The rationale for this choice cannot be purely economic; quite to the contrary, it is likely to be to a large extent political in nature, as the authorities may be motivated by what they perceive to be paramount considerations of national sovereignty.

Economic interdependence is a fundamental phenomenon of the contemporary world and for most, if not all, countries economic progress is hardly possible independent of the world economy except at unacceptable economic and social costs. But while it is agreed that international trade and, more generally, international economic relations, provide the basis for growth at a much faster rate than would otherwise be the case, there is no common agreement as to the most appropriate forms of international economic intercourse, and indeed as to the extent to which an individual economy should integrate with the world economy. The reasons for diverging beliefs in this respect are both economic and non-economic. Economic reasons pertain to different conceptions of the optimal degree and forms of integration: bilateral vs multilateral relations, outward vs inward looking industrialisation etc. But these are also issues which often are decided upon in a political context, in so far as they relate to the independent status of nations or to the degree of dependence (real or imaginary) they are willing to tolerate in an interdependent world.

Factors influencing economic interdependence

We shall examine three interrelated factors of interdependence: (1) the resource endowment of an individual economy and the extent to which it can be developed domestically through the expansion of the domestic market, (2) the policy stance on the desirable degree of openness of the national economy and (3) the degree to which the economy is public or private sector oriented. The interrelations of these factors should be properly recognised, as evidenced, for example, by the generally high correlation between the last two of them.

The capacity of the domestic economy to support self-sustained development on its own is expected to influence its degree of reliance on international trade. This capacity is based on the availability of both human and material resources as well as the level of technology attained. In today's world, only a few countries claim to be able to follow a developmental strategy based on relative insulation from the rest of the world economy. And even these few, if they tried to insulate, would find that the cost of development, especially in terms of consumption sacrifices and loss of the benefits which are normally derived from international specialisation and trade, becomes excessively high and unwarranted. Many countries rely on the world economy to an extreme extent precisely because their domestic markets are incapable of supporting self-sustained development on their own. Other countries may be less reliant on the international economy, depending upon their resources and the ability of the domestic market to develop. Where relative abundance of human and material resources exists, and the domestic market can be developed rapidly, the propensity to be more self-reliant or less dependent upon the outside world may increase. In practice, though, this need not be the case.

The degree of openness of an economy is also obviously influenced by the policy stance of the national authorities. When there are no restrictions on current and capital transfers and restrictions on trade are relatively few, or the country is a member of a large free trade area, the economy is likely to be more integrated, and hence more dependent upon the world economy, than is an economy characterised by various types of restrictions. Put somewhat differently, countries which tend to co-ordinate their economic policies with other countries, or permit a necessary domestic adjustment in response to balance of payment developments, normally exhibit a higher degree of interdependence than do countries which attempt to insulate their domestic economies from the effects of economic developments and policies abroad. The degree of economic interdependence is, therefore, influenced by the type of international economic policies which individual countries pursue.

The relative importance attributed to the public vs private sector is closely related to the attitude towards international interdependence. Generally, the more public sector oriented economies tend to follow less liberal international economic policies than do private sector oriented economies. The interaction of the former countries with the world economy is normally more restricted than that of the latter group. For this reason the public sector oriented economies may generally exhibit a lesser degree of dependence upon the outside world than do other countries. It should not be concluded, however, that this need be the case. In my view, the option of greater or lesser interdependence with the world economy is open to both public and private sector economies and the choice is one which the national authorities have to make.

ECONOMIC POLICY IN AN INTERDEPENDENT WORLD

While economic interdependence may be identified at several levels, a major aspect which deserves to be highlighted is economic policy in an interdependent world. Policy actions influence, albeit to varying degrees, all forms of economic interdependence. Irrespective of the given characteristics of a particular economy, the extent and form of its linkage with the outside world are greatly affected by the economic policies pursued by the national authorities.

Granted some countries may be able to use their economic policies more effectively than others. Larger countries exercise a greater degree of autonomy in policy-making than do smaller countries. None the less, they also have to account for developments elsewhere in the world, especially in the other larger countries.

Policy action by governments is an expression of national sovereignty. The extent to which such action, on its own, is effective

323

in achieving its target, reflects the degree of autonomy with which governments can pursue their stated objectives. The more integrated national economies are, the smaller the degree of policy autonomy. This fact, as pointed out above, lies at the core of regional attempts of industrialised economies to achieve proper policy co-ordination.[3]

For developing countries which want to achieve regional integration, policy co-ordination is equally important. In a regional context, the question of interdependence becomes significant. However, in their relations with the industrialised world, the issue of dependence becomes dominant.

Foreign exchange markets are the link between domestic and international economies. But it is the aggregate of the international economic policies of each country which, in substantial measure, determines the extent and nature of this link. The more liberal these policies are, the greater is the potential interaction between national economies and hence the greater the policy interdependence. This, in turn, may lead to increasing restrictions on the autonomy of domestic policy.

Restrictions on trade and payments, which take many forms, tend to insulate the national economy from the rest of the world. To that extent they may, in principle, increase the independence of domestic policies. In practice, however, restrictions do not necessarily insulate the domestic economy to the degree which is desired, in so far as they give rise to 'unofficial' and/or illegal markets which may be difficult to control. Accordingly, autonomous policy-making in economies which are externally restricted or protected is not necessarily greater than that enjoyed by economies with liberal policies.

Assuming substantially free foreign exchange markets, do certain international economic policies provide more autonomy to domestic policies than others? It has been argued, for example, that freely floating exchange rates insulate the domestic economy from the impact of external developments while fixed exchange rates are supposed to bring about greater interdependence between national economies. However, empirical evidence does not fully support this statement. Other factors need to be considered, it would seem, which may be more relevant than exchange rate regimes as explanatory variables of interdependence (Swoboda, 1983: 98–100).

What should be emphasised is that in an increasingly inter-dependent world the autonomy of economic policymaking in individual economies — viewed in terms of its ability to attain desired objectives on its own — has become severely restricted. But if growing interdependence is especially applicable to the larger industrialised economies, the dependence of smaller economies on the markets and policy actions of the industrial world has also increased. Repeated demands on the part of developing countries for greater access to the markets and technology of the industrialised countries illustrate their growing dependence. Growth, diversification of the economic base and the development of the material and human infrastructures are the major aims of developing countries. In all these areas, and in others, their need for interactions with the industrial world is immense. At the same time, their policies (with few exceptions) do not materially affect the larger countries, whereas they have to bear the consequences of the latter's policies in their countries.

In this context, developing countries are faced with three basic issues: (1) to what extent are the prerequisites of their own development a function of their economic interdependence with industrialised countries; how strong are their ties with the outside world? (2) to what extent are their own domestic policies autonomous in terms of achieving stated targets, both internal and external; are certain domestic policies more autonomous than others? and (3) what significance do regional groupings among developing countries have with respect to the sovereignty/interdependence dilemma? Once these questions have been examined, it will be possible to discern some of the basic interrelationships between national sovereignty and economic interdependence. In order to address the questions we just posed, it is obviously necessary to examine the specific characteristics of the particular economy and of the regional grouping to which it may belong. This we shall attempt to undertake with respect to Arab countries.

THE ARAB ECONOMIES

We shall classify the Arab economies into: (i) primarily oil exporting economies,[4] (ii) private sector oriented economies;[5] and (iii) public sector oriented economies.[6] The reason for adopting this classification is that it will serve the purposes of our analysis when considering the questions raised in the preceding section. Three topics will be examined: (i) links of the Arab economies with the world economy; (ii) inter-Arab economic links and (iii) policy

325

dependence and interdependence in relation to the world and regional economies. Some of the data presented refers to selected countries in each of the three groups.

Links with the world economy

Important links connect the Arab economies to the rest of the world, and particularly to the economies of the industrial world. These links reveal the relatively high degree of Arab dependency.

The latter is most obvious in the field of technology: the majority of Arab imports are manufactured goods which embody advanced technologies developed elsewhere. All Arab countries rely, to a great extent, on foreign inputs of technical know-how, patents and technical management. Reliance on foreign technology has not been accompanied, it would seem, by the required growth in R and D activities and technological management. The adaptation of acquired technology and its integration in the development process, to serve appropriately the developmental requirements of these countries, seems to be lagging behind (Zahlan, 1978). Thus, Arab technological dependency on the industrial world will continue in the foreseeable future with all its socio-economic and political implications. Unlike dependency in trade or capital movements, technological dependency is almost total. At this stage of their development the Arab countries can only be receivers of technological know-how, though some progress in building national institutions devoted to the development of indigenous technology is being made. In other words, the scope for autonomous action in this field appears much more restricted than in other fields.

The nature of trade links with the outside world is manifested by (i) the importance of foreign markets, especially those of the industrial countries, for Arab development and (ii) the position which trade occupies in national income. Table 13.1 shows that for the Arab countries as a whole, roughly three-quarters of international trade is with the industrial world. For individual countries this proportion varies. Table 13.2 indicates, in turn, that industrial goods supplied by the industrial countries account for over two-thirds of combined Arab imports again with varying shares for individual countries.

These two tables reflect, of course, a common phenomenon of developing countries, namely, their heavy dependence on the markets of the industrialised countries to acquire goods essential to

Table 13.1: Total Arab foreign trade: composition (%)

	1980		1981		1982	
	Exports	Imports	Exports	Imports	Exports	Imports
Agricultural products and beverages	1	16	1	18	1	14
Raw materials, petroleum	96	11	96	9	97	13
Chemicals	1	6	1	5	1	5
Industrial goods and transport equipment	2	67	2	68	1	68

Source: *Joint Arab Economic Reports 1981 and 1985.*

Table 13.2: Total Arab foreign trade: geographical distribution (%)

	1980		1981		1982		1983	
	Exports	Imports	Exports	Imports	Exports	Imports	Exports	Imports
Arab countries	5	11	1	8	8	10	8	8
Industrial countries	74	72	70	68	65	74	66	75
of which:								
EEC	34	46	33	38	31	40	29	40
US	14	12	13	12	7	13	6	13
Japan	17	14	18	12	19	13	20	13
Comecon countries	1	3	1	9	1	2	1	2
Developing countries	20	14	23	15	26	14	25	15
Total	100	100	95	100	100	100	100	100

Source: *Joint Arab Economic Report, 1984–1985.*

their developmental process. In contrast, oil apart, the dependence of the industrial countries on the Arab markets as a source of needed goods is very limited.

Oil trade is clearly essential for many countries. Its importance to the oil countries however is directly related to the proceeds it generates which in turn are dependent on the need of the primarily industrial countries for oil imports. Further, as mentioned below, it is the capital markets of these countries which, so far, have constituted the most important outlets for the investable surpluses of the oil exporting countries.

Oil trade, it may be said, reflects a certain degree of interdependence between Arab oil and the industrial countries not applicable to other forms of trade between the two groups. At the same time, the almost exclusive reliance of certain oil countries on exports of oil, a depletable natural resource, renders them nearly completely dependent upon the world economy. This applies to their need to both market their oil and to place the larger portion of their investable surpluses abroad. In the long run, they will have to contend with the depletion of oil resources and their reduced role in world industrial development.

Table 13.3 illustrates the ratio of exports and imports to GNP in selected Arab countries. On the import side, the oil countries and the private sector oriented economies exhibit higher ratios than do public sector oriented economies. This partly reflects the more liberal foreign exchange policies followed by the first two groups of countries. On the export side, a generally similar pattern appears though the differences between the second and third group is less pronounced than in the case of import ratios. While these ratios do not, on their own, convey a complete or sufficient picture of the relative degrees of interaction with the world economy, they point to the relatively greater dependence of the first two groups. This stems from both the given characteristics of the particular economies and the policy stance adopted by the national authorities.

Capital movements shed additional light on the issue of dependence (see Table 13.4 and 13.5). For the oil-exporting countries, outward long-term and short-term capital movements are a direct result of limited absorption capacity, which gives rise to substantial investable surpluses. The larger part of these surpluses has been attracted to the capital markets of the industrial countries, in particular the US and UK (IMF, 1982: 165), as these (especially the US market) appear to be the ones which can readily absorb huge investable surpluses. It should be noted that both direct investments

Table 13.3: Selected Arab countries: ratios of exports and imports to GNP (%)

Country	1980 Exports/GNP	1980 Imports/GNP	1981 Exports/GNP	1981 Imports/GNP	1982 Exports/GNP	1982 Imports/GNP	1983 Exports/GNP	1983 Imports/GNP
1st group								
Kuwait	67	29	71[1]	40[1]	59[1]	56[1]	56[1]	50[1]
Saudi Arabia	66	34	69	29	67	36	57	47
2nd group								
Jordan	39	81	42	92	39	89	35	79
Lebanon[2]	30	71	32	68	34	84	16[3]	93
Tunisia	40	46	41	49	36	47	35	43
3rd group								
Algeria[1]	34	30	34	31	30	29		
Egypt			28	36	27	38	28	36
Syria[1]	18	33	15	31	13	24	12	25

Notes: 1. GDP is used instead of GNP.
2. Rough estimates.
3. Substantial drop due to political and military events of that year.
Source: *IMF — International Financial Statistics*, April 1985.

Table 13.4: Selected Arab countries: net long-term capital movements (millions of SDRs)

Country	1980					1981					1982				
	DI	PI	OLT	TLT	CAC	DI	PT	OLT	TLT	CAC	DI	PI	OLT	TLT	CAC
Kuwait	−313	−253	537	−28	11757	128	−106	304	325	11684	−98	167	−289	−220	4414
Saudi Arabia	−2453	−18128	−457	21038	32849	5468	−27820	−1203	−23555	36264	10080	−12775		−2695	6862
Algeria	242		448	690	191	−1		6	5	72	−59	−3	−804	−866	−166
Egypt	416	4	311	731	−336	633	6	1081	1720	−1812	258		1001	1260	1677
Syria			−19	−19	−31	−193		41	41	−233			−7	−7	−228
Jordan	24		58	82	287	126		58	186	−33	51	−238	288		−304
Tunisia	180	11	199	391	−272	249	−2	292	539	−314	307	−57	336	699	597

Country	1983					1984					1985				
	DI	PI	OLT	TLT	CAC	DI	PT	OLT	TLT	CAC	DI	PI	OLT	TLT	CAC
Kuwait	−225	−199	−420	−844	4949	−92	204	−1160	−1048	6136	−56	−347	−655	−1058	5531
Saudi Arabia	4714	5448		10162	−15031	5100	14222		19322	−18580	2474	8541		11015	−12769
Algeria	−13	2	−782	−793	−80	−14		−381	−394	73	−2		−34	−36	
Egypt	440	6	167	614	−385	696	1	514	1210	−2030					
Syria			289	289	−762			318	318	−831					
Jordan	28		376	404	−364	72		90	163	−263	24		319	343	−248
Tunisia	174	36	378	587	−536	112	89	320	521	−711	107	30	437	574	−528

DI: Direct investment
PI: Portfolio investment
OLT: Other long-term
TLT: Total long-term
CAC: Current account
Source: *IMF Balance of Payments Statistics (1983: 34).*

and portfolio investments abroad are substantial and that they are mostly accounted for by governmental or public sector organisations.

For the second group of countries, long term capital inflows (largely drawings on official loans) are important in sustaining development plans and rates of growth which otherwise would not be attainable. Some of this inflow originates in the oil countries but a large part comes from industrial countries. Lebanon has traditionally relied on substantial private inflows but in recent years these have been greatly reduced due to the prevailing political situation. Direct investments have played a lesser role in these countries, while portfolio investments hardly appear. The explanation is that these countries do not possess investable surpluses and do not have highly developed capital markets which would attract funds from abroad. To a certain degree Lebanon is an exception in that relatively important portfolio investments abroad have been made by Lebanese residents. Some of the short-term capital movements of the other two countries refer to official loans or short-term trade credits.

The third group of countries (Tables 13.4 and 13.5) also relies on official loans to support its development plans. Algeria, an oil exporting country, has been less dependent on foreign loans than other countries in this group. In contrast with Syria, Egypt has relied on substantial direct investments from the rest of the world in recent years. Portfolio investments are either non-existent or very limited. Short-term capital movements appear to play a more significant role in Syria than Egypt. For the former country they include trade credits to the private sector and official movements under payment agreements concluded with foreign countries.

For the non-oil countries, capital inflows undoubtedly sustain levels of imports and of developmental expenditures which otherwise could not be attained. For the primarily oil exporters, capital outflows are in search of investment outlets not available domestically. The degree of dependence of either group on international capital movements is obvious and needs no further emphasis.

Inter-Arab economic links

Three aspects of inter-Arab economic links will be touched on briefly: (i) trade, (ii) capital movements and (iii) attempts at regional integration.[7]

Inter-Arab trade comprises a relatively small portion of total

Table 13.5: Selected Arab countries: balance of payments items (million SDRs)

	1980			1981			1982		
	CA	LTCA	STCA	CA	LTCA	STCA	CA	LTCA	STCA
1st group									
Kuwait	11757	−28	−8658	11684	325	−7365	4414	−220	−2526
Saudi Arabia	32849	−21038	−8778	36264	−23555	−4571	6862	−2695	−6259
2nd group[1]									
Jordan	287	82	171	−33	186	76	−304	288	60
Tunisia	−272	91	99	−314	539	−143	−597	699	−18
3rd group									
Algeria	191	690	43	72	5	9	−166	−866	142
Egypt	−336	731	47	−1812	1720	31	−1677	1260	75
Syria	193	−19	331	−233	41	450	−228	−7	134

	1983			1984			1985		
	CA	LTCA	STCA	CA	LTCA	STCA	CA	LTCA	STCA
1st group									
Kuwait	4949	-844	960	6136	-1048	-6037	5531	-1058	-1641
Saudi Arabia	-15031	10162	3429	-18580	19322	-2207	-12769	11015	1063
2nd group									
Jordan[1]	-364	404	119	-263	163	171	-248	343	54
Tunisia	-536	587	-185	-711	521	-4	-528	574	-14
3rd group									
Algeria	-80	-793	299	73	-394	189		-36	-83
Egypt	-385	614		-2050	1210	566			
Syria	-762	289	290	-831	318				

Note: 1. Reliable data for Lebanon not available.
CA: Current account
LTCA: Long-term capital account
STCA: Short-term capital account (excludes exceptional financing and changes in reserves)
Source: *IMF Balance of Payments Statistics* (1986: 37).

Arab trade: less than 10 per cent in recent years (see Table 13.2). Even if oil trade is excluded, the proportion remains relatively small. For individual Arab countries such as Jordan, Lebanon and Syria, however, Arab markets are much more important, particularly on the export side and with respect to manufactures. Indeed, the rationale for the establishment of an Arab regional market partly rests on the potential which such a market is expected to have in stimulating Arab industrial development. But apart from these limited exceptions, inter-Arab trade continues to be relatively restricted.[8]

Inter-Arab capital movements are also minor in relation to the combined Arab capital flows to the rest of the world, and in particular to the industrial countries. In the period 1974–81, for example, about 15 per cent of the Arab oil countries' cumulative current account surpluses of US$360 billion were directed as official aid to the Arab countries. Of this amount about 85 per cent was bilateral (government-to-government) and the rest originated in multilateral sources (regional funds). What is noteworthy, however, is that Arab aid covered about one-third of the external resources required for the combined investment programmes in the Arab countries — about $80 billion for the period under consideration (Makdisi, 1985). The pattern of investment flows of the Arab oil countries is familiar: the capital markets of the industrial countries act as powerful magnets for investable surpluses; the smaller portion of investment flows to the Arab region are primarily official loans and grants. But while in relative terms the investment flows to the Arab countries may be small, in terms of their support of Arab developmental programmes they play a substantial role.

Several attempts at regional economic integration have been made. In practice, no substantial progress in this direction has, so far, been achieved, except perhaps recently among the Arab Gulf countries (members of the Gulf Cooperation Council).[9] At present pan-Arab economic co-operation is essentially manifested in various regional and national funds which extend loans to Arab countries, as well as in joint Arab investment projects which involve combinations of Arab countries. But neither a unified Arab market nor closer co-ordination of Arab financial policies have been achieved.[10] Moves towards closer economic and financial integration will gradually bring about a greater degree of interdependence among the Arab countries especially at the policy level. Inter-Arab financial flows and investments, in particular from the oil to the non-oil economies, are likely to increase and come to assume a growing role in the economic development of individual Arab countries. At the trade level, however, the unification of the Arab market will only gradually bring about a greater degree of interdependence among the Arab economies. Given their present characteristics and development, the trade links with the outside world will not be significantly affected except gradually and over a period of time. In any event, closer Arab economic integration is likely to manifest itself more markedly in the monetary than in the trade fields.

The issue of interdependence is therefore expected to be more significant in the area of monetary policy than in trade. Monetary integration would gradually provide the Arab economies with a larger degree of policy autonomy to the extent that they can act as an effective regional block *vis-à-vis* the rest of the world.

Economic policy: autonomous, dependent and interdependent

Policy formulation requires the drawing up of national targets and the identification of policy instruments to be employed in attaining them. The crucial issue that national authorities have to consider at any time is that they face restrictions in formulating economic policy. What instruments are available and what targets are attainable during a given period of time? Existing restrictions vary not only from country to country but from one policy to another in the same country. In what follows preliminary observations will be made concerning: (i) the dependent or autonomous nature of Arab economic policies under existing conditions, in which the three categories of Arab countries discussed earlier will be treated separately and (ii) the implications for inter-Arab policy interdependence of closer integration among the Arab economies.

The primary oil exporting countries

Externally, these are fully open economies with no restrictions on current and capital transfers. Their exchange rates are formally linked to the SDR but effectively to the US dollar with the exception of Kuwait whose dinar is linked to a basket of currencies including the US dollar. Their foreign exchange rate policy, accordingly, is dependent upon the behaviour of the US dollar.

In principle, they do possess a degree of autonomy in so far as they can vary their own parities *vis-à-vis* the dollar. Parity changes have been made infrequently, though. They can also exercise some autonomy in their rate policies by varying the margins around parity. Indeed, Kuwait excepted, they maintain in principle, margins of 7.50 per cent around their parity with SDR but, in practice, the rate is not allowed to vary except within narrow margins.

Given their dependence on oil exports which are priced in dollars, the oil countries have sought to achieve relative stability in their exchange rates and in the foreign exchange market. In the first half of the 1980s their exchange rates *vis-à-vis* the dollar have remained virtually unchanged while the Kuwait dinar and to a lesser extent the Saudi rial have shown modest variation.[11] In 1985 and 1986 however, some of these countries reacted to the collapse in oil prices and revenues with devaluations relative to the dollar that served the purpose of reducing the imbalance in government budgets.

While some exchange rate policy options are available to the oil countries, their choices must be considered in relation to specific economic targets. A policy of appreciation of the national currency can be used, for example, to counter imported inflation. On the other hand, longer-term considerations of industrial development may require gradual depreciation of the national currency. Any changes in the prevailing exchange rate policy must be justified in terms of the targets the proposed change is supposed to serve. The advantages of choosing the exchange rate over alternative policy tools must be carefully evaluated. Unless the option of independent float is chosen (which does not seem to suit the case of the oil exporters), their ability to vary their exchange rate is limited. They effectively peg to the dollar for the purpose of maintaining stability in their foreign exchange market. Significant and frequent parity changes could undermine this objective, and render the process of domestic planning more cumbersome.

As for their policy concerning capital movements, the oil countries are obliged to permit the freedom of outward movements because they are in need of the capital markets of the industrial countries. The extent of this dependency will change gradually over time should the Arab region succeed in integrating economically and financially.

Domestically, the most important factor determining the pace of economic activity is the level of net government expenditure which is directly decided upon by the national authorities. As long as substantial oil revenues are being generated, the major constraint facing governmental expenditures is domestic absorptive capacity. Budget revenue, of course, is essentially dependent upon oil exports primarily to the industrial countries.[12] Given a stable foreign exchange situation, the authorities possess a substantial degree of policy autonomy in varying domestic expenditure and hence the level of domestic activity to attain specific domestic targets. In the long run this may not be the case, should oil revenues lose their present importance as a source of revenue.

Concerning economic relations with the Arab world, the policy dependence of the oil exporters is relatively small if not negligible. Arab markets are not, overall, significant as outlets for their exports or as sources of their imports. This is equally true in the area of capital movements. The one area where the dependence of the oil countries on other Arab countries has manifested itself is the supply of manpower, both skilled and unskilled. The nature of this dependence, is explored elsewhere in this volume.

The private sector oriented economies

This category comprises a heterogeneous group of countries, especially concerning their external economic policies. What they have in common is that the prominent role played by the private sector requires the national authorities to rely more heavily on traditional economic tools than is the case in other Arab countries.

Most of the countries in this group, if not all, maintain relatively liberal exchange systems. However, with the exception of Lebanon, which maintains no restrictions whatsoever on current or capital transfers, and of the Yemen Arab Republic, which permits free capital movements, they all impose certain controls with more liberal treatment being accorded to current rather than to capital transfers.

Their exchange rate policies differ: Lebanon maintains an independent float; the others peg either to the SDR, to the US dollar or to a basket of currencies.[13] Lebanon, and to a lesser extent, Morocco, have opted to retain some autonomy over their exchange rate policies in that they try to influence the floating of their currencies *vis-à-vis* other currencies. Despite the controls which some of the countries in this group maintain, all of them have opted to accept a relatively high degree of interaction with the world economy and especially with the industrial economies. Those with fixed pegs have chosen to bear the consequences of the movements of the currency to which they are linked, i.e. the currency or currencies in which their trade is primarily denominated. This policy has been chosen for the purpose of maintaining stability in their foreign exchange markets. Those which maintain an independent or managed float do not necessarily insulate their domestic economies

337

from the impact of balance of payments developments, particularly since they are open economies dependent on world trade and foreign capital, but they do possess a certain flexibility in their exchange rate policies.

The relative openness of the private sector oriented economies increases the difficulty of domestic macro-economic management. The authorities' tendency to rely on traditional monetary and fiscal tools to influence the level of economic activity and economic policy in these countries is probably greater than it is in other Arab countries. Reliance on market oriented policies implies, however, dependence on policy developments abroad especially in industrial countries. To illustrate, domestic interest rate policy cannot be set independently of interest rate policies abroad and similarly the level of monetary expansion as a tool of macro-economic management cannot be controlled independently of balance of payments developments. While a limited degree of policy manoeuvrability may exist, especially if external restrictions are effectively maintained, their domestic monetary management remains strongly influenced by world monetary developments, particularly inasmuch as they lack developed financial markets.

It is in the fiscal area that greater policy autonomy may be achieved. National authorities can vary the level of taxation and/or public expenditure. But this autonomy is limited as well, in view of the fact that most of the countries concerned rely on public capital inflows to support their development programmes or their general budget. The degree to which this autonomy is restricted depends in part on the growth targets which have been set by the authorities: the more ambitious they are, the greater is their fiscal dependence on other countries.

Economic interdependence with the rest of the Arab world exists in both trade and capital movements. For some of the countries in this group (e.g. Lebanon, Jordan, Yemen Arab Republic), the Arab markets are important export outlets. All of them seek to attract Arab capital with varying degrees of success. Their economic policies, however, do not seem to be influenced by the extent of their economic or monetary interaction with the rest of the Arab world. Neither their domestic policies nor exchange rate policies are formulated with the Arab economic dimension in mind. Arab capital is primarily sought through bilateral negotiations with the donor countries or regional funds.

The public sector oriented economies

All the countries included in this category maintain comprehensive controls over their economic relations with the rest of the world, especially as regards capital movements. With the exception of Algeria, which pegs its currency to a basket of foreign currencies, all of them peg to the US dollar with infrequent changes in their official parities. Some countries (Egypt, Sudan and Syria) maintain multiple exchange rates: official, parallel and free markets. The exchange rate pertaining to the official market is fixed, while in other parallel markets it is either fixed at a more depreciated level, or allowed to float either freely or within certain limits.

Without going into the merits and demerits of multiple exchange rates, they are supposed to offer more autonomy over domestic economic policies. Whether, in fact, this is true is more of an empirical than a theoretical question.

Ineffective controls invariably lead to illegal markets which tend to defeat the purposes for which controls were set up in the first place. To the extent that they are successful in insulating the domestic economy as planned, the national authorities can perhaps rely on domestic policy tools more effectively than can governments in private sector oriented economies.

Experience shows, for example, that monetary policy plays a minor role in public sector oriented economies; indeed, it often tends to accommodate the requirements of public sector operations. Fiscal policy, as part of overall planning, plays a more important role than does monetary policy. The authorities can formulate fiscal targets fully well knowing that monetary policy will respond to the requirements of fiscal policy. None the less, fiscal policy autonomy is restricted, as in the case of private sector economies, by two external factors, namely (i) the availability of foreign financing and (ii) balance of payments developments which can vary dramatically from year to year. For both aspects, the dependency of these economies on the outside world is clear, and there is little they can economically do to influence the outcome in their favour. The policy autonomy which governments in public sector oriented economies possess is constrained in a major way by external monetary developments beyond their control.

Regional integration

Let us assume, for purposes of analysis, that the Arab countries succeed in forging close regional integration consisting in (i) free trade between the Arab countries (ii) free movement of capital and

(iii) greater policy co-ordination in trade and monetary policies including exchange rates. On this assumption the implications for Arab policy interdependence may be summarised as follows:

(a) The effects of any integration are likely to be felt gradually over the longer term. The evolution of the productive and absorptive capacities of the Arab economies will be relatively slow. In consequence, any increase in the level of Arab economic interdependence is likely to be gradual.

(b) The emergence of a unified Arab market is expected initially to benefit the more industrialised Arab countries. However, until the Arab economies can achieve advanced levels of industrial development, their dependence on the markets of the industrial countries as sources of imports, possibly also as outlets for investments will remain immense. In any event, as the literature on the product life-cycle implicitly points out, the form of dependency on the more advanced industrial countries will shift from standardised technologically mature products to high technology products.[14] Should a unified Arab market eventually lead to greater inter-Arab industrial trade, then the level of Arab industrial interactions will, in turn, increase and so will the interdependence between Arab trade and exchange rate policies.

The implications for the oil countries are not necessarily clear. The net effect would partly depend on (i) the evolving significance of oil in world industrial development and (ii) the extent to which oil countries succeed in building an industrial base which can compete with industries based in other Arab countries. The more they succeed in this latter endeavour, the less will be their future dependence on trade with Arab countries, at least as far as the technologically mature products are concerned.

(c) At the investment level, closer monetary integration including free capital movements between the Arab countries and co-ordinated exchange rate policies may not have a substantial impact initially. Inter-Arab investment flows will continue to be governed by (i) the availability of suitable investment outlets (ii) the maintenance of a relatively stable financial environment and (iii) freedom of further transfers of capital within as well as outside the region.

Even if the last two conditions are fulfilled, the availability of suitable investment opportunities will partly depend upon the growth of the Arab domestic economies and of Arab financial markets and intermediation, all of which evolve gradually. Closer Arab monetary integration may thus not lead to a dramatic redirection of Arab investments toward the Arab region.

One should bear in mind that Arab investment behaviour is, to a large extent, governed by the behaviour of public investment institutions whose criteria are political as much as they are economic. The influence of purely economic and financial considerations, none the less, should not be ignored.

In brief, in the short term, closer Arab monetary integration would not dramatically reduce the flow of Arab funds to the capital markets of the industrial countries. In the longer term, a redirection in favour of the Arab economies may very well occur. This, in turn, will bring about closer Arab financial interdependence and will afford the Arab region more policy autonomy *vis-à-vis* the rest of the world.

(d) At the macro-economic policy level, greater economic interactions will result in greater policy interdependence. Indeed, proper policy co-ordination among the Arab countries will promote inter-Arab trade and investment flows. Trade, monetary and policy integration reinforce one another. To the extent that integration takes place. Arab policy dependence upon the outside world will correspondingly decrease. The speed and extent of this transformation is uncertain, being influenced by the evolving strategy and pattern of Arab industrial development, i.e. whether it tends to be integrative with world industrial development or relatively inward looking.

ECONOMIC INTERDEPENDENCE AND SOVEREIGNTY WITH REFERENCE TO THE ARAB STATES

Economic sovereignty, i.e. the ability to develop independently and to take policy actions without regard to developments and/or reactions elsewhere, is a fundamental component of national sovereignty. In an economically interdependent world absolute economic sovereignty probably does not exist, and if it did it could only be sustained at a very substantial cost in terms of economic growth and welfare. Wealth and power, it has often been pointed out, are complementary: the one leads to the other (Keohane, 1984: 22–4). Hence the wealthier a state, the more powerful it is and the greater is its say in international economic matters. Generally speaking, wealthier or more advanced countries enjoy fuller economic sovereignty than do less wealthy or less advanced countries. But the level of wealth attained does not, on its own, necessarily determine the degree of economic sovereignty a country can enjoy. The latter would also partly depend upon the extent to which the process of wealth accumulation is itself a function of the country's dependence upon the world economy. Given the linkage of wealth and power, the more dependent a country's economic development is on the world economy, the less the degree of economic sovereignty it is likely to enjoy.[15] Japan and the United Kingdom are relatively wealthy and advanced countries. They are both, however, highly dependent upon world trade and to that extent their economic sovereignty is constrained by this dependence. Had they been able to attain the level of wealth they enjoy today largely independently of world trade, they could have achieved a higher level of autonomy in terms of economic decision-making than they presently enjoy.[16]

The degree of economic sovereignty is closely linked to the objectives which a country sets for itself, and the means it employs to attain them. If one accepts the notion that a country's growth potential is enhanced by interactions with the world economy via trade and investment flows, and that the country wishes to take advantage of the interactions, then it follows that the country's economic sovereignty cannot be absolute.

The degree of its reliance on the world economy will vary depending on a number of factors, including its economic objectives. For example, certain growth targets may not be attainable without substantial levels of foreign trade. Or the potential to develop industries may be greater under appropriate forms of protection than in their absence. The objectives which a country sets for itself and the means it employs to attain them have an important bearing on the degree of integration of its economy with the rest of the world, and on the degree to which it can maintain its economic sovereignty in an economically interdependent world.

Economic dependence implies political dependence. Controversies regarding the extent to which the domestic economy should integrate with the world economy are as much political in nature as they are economic. This is an area where economic and political issues are closely intertwined. Political considerations may override considerations of economic efficiency and growth and vice versa. Trade-offs between political sovereignty and economic welfare may have to be made. A country may choose to be politically more independent at the cost of economic benefits.[17] On the other hand, political independence may present a country with the potential for faster economic development if this also implies sovereignty in the choice of economic policy.

Issues relating to the interrelationship between political and economic sovereignty, on the one hand, and economic welfare on the other may not be readily settled. One can argue that political and economic sovereignty is or should be the primary objective of all national policies. But to what extent can a country reconcile the objectives of sovereignty and growth in an economically inter-dependent world?

The answer to this question is obviously complex and varies from one country to another. Many factors have to be considered and properly weighed before attempting an answer. They include the level and pattern of development achieved by the country concerned, its national and human endowment, reliance on outside markets, economic and social objectives to be realised, the size of the economy, the political power it enjoys internationally, etc. The relative importance of each of these factors cannot be determined *a priori* and is expected to vary from country to country. And for each country it would be difficult to quantify the relative significance of each of the factors involved. Still, they have to be borne in mind when assessing a single country's situation or that of a regional grouping.

In the case of the Arab states, two general observations can be made: first, given their present endowment, level and pattern of development and the economic objectives which they have set for themselves, their reliance on world markets for trade, investment and technology is very substantial indeed. To that extent, their economic sovereignty is highly constrained. Secondly, the extent to which this sovereignty is practised may vary considerably from one Arab state to another, though as stated above, no *a priori* comparisons can be made in this respect.

The highest degree of economic dependence among Arab countries is found in the oil exporting countries, while the public sector oriented economies occupy the opposite end of the scale. How does this translate in terms of sovereignty? There is no clear-cut answer. Acting within the framework of OPEC, the Arab oil countries have been able to influence the world price of oil and hence the level of their export earnings. To that extent, joint action allowed them to maintain a degree of sovereignty which would not have been attainable otherwise.[18] None the less, individual national sovereignty has been subjugated to joint OPEC sovereignty. And while the huge oil revenues provide them with sovereignty in deciding economic and development priorities in the relative absence of financial constraints, their ability to generate revenue via oil exports and to dispose of this revenue as they choose has been directly linked to markets — primarily of the industrial countries — and to policies enforced by these countries. Given the need of the oil countries for the markets of the industrial countries, they hardly possess any policy options as to where to direct the bulk of their oil revenue except to these countries, and they cannot influence the policies which these countries choose to implement with respect to prices of goods or prevailing returns in the financial markets.

The dependence of the oil countries on the world economy is almost totally in contrast with the situation of the non-oil Arab countries endowed with domestic resources other than oil. Undoubtedly, substantial oil revenues imply financial power. But the financial resources the oil countries presently enjoy do not translate, in equal measure, into economic sovereignty in the sense of the ability to develop independently and take policy actions without regard to reactions elsewhere, specifically in the industrial countries. The real sovereignty they presently enjoy, as made possible by the huge financial resources at their disposal, pertains to decisions concerning the choice of national economic targets.

The Arab non-oil countries also depend heavily upon world trade and investments. But their economies are not as fully integrated with the world economy as are the oil economies. While a curtailment of economic links with the outside world would affect their economies adversely, they are in a relatively stronger position than the oil economies in choosing this option should the need arise. The domestic resources they possess afford them a better fall-back position than does a depletable resource such as oil. Admittedly, strict insulation of the domestic economy may not be implemented except at substantial economic and social costs. But such costs are incomparably greater for the oil exporting economies than for the non-oil economies.

In this respect it may be argued that the latter group of countries enjoys relatively greater sovereignty in decisions pertaining to foreign economic policies. However, since these countries aspire to achieve rapid rates of growth accompanied by relative financial stability, reliance on world trade and capital inflows is an important component in their development plans. Moreover, they do not possess the required financial strength which would permit them to have a wide range of policy options in setting their national economic targets.

It may be difficult to compare the relative degrees of national economic sovereignty enjoyed by each of the oil, public sector and private sector oriented economies. In the final analysis any judgement would have to be based on the weight one assigns to the various factors which influence the interrelationship between sovereignty and economic interdependence. When all factors are considered, one tentative conclusion may be that, potentially, public sector oriented economies have or can enjoy relatively more sovereignty than oil economies, or for that matter, private sector oriented economies.

This conclusion is predicated on the implicit recognition that one major element influencing the question of sovereignty is the potential economic and political ability of a country to withstand the repercussions of relative economic insulation or an attempt to pursue a more independent economic development. The public sector oriented Arab economies appear to have greater capability in this regard than do the other economies. In practice, however, given the national objectives of the various Arab states such a potential has not yet been really tested.

Closer Arab economic and financial integration, as pointed out above, is expected to gradually promote inter-Arab trade and investment, depending upon the rate and pattern of domestic transformation of individual Arab economies and the policies they pursue. Closer integration, however, implies closer policy co-ordination among the integrating countries. This, in turn, will have implications for the issue of sovereignty. At the individual level, the loss of some sovereignty in policy-making is a major cost which has to be borne by the individual countries. The argument in favour of economic integration is based on the fact that for any single economy, the benefits from integration outweigh its costs. On the other hand, closer integration would lead to the emergence of collective Arab sovereignty *vis-à-vis* the rest of the world and consequently, to an enhancement of individual countries' stature and say in international economic affairs. They will come to acquire potentially greater collective independence in setting their economic policies. At the same time, as long as the Arab countries continue collectively and individually to rely on world markets for trade, investment and technology, their dependence on the world economy will remain substantial.

The gradual industrialisation of the Arab economies and the concomitant growth in the inter-Arab trade and investment will gradually permit the Arab economies to develop the basis for more independent economic development. But, to a large extent, this will depend upon the future pattern of Arab development, i.e. whether Arab industrialisation tends to be internally or externally oriented, and the extent to which Arab industrial processes tend to rely on domestic rather than foreign resources. Irrespective of the purely economic merits and demerits of either orientation, an inward looking strategy is likely to create a greater potential for the exercise of economic sovereignty than an outward pattern of industrialisation with its integrative orientation toward the world economy. In making a choice, purely economic considerations may or may not indicate the need for an outward looking development. The choice of any path however, will be determined by both economic and political considerations.

NOTES

1. Technological flows manifest themselves through factor movements (skills, technical management) and trade flows (movement of goods embodying technology) or acquisition of patents. Technology, however, has come to occupy a very significant position in trade and economic growth and has come to be considered as a separate category in international economic relations.

2. Theories of dependency, expounded primarily by Latin American writers, emphasise the constraints and distortions which the prevailing international (capitalist) economic system places on the development of developing countries, putting them in a state of economic, social and cultural dependency on the industrial (capitalist) countries. What is required is a new international economic order which would permit the developing countries to achieve independent national development. Dependency theories, or some of them, argue for a relative insulation from, or less reliance on, the present international economic system via the pursuit of autarkic policies. For an examination of dependency theories see D. Seers (ed.) (1981) *Dependency Theory, A Critical Reassessment*, Frances Pinter, especially the articles by G. Palma and D. Seers. However, delinking from the international economic system, as Seers has pointed out could be very costly and raise major problems for the delinking country.

3. Policy co-ordination refers, in its essence, to the formulation of national targets and policy instruments required to achieve them. As already pointed out by Tinbergen many years ago, a given number of targets requires an equal (effective) number of instruments. See J. Tinbergen (1952) *On The Theory of Economic Policy*, North Holland. Policy instruments and targets should also be properly matched. See R. Mundell (1968) *International Economics*, Macmillan, London, p. 203.

4. Saudi Arabia and the Gulf countries.

5. Jordan, Lebanon, Morocco, Tunisia, Yemen Arab Republic.

6. Algeria, Egypt, Iraq, Libya, Sudan, Syria, the Democratic Republic of Yemen.

7. Labour movements have also come to constitute an important economic link between several Arab countries, especially the movement of

skilled and semi-skilled labour to the Arab Gulf countries. They will not be discussed here, however.

8. In 1982 a multilateral agreement facilitating and promoting inter-Arab trade came into effect. Nine Arab countries are so far signatories to this agreement.

9. For an analysis of various plans and proposals to achieve closer Arab economic and monetary integration, and of a cost-benefit analysis of closer integration see (i) *Horizons of International Monetary Developments and Arab Monetary Cooperation in the Eighties*, proceedings of a conference held in Amman in January 1984 organised by the Central Bank of Jordan, the Arab Monetary Fund and the Arab Thought Forum and (ii) K. Haseeb and S. Makdisi (eds) (1982) *Arab Monetary Integration: Issues and Prerequisites*, Croom Helm, London.

10. There are a number of reasons which explain the limited progress made towards closer Arab economic integration. A principal reason is the lack of the required political will to move in this direction. Other reasons pertain to the potential loss of sovereignty over economic policy, lack of conviction on the part of certain Arab countries of the benefits of integration, or the belief that national industrial development may be adversely affected and an unwillingness to effect the domestic adjustments required by economic integration. For a discussion of these points, see Haseeb and Makdisi (1982).

11. Admittedly, this observation refers to annual trends and not to possible short-term variations around the trend.

12. Returns on investments abroad are, however, assuming a gradually increasing role as a source of revenue. In the case of Kuwait, for example, investment income accounted in 1979/80 for 12.6 per cent of total public revenue, compared with shares of 39.0 per cent and 22.2 per cent in 1982/83 and 1983/84, respectively. This relative increase is partly explained by the drop in oil revenues during the first half of the eighties. See Central Bank of Kuwait, *The Kuwaiti Economy 1980–84*, pp. 47–8.

13. The Moroccan dinar is pegged to the currencies of the country's principal trading partners. The authorities follow a policy of managed float.

14. It is assumed that, in the foreseeable future, the Arab world will not be able to catch up in the technological field with the presently industrialised countries.

15. Unless a single state is sufficiently powerful to impose its economic will on the rest of the world without regard to any possible reactions from other states. This situation does not exist in today's world and it is unlikely to have existed earlier, though the US came to exercise, especially in the early period after the Second World War, immense influence on international economic affairs (Keohane, 1984).

16. As the world's most important single economy the US, as pointed out earlier, enjoys a high degree of economic sovereignty and major say in international economic affairs. To a large extent this is derived from the political and military power at its disposal. But it is also derived from the fact that, to a substantial degree, it can rely on its resources for purposes of development.

17. An extreme illustration would be a totally closed economy with no links whatsoever with the outside world. Such an economy can enjoy

absolute economic sovereignty. However for most, if not all countries of the world, such a situation carries with it unacceptable economic and social costs. The international economy has been described as a non-zero sum game, i.e. the sum of winnings may be greater than (or less than) zero, and all players (countries) may gain (or lose) simultaneously, though not necessarily in the same proportions. Under prevailing international economic relationships, however, the dominant capitalist nations have considerably greater bargaining power than do other countries, with all its implications on the issues of exploitation and dependence. See Cohen, (1973: 211–17).

18. In recent times the power of OPEC to influence the world price of oil appears to have been checked by policies enforced by the industrial countries.

14

Immigrants in the Arab Gulf Countries: 'Sojourners' or 'Settlers'?[1]

Georges Sabagh

An increasingly important aspect of the study of international migration from one Arab country to another, mainly capital-poor to capital-rich, is the relationship that may exist between this migration and patterns of integration. Yet, this is the aspect of international migration in the Arab world which appears to be least systematically studied. Thus, Fargues writing in 1980 (pp. 116–17) argued that the social effects of labour migration to the Gulf are least known and that there is the greatest deficiency of field studies of these effects. Nevertheless, he ventured the opinion that this migration has had more 'disintegrative' than 'integrative effects', particularly in the receiving oil-rich countries where there is extreme separation between natives and migrants. While more research and field studies of the social impact of international migration are now available, most of them pertain to sending countries such as Egypt, Jordan, and Lebanon (Amin and Awny, 1985; Fergani, 1987a and 1987b; Keeley and Saket, 1984; Sa'd Eddine and 'Abd al-Fadil, 1983; Zurayk and Ghulmiyah, 1985).

The objective of this chapter is to explore some apects of the relationship between international migration and integration in Arab states. First, a general discussion will be presented on: (i) inter-Arab migration and integration between Arab states, (ii) inter-Arab migration and integration within the labour-exporting Arab states, and (iii) integration of immigrants within the labour-importing Arab Gulf states. Secondly, the chapter will give a more detailed analysis of the socially and politically important process of the integration of immigrants in the Arab Gulf countries, with particular reference to Kuwait. The main issue is whether immigrants in some Arab Gulf countries are 'sojourners' or 'settlers'. The political aspects of this issue are discussed at length in Chapter 15 by Sharon Stanton Russell.

349

THE RELATIONSHIP BETWEEN MIGRATION AND INTEGRATION: MACRO AND MICRO APPROACHES

Migration and integration between Arab countries

There are a number of different ways of conceptualising the relationship between migration and integration. At the most general macro level, one may consider the possible impact of international migration on the integration of sending and receiving Arab countries, with a particular emphasis on political and economic integration. There is no doubt that substantial migration streams from country A to country B, and the reverse movement of migrants' remittances from country B to country A, increase the economic interdependence between these two countries. But economic interdependence is far from being equivalent to economic integration or from leading to political integration. One need only consider the case of Egypt and the capital-rich Arab states which are importers of Egyptian labour. While estimates may differ widely (Amin and Awny, 1985; Sa'd Eddine and 'Abd al-Fadil, 1983), a sample survey completed in Egypt in 1985 showed that as many as 2.4 million Egyptians had emigrated for work or were currently labour migrants in Iraq, Saudi Arabia, Kuwait, Jordan, and Libya (Fergani, 1987a). Remittances have grown rapidly from about 3 per cent of the Egyptian Gross Domestic Product in 1974 to around 10 per cent in the late 1970s and early 1980s (Amin and Awny, 1985). One can hardly argue that, as a consequence, Egypt is now any closer to political and economic integration with the capital-rich states than it was in 1974. There is no doubt that the exchange of people and capital at the present scale would facilitate such a move to integration, but other factors are likely to be of greater importance. Sherbiny and Serageldin (1982: 255) argue that the 'growing interdependence between' Egypt and Saudi Arabia 'which is being fostered by the interlinkages of their labour markets . . . does not automatically translate into a symbiotic economic relationship which will magically overcome political differences and regional geo-political considerations'. Yet, in another paper, Serageldin *et al.* (1984: 617–18) write that 'international migration . . . could work to create an integrated economic region'. Similarly, in a summary of a roundtable discussion at the 1981 International Migration Conference in the Arab World, Tabbarah (1982: 1167) summarised the view that 'migration among Arab countries was generally viewed as a positive phenomenon' that helps 'in the social and economic integration of Arab world'.

Although the subject of the effect of inter-Arab migration on Arab unity is certainly of great economic and political interest one can only be impressionistic at the present state of knowledge about the relative importance of inter-Arab migration as compared to other factors, such as regional political alliances or economic and political dependency. Serageldin *et al.* (1984: 625) have recently indicated the importance of the question: 'Will the contacts by Arab migrants with other Arab migrants and host country nationals instil or strengthen a pan-Arab view of a single Arab nation in which labour 'circulate'?' But there are no 'sensible answers' to this question since 'much more research is required'. Thus, while we have an excellent analysis of a multi-nation survey of Arab public opinion on the issue of Arab unity (Ibrahim, 1982), it does not provide us with any answers to the question posed by Serageldin *et al.* Somewhat more pertinent is the small-scale study by Leila (1983), but it is inconclusive. It would seem more fruitful at the present state of our knowledge to explore somewhat less general relationships between migration and integration by focusing on the impact of international migration on national political, economic, and social integration in countries of origin and destination of migrants. The type of study needed is exemplified by the 1985 Egyptian national sample survey of households without emigrants, with return migrants, and with current emigrants (Fergani, 1987a and 1987b). This unique survey provides us not only with the best current estimates of the size and characteristics of Egyptian international migrants but also with the most systematic information on the views of return migrants and non-migrants about Arab unity and integration. Comparisons between non-migrants and return migrants and between groups of return migrants with work experience in different Arab countries provide a basis for assessing the effects of migration on these attitudes (Fergani, 1987a).

Migration and integration with Arab countries

In considering the possible linkages between international migration and integration within a country one should distinguish between countries of origin of migrants (sending countries) and countries of their destination (receiving countries).

Sending countries

There are both macro and micro aspects of the possible connections between migration and integration in sending countries. The substantial literature on the macro impacts of international migration, particularly for Egypt and Jordan, provides some clues as to the nature of some of these connections, but it has to be supplemented by micro studies (Amin and Awny, 1985). The most salient aspects appear to be shortages of labour in certain areas such as construction and the increase in money supply, consumer demand, and available capital as a result of migrants' remittances (Aliboni *et al.*, 1984). With the slowdown in the development programmes of the capital-rich countries and the possible return of large numbers of migrants, there is a heightened interest in the possible consequences of this process. Will returnees contribute to or detract from any on-going process of political, economic, or social integration? Answers to this question depend in part on the scale and tempo of return migration. For example, if a large number of Egyptians were to return home within a short period of time, it could have a dislocating effect on Egyptian society and economy, particularly if they opt to settle in large cities. Aliboni *et al.* (1984) challenge the idea that this could happen. Nevertheless, there is a need to study the comparative patterns of social and economic adjustments among families with heads and other members abroad, families that never had migrants and those that have returnees. Similar comparisons are needed for non-migrants and returnees. This is precisely the design of a sample survey carried out in Jordan in 1980 (Keeley and Saket, 1984). The first results of this study do not suggest that migrant families tend to invest any of their savings 'in small firms and professional activities' and thus 'generate a process of unprecedented primitive accumulation' (Aliboni *et al.*, 1984: 10). While remittances in 1981 constituted nearly 28 per cent of Jordan's GNP and 35 per cent of its M2 money supply, the micro behaviour of migrant households suggests that the Jordanian state cannot count on these funds for development projects (Keeley and Saket, 1984: 696).[2]

The study also points to some changes in women's roles and family relationships. Still, it is hard from these preliminary results to envisage what might be the consequences of labour emigration for the integration of Jordanian society. The conclusion by Keeley and Saket (1984: 698) that 'migration has meant a major course change for Jordan and most Jordanians, even if no one is quite sure where they are headed', while not helpful in this respect, may reflect the state of our knowledge. After a review of existing studies on the social consequences of emigration in Egypt, Amin and Awny (1985:

155) concluded that 'only one area, that of the impact of migration on family structure, has been to any degree substantially researched'.[3] This gap has been recently filled, however, by the 1985 Egyptian national sample survey of emigration (Fergani, 1987a and 1987b).

Receiving countries

Theoretically and practically one of the most interesting aspects of the migration-integration relationship is what is happening or will happen in receiving countries (Farah and Al Salem, 1980; Farah, 1982). While there is no doubt that international migration has contributed to economic development in most of the receiving countries, it is not clear what it has done to their political, social, and economic integration (Fergani, 1985). Opinions and informal observations abound on this issue and they generally tend to be 'pessimistic'. Following a study tour of the Gulf areas, Weiner (1982: 26), an American political scientist, reached the following conclusion:

> Migrants are incorporated into the economic structure, but are excluded from the social structure. Separation, not integration or assimilation, is the goal . . . Social contacts between Arabs and expatriates are minimized . . . An increasing number of migrants stay for extended periods, and some may remain legally 'temporary' residents, with little notice they can be asked by the government to leave.

Franklin (1985: 11 and 13) paints a similar bleak picture of the status of migrants in Bahrain with 'the emergence of a large foreign presence significant economically but discriminated against legally, socially, and culturally . . . in a country noted for its tolerance, the tone of relations between "locals" and "expats", especially Asians, is rising to xenophobic pitch'. But how does this differ from the status of the current undocumented Mexican labour migrants in the United States or 'guest workers' in Western Europe or from the status of Asian migrants in California in the nineteenth century? The living conditions of the latter were far worse than the poorest migrants in the Gulf, and they suffered all types of discrimination. It is clear that we need to look at the situation of migrants in the Gulf from a comparative and historical perspective.

But more than opinions, however well-intentioned, we need studies of the extent and patterns of integration and segregation of migrants in Gulf and other receiving countries. Yet, such studies would, in their essence, contradict official policy. Migrants are 'guest workers' who will presumably leave, or be deported, when they are not needed or have violated the conditions of their stay. Furthermore, in some Gulf states migrants constitute a majority and both governments and their constituencies fear that if they are allowed to settle they could upset the balance of power. Some of these fears are documented in a multi-country survey carried out in Bahrain, Kuwait, Qatar, Saudi Arabia, and the United Arab Emirates (Dhaher, Al-Salem, and Al-Salem, 1984). The experience of West Germany is instructive in this respect. After all, 'guest worker' is a translation of an expression (*gastarbeiter*) which was coined by West Germans to convey the temporary nature of labour migration to West Germany. Yet in 1980, there were 1.5 million Turks settled in West Germany (Basa, 1983: 143). There has been a real 'explosion' of West German studies on the integration of those who were once *gastarbeiter* (Herfurth and Haart, 1982; Hoffman-Nowotny and Hondrich, 1982). What will happen in the future to the presumed 'guest workers' of the Gulf when most development projects are completed and oil revenues are no longer adequate to sustain the same level of state expenditures? Four scenarios may be envisaged:

(a) In the first scenario, migrants now in the Gulf will start leaving and will not be replaced by other migrants, and nationals will slowly replace migrants in the economic sectors where the latter were dominant. This represents, in one sense, a continuation of the *status quo*. As stated by Aliboni *et al.* (1984: 111), 'to date migrants have not been able to settle in their host countries, and this situation is not likely to change'. This scenario assumes that the following needed demographic and socioeconomic changes will occur: fertility will decline markedly leading to an increase in the relative importance of labour force ages; women will enter the labour force in greater numbers; nationals will be willing to take semi-skilled and unskilled jobs which they have so far shunned.

(b) Migrants who are now in the Gulf will leave and will be replaced by other migrants to fill all the menial jobs. Nationals will replace migrants in the skilled and higher status jobs. To some extent, this process has started with the replacement of Arab by Asian migrants. It is a process that is well-known in developed receiving countries such as the United States and France and it could lead to the formation of a permanent under-class (Talha, 1983; Sayad, 1983). This would have far-reaching consequences for the political and social integration of Gulf countries.

(c) There will be a relaxation of current restrictive legislation, and many of the migrants, or their children, will settle in the Arab Gulf countries. At present, this scenario seems more applicable to Iraq, with its liberal naturalisation laws for Arab migrants, than to the Gulf. One more likely version of this scenario will be a tacit acceptance by Gulf governments of illegal migrants who are allowed to settle, but would still experience social and economic discrimination and segregation. This scenario would then be equivalent to the previous one and could also lead to the formation of a permanent under-class.

(d) There could be an important shift in technology which would lead to an increase in the use of robotics. But the nature of the economic activity of many immigrants is precisely in areas that are least likely to be affected by robotics (small business or services).

While it is difficult to state with any certainty which of these scenarios is most likely to unfold, it is possible nevertheless to examine the current status of migrants in receiving countries and estimate the degree of their political, economic, or social integration. Since Kuwait is the Arab Gulf country for which we have the most systematic information on this subject, it was selected for a preliminary assessment of the extent of integration of immigrants.

IMMIGRANTS IN ARAB GULF COUNTRIES: 'SOJOURNERS' OR 'SETTLERS'?

Even though the official policy of most Gulf countries is to treat the immigrants as 'guest workers', an increasing number of recent discussions of the fate of immigrants has focused on the issue of their possible integration within Gulf society. With the decline of oil prices and the dwindling of investments in the Gulf, this is a very important political and economic issue. While it might be assumed that the economic downturn in the Gulf may lead to an exodus of migrant labour, Birks, Seccombe and Sinclair (1986: 813–14) draw a parallel with Western Europe and suggest that 'effectively the Gulf states would repeat the experience of Western Europe where immigrant labour stocks also proved exceptionally resistant to the pressure of economic recessions'. Writing in 1986, Longuenesse (1986: 8) asserts that 'it is clear today that not a single Gulf country could do without the foreign manpower and that the presence of an important immigrant population is irreversible'. Owen (1985: 17)

355

goes further and calls for recognition by the Gulf governments of 'the permanent nature of much of the foreign labour force', thus forcing them to address the issue of 'how to best integrate the long-stay workers in their own societies'. On the other hand, Galal el Din (1984) asserts that 'all surveys conducted so far seem to indicate that the majority of immigrants including those with their families intend to go back'. Thus, the issue of 'integration' of the foreign workers and their families is still controversial. But it is also a sensitive one in Gulf countries where non-nationals comprise close to or even over half of the total population. While Gulf states have been concerned for some time about the 'threats to their national identity', they are similar in this respect to other labour-importing countries in other regions of the world.

Conceptualisations of the integration of immigrants

According to Bohning (1972), Piore (1979), and Massey (1986) labour migration matures over time as immigrants gain more experience in the host society, and this eventually results in their settlement. Similarly, Birks and Sinclair (1981: 449) have asserted that 'while migration for employment is always seen as a temporary phenomenon by both the receiving country and by the individual migrant, a metamorphosis into permanence generally occurs sooner or later'. Massey (1986: 671) identifies the following 'basic phases' of the integration and settlement of Mexican immigrants in the United States: (a) 'in the initial ''sojourning phase'', male migrants enter the host country to work without dependents' (b) 'as migrants spend more time abroad, either through continuous residence or repeated trips, they enter the ''transition'' phase during which the sojourner-settler distinction becomes increasingly problematic . . . many acquire legal residence documents, and as their experience grows, they get more stable, better paying jobs and (c) 'in the final ''settlement phase'', migrants come to see themselves as residents of the host society'. This *settlement phase* is further characterised by the presence of immigrants' wives and children, 'widespread contacts with people and institutions in and out of the immigrant enclave', the declining importance of remittances and the nearly universal acquisition of legal residence. Massey (1986) documents this process with extensive life histories collected in four Mexican communities.

Three types of immigrant integration may be identified. First, there is the *economic* integration of immigrants in the occupational structure of receiving countries so as to allow occupational mobility and access to economic advancement and opportunity. The degree of occupational mobility is perhaps the best measure of this aspect of integration. Second, *social* integration occurs when immigrants are incorporated in the social life of the society. The lack of segregation and the presence of immigrants in voluntary association alongside natives are some of the indicators of this type of integration. Finally, *political* integration refers to the political participation of immigrants in the receiving society. One measure of this type of integration is the acquisition of citizenship. Political integration is the focus of Chapter 15 in this volume.

Indicators of integration and settlement of immigrants in the Gulf

In a study of the settlement of Yemenis in the United States, Sabagh and Bozorgmehr (in press) suggest that naturalisation is one of the best indicators of settlement and integration of immigrants. Unfortunately, as indicated in Chapter 15, citizenship is difficult to acquire in the Gulf countries and often does not give the naturalised citizen the same rights as other citizens. Nevertheless, there is some indication that naturalisation is becoming an important aspect of the process of integration and settlement in Kuwait. Russell, in Chapter 15 of this volume, estimates that 212,000 persons were naturalised between 1961 and 1984. This compares to a non-Kuwaiti population of 1,016,013 in 1985 (State of Kuwait, 1986). Even though many of these naturalised persons were Beduins who had lived many years in Kuwait, it appears that naturalisations should be used in an analysis of the process of immigrant integration in Kuwait. Unfortunately, the Kuwait censuses do not provide tabulations on naturalised citizens.

As suggested by Massey (1986) and others, the maturation of temporary migrants into a settled population involves demographic, economic, and social transformation of the immigrant population. These transformations provide the basis for the selection of indicators of settlement which are relevant to the experience of the Arab Gulf countries. The demographic measures pertain to the age, sex, and marital structure of the immigrant population. In the early stages of labour migration, the young and single males predominate. Later, married men join the migration stream. Feeling torn from

357

immediate family members, these men bring over their wives and children, followed by brothers and sisters. Since married people in general are older, this partially accounts for the aging of the migrant stream. The original sex imbalance is somewhat corrected with the occurrence of family reunification. In the long run, the unit of migration changes from single individuals to families involving chain migration and a self-feeding process, independent of the demand for labour (Bohning, 1972: 54–71).

Parallel to the process of demographic settlement there are processes of economic and social integration which provide a rationale for utilising indicators of these aspects of integration. Thus, increased participation in the labour force, more stable and higher level occupations, and higher earnings are all factors that would increase the propensity for settlement (Massey, 1986). Other important variables are friendship ties with members of the host society, proficiency in the language of the host country, access to public or private social services (e.g. unemployment compensation and medical facilities), and payment of taxes (Massey, 1986).

While there are extensive qualitative materials such as novels and biographies that provide many insights into the lives of immigrants in the Arab Gulf countries, this chapter will be limited to an analysis of available quantitative data from censuses and sample surveys. But since these quantitative data are presently available mostly for Kuwait, the focus of this analysis is on Kuwait. This will be supplemented, however, with some pertinent data from other Arab Gulf countries.

Demographic settlement of immigrants in Bahrain, Kuwait, and the United Arab Emirates

As labour migrants and sojourners become settled, they tend to bring over their wives, children and older relatives. Consequently, we would expect that, compared to a predominantly sojourning immigrant population, settled immigrants will have a much higher ratio of males to females (sex ratio) and a much more balanced age distribution including more children and older persons. Birks and Sinclair (1981) contend that this process constitutes the 'demographic settling' of immigrants.

Table 14.1 presents data on length of residence, sex ratio, and percentage in ages 15–59 for Kuwait, Bahrain, and the United Arab Emirates (UAE). In the mid-1980s the UAE had the highest percentage of immigrants (75.4) and Bahrain the lowest (34.8) with Kuwait in-between (59.8).

Table 14.1: Demographic indicators of settlement of non-nationals, Bahrain, Kuwait and United Arab Emirates 1957–1984

Country and year of census or estimates	% Non-nationals	% with residence of		Non-nationals Ratio of males per 100 females	% in age group 15–49	Crude activity rate
		10+ years	15+ years			
Kuwait censuses						
1957	45.0	6.4	2.4	424	83.4	65.8
1965	52.9	12.1	3.1	236	69.5	56.2
1970	53.0	21.4	6.6	166	61.8	44.6
1975	52.5	29.1	12.7	142	59.1	40.4
1980	58.3	32.2	16.2	167	66.8	48.4
1985	59.8	35.4	21.1	161	65.2	53.5
Bahrain						
1971 census	18.6			234	72.7	59.0
1981 census	31.0	14.4		308	83.6	72.5
1984 est.	34.8			303	80.7	70.2
UAE						
1984 est.	75.4			292	78.5	66.5

Source: Bahrain, n.d.; State of Kuwait, 1983, p. 47; United Nations Economic Commission for West Asia, 1985.

If the sex ratios and percentages of the population in the labour force in the 15–64 age group, which are available for the three countries are used as indicators of settlement, it is clear that sojourners or temporary migrants constitute a much more important segment of the non-national populations of Bahrain and the UAE than of Kuwait. There is a marked trend toward settlement in Kuwait as sex ratios decreased from 424 in 1957 to 142 in 1975 and the percentage in the 15–59 age group declined from 83.4 to 59.1 in the same period. It may be noted that the levels of these indicators for Kuwait in 1957 are comparable to those for Bahrain and the UAE in the mid-1980s. Interestingly, on the basis of the same measures, there is a slight reversal of the settlement trends in Kuwait between 1975 and 1980. A similar trend occurs in Bahrain between 1971 and 1981. The last column in Table 14.1 gives crude participation rates (labour force as a percentage of the total population) which have been used by Birks and Sinclair (1981) as an indicator of settlement. Except for the period 1980–85 in Kuwait, the changes in these rates parallel the figures on the percentage in the 15–59 age group. In this most recent period in Kuwait, the crude labour force participation rate goes up markedly from 48.4 to 53.5, but the percentage in the 15–49 age group declines slightly from 66.8 to 65.2. The increase in crude labour force participation reflects a sharp increase in labour force participation of non-national females (Fargues, 1987).

The data on length of residence of immigrants tend to confirm the patterns for the sex ratios, age distribution, and crude participation rates. Thus in 1985, 35.4 per cent of non-nationals in Kuwait had resided in that country for 10 years or more. By contrast, 14.4 per cent of immigrants in Bahrain in 1981 had lived there for 9 years or more. In Kuwait, the percentage with 15 or more years of residence increased from 2.4 in 1957 to 21.1 in 1985.

The data in Table 14.1 suggest that any findings on the process of settlement in Kuwait would not necessarily apply to other Arab Gulf countries. But, in spite of the different socio-historical and political contexts, it is possible that Kuwait could provide us with a scenario that might be applicable to other Arab Gulf countries in the future.

Differentials in demographic settlement in Kuwait

Birks and Sinclair (1981) have documented significant differentials in demographic settlement between various nationalities in Kuwait in 1965, 1970, and 1975. Their analysis, however, is based only on

Table 14.2: Years of residence in Kuwait, non-Kuwaiti male and female population, Kuwait 1965–1980

Year and sex	% years of residence				Total	Number of non-Kuwaitis
	0–4	5–9	10–14	15+		
Males						
1965	58.4	28.2	10.0	3.4	100	173,743
1970	49.8	25.6	16.4	8.1	100	244,368
1975	41.7	26.5	16.3	15.4	100	307,168
1980	49.2	20.8	13.4	16.5	100	495,990
Females						
1965	64.6	26.5	6.6	2.3	100	73,537
1970	55.3	28.6	12.2	3.9	100	146,898
1975	42.8	31.9	16.5	8.8	100	215,581
1980	38.7	25.4	20.2	15.6	100	296,349

Source: State of Kuwait, 1983, p. 47.

crude rates of labour force participation. There is a need to consider other indicators as well as more recent data from the 1980 and 1985 censuses of Kuwait. Table 14.2 gives various indicators of demographic settlement for Arab and Asian immigrants in 1975, 1980, and 1985 in Kuwait. It may be noted that these two groups comprised 98 per cent of all immigrants in Kuwait in 1985. In 1975, 1980 and 1985, Arab as compared to Asian immigrants had resided for a longer time in Kuwait, had a higher percentage of children under 10, and proportionately more women. For example in 1985, 59.8 per cent of Arab non-nationals 40 years or older had resided in Kuwait 15 or more years as compared to 28 per cent for Asians in the same age group. Children (ages 0–9) constitute 26.9 per cent of the Arabs and 9.7 per cent of Asians. The former group had 144 males for 100 females and the latter 202 males for every 100 females.

In 1975, there were important differences in rates of demographic settlement between specific immigrant groups (Table 14.3). In general Palestinians have the longest residence in Kuwait, the highest percentage of children and the lowest sex ratios and Egyptians have the shortest residence in Kuwait, one of the lowest percentages of children, but not the highest sex ratio. Iranians and Pakistanis have even higher sex ratios. These differences, however, may reflect more the timing in migration to Kuwait rather than any propensity for settlement. Furthermore, the Palestinians constitute a special case. Their aspirations are to go back to a Palestinian state and even the presence of a third generation in the Gulf does not stifle

361

Table 14.3: Length of residence of selected nationality groups by age group, Kuwait 1975

Length of residence, sex ratios and ages	Jordan and Palestine	Egypt	Iraq	Syria	Iran	India	Pakistan
% with 15+ years of residence in Kuwait							
Age 10–19	11.9	4.3	17.8	6.1	7.4	8.4	7.0
Age 20–29	7.4	2.3	15.8	4.0	3.5	1.5	5.4
Age 30–39	27.8	3.0	24.3	16.7	24.9	10.4	16.9
Age 40+	50.6	11.3	42.7	34.2	41.5	29.4	27.1
% with 10+ years of residence in Kuwait							
Age 10–19	65.5	24.1	56.1	34.3	28.2	22.4	46.7
Age 20–29	27.7	3.3	28.0	16.3	12.3	4.8	14.2
Age 30–39	68.0	12.7	42.8	45.6	43.5	22.1	35.9
Age 40+	72.0	12.4	60.5	56.9	54.7	39.9	35.4
% aged 10–19	42.4	17.3	25.6	31.3	15.0	16.3	24.8
Males per 100 females	112	145	143	151	425	109	187
Number of persons	204,178	60,534	45,070	40,962	40,842	32,105	23,016

Source: State of Kuwait, 1978 and 1983.

this desire to go back. Thus Qutub (1982: 644–6) reports on the results of a study of 300 Palestinians in Kuwait in 1978. Even though about one-third had been in Kuwait for 10 years or more, 'only 8 per cent expressed their readiness to stay permanently in Kuwait if given the opportunity'. The findings on the Palestinian's desire for settlement suggest that, for this group, 'settlement intentions' may be preferable to demographic indicators. But the results of survey in Kuwait in 1981 indicate that it is difficult to obtain information on this subject from immigrants. Of those interviewed, 82.3 per cent stated that they didn't know in response to a question on 'intentions to stay'. At the same time, however, 89.9 per cent stated that they were perfectly settled.

The data given in Table 14.2 for both Arab and Asian nationals show that the process of 'demographic settling' of these two major immigrant groups in Kuwait is much more complex than is suggested by the data on all immigrants given in Table 14.1. Among Asian immigrants, the paradoxical and noticeable decrease in sex ratio and the increase in the percentage of the 20–39 age group between 1980 and 1985 (from 58.1 to 66 per cent) reflect the rapid expansion in the immigration of Asian women in the 20–39 age group who work as domestic help. The data on length of residence by age groups confirms this trend. While there are similar contradictions in the demographic measures of the settlement of Arab immigrants, the data in Table 14.2 suggest that there are two groups of Arab immigrants. One group consists of older and more settled immigrants and the other comprises recently arrived young workers in their twenties. This trend is particularly marked for the period 1980–85. Does this mean, as indicated by Choucri (1986), that the years since 1983 have been characterised by increasing restriction on the importation of labour, by an increasing shift from Arab to Asian labour, and by return Arab migration? In a recent article, Birks, Seccombe, and Sinclair (1986) also address this issue. Between 1980 and 1984, there was a decline in new work permits issued to new immigrants in Kuwait. On the other hand, during the same period renewals of existing permits show a sharp increase from 54,905 in 1980 to 139,578 in 1980 (Birks, Sinclair, and Seccombe, 1986: 819). While this increase may be attributed to many factors, including labour hoarding by employers, it is also indicative of some settlement. One indirect measure of the 'retention' of immigrants is given by an analysis of the 'survival' of age-duration of residence cohorts (Fargues, 1987). For example, the 'survival rates' between 1975 and 1985 for persons who had already resided 15 years or more in Kuwait in 1975 were 74, 76 and 65 per cent for Arab immigrants in the 10–19, 20–29, and 30+ age groups respectively in 1975 and 62, 85 and 65 per cent respectively for Asian immigrants in the 10–19, 20–29, and 30+ age group respectively in the same year.[4] As Fargues (1987) has noted, those who do not survive include deaths, emigrants, and naturalisation. Nevertheless, the data suggest that both Arab and Asian 'established' immigrants have tended to remain in Kuwait between 1975 and 1985. There is additional evidence to support the view that while there is a decline in new immigration to the Gulf and some emigration, many labour migrants already in the Gulf may be in the process of becoming settled. Thus in Kuwait, the decline in labour permits in the 1980s has been accompanied by what appears to be a contradictory trend of non-national population growth. While this trend may partly reflect undocumented migration and economic activity, it is mostly a consequence of the increasing importance of the natural increase of the non-national population. During the period 1982–85, for non-Kuwaitis natural increase was almost equal to net migration (81,172 as compared to 82,828).[5] By contrast, during 1975–80, the estimated number of net migrants was substantially higher than the number of births to immigrants (Fargues, 1987). Data from the 1985 census reveal the numerical importance of non-Kuwaiti children and adolescents born in Kuwait, particularly among non-Kuwaiti Arabs. Kuwaiti-born persons comprised 81.7 per cent of non-Kuwaiti Arabs and 62.6 per cent of non-Kuwaiti Asians under 20 years.[6] It may be noted that persons under 20 years of age constitute 47 per cent of the non-Kuwaiti Arabs, but only 16 per cent of non-Kuwaiti Asians. But even for long-term foreign residents and their Kuwaiti-born children, favourable prospects for higher occupational achievement and mobility will increase their propensity to settle.

Occupational achievement and mobility of immigrants

An increase in the occupational achievement of immigrants in a receiving country is likely to increase their propensity to settle (Massey 1986). This propensity is reinforced when the occupational achievement of immigrants is higher than their occupational status in the country of origin. Thus, the analysis has to include both occupational changes in Kuwait and variations in occupational status between the country of origin of immigrants and Kuwait.

Table 14.4: Occupational distribution of males in non-agricultural occupations, Kuwaitis and non-Kuwaiti Arabs and Asians, Kuwait 1975 and 1985

Occupational groups	% in occupational groups					
	non-Kuwaiti males				Kuwaiti males	
	Arabs		Asians			
	1975	1985	1975	1985	1975	1985
Professional, technical and related workers, administrative and managerial workers	15.8	21.8	5.0	7.4	7.0	17.2
Clerical and related workers	11.4	13.0	6.6	5.1	20.9	24.8
Sales workers	9.7	9.3	10.4	5.3	8.1	5.9
Service workers	16.9	14.5	17.8	22.3	42.0	39.3
Production and related workers, transport, operators and labourers	46.1	41.4	60.2	59.1	20.2	10.3

Sources: State of Kuwait, 1983 and 1986.

Data from the 1975 and 1980 censuses of Kuwait provide information on the occupational distribution of Kuwaitis and non-Kuwaitis. Since there are no published tabulations from the 1985 census on the occupations of specific nationalities such as Palestinian, Egyptian or Pakistani, the only distinction that can be made is between Arab and Asian non-Kuwaitis. An unpublished paper by Shah (1987) based on analysis of two sample surveys in 1977–78 and 1983 suggests, however, that there are important differences in occupational trends for specific nationalities. Nevertheless, the occupational data for male Arabs and Asians given in Table 14.4 reveal some important differences between two groups. It is clear that the occupational achievement of non-Kuwaiti Arabs improved between 1975 and 1985. The percentage in the two bottom occupations decreased from 63.0 to 55.9 and the percentage in the top professional and managerial occupations increased from 27.2 to 34.8. Census data on occupational levels indicate that service workers have about the same low educational levels as production workers, operators and labourers, and that levels of education increase rapidly from the bottom to the top occupations in Table 14.4. Consequently, a move from the bottom to the top occupational categories in Table 14.4 reflects higher achievement. As compared to Arab immigrants, Asians experienced a *downward* structural mobility between 1975 and 1985, with an increase in the relative

365

Table 14.5: Occupational profile in Kuwait 1981 and occupational profile in country of origin of migrants and index of structural mobility, by nationality, Kuwait 1981

Nationality and country where occupation is reported	Occupations							N	SM
	1	2	3	4	5	6	7		
Palestinians and Jordanians									
Origin	27.7	1.2	9.2	8.2	6.5	19.9	22.3	(760)	
Kuwait 1981	35.8	4.4	19.0	7.5	7.0	1.3	25.1	(760)	19.6
Gulf Arabs									
Origin	9.1		36.3	27.3	3.8	9.1	18.2	(28)	
Kuwait 1981	28.6	7.1	25.0	16.7			25.0	(28)	34.1
Egyptians									
Origin	66.6	6.4	14.1	3.1	4.0	.9	4.9	(404)	
Kuwait 1981	68.3	2.0	14.9	2.5	7.2	6.0	5.2	(404)	7.6
Other Arabs									
Origin	33.8	3.8	10.2	14.5	3.6	8.4	25.0	(306)	
Kuwait 1981	23.8	5.6	15.2	17.9	12.6		24.8	(306)	22.5
Indians									
Origin	38.7	7.5	26.9	3.1	1.5	1.5	20.9	(84)	
Kuwait 1981	33.3	4.8	29.8	8.3	9.5		14.3	(84)	12.2
Pakistanis									
Origin	33.3		9.1	4.8	9.5		52.4	(34)	
Kuwait 1981	24.2	6.1	15.2	9.1			45.5	(34)	21.0

Other Asians

	1	2	3	4	5	6	7	SM	N
Origin	13.6	4.5	9.1	13.6	33.3	13.6	45.6	32.7	= 42)
Kuwait 1981	19.0	4.8	7.1				35.1		= 42)

Occupational categories:
1. Professional and technical
2. Administrative and managerial
3. Clerical
4. Sales
5. Services
6. Agriculture and fishing
7. Production and labourers

SM = (index of structural mobility)

N = ½ [(origin per cent) − (Kuwait 1981 per cent)]

Source: Prepared from data given in Tables 1, 21, and 23 in Al-Moosa and McLachlan, 1985, pp. 138 and 150.

Table 14.6: Percentage distribution of migrants' main occupations in Kuwait in 1981 and main occupation in country of origin, Kuwait 1981

Occupation in country of origin	Occupation in Kuwait in 1981							Total	(N)
	1	2	3	4	5	6	7		
1. Professional + technical	88.7	2.2	6.3	1.7	0.2		0.9	44.4	(463)
2. Administration + managerial	45.5	36.3	15.9	2.3				4.2	(44)
3. Clerical + executive	20.6	7.9	55.6	3.2	4.8		7.8	12.1	(126)
4. Sales	15.6	7.8	10.4	45.4	6.5	1.3	13.0	7.4	(77)
5. Services	2.2	4.4	11.1	4.4	46.8		31.1	4.3	(45)
6. Agriculture + fishing	2.8	2.0	12.7	8.8	22.6	7.8	43.2	9.8	(102)
7. Production + labouring	6.5	2.7	1.6	7.5	3.8	.8	77.9	17.8	(186)
Total	46.5	4.9	12.9	7.0	6.0	.8	21.8	100.0	
N	(485)	(51)	(135)	(73)	(63)	(9)	(227)		(1,843)

Source: Prepared from data in Table 43, Al-Moosa and McLachlan, 1985, p. 73. Based on a sample survey in Kuwait in 1981.

importance of the two lowest occupations (from 78.0 to 81.4 per cent). The percentage of Asians in these occupations in 1985 is much higher than among non-Kuwaiti Arabs. It is significant that the number of Kuwaiti nationals in the industrial and manual worker stratum decreased from about 20 to about 10 per cent. While it might be argued that the increasing importance of white-collar occupations among both Kuwaiti and non-Kuwaiti Arabs reflects the structural changes in the Kuwaiti economy, this is not supported by the experience of Asians. It appears that Asian immigration in the 1980s provided the required manual and unskilled labour force replacing non-immigrants and some Arab immigrants.

Some survey data are available on the occupational distribution of immigrants in Kuwait in 1981 and in their country of origin. Unfortunately, these data are not controlled for length of residence in Kuwait. On the basis of the percentages in Table 14.5 and the indices of structural mobility, it is clear that, with the exception of Egyptians and Indians, all nationalities have experienced a noticeable change in their occupational structure. In general, there is upward mobility for Arabs and downward mobility for Asians. For Egyptians, the high percentage of professionals both in Egypt and Kuwait (66.6 and 68.3 respectively) may reflect the nature of the sample. Another survey conducted in 1983 reveals a much lower occupational profile for Egyptians in Kuwait (Shah, 1987).

In order to disentangle the structural from the exchange aspects of occupational mobility, it is necessary to have a cross-tabulation of occupations in country of origin and country of destination. These cross-tabulations are available for all immigrants in the 1981 sample survey and are given in Table 14.6. The percentages along the diagonal show the extent of *non-mobility* which appears to be fairly high, particularly for the top and the bottom occupational strata 1 and 7. This could reflect, however, the experience of both Egyptians at the top and Indians at the bottom.

SUMMARY AND CONCLUSION

There are three major conceptualisations of the relationship between Arab international migration and integration. First, international migration between Arab countries has been viewed by some social scientists as having an impact on economic, political or social integration between Arab states. It is not clear from the literature whether this effect is positive or negative. Secondly, there is an extensive literature on the macro-economic effects of international migration on labour-exporting countries, particularly in Egypt and Jordan. More research is needed however, on the political and social effects of international emigration and on the consequences of return migration in sending countries. Finally, there is a growing literature on the political, economic and social impacts of migration in the labour-importing countries, particularly the Arab Gulf countries where migrants often comprise the majority of the total population.

The main objective of this chapter is to address an issue which Arab Gulf countries will increasingly face in the future: will migrants remain sojourners or will they become settlers? While the future is obviously uncertain, existing data and studies may provide some clues as to the nature and extent of the settlement of migrants in the Arab Gulf countries. While the goals of sojourners or temporary labour-migrants in these countries are mainly economic, continued stay in these countries may lead to their transformation into settlers. According to studies of labour-migrants to the United States and Western Europe, it is possible to make quantitative assessments of this process. But this assessment requires the availability of longitudinal demographic, economic and social data. While there is no published longitudinal information on migrants in the Arab Gulf countries, a series of censuses or surveys as are available for Kuwait provide an approximation to this information. This is the main reason why the analysis in this chapter is mainly for Kuwait.

Data on sex ratios, crude rate of labour force participation and age structures of immigrants for Bahrain, Kuwait and the United Arab Emirates around 1980 suggest the demographic settlement of migrants is much more pronounced in Kuwait than the other two countries. Thus, any conclusions pertaining to Kuwait may not be applicable to other Arab Gulf countries, but Kuwait may give us a glimpse into the future of migrants in these other countries. Within Kuwait, however, there are important differentials between Arab and Asian immigrants.

Cross-sectional data from the 1975, 1980 and 1985 Kuwait censuses on length of residence, sex ratios and age structure, and longitudinal data on the 'survival' of immigrant cohorts between 1975 and 1985 indicate that (a) the degree of demographic settlement is much higher for Arab than Asian non-nationals, (b) Arab immigrants included both an older settled group and younger newly arrived migrants and (c) while there is an older settled Asian immigrant group, it was overwhelmed in this period by newly arrived migrants, particularly young women. The presence of a second generation among immigrants is a strong indicator of settlement despite restrictive naturalisation policies. The large number (41 per cent in 1985) of Arab non-nationals who were born in Kuwait, most of whom were under age 20, constitutes additional evidence of a fairly high level of settlement in this population. This indicator also shows Asians to be less settled than Arab immigrants (16 per cent born in Kuwait). It should be noted, however, that many Arab non-nationals born in Kuwait are Palestinians whose parents were forced out of their country and aspire to go back to a Palestinian state.

From the standpoint of the analysis of the impact of occupational mobility and achievement on the likelihood of settlement, the most telling data on first and current occupations of migrants are not available. Nevertheless, the occupational data presented in this chapter suggests that Arabs are more likely to settle in Kuwait than Asians. It is likely that knowledge of the language of the host country provides a basis for occupational mobility and an additional impetus for settlement.

The policy of many Arab Gulf countries involving a shift from Arab to Asian labour is based on the premise that Asians are more likely to be sojourners than settlers. While the data presented in this paper provide partial support for this assumption, they also reveal that the process of settlement has also started among Asians. The experience of other labour-importing countries such as the United States, France or the Federal Republic of Germany implies that, in spite of adversity, the longer Asians stay in the Arab Gulf countries the more likely they are to start a family and establish themselves in these countries. It is true that temporary labour-migrants, many of whom arrive under a contract, are subject to deportation. While this mechanism could be used to enforce a 'revolving door' migration policy, the experience of Kuwait suggests that such a policy cannot be easily implemented.[7] Miller's (1986: 744) observation that 'the post-war European guest worker policies resulted in unanticipated, and, to a certain degree, unwanted settlement by aliens admitted as temporary workers' may well apply to the Arab Gulf countries in the 1990s.

NOTES

1. The research for this paper was made possible, in part, by a grant

from the UCLA Academic Senate. The assistance of Mr Elie Chalala is gratefully acknowledged. I would also like to thank the following persons for their many helpful comments and suggestions: Mehdi Bozorgmehr, Ursula Brown, Marwan Buheiry, Alex Cudsi, Tawfik Farah, Giacomo Luciani, Abdel Moneim al-Mashat, Samir Makdisi, Afaf Marsot, and Ghassan Salamé.

2. One important reason for the lack of productive investments by migrants in their countries of origin is the economic and monetary policies of these countries.

3. See also El Dib, Ismail and Gad (1984) and El Sakka (1984).

4. Calculated on the basis of data given in State of Kuwait, Central Statistical Office, *Population Census 1975*, Safat, 1977 and State of Kuwait, Central Statistical Office, *At-Ta'dad al-'Am: As-Sukkan wa al-Masakin wa al Munsha'at 1985*, Safat, 1986.

5. Calculated on the basis of data given in State of Kuwait, Central Statistical Office, *Monthly Digest of Statistics*, vol. 7, October 1986, pp. 1, 10, and 21.

6. Calculated on the basis of data given in State of Kuwait, Central Statistical Office, *At-Ta'dad al-'Am: As-Sukkan wa al-Masakin wa al Munsha'at 1985*, Safat, 1986, Tables 23 and 135.

7. In 1984, 15,549 Asians were deported, but in the same year 31,720 Asians were admitted for the first time (State of Kuwait, Central Statistical Office, *Social Statistics 1985*, Safat, 1985, pp. 118–119). These figures compare to an Asian employed population of 282,843 in 1985 (State of Kuwait, Central Statistical Office, *At-Ta'dad al-'Am: As-Sukkan wa al-Masakin wa al Munsha'at 1985*, Safat, 1986, Table 120).

15

Migration and Political Integration in the Arab World

Sharon Stanton Russell

Since the first oil price rise of 1973, migration across state boundaries has become a significant phenomenon in the Arab world. Much has been written about the economic causes, demographic dimensions and social and economic consequences of these recent population movements.[1] Substantially less attention has been given to the political dimensions of migration.[2] Indeed, perhaps because the very word 'political' evokes sensitive issues of internal stability and security from outside threat, there has been a general reluctance, particularly in the Arab world, to consider the broader political aspects of migration, such as the long-term political factors that shape the process of migration and its consequences, or the policy responses of both sending and receiving countries, or the role of migrants in the day-to-day political life of their host countries. Yet the political ramifications of migration are likely to be of increasing importance. As the economies of principal migration-receiving countries have experienced structural shifts resulting from the completion of major development projects and the decline of oil prices, and as labour markets have begun to adjust accordingly, concern over the future of migration and of migrants in their societies has deepened in both sending and receiving countries.

The assumption — held by many policy-makers, migrants and scholars alike — has been that migrants within and to the Arab world are temporary residents of the countries hosting them. The data, however, challenge this assumption and, in so doing, raise the central question which this chapter explores: what have been the consequences of migration for political integration? To what extent have migrants (or may they in future) become not only *de facto* stabilised but also legitimately involved in the political processes of the countries in which they reside? Introducing these questions, the discussion will focus in particular on the political significance of naturalisation as it may pertain to migrants in the Arab world but will touch as well on other forms of political integration.

DIMENSIONS OF MIGRATION

Migration within the Arab world is, of course, not a new phenomenon. As the cradle of civilisation and the crossroads of commerce in the ancient world, as the wellspring of Islam and the nexus of successive imperial conflicts, the region has long been characterised by population movements in response to the conjunction of political and economic forces. Nor is migration for wage employment merely a recent phenomenon. Since the establishment of the oil industry in the 1930s, the Gulf has been a magnet for migrant workers from within the Arab world and from Western Asia and the Indian subcontinent (see Seccombe and Lawless, 1986), to staff both the nascent oil sector and the growing social service sectors.

Underlying economic and demographic conditions, in both sending and receiving countries, helped to shape the directions and magnitudes of the major migration streams which began during the 1950s and 1960s. Among the receiving countries, particularly Saudi Arabia and Kuwait, expansion of the oil sector was accompanied by adoption of development strategies that increased demand for labour in social and physical infrastructure development as well. Relative to demand, indigenous manpower was (and remains) in short supply as a consequence of small absolute population size and low levels of crude labour force participation which, in turn, are linked to low female labour force participation, high proportions of the population under working age, and increasingly high rates of enrolment in secondary and post-secondary education. With fewer natural resources, slower industrial expansion and relatively skilled populations, other countries of the Arab world were well positioned to help meet growing labour demand in the major oil-producing countries.

The composition of Arab migration streams during the past forty years, however, is by no means the consequence of economic and demographic 'push-pull' factors alone. Political changes in the region have played a major role in shaping that composition. The war of 1947–48 displaced an estimated 700,000 Palestinian Arabs. While a significant number relocated to the West Bank, others fled to Lebanon and Syria or to Amman, which grew from a town of less than 60,000 in 1945 to a city of approximately 200,000 by the early 1950s (Abu Lughod, 1985: 178). Still others found employment in the Gulf, principally in Kuwait, where, between 1949 and the census of 1957, total population more than doubled; between 1957 and 1965, the proportion of non-Kuwaitis in the total population rose from nearly 45 per cent to almost 53 per cent, with Jordanians and Palestinians comprising over 30 per cent of all non-Kuwaitis by 1965.[3]

The June 1967 war resulted in additional population migrations. Abu Lughod (1985: 180) has linked both rapid population growth in Cairo and the increasing propensity of Egyptians to migrate for employment after 1967 to the war, and has estimated that between 150,000 and 250,000 Palestinians crossed the Jordan river to the vicinity of Amman in the aftermath of Israeli occupation of the West Bank. Reverberations from these war-induced population migrations were felt in the Gulf as well. In Kuwait the number of Jordanians and Palestinians nearly doubled between 1965 and 1970 and the number of Egyptians (although considerably fewer than the number of Jordanians and Palestinians) nearly tripled in the same five year period (State of Kuwait, 1977: 25–9, 59).

Even as the oil price rise of 1973 began to generate economic changes that would induce the spectacular increase in migration for employment during the following decade, regional policy changes and political conflicts continue to exert an effect on population movements. The restrictive character of Egypt's emigration policies from the mid-fifties to 1967 was altered significantly with the adoption of the open door policy (*infitah*) in 1973 and the abolition of exit visas in 1974, facilitating the movement of large numbers of Egyptians into the expanding regional labour market (Dessouki, 1982). Receiving countries enacted policy changes as well: in 1974, Kuwait's Council of Ministers adopted a resolution loosening the previously restrictive immigration policies imposed by the Ministry of Interior during the late 1960s (State of Kuwait, 1979: 46, 136), effectively enabling a new inflow of immigrant workers. Such policy changes, together with the 1973 war, the Lebanese civil war, and the Iran-Iraq war have all contributed to the size and composition of recent migration in the Arab world.

Whatever their effects on various types of integration, the population movements that followed structural changes in the regional economy after 1973 were unprecedented in the degree to which they brought Arabs from different states into contact with one another and with other nationalities. Around 1970, there were approximately

375

648,000 Arabs working abroad in other countries of the region; by the early 1980s, their numbers had swelled to approximately 3.7 million (Choucri, 1983: 3–2 ff, Tables 3.1 and 3.7). Although Arabs have continued to comprise the majority of all migrant workers in the region, since the mid-1970s the proportion of Asians has grown dramatically: from approximately 12 per cent of all workers in 1970 to an estimated 30 per cent in the early 1980s. By the latter date, migrants of all nationalities accounted for a significant portion (40–46 per cent) of the total labour force in the region; in the Gulf countries alone, migrants represented three-quarters of all workers (Choucri, 1983: 3–2, 3–12 ff). These rapid and dramatic changes in the size, composition and proportions of migrants converged to make the migration phenomenon itself a major political, as well as social and economic issue in the Arab world.

This brief overview of the roots and patterns of migration raises several points of importance with regard to understanding the role of migration in political integration within the region. First, the population migrations of the past forty years cannot be explained by economic factors alone; political factors, ranging from wars to government policies concerning immigration and emigration, have affected the timing, size, and composition of population movements. Conversely, changes in the economic conditions shaping the directions of migration flows are not likely to signal an end either to the migration phenomenon or to the presence of migrants in the host countries of the region. Indeed, the presence of proportionately significant numbers of migrants in many societies of the region is not a 'new' phenomenon, as many discussions of the post-oil migration streams would seem to suggest. As a result, substantial numbers of migrants are not 'temporary' in any meaningful sense of the term; rather, they are long-term residents or, increasingly, native-born alien residents of their host countries. In the case of Kuwait, nearly a third of all non-Kuwaitis counted in the 1980 census had been resident for 10 years or more; 16 per cent had been resident for 15 years or more (State of Kuwait, 1985: 51, Table 36). By the census of 1985, 303,938 aliens — nearly 30 per cent of the non-Kuwaiti population — had been born in Kuwait (National Bank of Kuwait, 1986: 10).

STATEHOOD INTEGRATION: THE ISSUE OF CITIZENSHIP

One of the most fundamental forms of political integration is the development of a sense of identity with a particular nation or state.[4] Political integration in the Arab world must be considered in the context of the dual nature of Arab states: most subscribe to the principle that Arabs constitute a single people (*Ummah*), a conviction that finds expression in the constitutions of Syria, Egypt, Jordan, Kuwait, and the United Arab Emirates (Dib, 1978: 43). At the same time, as the League of Arab States has acknowledged (1983: 3), they are multiple, separate sovereign states, each of which in turn faces its own challenges to political integration. It is the role of Arab migrants in what may be called 'statehood integration' that will be considered first here.

Citizenship constitutes the most basic mechanism for statehood integration. Plender (1972: 3–4) has observed that 'citizenship, subjecthood and nationality are all descriptions of the status of a legal person *vis-à-vis* a political environment' and that, although a concept of citizenship existed in ancient times, the modern use of the term as synonymous with nationality coincides with the emergence of the nation-state as a political entity. Ebraheem has emphasised the Western origins of the nation-state concept and the role of colonialism in the relatively recent emergence of many Arab states, 'some of which were artificially created at the end of the First World War as a result of the disintegration of the Ottoman Empire and the compartmentalization of the Arab world by the Western powers' (Al-Ebraheem, 1975: 19). But these facts should not obscure the historical origins of the concept of citizenship from within the region.[5] During pre-Islamic times, primary affiliation was tribal and an 'alien' was, by definition, anyone who did not belong to the tribe. With the coming of Islam and establishment of the principle of Ummah, religious identification became intrinsically tied to the concept of nationality. *Dhimmis* or Peoples of the Book (mainly Christians and Jews) were incorporated into the Islamic world by virtue of the status accorded them by the Qu'ran and by their payment of a special tax (the *jizya*) as well as of the land tax (*kharaj*) which Muslims also paid. Temporary residents (*musta'minun* or *mu'ahadun*) possessing safe-conduct agreements were permitted to remain in the Islamic world for a year and a day, after which time they became *ipso facto* dhimmis and subject to the jizya tax.

Many of the principles of the Islamic caliphate, including the implicit linkage between religion and nationality, were continued during the Ottoman period. Then, in 1869, the Sultan promulgated the first nationality law. This separated the concepts of religion and nationality, and adopted instead the concepts of *jus sanguinis* and *jus soli* as the bases for the definition of citizenship. The principle of *jus sanguinis* holds that citizenship of an individual is determined by the citizenship of his or her parents, while that of *jus soli* holds that citizenship of an individual is determined by his or her own place of birth.

The Treaty of Lausanne, signed 24 July 1923, established the legal status of the populations which were detached from the Ottoman Empire at the end of World War I and adopted the territorial principle (*jus soli*) as the basis for determining citizenship. As Dib has observed, however, despite the provisions of the Treaty, today,

> The Arab states — especially Lebanon, Syria, Jordan, Egypt, Kuwait, and the UAE — take a middle road between these two principles in their legislation: they employ *jus sanguinis* as the basic principle and *jus soli* as an auxiliary principle. The reason is that together these two principles forge the strong bond that is needed in every modern citizenship, the bond that integrates loyalty to blood and loyalty to the land. (Dib, 1979: 3)

While these principles are noteworthy in that they constitute the backbone of modern Arab citizenship laws and are of particular importance when considering the status of the children of migrants (a point to which we shall return below), the main reason for considering the regional historical roots of citizenship law is to stress that the concept is not merely an 'imported' one; rather, Arab states themselves have adopted and adjusted historical concepts to address the task of statehood integration. The major question to which we may now turn is: to what degree have Arab migrants participated in the process of statehood integration through the acquisition of citizenship by means of naturalisation?

The naturalisation laws of the states of Bahrain, Egypt, Iraq, Jordan, Kuwait, Lebanon, Syria, and the United Arab Emirates all stipulate the length of residency and the personal characteristics required of qualified applicants for naturalisation. Most also provide for special conditions, under which applicants may be granted citizenship regardless of whether or not they have fulfilled the usual requirements.

These laws themselves differ in the extent to which they facilitate Arab integration by making special provisions for the naturalisation of Arabs. Most countries have reduced residency requirements for Arab applicants, although the extent of the reduction varies considerably: in Kuwait, the UAE and Bahrain, Arab applicants must have from 10 to 30 years or more of residency in addition to possessing other personal qualifications; in Syria and Jordan, on the other hand, the residency requirement may be waived entirely for qualified Arabs. Several states treat at least some Arab applicants for citizenship as exceptional cases altogether. Following the principle of *jus sanguinis*, Egypt, Jordan, Lebanon and Syria make special provisions for the 'émigré-national' — that is an Arab national who is not a resident of an Arab country or a citizen of an Arab state but who can trace his or her origins to the prospective host country. Egypt has additional special conditions for applicants of Syrian or Egyptian origin. In accordance with the principle of *jus soli*, Syria also considers on a case-by-case basis any applicant who was formerly a citizen of an Arab state. Jordan is unique in its treatment of Arab applicants in one important respect: while most states reserve the right to grant or not to grant citizenship as a matter of state sovereignty, Jordan has stipulated that the citizenship application of an Arab may not be denied as long as the applicant fulfils the personal qualifications for naturalisation. Several states consider as special cases the applications of those who have rendered distinguished service to the state but Syria and Egypt are distinctive in considering also distinguished service to the Arab Nation, to Arab Nationalism or to the Arab people.

The possibility of children of Arab migrants attaining citizenship in their host country is generally covered by the provisions mentioned above. For minors, citizenship status often follows upon naturalisation of the father and may be retained upon application when the children reach adulthood. Egypt, however, has recognised the principle of *jus soli* to the extent that any alien born there who is a regular resident and meets the personal qualifications required is eligible to apply for naturalisation, regardless of the citizenship of his or her parents.

The attainment of citizenship itself is only one aspect governing the potential participation of migrants in statehood integration, for states differ in the extent to which naturalised citizens may exercise fundamental citizenship rights or political rights. In Jordan, a naturalised citizen is considered a Jordanian in every respect. In Egypt, an émigré-national who has been resident at least one year enjoys rights nearly identical to those of an original citizen, but other naturalised citizens may not exercise full citizenship or political rights until five years after naturalisation and may not be elected or appointed to a representative body (e.g. parliament) until ten years have passed. Similarly, in Syria, candidates for parliament must have been citizens for ten years and there are time restrictions on eligibility for civil service employment and the practice of law for all but naturalised citizens from Arab States. In Lebanon, a naturalised citizen who is not an émigré-national is restricted from civil service or other publically financed employment, from nomination to parliament, and from the practice of law until ten years following naturalisation; the practice of medicine is restricted until five years have passed.

In the Gulf states considered here, restrictions on the rights of naturalised citizen tend to focus on political rights. Naturalised Bahrainis may not vote or nominate themselves for election until ten years after naturalisation. Naturalised Kuwaitis are free to enjoy such fundamental citizenship rights as civil service employment, retirement and educational benefits and property ownership, but do not have the right to vote for any representative body until twenty years after the acquisition of citizenship and are ineligible for nomination or appointment to a representative body or ministerial position. In the UAE (with the exception of those of Bahraini, Omani or Qatari origin), naturalised citizens do not have the right to vote in any election for a representative or popular body, or to be nominated, elected, or appointed to such a body or to a ministerial post.

In summary, states have differed in the extent to which they have used naturalisation as a means to involve immigrants in the process of solidifying their own sense of identity as a state. Conversely, where the granting of citizenship has been used extensively for this purpose, naturalisation has been a prominent vehicle for Arab integration; in other cases, where even the granting of citizenship does not confer full rights, naturalisation has played a more limited role as an integrating factor. Jordan exemplifies the first approach, one end point along a spectrum of possible strategies: it has a short (4-year) residency requirement (which may be waived for Arabs), imposes upon itself a requirement to grant citizenship to any Arab with the requisite qualifications who seeks to become naturalised, and extends full citizenship rights to all naturalised persons. Kuwait and the United Arab Emirates illustrate the second approach and the other end point along the spectrum: they have adopted long residency requirements (although somewhat shorter ones for Arabs), limited political participation of naturalised citizens, and (in the case of Kuwait) chosen to limit the number of persons who may be naturalised through non-exceptional procedures.

It is beyond the scope of this chapter to consider fully why a given state chose the particular strategy it did, but it is clear that historical events, demography and political calculations all help to explain such choices. In the case of Jordan, the population census of 1952 enumerated a total population of 1.33 million persons, 587,000 of whom were residents of the East Bank and 743,000 residents of the West Bank (Hashemite Kingdom of Jordan, 1979: 3). Of those on the East Bank, a substantial number had immigrated earlier from Palestine. Given Jordan's strategic position, the presence of Palestinians on both banks, and the difficulties and costs likely to be associated with forging a state identity by differentiating among the populace on the bases of tribal or ethnic affiliations, it is not surprising that Jordan extended full citizenship to Palestinians after annexation of the West Bank in 1950, and subsequently (in 1954) adopted a naturalisation law consistent with this approach.

In the UAE and Kuwait, the historical, demographic and political conditions surrounding adoption of the nationality law and the strategies it embodied were different in several respects. In 1968, the population of the seven trucial states which later comprised the UAE stood at nearly 181,000, of which 63 per cent were citizens and 37 per cent non-citizen immigrants (Birks and Sinclair, 1980b: 74, Table 4.3). Over the following few years, the States faced the dual challenges of coping with a significant increase in the number of immigrants and, at the same time, of forging a united political entity out of disparate indigenous groups. The decision to naturalise some 55,000 Arabs between 1968 and 1975 (Birks and Sinclair, 1980b: 73) helped to address the first problem by bolstering the proportion of citizens in the population,[6] while the restriction of political rights for those naturalised helped strengthen the indigenous citizens' identification with the new state which resulted from the political union of 1971.

Similarly in Kuwait, the fundamental decisions to limit naturalisation in all but exceptional cases and to restrict the political rights of naturalised citizens were taken in the context of substantial levels of immigration (during the 1950s and early 1960s) and state independence (in 1961), both of which factors created new challenges to statehood identification. As in the UAE (and in contrast to Jordan), it was politically feasible to distinguish between the indigenous population and immigrants, in part because at the time basic nationality laws were promulgated (if not for long thereafter) original citizens outnumbered the newcomers. The restriction of political rights may also have been more acceptable on the grounds that many of the new immigrants and potential citizens were Palestinians whose political interests were focused on their own homeland. Be that as it may, official statistics record some 139,603 persons naturalised between 1967 and 1984 (State of Kuwait, 1977: 62, Table 54 and 1985: 51, Table 35). Analysis of census data on changes in the size of already-born cohorts suggest that approximately 73,000 persons became Kuwaiti citizens between 1961 and 1967 (State of Kuwait, 1972: Table 2 and 1977: 62, Table 54). Together, these estimates imply that approximately 212,000 naturalisations occurred between 1961 and 1984; without adjustments for deaths, this figure constitutes more than 30 per cent of the Kuwaiti population in 1985. While citizenship of origin is not recorded, and it is likely that a proportion of these were originally immigrants from other Arab states, a substantial number of those naturalised during the 1960s were Bedouin.[7]

In summary, the extent to which migrants have played a major role in forging statehood integration by acquiring citizenship and political rights in their host countries has differed across the region. In Jordan, data are not readily available on the total number of naturalised persons among the citizenry. However, it is clear from the discussion above that naturalisation was a major vehicle for integrating immigrant groups into the society and, conversely for achieving statehood integration. In the UAE and Kuwait, the use of naturalisation to achieve statehood integration has been much more limited and naturalisation has not served to fully integrate new citizens into the society. None the less, naturalised persons do account for a substantial portion of the citizen population in Kuwait.

MIGRATION AND TERRITORIAL INTEGRATION

Territorial integration differs from statehood integration in that it concerns not identity of the citizen with the state, but rather the process of strengthening both the geographical or territorial boundaries of the state and the legitimacy of central government's jurisdiction over and within the designated area. To see the effects of migration on territorial integration, we need to consider the regional, as well as the state levels.

As the Arab labour market has become regional in character, there have been efforts to view the Arab world as one territorial unit, with migration as one among several forms of interaction amenable to co-ordination under the framework of regional institutions and thus likely to strengthen the territorial integrity of the region. The Agreement on Economic Unity drafted by the League of Arab States' Economic Council in 1957 specifically endorsed the principle of freedom of movement among member states. Similarly, the principle of freedom of movement was endorsed by the first conference of Arab Labour ministers in 1965 and by a subsequent conference in 1967. It is noteworthy, however, that few states have actually ratified these agreements[8] and, although migration has had observable effects on institutional integration (discussed below), it has had little evident effect on *territorial* integration at the regional level. The situation is quite different at the state level. Despite the prevailing impression that 'migration occurs in a fundamental laissez-faire environment' (Richards and Martin, 1983: 460–1), both sending and receiving states have in fact been active in developing policies to govern entry, exit and residence of migrants. Egypt's abolition of exit visas and introduction of policy changes promoting migration were noted earlier. From the late 1970s, Jordan had permitted relatively free entry of migrants to work in the agricultural and service sectors. But in June 1984, as the number of non-Jordanian workers swelled to more than 150,000 and concern grew over unemployment among Jordanians, government amended the labour law to require all immigrant workers to register with the Ministry of Labour (Hashemite Kingdom of Jordan, 1984).

Kuwait has carefully controlled entry, exit and residence, under provisions of the Aliens Residence Law (Decree no. 17) of 1959 and migration has only stimulated further development and implementation of these controls: amendments and regulations under the Law were issued five times between 1963 and 1969 and ten times between 1974 and 1985.[9] The Labour Law (no. 38) of 1964 has similarly served as a vehicle for regulating migration, by tying conditions for legal employment to those for entry, exit and residence; Decrees no. 37 and 39 of 1979 were not only a major effort to organise the labour market, they were also closely linked to measures enforcing the Aliens Residence Law enacted the same year.

Although the desire to regulate internal labour market conditions explains the adoption of some state policies, the more fundamental reason migration has served to increase governments' control over their territorial boundaries has been clearly articulated in the Explanatory Memorandum accompanying Kuwait's Law no. 55 of 1982:

> The most prominent aspects of the State's sovereignty over its
> lands is the protection of its territories from any offender [who]
> daringly violates the said sovereignty by infiltration and residing
> in [it] without having secured a proper residence permit.
> (Hamdan: n.d.: 172–3).

Although the vast majority of migrants have been legally admitted
to and are law-abiding residents of their host countries, the sheer
size of the population movements involved has raised issues of
sovereignty and security which in turn have strengthened territorial
integration at the state level.

POLITICAL VALUES, CONSENSUS, COMMUNICATION AND MIGRATION

Formal political institutions (such as parliament) come to mind most
readily as examples of mechanisms for political exchange. Yet, in
any society, such institutions represent only one means for accom-
plishing some of the most fundamental tasks of political integration:
transmission of the basic values on which social and political
consensus is built, communication of views between the governed
and those who govern, and the formulation and implementation of
public policy.

Particularly in the case of the Gulf States, attention has tended to
focus on the absence or weakness of informal, non-governmental
political institutions. The status of political parties, labour unions
and voluntary organisations in the Arab world generally has been
characterised as 'either not allowed, repressed, or at least dismissed
as irrelevant' (Barakat, 1983: 173). As regards the UAE, Koury has
noted the absence of political parties, trade unions, non-religious
associations (apart from the Chamber of Commerce) and, in
particular, the lack of 'institutional intermediaries' between the
indigenous and migrant populations (Koury, 1980: 78, 131). But
these characterisations should not preclude examination of the
variety of ways in which the crucial tasks of political integration
identified above are, in fact, promoted by existing formal and non-
formal institutions. Institutions such as cultural, civic and religious
associations, the media, schools and universities, and the civil
service are not primarily political institutions, but they do play an
important role in the political process. And it is through these institutions that migrants have become most fully integrated into the

political fabric of many host countries.

Professional, cultural, civic and religious associations serve a number of functions that are political in nature. They help to meet specific needs of migrant communities, provide informal channels for communicating the views and concerns of migrants both to government and to the society at large, and provide a focal point for participation in community life. While there is little evidence to suggest that migrants participate to any significant degree in the informal socio-political groups (such as the *diwaniyyah* in Kuwait) which serve an important consultative function in Gulf societies, migrants have for some time been active participants in youth clubs and cultural associations. The potential for such associations to assume a more direct political role is only underscored by the fact that host governments have found it necessary to restrict cultural groups from time to time (see Moubarak, 1979: 125). Migrants are also active in religious groups, many of which seek to incorporate Islamic principles into political life: the leaders of Al-Usuliyyun movement, for example, are Egyptians living and publishing in Kuwait (Haddad, 1986: 146). A recent study of Palestinians in Kuwait suggests that village and town associations, as well as established groups like the General Union of Palestinian Women, play important roles in identifying and meeting community needs and articulating community opinion (Al-Ghabra, 1986). In short, it is likely that the full extent to which informal organisations exist among migrant communities in many host countries and the roles such groups actually play in political integration are in fact both poorly understood and underestimated.

It may be argued that the openness and effectiveness of the media as a vehicle for public debate are limited, particularly so following recent restrictions on the press in Kuwait. But again, this should not obscure the fact that — to the extent the print and broadcast media have served to promote dialogue and build consensus, migrants have been active in the process: of the 49 top editors and journalists relieved of their positions in Kuwait during the summer of 1986, all were expatriates (*Christian Science Monitor*, 1987: 12). As publishers, writers and public figures, migrants have contributed to the exchange of views on a wide range of political issues, to the communication of public opinion concerning the policies and actions of government and to debate over social goals and the means to achieve them.

One of the most basic roles of education is the transmission of political as well as social and cultural values. Since the 1930s, expatriate teachers from Egypt, Jordan, Syria and Sudan have played a major role in the expansion of educational systems throughout the Gulf and in Saudi Arabia and this pattern has continued to the present time. In Qatar, non-Qatari Arabs comprised 75 per cent of all teachers in 1976/7 (Birks and Sinclair, 1980: 61, Table 3.6); non-Saudis were 48 per cent of teachers at all educational levels in Saudi Arabia as of 1983 (Kingdom of Saudi Arabia, 1983: 51, Table 2–3). In Kuwait, although the proportion of Kuwaiti teachers has increased rapidly in recent years, non-Kuwaitis comprised nearly 68 per cent of all teachers in government schools in 1984/5 and over 69 per cent of all teaching staff at the university level (State of Kuwait, 1984a: 302, Table 262 and 324, Table 282). As teachers of future citizens, Arab migrants have had considerable influence in shaping the political values and attitudes in their host countries.

Civil service employment is another means by which migrants are integrated into the political life of the countries in which they work. This is not to say that the civil services are 'politicised', but merely to acknowledge the fact that civil servants play a significant role in political processes through participation in the day-to-day business of running the government bureaucracy: planning policies, supporting the work of elected officials, and generally ensuring that governmental policies are implemented. These are not inconsequential roles, particularly in the receiving states which have explicitly used government programmes to distribute benefits of oil wealth and thereby build political support among their citizens. In many countries, despite the fact that citizens tend to be concentrated in public sector employment, migrants provide substantial numbers and proportions of civil service manpower: in Qatar, expatriate staff (mostly Arabs from Egypt and the Levant) were 38 per cent of all public sector employees in 1975, while in Oman more than a quarter of all public sector employees were expatriates in 1976/7 (Birks and Sinclair, 1980. 68, Table 3.15, 69 and 185); in Saudi Arabia in 1985, there were approximately 100,000 expatriates in the civil service, comprising 22 per cent of public employees (Al-Sadhan, 1985); in Kuwait, expatriates comprised nearly 58 per cent of public sector employees (National Bank of Kuwait, 1986: 10, author's calculation).

In summary, even as non-citizens, and despite the limitations on intermediary or non-governmental institutions, migrants are integrated into the political life of their host communities through participation in a variety of formal and non-formal institutions which serve essential political functions: channelling communication between those who govern and the governed, shaping fundamental political values and providing stability and continuity in the social order.

MIGRATION AND INSTITUTIONAL DEVELOPMENT

A final dimension of political integration is the capacity of people to develop new institutions in response to change. To fully measure the effects of migration on institutional development in the Arab world is a daunting task, beyond the scope of this chapter. But a brief look at the role of migration in the emergence of a few new institutions will serve to suggest the force of migration in this integrative process.

One of the new challenges facing sending countries as a consequence of migration has been the task of maintaining meaningful contact with citizens abroad in order to assure the migrants' continuing identity with and loyalty to their home country, to promote the remittance of earnings and, potentially, to ease the reintegration of migrants upon their return. This challenge has been met in a number of ways, through new institutions or the adaptation of existing ones. Dessouki (1982) has documented some of Egypt's institutional responses to migration: since 1967, a proliferation of governmental committees dealing with migration; the establishment of an emigration department in the Ministry of Foreign Affairs in 1969; the reinstitution during the 1970s of Egyptian labour attachés in major receiving countries. Similar institutions have developed in Jordan: since 1976, the Ministry of Labour has posted labour attachés in Jordanian embassies abroad; since 1981, the Ministry of Foreign Affairs has had a 'Section for Emigrants' (Hashemite Kingdom of Jordan 1982: 2–5). In 1985, the government sponsored Jordan's first conference of migrants.[10] Representatives to the conference were nominated by Jordanian embassies in numbers proportionate to the size of the Jordanian workforce in each country, on the basis of recognised leadership in the Jordanian community and with regard to achieving broad representation from various occupational and sectoral groups as well as professional syndicates and cultural associations. The migrant representatives themselves, in consultation with other members of their communities, prepared written reports detailing with considerable candor the concerns of Jordanians in their host countries, problems they face on returning home

387

and concrete recommendations concerning actions the Jordanian government could take to address these issues. For its part, the government (with representatives from all ministries) presented issue papers as the basis for discussion of matters ranging from economic and social conditions to regional political affairs. The resulting frank exchange of views was an altogether new form of political interaction, under the framework of a new type of political institution.

Sending countries have also sought collectively to facilitate migration through new initiatives under the framework of existing institutions. A project begun in 1983 under the Arab Labour Organisation (and co-sponsored by the Arab Fund and the United Nations Development Programme) has established the Arab Employment Institute in Tangier and undertaken development of a Pan-Arab Labour Market Information System. These efforts are aimed at disseminating regional labour market information and promoting Arab migration (Arab Employment Institution, 1983; UNDP, 1984; Helmy, 1985).

Among receiving countries as well, migration has become a matter for co-ordination under the rubric of new institutions. The Gulf Cooperation Council (GCC) was founded in 1981 to facilitate co-operation among member states on a wide range of economic, social and political issues and migration has figured prominently among the topics addressed. Indeed, GCC Secretary General Abdullah Bishara has called 'the population problem' induced by migration 'the greatest problem facing the Council' (*Al-Mujtama'*, 1984. 17).

Migration within the GCC region has been the subject of several measures. Free movement of GCC citizens among member countries is provided for under the unified economic agreement signed in 1981 and had been largely implemented by 1985 (*Arab Times*, 12 May 1985; 5 and 31 March 1985: 5). Agreement was reached in May 1985 to equalise the rights and duties of GCC citizens working in the private sector and free professions in other member states (GCC, 1985).

Migration from outside the GCC region has been the major concern within the Council, however. At their April 1984 meeting, the GCC Ministers of Labour and Social Affairs explicitly recognised 'the necessity of creating a Gulf apparatus to supervise the movement of non-GCC Arab labour in the region in a way to best serve both the GCC and labour-supplying states' (Kuwait News Agency, 1984: 126). At their meeting the following year, the labour ministers reviewed findings of a study commissioned to propose ways of unifying regulations governing the importation of man-power, established a committee to prepare specific recommenda-tions on the subject and reached agreement on co-ordinated measures to protect the rights of migrants and their dependents (GCC, 1985). Nor is migration solely a matter of concern to the Ministers of Labour, under the Council's Man and Environment Affairs Sector. According to Dr Ebrahim Homood Al-Subhi, Assis-tant Secretary General for Political Affairs, the issue of migration and migrants is part of the programme of work of the Political Affairs Sector as well: since 1984, member states have begun to consult collectively, through the GCC, with some Asian labour-exporting countries (As-Subhi, 1985) and, in an effort to reduce perceived political and security risks associated with migration, mechanisms are being established to enable GCC member countries to share information about individual workers (Al-Jasr, 1985, and *Middle East Times*, 6–8 October 1985: 1).

Thus, in both sending and receiving countries and at the regional and sub-regional levels, the issue of migration itself has evoked the development of new institutions and the responsive adaptation of existing ones. The degree to which these institutions have been or may become effective in attaining their migration-related objectives is a separate question. The point is that migration has induced new forms of political integration at the institutional level.

CONCLUSION

This chapter has explored the consequences of migration for political integration in the Arab world and particularly for the integration of migrants into the political fabric of their host coun-tries. These issues are likely to be of growing importance, as both sending and receiving countries come to grips with the fact that large numbers of migrants and their dependents may well continue as settled, long-term residents outside their countries of origin.

The acquisition of citizenship has been one vehicle for the political integration of migrants, but its use has been affected by the strategies which individual states have adopted towards the role of immigrants in building state identity. Indeed, in some cases, states have promoted statehood integration by differentiating between 'original' and naturalised citizens. The fact that acquisition of citizenship has been limited in the major receiving states of the Gulf, or has not resulted in full political participation where it has occurred, does not mean, however, that political integration of migrants has not taken place. As Al-Ebraheem has observed (1984: 80) participatory government is not the prevailing pattern in the Gulf in any case.

On balance, and particularly in view of the authoritarian nature of the Gulf regimes, a more important mechanism for integration of migrants has been their participation in host country institutions that — despite the real constraints upon them — none the less serve to build consensus, transmit values and promote dialogue between government and society. Through their involvement in schools and universities, the media, community associations and the civil service, migrants have played a role in the political integration of the countries in which they reside and have themselves achieved a measure of political integration in the process.

The political integration of migrants in their host societies is one level of concern; the effects of migration on integration at the state and regional levels is another. There is little evidence that migration has succeeded in making the Arab world a single territory without boundaries; in fact, as migration has induced states to develop policies to control their borders, the process has contributed more to territorial integration at the state level. But migration has evoked an array of new institutions and of adaptive responses by existing ones. With large numbers of their citizens resident abroad, sending countries have developed new ways of linking government with society. Shared concerns for labour force stability and the future of migration have prompted new regional efforts at co-ordination among sending countries, while political and security as well as manpower concerns have made migration an issue for co-ordination among receiving countries. While the effectiveness of these efforts remains untested, it is clear that institutional development has been stimulated by the migration process.

Whatever the degrees and types of political integration resulting from migration observable today, there will be others to follow. The degree of day-to-day interaction among Arabs of different origins has never been greater. The numbers born and growing up outside their home countries are increasing. Manpower and population policies are no longer of purely domestic concern: they carry bilateral and regional political as well as economic consequences.

For the countries of the Gulf, the future position of migrants is an especially sensitive one, not only because of the proportionate size of the migrant communities there, but because these states are at a critical juncture with respect to the very issue of political participation itself. As Roger Owen has observed, the long-range tasks of building diversified, export-oriented economies, of achieving public consensus on the use of national resources (especially oil and investment earnings) and of facilitating technology transfer, all require greater political expression, freer exchange of ideas and less authoritarian rule (Owen, 1983: 143ff). Yet, under the immediate pressures of budget constraints, internal political dissent and security risks — including those posed by the Iran–Iraq wars — constraints on popular political participation by citizens, let alone non-citizens, have seldom been tighter. The future status of migrants in the politics of the Gulf must be determined in the context of rethinking how long-range political stability and economic prosperity are best achieved. The underlying assumptions on the bases of which Gulf states chose to ensure domestic political stability and regime support by differentiating sharply between citizens and non-citizens have changed. In many places, citizens are not the majority they were when basic nationality laws were passed, nor are they as homogeneous as they once were. Both past naturalisations and rising levels of education and technical skill have introduced new subgroups, expectations and complexities among the citizenry itself. The increased sensitivity of the population to basic Islamic principles has only deepened the moral dilemmas inherent in differential treatment of Muslim Arab naturalised citizens and non-citizens alike. Nor are migrants merely the temporary sojourners they were once expected to be. They are long-term residents who, it has been argued here, have already achieved a degree of political integration in their host societies. They are, increasingly, native-born sons and daughters whose commitment to their country of birth remains an unchannelled resource for stability. Together, these factors pose new challenges to the internal coherence of Gulf societies, argue for a careful reassessment of the role of migrants in their host countries and will make migration a continuing factor in political integration for years to come.

ACKNOWLEDGEMENTS

The research on which this chapter is based was supported in part by a grant from the Social Science Research Council with funds from the Ford Foundation and the National Endowment for the Humanities. The author extends special thanks to David Partington and Ahmed Jibari of Widener Library,

391

Harvard University for their assistance with Arabic texts consulted in preparation of this chapter.

NOTES

1. Major studies of the economic, demographic and social aspects of recent Arab migration include: Birks and Sinclair, 1980; Serageldin *et al.*, 1981 and 1983; Ibrahim, 1982; Abdallah and Abd al-Fadil, 1983; Choucri *et al.*, 1983; Fergany, 1984; Amin and 'Awny, 1985.

2. Some recent studies that have addressed the political dimensions of migration (both Arab and non-Arab) are: Dib, 1978, 1979; Montgomery *et al.*, 1979; Khoury, 1981; Zolberg in Kritz *et al.*, 1981; Dessouki, 1982; United Nations, 1982; Bhagwati, 1984; Zolberg and Suhrke, 1984; Abu Lughod in Ibrahim and Hopkins, 1985; Choucri, 1986; Russell, 1986a; Weiner and Choucri, 1986.

3. Kuwait's population in 1949 has been estimated at 100,000 (Ismael, 1982: 60, 117); total population was 206,473 in 1957, and 467,339 in 1965 (State of Kuwait, 1984b). In 1965, Jordanians and Palestinians in Kuwait numbered 77,712, out of a total non-Kuwaiti population of 247,280 (State of Kuwait, 1977: 25–6, 59).

4. Weiner (1965: 53–4) has identified five dimensions of political integration. The first, which he calls *national integration*, addresses 'the problem of creating a sense of territorial nationality which overshadows — or eliminates — subordinate parochial loyalties'. The second dimension is *territorial integration*, or the response to a government's need to establish control over the geographical area (and political sub-units) under its claimed jurisdiction. *Elite-mass integration*, addresses the problem of linking the interests of government with those of the governed by means of institutions in and through which members of society express their views. *Value integration* serves to maintain social order through achievement of a minimum level of consensus about basic values, a process generally accomplished through involvement of the populace in a common political process. The fifth and final dimension is *integrative behaviour*, or 'the capacity of people in a society to organize for some common purposes' and particularly to create new organisations adapted to changing social circumstances. Weiner's typology has been loosely adapted in the discussion which follows.

5. The following discussion of the historical origins of citizenship law in the Arab world and the characteristics of naturalisation law in selected countries is drawn from Dib (1978: 42ff and 1979: 3ff); the *International Encyclopedia of Comparative Law*, vol. I, National Reports; and The Hashemite Kingdom of Jordan, 1954 (Nationality Law); and State of Kuwait, 1959 (Nationality Law as amended through 1982).

6. By 1975, the total population of the UAE had risen to 655,000, and non-nationals (numbering nearly 456,000) had come to comprise 70 per cent of the population. Without the naturalisation programme, citizens would have been only 22 per cent of the population, rather than 30 per cent.

7. Estimates as to the number of Bedouin naturalised prior to the 1967

elections run as high as 100,000–200,000 (Crystal, 1986: 198).

8. Jordan, Iraq, Egypt and Syria ratified the 1967 agreement but (with the exception of Iraq) none of the receiving countries ratified it (Dessouki, 1982: 64). Kuwait initially supported the Economic Council's proposal but later withdrew, reportedly over the issue of free movement (Moubarak, 1979: 89).

9. The relevant amendments and regulatory changes were Law no. 1 of 1963; Law no. 26 of 1965; Decree no. 10 of 1965; Law no. 17 of 1968; Decree no. 3 of 1969; Decree no. 22 of 1975; Decree no. 70 of 1976; Decree no. 84 of 1977; Decree no. 54 of 1979; various orders issued April 1980; Law no. 55 of 1982; Decree no. 262 of 1982; various orders issued September 1982; orders issued April 4 1985; and orders pertaining to dependents of 1985.

10. Material concerning the First Conference of Jordanian Migrants Abroad, held in Amman 20–24 July 1985, is drawn from background papers and conference proceedings provided by the Ministry of Labour and from the author's interviews with officials and migrant representatives during the spring and summer of 1985.

16

The Politics of Arab Integration

Giacomo Luciani and Ghassan Salamé

In its examination of the foundations and stability of the Arab states, the prevailing message of this book has been that Arab states as 'sovereign', internationally recognised entities, contrary to the hopes of many, appear to be more resilient than they have often been portrayed. The analyses of the historical foundations, the economic bases and the interplay between state and society lead to an overall impression of progressive consolidation of the state structures that formed at various times during the first half of this century.

The most common image of the Arab states in the media and in most of the literature is, in contrast, one of weak states precariously ruling over highly segmented societies. The emphasis is laid on the multiple lines of division honeycombing Arab politics along ethnic, religious and linguistic grounds. The 'mosaic' framework is easily accepted and often aggravated by those political forces that have among their objectives that of showing the Arab governments as 'unreliable' or 'shaky'. Lebanon is viewed as the forerunner of the inevitable disaggregation of all Arab states.

At the same time, the demise of pan-Arabism is recorded time and again, as if some found pleasure in constantly writing its obituary. Yet somehow the ideal and call of the Arab nation refuses to die. The reality of Arab politics is there for everybody to see, and it is a different reality from the politics of each individual Arab country. While obituaries are being written, new, intense forms of Arab interaction are emerging.

Thus, our inquiry into the Arab state could not possibly avoid a discussion of the politics of integration, both at the domestic (state) level and at the regional (pan-Arab) level. The first aspect was dealt with in earlier chapters. This chapter concludes the discussion of the regional dimension of integration that has been developed throughout the last four chapters.

Integration — from the Latin *integer* — is the process whereby differences are gradually overcome and homogeneity is created. It is convenient to differentiate between integration and unification; the former refers to economic, cultural or societal processes, the latter has a predominantly institutional content. A country may be politically unified and still be socially or economically disintegrated; a nation or a group of nations can be highly integrated while not politically unified. Integration is a multidimensional process and need not happen in parallel at all levels: economic integration is largely independent of linguistic or cultural or religious or social integration.

At the same time, integration is more than the mere existence of some common ground (similarities) or linkage (interaction) between different actors. The latter may be sufficient to establish a relationship of interdependence between the actors sharing common traits; but interdependence may be a conflictual as well as a co-operative relationship. It is only in the latter case, that of co-operative interdependence, that we should speak of integration. Thus, several countries have in common the fact that they possess nuclear weapons, but in most cases this creates mere interdependence, not integration. Even an intense trade relationship can sometimes lead to conflictual interdependence, rather than integration — as in the case of trade between oil-exporting and oil-importing countries. But when the sharing of a common interest is accompanied by co-operative behaviour (a regime) then it leads to integration, as in the case of trade between countries which are members of the European Community. Integration is thus the result of a component of *voluntarism* rather than simply of facts of geography, culture etc.

Also, integration is always relative to some specific interest, and as we shift analysis from one interest or set of interests to another the geometry of integration changes: countries that are integrated with respect to trade may not be integrated in matters of defence or language or religion. Thus, while members of the EC are integrated in matters of trade, agriculture etc., in matters of defence some, but not all, are integrated in NATO; the latter comprises also countries that are not members of the Community. With respect to international monetary affairs the relevant integrative scheme (admittedly a weak one) is the Group of 7, in which Japan participates as well. If language is chosen as a variable, then Europe is disintegrated, while France promotes schemes to achieve cooperation among the French-speaking countries. In matters concerned with the international forwarding of mail, a large number of countries are integrated in the World Postal Union. In short: the geometry of integration/interdependence between states varies with the specific interest or set of interests under consideration. While some interests may be perceived as more important than others, there is little reason to argue that one integrative project relative to one interest should not coexist with a different integrative project for a different interest. Neither is there evidence to prove that integration relative to one interest will tend to encourage integration relative to other interests, eventually leading to the emergence of one pre-eminent integrative project spanning a broad range of interests simultaneously: this may occur, but it is certainly not a necessary outcome.

Supposedly, a nation is integrated, and it is the fact of integration that distinguishes one nation from the other. This postulates that there is one overriding character, or a set of common interests that is shared by all individuals belonging to this nation, and not by others. Integration should thus define the boundary of any nation. This is particularly evident in the German tradition (*Fichte*), according to which a nation is the result of an integrated people; the French tradition (*vouloir vivre en commun*) views the nation as the vehicle for integration, rather than the result of it, but nevertheless in both traditions a strong association is posited between nation and integration. However, because commonly the geometry of integration varies with the character that is posited as definitional, and several characters may be equally important in shaping political life, nations seldom are defined in an empirically measurable way, as entities which are integrated with respect to one or another well defined and quantifiable character. Nations are *myths* that politicians manipulate to achieve their political goals: while there *must* be something in common that helps define a nation, very profound segmentation is frequent. In historical experience, nations are more often than not integrated *ex post*, by the conscious effort of the political structure that was created in their name.

Ethnic and cultural factors, more rarely religious or economic ones, are commonly invoked to define a nation. But in no case in the real world are boundaries so neat as to identify clearly a set of contiguous groups: overlaps and ambiguity prevail, and not only in the newly independent states, but in old Europe as well. While there may be some core group which is indeed strongly integrated with respect to several characteristics, as we move towards the edges of this group the coherence of the integrative pattern will gradually fade away, and commonality will become dubious, or the pattern of integration according to one characteristic will conflict with those based on different characteristics. Very often a single core group cannot even be clearly identified. Yet, nationalistic discourse dominates contemporary international relations, and the very usage of the adjective *international*, where inter-statal would certainly be more accurate, is a manifestation of such domination.

Shying away from the issue of definition, the discourse on nationalism and the nation often personalises the latter. Nations, or countries, are assumed to be living entities that one can readily recognise; to have a soul, a conscience, a will, a personal history of maturing and becoming more sensible. They are assumed to have a character to which they may be true or unfaithful (as in the Ba'th slogan 'One single Arab nation with an eternal mission'): hence the debate on authenticity, which is so overwhelmingly important in the Arab countries today.

This personalised approach is common both in the nationalist literature (Bensaid in Salamé, 1987) and in the 'scholarly' literature on Arab nationalism (such as in *The Arab Predicament*). Within this line of thinking, we may include all those who maintain that the distinction between East and West has significant scientific value left to it (including most of the orientalists and all kinds of *salafi* nationalists or religious writers in the Arab world), and that humankind is not singular, but plural.

Contrary to this approach, the authors of this chapter are inclined to confess their unabashed illuministic belief that men are primarily just that, and groupings of men are a matter of convenience and adherence to observable facts, and, to a large extent, the result of accidents of history and geography. Thus in discussing a highly emotional topic such as the definition and future of the Arab nation, this volume tries to adhere as much as possible to reality and measurable facts and concentrates on the non-ideological aspect of the problem, i.e. integration.

Any society, large or small, has divisive and integrating factors, and integration is a political problem at any level of political action. Politics of integration exist even within the family, although admittedly the concrete meaning of integration vs. disintegrative behaviour changes with the dimensions and nature of the group it refers to.

Political life takes place at various levels: the common distinction between local (municipal), national and international political affairs

— which is reflected in the layout of many a morning paper — is as good as any other. In fact, we know that there are many more than three levels: but for the sake of clarity let us stick to these three.

Integration is a problem at all levels, and there is normally a trade-off between integration/disintegration at each of them. Because integration is achieved not only by reducing differences within, but also underlining differences with the rest of the universe, the dictates of integration at any one level contrast with the same at levels above or below. This is the essential reason why the issue of integration should be simultaneously considered with reference to the various levels. Integration within the existing Arab states is logically and politically connected to integration between these same states, and very frequently policies that are adopted with a view to promoting integration at one level are opposed as jeopardising integration at other levels. Thus, for example, to insist on a 'Lebanese' identity serves the purpose of integrating the various confessions within Lebanon and isolating the country from the environment, while insisting on the Arab and Islamic dimension of the Sudan has disintegrative consequences on relations between the north and south of the country. This is a common problem in any subregional system, as well as globally and within each state (when the dialectical relationship between central and local government is considered).

Arab societies are divided: this point has been extensively dealt with in the literature. In most cases the divisions that are described and analysed with greatest accuracy are those that are the closest to heart and mind of the orientalist tradition and of its local followers: the communal and religious differences. Thus considerable attention is paid to the differences between Sunnis and Shi'is, Druzes and 'Alawis, Maronites and Greek Orthodox, Copts and Protestants, and so on; or to communal identities such as Kurds, Berbers, southern Sudanese. The various identifications combine to form multiple groupings, and the image projected is of a regional political system of baffling complexity, that only devotees of an esoteric science can understand. The insistence on complexity implies that the region is a natural ground for foreign intervention.

This line of analysis is often elegant and may make fascinating reading. Of course, no one would ever deny that these factors play an important role in Arab politics, and yes: the Middle East is an anthropologist's paradise. However, that Arab societies are in any significant and measurable sense more divided than societies in other parts of the world is questionable. Religious or communal differences exist in all countries, and are the rule rather than the exception. Examples in the Third World are extremely abundant, but one should not forget the tendency for ethnicity to push aside the old melting pot, while segmentation persists in centuries old European states. A Scot is not the same thing as a Welshman, a Lutheran Hamburger is not the same as a Catholic Münchener, and a Sicilian is not to be confused with a Milanese. It is hard to argue that European politics is in any meaningful sense less complex and involute that Arab politics: American political scientists sometimes lose the perception of this fact, because of the widespread lack of interest in European affairs and the well-known American impatience with anything complex. But they only have to consider their own country: in the US citizens are on many occasions requested to state whether they are white or black, Asian or latino, while ethnic lobbies are increasingly influential in culture and politics.

That existing societal divisions have a greater impact on Arab politics than on politics in non-Arab countries is again questionable. One need only recall that in Belgium parties are differentiated along linguistic as well as ideological lines, that regionally defined parties exist in West Germany and Italy, and communal irredentism fuels intense terrorist activity in the United Kingdom (Northern Ireland), Spain (the Basques) and France (Corsica). In the United States, the influence of ethnically or religiously defined lobbies has gradually overshadowed the more traditional, economically defined groupings (labour vs. capital, industry vs. agriculture or finance, small business vs. big business etc.). Indeed, while in Europe ideology still plays an important role in politics, in the United States ethnic and religious factors have, for all practical purposes, made ideology irrelevant to political life. Finally, examples of the political impact of societal segmentation in non-Arab developing countries are so numerous that we do not need to elaborate. How can one seriously argue that the Arab case is quantitatively or qualitatively different?

The need to integrate, i.e. to establish a common basis of allegiance to the state and the political process is common to any country. The way this need is addressed, however, is different. In particular, integration through the acceptance of a constitutional pact may be considered a superior and more stable solution to the problem. Indeed, while disintegrative movements may surface in any country, they may be expected to have less of a conflictual character if the latter enjoys well-established democratic institutions. Yet it is a fact that even the United Kingdom, the land of the Magna Carta, still faces rebellion in Northern Ireland. Furthermore, whenever the authoritarian nature of the regime creates conditions that are more conducive to disintegration, the blame should logically be laid on the character of the regime, not on some supposedly extra-ordinary degree of segmentation.

Although the acceptance of a national myth is certainly more widespread in certain countries than it is in others (*les Français sont chauvins!*), no national myth is able to monopolise the hearts and minds of the people. It is inevitable that individuals realise that they sometimes have differences with their fellow countrymen, while at the same time sharing interests with individuals or groups elsewhere in the world. But if individuals have multiple identifications, and they all do, the ranking of the latter and the attempt to find one that may be said to be predominant is largely arbitrary. Such rankings only acquire a meaning when identifications become mutually exclusive and people are requested to choose. But this is a rare occurrence, although it may help explain why so many Egyptian intellectuals have been obsessed by the need to return to the Arab fold following Camp David, while most intellectuals outside of Egypt derive very little satisfaction from being in the same Arab fold, and even wonder what the Arab fold is anyhow. In any case, the vast majority of the people probably never felt this contradiction, simply because they quite naturally identify as both Egyptian *and* Arab, independently of what their government or the Arab League may say in this respect in their official declarations.

Thus it is not surprising that citizens of the Arab countries typically identify with subnational groups defined along ethnic, religious, linguistic or cultural lines; while at the same time they also identify with their country of birth as well as with an Arab dimension, or nation. If it is acceptable to be *bruxellois-wallon-belge-catholique-européen-occidental*, why should there be a problem in being a Damascene-Greek Orthodox-Syrian-Arab? Such multiple identifications would hardly be as controversial as they are if the Arab states were ruled by legitimate, democratic governments. But because this is commonly not the case, particularism and/or Arab nationalism have at times become vehicles of opposition, threatening governments in power.

It is entirely predictable that whenever political discourse *per se* is suppressed, individuals will attribute political functions to aggregations that would normally perform altogether different roles. Social, cultural, communal and religious groups will be used as covers or alternative avenues for political action. This surrogate role may lead to the impression that segmentation thus defined plays a fundamental role, but it is only after freedom of political discourse is restored that one can pass judgement. Admittedly, this freedom may never be restored, and the political role of non-political agents may become entrenched; but surprising changes in the perceived structure of the political system are common whenever countries return to democracy. Thus, it was commonly believed in the last years of Franco's rule that the Catholic church would play a crucial role in post-Francoist Spain: yet we witness an entirely different reality, one which was unpredictable as long as authoritarian rule suppressed political discourse.

The same Catholic church that provided technocratic expertise through the Opus Dei in Spain, has often been a vehicle of opposition to authoritarian rule in Latin America. However when democracy was reinstated, e.g. in Brazil, entirely secular political parties came to dominate the political debate, and the role of the church was redefined. In the Arab region it is Islam that has sometimes played a prominent role as the language of opposition (while generally being used to support and legitimise authoritarian governments). Not surprisingly, governments in power have tended to portray this opposition as being a threat to the state, and this view has often found its way in to the literature. In fact, there is little evidence that this opposition is aimed at the state rather than at the regime or government. Thus, it is not clear that the prominence of particularism or universalism is a manifestation of state weakness, while it may be a manifestation of the weakness of the government and institutions (more on this in Hermassi, 1987: 75–85).

Opposition to established rule has always been coloured by local, religious or ethnic considerations in the region. In many cases it is difficult and arbitrary to dissociate opposition (i.e. the wish to see an alternative to the present use of power) from separatism (the wish to subtract oneself from submission to that power). Most opposition movements, being unable to achieve results *qua* opposition have reverted or contented themselves with separatism.

From a theoretical point of view, a segmented polity may provide an authoritarian government the opportunity to consolidate its position through *divide et impera*. However, it would obviously be preposterous to derive the conclusion that authoritarian governments are better equipped to address the problem of segmentation: they may deliberately maintain it rather than promoting integration. This is not reflected, however, in their official rhetoric nor, in most cases, in their deeds: most authoritarian governments are inclined to deny the existence and legitimacy of communal identifications,

401

while at the same time trying to manipulate universalistic ones. Thus in most Arab countries the existence of politically or sociologically defined minorities is ignored, and the power of the central state is affirmed over regional or municipal autonomy. At the same time, almost all governments resort to pan-Arab or pan-Islamic rhetoric to support their dubious legitimacy.

At the same time, it must be recognised that the formal existence of democratic institutions in no way guarantees *per se* that a segmented society will be able to maintain political unity and evolve towards integration. The case of Lebanon is an obvious example of this, and certain of its peculiarities need to be underlined at this point. While the Lebanese regime was a democratic one, it was based on the official recognition of sectarian cleavages, and tended to consolidate them. In fact, sectarianism was a political objective sought by the ruling elite (basically Maronite). At the same time, the constitution strongly centralised power in the hands of the president, naturally concentrating attention and controversy on presidential politics. Indeed, because the lack of integration was officially recognised in the National Covenant, attempts to make up for it through constitutional centralisation (the powers of the President reflecting the privileged position of his sect) were made. The alternative approach — a deliberate attempt to play down the political significance of sectarian connotations coupled with a fairer institutional power-sharing formula — was systematically blocked by the ruling elite. Partly because of the strongly centralised definition of the state, the role of the latter in the economy and society tended to be limited. Had the state attempted to permeate society and perform all the crucial roles (education, information, allocation of resources) that it plays in most Arab countries, the concentration of power in the hands of a Maronite president would probably have become unacceptable to the other sectarian groups. Hence the state was centralised but confined, and consequently the dependence of the individual on the state was also limited.

It is interesting to underline, at this point, the current paradox of the Lebanese civil war: none of the major factions proposes liquidation of the Lebanese state nor partition, nor absorption by neighbouring Syria. True, Lebanese militias that confront each other in the civil war do not normally engage in issue politics: yet the absence of a real debate on the redefinition of the Lebanese state is significant. The idea that a territorial redefinition of the Lebanese state is possible, whereby Tripoli and the Beqa' would be annexed by Syria, and the remaining territory would have a clear Maronite majority, is found in the writings of Israeli scholars, but is not publicly entertained by any of the Lebanese forces nor does it seem to appeal to Damascus; this creates a paradox which has left an important mark in the domestic debate in Israel (as documented by Shlaim, Luciani and Salamé, 1987, Chapter 9).

The experience of all other Arab states is entirely different. Centralisation has been coupled with the official downplaying of sectarian identifications and with a tremendous growth in the role of the state, that has greatly increased citizens' dependence on it. While sects have certainly not disappeared, their influence must be weighed against dependence on the state, and the expectation that Arab states will blow apart has not been supported by facts. Thus, notwithstanding the fact that in Iraq the Shi'a do not participate in power — while being the majority — has not led to opposition and massive desertions, as the Iranian Islamic government had hoped. In the early stages of war, the speculative expectation that the Arab population in southern Iran might come to support the Iraqi invasion was proven equally unfounded.

The next candidate for disintegration along sectarian lines is Syria. Indeed, the authoritarian nature of the Syrian regime, coupled with its own sectarian dimension, abundantly justifies the continuing importance of sectarian identifications as an expression of opposition. Yet, one should not forget that the Syrian state has come to be something much more complex than simply the regime of Hafez al-Asad, and that this same regime relies on numerous support structures, not just the 'Alawi 'asabiyya (see on this Hinnebush, in Dawisha and Zartman, 1987). The expectation that Syria will disintegrate whenever the current regime comes to an end may therefore be unfounded. Authoritarian governments create conditions that do not allow measurement of the transformations that occur in societies and individual perceptions; but transformations do occur.

In the case of the Sudan, the attempt on the part of the authoritarian government of Ga'far an-Nimeiry to play the game of divide and rule has gradually brought it to isolation and downfall. The armed revolt in the south has played an essential role in bringing about this result. Restoration of democratic government has not led to an end of the civil war, partly because of the fact that the Islamic legislation approved in 1983 has not yet been repealed (An-Na'im, 1987).

The Sudan is a graphic example of the contradiction between domestic and regional integration. The proposition of wider integrative projects — be they Nilotic co-operation with Egypt, pan-

Arab sympathy or adoption of the *shari'ah* — has a disintegrative impact on the domestic polity. The Ba'th pan-Arab vocabulary is no more adequate in Iraq: indeed examples can be given for almost any Arab state. Faced with the need to achieve greater domestic integration, a majority of the Arab states have paid little more than lip service to the goal of Arab integration. Yet some pan-Arab integration nevertheless exists, at least enough of it to keep the Arab national dream alive. The next question is to see what is the concrete, measurable content of Arab integration.

Who is an Arab? Clearly the shortest acceptable definition is: any individual whose native language is Arabic. Thus, the Arabic language must be the backbone of any attempt to define an Arab nation, and is anyway the common point of departure for most Arabists.

In recent times, as noted, Islam has played an increasing role as an universalistic language of opposition, eroding the impact of Arab nationalism. However, although some speak of an Islamic nation, on the basis of a misleading if possibly unavoidable translation of *umma*, it is obviously inaccurate to speak of Islamic nationalism. Islam, thus, may be a language of opposition, but it is not a language of integration, in the sense that it does not *per se* define a credible dimension for intense co-operation between states. The tendency to create Islamic institutions is not to be denied, but is a qualitatively different phenomenon from the growth of pan-Arab institutions. While for the Arabs the ideal is that of one nation one state, for the other Islamic states such an ideal is marginal, or a mere sanctified utopia.

For this reason, we felt it was necessary to start from Arabic. If Arabic is the backbone of the attempt to define the Arab nation, then the question must be asked: is there *one* Arabic language? Zakaria Abuhamdia feels strongly that indeed Arabic provides language unity, notwithstanding the regional and social variations that are common in any language. He notes the opinion of those who believe that Arabic as a unified language is dead or doomed and sees a lack of supporting evidence and a political intention in them.

The fact that Arabic in its standard form has become the prevailing political language in the Arab countries, and that Arabisation programmes explicitly exist in many of them, although implementation is far from uniform, will probably tend to consolidate the unity of Arabic and its integrating role. At the same time, does this fact *per se* carry political consequences? Arabic certainly is not the only language utilised in more than one country: English, Spanish, Portuguese, German and French are all examples of languages similarly conserving unity across political boundaries. With the possible exception of German, such commonality of language justifies limited common undertakings and co-operation, but does not impinge upon the definition(s) of nation and the strictly political realm. (Even in the case of German, World War II killed pan-Germanism in its broader definition, and what is left of it is only the aspiration to eventual reunification of the FRG and GDR in a very distant future). On the other hand, we have examples of countries in which multiple languages are officially spoken, and even of countries in which an altogether foreign language is the common vehicle for political life. In what sense can the use of English in India be portrayed as a limitation of sovereignty or a factor negatively affecting the stability of the Indian state? Finally, the most successful experience of regional integration to this date (notwithstanding its failures and limitations), i.e. the European Community, is not based on a commonality of language. Many Arab nationalists try hard to show that the case of the Arabic language is different, primarily because of its association with Islam. Arabic, in this view, is not like any other language, and acquires greater importance for the Arabs as an integrating factor. The latter remains a respectable subjective opinion, but we see little empirical evidence to support it objectively.

Thus, international evidence points to a separation of language and politics: commonality of language can help consolidate a political entity which historical and political forces create and sustain, but is neither a sufficient nor a necessary condition for its birth and viability.

Surely there is more to it than pure language. Language unity permits the circulation of information and cultural inputs, which would be obviously hindered by language barriers. More generally one may argue it is the knowledge of the Arab culture in its historical dimension that is important. The continuity of Arab culture and its commonality as the source of contemporary cultural life in all Arab countries is an important integrating factor. At the same time, the European experience once again shows that commonality of language is neither a necessary nor a sufficient condition for commonality of culture. Homer, Dante, Shakespeare and Goethe belong to a same cultural tradition independently of the fact that they use different languages. Europe has had an integrated culture for a very long time, indeed centuries, and her contemporary process of integration is nevertheless progressing at a snail's pace, and no common language is involved.

Furthermore, and notwithstanding the progress of education, how many Arabs are aware of past and present Arab culture? In addition, if we shift our attention from culture in the sense of learned intellectual life, to culture in the anthropological sense of daily values, interests and behavioural codes, is it not the case that Arabs, as indeed the citizens of almost any country except possibly Albania, are increasingly participating into an international culture, promoted by media and advertising agencies? A culture made of jeans, soft drinks, diapers and aspirin: possibly uninspiring, but for those who can afford it, marking a very substantial increase in the standard of living by any reasonable objective measure.

Common, or popular, culture is thus internationalised, and so too is learned intellectual life. While there is no doubt a domain in which a specifically Arab culture can flourish, knowledge is universal and the international circulation of it, as well as of intellectuals, is continuously increasing. In fact, it is a common experience that Arab intellectuals have easier access to non-Arab sources, and can more easily travel to non-Arab countries than within the Arab region itself. The influence of the French and Anglo-American cultures created a cleavage which the explicit will to Arabise and increase communication among Arabs has not yet erased.

In fact, even Salafi Islamist writers participate in this acculturation. Some of them discuss Marx as if he were their neighbour and Newton as the neighbourhood shopkeeper. The real problem with Islamist writers (and some Arabist writers as well) is that their knowledge of the 'West' they curse daily is ashamedly nil, or in any case much more superficial and equally if not more biased than the way the 'Orient' is presented in the orientalist literature.

At the cultural level, the Arab identification is strong enough to deny credibility to alternative universalist doctrines, and even acts as a limiting factor on the impact of Islam. At the same time, it is not powerful enough to overcome the obstacles that illegitimate *governments* (not states) raise to prevent it from becoming an instrument of the opposition. One gets the impression that the potential for a rebirth of Arab nationalism is there, but political conditions are not ripe for it. What is becoming clear at last, two decades after the 1967 defeat — the greatest blow to Arab nationalism — is that the 'Arab idea' is not the creation of any individual political party or leader, such as the Ba'th or Nasser or al-Husri. Following the reaction to one form of Arabism, a reaction well illustrated in Ajami (1981), a time for the reappearance of other forms, other expressions of the idea, has come.

In the post-World War II era the importance of cultural factors in the conduct of international affairs, and as a determinant of integrative processes, has often been downplayed to the benefit of economic factors. While nationalism based on ethnicity or cultural heritage led to the worst conflicts in the history of humankind, trade and investment were expected to cause reciprocal interest and dependence, mutual knowledge, respect and confidence. On the basis of this belief, an international economic order was put in place which explicitly aimed at increasing economic intercourse to reinforce stability and peaceful co-operation. It is clear that this system did, in fact, succeed in increasing interdependence among industrial countries; in Europe, in particular, the economy has provided a convenient base to launch and sustain an important experiment in regional integration, i.e. the European Community. At the same time, other countries of the world have remained largely at the periphery of this process.

The increase in international economic intercourse is a fact, but it is not at all clear that the resulting interdependence necessarily leads to integration: countries may fail to agree on a regime, may fail to develop the co-operative and institutionalised environment that distinguishes integration from mere interdependence. Indeed, as we look at the evolution of economic relations since 1971, the year the Bretton Woods system collapsed, we see at one and the same time continued growth of interdependence and economic conflicts among the major players. If anything, the international economy has witnessed a decrease of integration, in the sense of coherent and possibly institutionalised conduct of economic policies, and a sharp increase in conflictual behaviour. That this has not led to a collapse of the international economy is proof of the fact that countries are indeed interdependent, and could no longer isolate themselves from international economic relations. Still, the fact remains that increasing interdependence does not necessarily lead to integration.

The European Community, in partial contrast, constitutes an attempt at integration inasmuch as it established common institutions and policies. That this integration is less than perfect is abundantly clear, as conflicts are the daily experience of the Community. It remains to be explained, nevertheless, why the members of the Community insist in being engaged in this integrative process, while conflict and disintegration prevail at the international level. Mere analysis of economic data does not provide an answer, as

Community members are not significantly more interdependent than they are individually with the rest of the world. Countries that have just as important ties with EC members, such as Switzerland and Norway, stay out of the Community. Any Community member could leave the Community at very little economist cost, as it would still maintain the possibility of engaging in economic intercourse with the rest of Europe to the extent it wished. Thus, pure economic interdependence does not suffice to explain economic integration.

When discussing the credibility of Arab economic integration, attention is often focused on trade and financial flows only, and one loses sight of the most important factor of economic interdependence between Arab countries, i.e. migration. This is partly a consequence of the impact of the European precedent, in which trade was the driving force; and in part as well a consequence of the fact that migration has attracted little interest on the part of the economic profession, and is viewed with considerable uneasiness in the political circles of both the countries of origin and the countries of destination. Yet the fact is, as Chapters 14 and 15 by Sharon Stanton-Russell and Georges Sabagh illustrate, migration is a massive phenomenon and a powerful factor of interdependence. (See also I.S.E. Abdallah in Luciani and Salamé, 1987.)

While the literature on inter-Arab migration has tended to stress the potential negative effects of this phenomenon, and has in some cases listed as negative certain consequences that from any reasonable point of view should be called positive, it is clear that migration is having a major and unmistakable impact on the economies of both the countries of origin and the countries of destination.

Countries of destination have been able to build up rapidly from scratch an administrative and services sector, and engage in massive infrastructural and residential construction, that has literally changed the structure of the countries themselves. Their dependence on the inflow of migrant workers is massive, as foreign workers constitute 90.3 per cent of the work force in the UAE, 84.5 per cent in Qatar, 78.6 per cent in Kuwait, 58.6 per cent in Bahrain, 48.7 per cent in Oman and 46.6 per cent in Saudi Arabia.

It has often been maintained by Gulf leaders that such immigration is a temporary and disposable phenomenon. Available data for the 1980s show, quite to the contrary, that migrants are displaying a tendency to stabilise, extend their period of residence, establish independent businesses and become self-employed in increasing numbers. Thus, the predicted massive outflow of migrants, who, some feared would be pushed back to their countries of origin, has not materialised, as the net flow remains positive in the direction of the major oil-exporters, albeit, not surprisingly, at a much reduced level relative to the previous decade. Much has also been made of the recent tendency of some of the Gulf countries to hire an increasing proportion of Asian immigrant workers, thus reducing their relative dependence on other Arab countries; this tendency is there, but it must be seen in the context of the extreme dependence of some of these countries on foreign labour. If 90 per cent of the labour force is foreign, and 40 per cent of immigrants are Asians, one is still left with a proportion of Arabs from other countries which is higher than 50 per cent of the labour force. Furthermore, it is the Arabs that tend to renew and extend their work permits, while the Asian immigrants exhibit a higher turnover.

In the face of these data, it is difficult to discard migration as just a passing phenomenon, that does not establish any long-term ties between the Arab countries.

As far as the effect on the countries of origin is concerned, attention has often focused on the balance of payments, and less so on the allocation of savings of the migrants. To the limited extent that they are available, empirical data on the utilisation of remittances underline the importance of expenditure on improving one's basic life conditions, especially on housing, and on investment goods. Such data probably underestimate the investment content of migrants' remittances, as expenditure that may appear to be for consumption is in fact a form of investment, such as may be the case when offspring or relatives are allowed to continue in school for more years than they would have otherwise. When all direct and indirect effects are considered, the effect of migration on economic and social mobility in the countries of origin will be shown to be very substantial indeed.

It is typically the private sector that leads economic integration across borders. It often does so to escape the control of the state in the country of origin, besides reaping the higher profits generally associated with international expansion. The state sector naturally thinks in terms of self-sufficiency, and national administrative controls seldom are mutually consistent. The experience of the European Community and of international trade negotiations proves that while it is relatively easy to reduce tariffs and other barriers to trade, it is extremely difficult to agree on common standards for national regulations and administrative systems, and the latter have by now become very important obstacles to a further deepening of economic interdependence. The recent history of the Arab countries is dotted with attempts at co-ordination and integration in situations in which states are the most important actors, and it is often the case that the original goodwill, which may in some cases be quite substantial, is rapidly eroded and the agreements collapse as each partner becomes intolerant of limitations on his sovereignty. But where the role of the state is more limited and the market is the primary mechanism for allocation, the opportunity for successful integration is increased.

Of course, one should beware of the mystique of the private sector, a category that includes several sharply different types of actors. We do not expect too much of the wealthy financiers and speculators who accumulated large fortunes in the years of the oil boom: Khashoggi's involvement in the Sudan is not our model of Arab integration. We believe in the potential of the millions who work and toil, who migrated and were able to accumulate a small capital and become aware of new opportunities, out of which a new entrepreneurial class with a strong interest in the regional dimension may emerge.

In Chapter 3 it was argued that the different economic bases of the Arab states act as important obstacles on the path to Arab integration. According to the conceptualisation proposed there, allocation and production states have different and conflicting interests with respect to integration, and progress would inevitably require a progressive transformation of the allocation states into production states. Current trends, with respect to both the effort for industrialisation and diversification on one hand, and the tendency to a stabilisation of the immigrant labour force, point to such a progressive transformation.

At the same time, it seems likely that, if these trends are consolidated, political problems will arise that may cause a crisis. In particular, none of the countries of destination offers immigrants a fully predictable way to acquire citizenship and political rights. As long as these states remain independent of domestic taxation, while providing a profitable business environment, it is possible that even long term residents might accept such political marginalisation. As Sharon Stanton Russell underlines, 'The fact that acquisition of citizenship has been limited in the major receiving states of the Gulf, or has not resulted in full political participation where it occurred, does not mean, however, that political integration of migrants has not taken place . . . in view of the authoritarian nature of the Gulf regimes, a more important mechanism for integration of migrants has been their participation in host countries institutions that . . . serve to build consensus'. However the writing is on the wall and the day will come when the state will need to appeal to the support of the established foreign resident community, and the latter will inevitably demand political rights as a result. Indeed, in some cases, e.g. in Bahrain, this support has been sought and obtained on a limited scale. The very lack of any discussion of the possibility of changing the rules for acquiring local citizenship in those countries, such as Kuwait, where there is already a long established immigrant community (mostly Palestinians) is proof of the uneasiness which this problem arouses. It is not by chance that the Kuwaiti political elite maintains a close relationship with the PLO, and tries to accommodate the latter's wishes on matters of interest to the Palestinian community.

That allocation states will in fact evolve to become production states is thus not clear. If current regimes start feeling threatened by this evolution, then they may cut down on industrialisation, diversification and immigration, and concentrate on oil revenues and financial investment on the capital markets of the industrial countries. This would be a setback for the cause of Arab integration. But if current trends are allowed to continue, then it is likely that the migrant community will gradually establish a network of regional ties that will involve trade and financial flows as well as movements of labour.

Thus the importance of migration as a link establishing interdependence between the Arab countries deserves to be stressed, and certainly adds to the credibility of regional economic integration. Increased regional interdependence may occur largely independently of state will and international agreement. This is in fact what has occurred with migration: attempts at regulating this essentially private phenomenon through international agreement have almost consistently failed. Under what conditions is the potentially growing regional interdependence going to stimulate a conscious effort at integration?

Makdisi's answer to this question is essentially linked to the politics of interdependence. He believes that regional integration will result from the realisation on the part of the Arab states that their individual weight is not sufficient to defend their economic sovereignty while pursuing their development goals. Only a regional dimension can provide an adequate base for the implementation of the optimal balance of inward looking and outward looking policies, striking a compromise between sovereignty and growth.

Indeed, the European experience seems to support this view. Progress is made on the lengthy and at times byzantine path to a united Europe only when the international environment evolves in such a way that the leading countries feel the need for support on the part of the other Community members in order to resist unwanted outside influences. The European Monetary System provides an excellent example in this respect, as it was brought about by the German determination to resist what were viewed as disastrous American pressures to reflate under the Carter administration. Generally, once some progress is made the Community then tends to defend it even under changed, frequently adverse, circumstances. Thus, the EMS survived the second oil shock, although the original project was realised only in part. Indeed, the tendency to defend the *aequis communautaire* under all circumstances has become one of the basic rules of Community life and a powerful obstacle to reform even for blatantly irrational common policies, such as the agricultural policy.

Can similar circumstances and processes arise in the Arab context? It is clear that the reduction in the price of oil may turn out to be a blessing for the cause of Arab integration. During the oil boom, the extraordinary complementarity of the Arab countries was repeatedly underlined (some countries offering agricultural potential, others a favourable environment for industrial development; some financial capital and others an abundant labour supply; some needing export markets and others reliable sources of supply); but this very same complementarity made a political approach to integration more difficult, as the issue of division of benefits was necessarily quite controversial, and the balance of inter-Arab power was tilting too heavily to the benefit of the oil countries.

The end of the oil boom creates conditions in which the emphasis is shifted from profit maximisation to damage limitation. The Arab countries presently face, individually and collectively, the spectre of disaster, and should be willing to pay a price to avoid it. The major oil exporters need the support and discipline of even the smaller and more densely populated exporters such as Tunisia or Egypt to effectively bargain in their difficult position within Opec. The currencies of all the Arab countries will manifest a tendency to depreciate in dollar terms, and consequently even more so relative to the Yen or the European currencies. This will act as a powerful incentive to increased regional trade. The oil exporters will look more carefully into the opportunities for cheaper imports from neighbouring Arab countries, and the latter need markets desperately, and may be willing to shed some of the administrative regulations that still hinder the establishment of export-oriented industries. As official surpluses shrink, emphasis will shift from the macro-recycling of officially-held funds to the micro-recycling of private savings, belonging to migrants or to the national bourgeoisie. These may be more easily attracted into regional investment if the appropriate conditions are offered. Thus trade liberalisation between Arab countries, formal or informal co-ordination of oil and exchange rate policies, and guarantees on the transferability of funds may all be much more attractive propositions today than they were some years back.

These are not impressive steps. It is not clear, however, that more impressive steps are needed. And neither is it clear that political conditions exist for more ambitious attempts at regional integration. Indeed, we noted before that the European Community cannot be understood as merely economically motivated, although the dismantling of trade barriers is at the heart of it. The existence of the Community can only be explained in the light of two major political circumstances:

(a) the institutional homogeneity of the original members, all of which are parliamentary democracies (with the three major original members, Italy, Germany and France, being republics); and
(b) the presence of a powerful external threat, and the traumatic division of Europe in two opposed groups, with contrasting ideologies, and the iron curtain in between.

The failure of most regional groupings in the Third World may be at least in part attributed to the absence of similarly compelling political considerations. It is not by chance that ASEAN, presently another success story, also displays similar features, and in particular the perception of a powerful threat following the US defeat in Vietnam and the latter's invasion of Cambodia. ASEAN however does not display homogeneous democratic governments, or at least not yet.

The importance of institutional homogeneity has been highlighted in the successive enlargements of the Community's membership. Indeed, in the last two enlargements — Greece and then Spain and Portugal — the basic criterion for acceptance as a member has been the establishment of democratic regimes after periods of authoritarian rule. In the case of Spain, the economic incentive of becoming a member was minimal, and the interest both on the side of the Community and on the side of Spain lay primarily in the consolidation of Spanish democratic institutions after forty years of Francoist rule. In current discussions about the status of relations between the Community and Turkey the question of Turkish democratisation and respect for individual political rights plays a crucial role.

What is the situation in the Arab region with respect to institutional homogeneity? The answer is very obviously that there is very little of it: most Arab countries are not democracies, the ideologies of the regimes in power are often mutually exclusive, and a number of them are ruled by monarchs or tribal clans, some of whom do not even feel the need for a constitution. That this lack of political homogeneity at the superstructure level is a practically unsurmountable obstacle to regional integration hardly needs to be stressed. A proof *per absurdum* comes from the relative success of the Gulf Cooperation Council, whose membership is clearly defined as a function of institutional homogeneity (a club of wealthy rulers, be they kings, sultans or amirs).

This point is so obvious that it does not require further analysis in this volume. The same cannot be said with respect to the role of an external threat. In the last forty years the Arab world has been subjected to a multiplicity of external threats, and it is interesting to see how their impact on Arab integration evolved.

Initially the main external threat was represented by genuine colonial domination. The idea of an Arab state that would include at least all of the eastern Arab region, was coincidental with the Hijazi-based 'Arab revolt' and the wish to detach the Arabs from Ottoman rule. When that disappeared, resistance to European colonial power and schemes came to the fore, and the Maghreb and Mashreq found themselves involved in the same struggle. The period of anticolonial struggle, culminating with the Algerian war, was one in which on the one hand the present system of states was confirmed, while on the other the Arabs were drawn significantly together. However, Algerian independence coincided with the breakdown of the UAR (1961), the beginning of Egyptian-Saudi confrontation in the Yemen (1962), the collapse of the tripartite unity talks (1963): the agenda of inter-Arab politics was substantially modified.

As all Arab states gradually achieved independence, Israel was left as the only immediate external threat confronting the region. The continuity between the anticolonial struggle and the struggle against Israel has often been underlined, and the Middle East conflict is in a sense the struggle for independence of the Palestinians. Indeed, some would propose that the creation of the Israeli state and the subsequent Arab-Israeli conflict has been by far the most important external threat confronting the region. The creation of Israel evidenced the weakness and precipitated the downfall of the 'traditional' regimes in Egypt and the Crescent (Kazziha, Chapter 12, pages 300–5). Subsequently, the Israeli state has been assimilated to a beachhead of Western, or specifically American, penetration in the Arab world, aiming at regional dominance. Israel has been equated to the Crusaders' state. The return of Palestine to Arab rule has been portrayed as the most important objective of Arab nationalism and co-operation among Arab countries, hence the famous slogan 'Unity is the road to Palestine', later turned by PLO publicists into 'Palestine is the road to Unity'.

Might Israel have played the same role in precipitating Arab integration as the iron curtain played in the establishment of the European Community? There is obviously a scale factor to be considered here, as the magnitude of the two threats is simply not comparable, and merely proposing the parallel constitutes a wild exaggeration of Israel's position in the region. However, it is a fact that many Arabs tend to portray Israel as *the* overriding preoccupation of all sincere Arab patriots.

With hindsight, it should be clear that, contrary to rhetorical utterances, Israel was never perceived as a threat equally by all Arab countries, and the call for co-ordinated Arab action has consistently been stuffed with explicit or implicit reservations. The Arab regimes became trapped in their own rhetoric and to this day have been unable to admit to their genuine interests and seek a compromise accordingly. Similarly, the Arab countries have become victims of the initial decision not to assimilate the Palestinian refugees, creating a factor of disintegration that has destroyed Lebanon and threatens Kuwait. (Not so Jordan, because the Palestinians are Jordanian citizens; the threat to Jordanian integrity is a consequence of competition for Palestinian allegiance between the PLO and the Hashemite monarchy.) Because of their marginalisation, and despite their role in pan-Arab politics, the Palestinians failed to become a factor of Arab integration, and became instead a source of conflict.

The isolation of Egypt following the Camp David agreements underlines the connection between Arab integration and peace with Israel. If, as Shlaim would argue, Arab integration is to some extent a necessary, though not sufficient, condition for peace between Israel and the Arab states, today the reverse is also true, and peace has become a prerequisite of integration. No attempt at Arab integration is credible if Egypt, by far the largest Arab country, is not a party to it. Egypt does not need to be the leader of Arab integration, but certainly cannot be left aside. Thus, the agenda for integration is indefinitely postponed until some kind of agreement is fashioned with Israel that is acceptable to all Arab sides.

One can speculate on the shape of such an agreement, but no agreement can solve the Palestinian problem in a simple way. Whatever the territorial solution for Palestine, and though the existence of a Palestinian political entity is an unavoidable component of any peace, a Palestinian diaspora will continue, and a solution to it, i.e. assimilation of a number of Palestinians in some of their countries of residence, is necessary if the Palestinians are to play a more integrative role in Arab politics.

In the immediate aftermath of the Second World War, and at least until the 1960s, the need to strengthen the stability of the international system through regional integrative schemes that would encompass the 'new' states which the process of decolonisation was bringing to independence, was commonly recognised and found expression in a multiplicity of institutions and agreements. Most of these attempts have not born the fruits that were expected of them. Indeed, most collapsed or lost effectiveness because states systematically privileged the demands of domestic integration over those of regional integration. Considerable disillusionment has thus arisen over the potential for regional integration: at the same time the need for it stands unaffected.

The fact that regional integration may be necessary to strengthen individual states in the face of superpower rivalries and broader international conflicts does not necessarily mean that it will take place. The functionalist fallacy is to believe that because an institution is necessary, it will develop. Rationality does not always belong to this world, and it is entirely possible that states will continue to engage in conflictual relations with each other. After all, European states engaged in many a long war before resigning themselves to co-operation; and to this date, it is not clear that this decision cannot be reversed.

At the same time, it should not be surprising that fresh attempts are periodically made to get regional integration off the ground. This is true of all regions, not just of the Arab countries: in south and southeast Asia, in Latin America and to some extent in Africa as well, new attempts at regional integration have been proposed, with mixed results, in the last 15 years. In this respect, the Arab countries are no different: what makes the politics of integration different in the Arab region is the nationalist undertone that is an ineliminable component of it. Elsewhere in the world, the politics of integration generally do not speak the nationalist language, but rather *de facto* contradict it.

It is the nationalist component that makes it so difficult to attempt a fresh start. What is peculiar about Arab integration is that, while little effective progress has been made, an array of institutions has been put in place, mostly under the general umbrella of the Arab League — an aspect which is explored in the concluding chapter of this book. While these institutions are mostly ineffective, they have served the existing state system well because they have provided international legitimation to the plurality of sovereign Arab states. At the same time, these institutions enjoy an undeserved legitimacy in terms of the nationalist discourse, leading to a situation whereby progress within the existing setup is precluded by sclerosis, while progress with some alternative setup is immediately perceived as being contradictory to the cause of building an Arab nation. At best, subregional schemes can be launched, such as the Gulf Cooperation Council, but their consistency with the objective of Arab integration is still questioned. Clearly, participation on the part of Arab states in integrative schemes that are openly at odds with the Arab idea is anathema.

Thus, while these institutions are likely to continue a subsistence life, they certainly cannot be expected to take the lead in future efforts to promote Arab integration. At the same time, new developments are occurring in the region which may establish a new basis for the process.

At the superstructural level, Arab nationalism now appears to have entered a third phase in its evolution. The first phase had been characterised by the affirmation of the existence and unity of the Arab nation as a theological statement. Total dedication was requested to the ideal of reuniting the Arab nation, and this was an objective more important than any other and one that encompassed all others. No problem could be solved unless the Arab nation was restored to unity and glory, and all problems would be easy to solve once this task had been accomplished. As reality did not support this vision, a second phase was ushered in, during which isolationist policies prevailed, states gave priority to their domestic integration rather than to inter-Arab integration, and disillusionment ensued. Intellectuals started to question the validity of the pan-Arab ideal, and proclaimed the end of pan-Arabism. The third phase, that we now witness, is marked by a revived and more serene assessment of the Arab idea: an idea which is seen as useful and realistic, but stripped of the theological tones that abound in the writings of Husri or 'Aflaq. This phase is marked by several concurrent phenomena. There is a new wave of writings on Arabism, which, however, are not related to political agendas and programmes. There is a fresh interest in the Arab idea outside the tense ideological climate of the Crescent, notably in the Maghreb and in the Gulf: writers from the 'wings' of the Arab world sometimes pretend to offer *their* view of Arabism, as opposed to the Syrian traditional school, but do not refute the idea itself. In parallel, Western-educated technocrats, bankers and businessmen have taken up the idea outside the ideological milieu in which it had been cultivated, and repropose it with new, more immediate, if more limited, contents. Finally, there is the growing perception of Iran as a strongly nationalist state, that constitutes a threat behind the veil of Islamism, and stimulates a growing support of the potential victims of Iranian expansionism.

Other factors are at work at the structural level. The progressive strengthening of existing Arab states points to the fact that states may possibly be less obsessed by the need to control centrifugal tendencies, and more open to a redefinition of the relative role of state and society. These structural tendencies are important because integration is very closely connected with democratisation. One may propose examples of forms of integration that have developed between states that are not democratic, and indeed the GCC is an example of this. However, there is always necessarily a limit to such integrative processes since eventually the evolution towards unity would entail a loss of power for all except whoever would rule the unified entity. The difficulties of the federal government in the UAE are a clear proof of this. It is only if the participants share democratic institutions that a process of integration may eventually — and if a strong political will prevails — lead to political unification. Inevitably, the objective of political unification will arouse as much resistance as it receives support, and it is only the support of a strong popular will that may possibly lead to a prevalence of the unitarian ideal.

If the Arabs, rather than the Arab states, become the protagonists of the drive towards integration, then the latter stands a chance of making real progress. It is unlikely that all Arab countries will experience similar political evolutions, although the tendency to a paring down of the states' ambitions seems to be quite widespread.

To the extent that only some of the Arab states will evolve towards democratisation and abandon the attempt to contol every aspect of society, integration will take place among a subset of the Arab countries. In many respects, it is the African Arab countries — with the possible exception of Libya — that are more likely to evolve in the direction that we are suggesting. In the Arab east, the negative impact of the Arab-Israeli conflict, the likelihood that the Gulf states will continue to be based essentially on oil rent and to be ruled by authoritarian governments, and the authoritarian character of the regimes in Syria and Iraq, all converge to make a society-based integrative process more difficult. Yet even there things are happening, changes are taking place, and surprises are not to be ruled out.

Society-based integrative processes do not need to endanger the independent existence of present-day Arab states, and may even find accommodation and political co-optation in the context of existing inter-Arab institutions. Yet this requires that the evolution be fairly generalised. If, on the other hand, Arab states experience divergent political evolutions, some possibly falling prey to Islamic fundamentalism, others continuing under authoritarian rule, and only a few evolving towards democratisation, then the Arab dimension will eventually lose its appeal, and attempts at regional co-operation that would explicitly contradict the Arab conception (i.e. that would tie some Arab states to other non-Arab states, in a co-operation motivated by homogeneity of domestic regimes rather than by the nationalist ideology), and that would aggravate the east/west polarisation in the region, might well emerge.

References

Abadha, F. (1975) *Al Hukh al-'Uthmani fi al-Yaman: 1872–1918*, Al-Hay'a al-Misriyyah al-'Amma li al-Kitab, Cairo

'Abd al-Fadil, M. (1983) *Al-Fikr al Iqtissadi al-'Arabi wa Qadiyyat at Taharrur wa at-Tanmiya wa al-Wahda*, (Arab Economic Thought and the Problems of Liberation, Development and Unity), Center of Arab Unity Studies, Beirut

'Abd al-Rahim, A. (1975) *Ad-Dawlah as-Sa'udiyya al-Ula*, 1745–1818, Al-Jami'ah al-'Arabiya, Cairo

Abd al-Rahman, U. (1982) *Al-Biruqratiyya al-naftiyya wa mu'adilat al-tanmiya* (petroleum bureaucracy and the dilemma of development), National Council for Culture and Arts, Kuwait

'Abd al-Raziq, A. (1925) *Al-Islam wa'Usul al-Hukm*, Egypt Press

Abdel Malek, A. (1962) *Egypte: Société Militaire*, Le Seuil, Paris

Abdullah, I.S.D. and Abd al-Fadil, M. (1983) *The Movement of Arab Manpower: Problems, Effects and Policies*, center for Arab Unity Studies, Beirut

Abu al-Futuh, A. (1905) *Ash-Shari'ah al-Islamiyyah Wa al-Qawanin al Wad'iyyah*, Cairo

Abu-Hakima, M. (1967) *Tarikh al-Kuwait*, Lajnat Tarikh al-Kuwait, Kuwait

Abuhamdia, Z. (1984) 'The dilemma of academies of Arabic', *Muslim Education Quarterly*, I, 4, 57–84

—— (1987) 'Speech diversity and language unity: Arabic as an integrating factor', in G. Luciani and G. Salamé (eds) *Politics of Arab Integration*, Croom Helm, London

Abu Lughod, J. (1985) 'Recent migration in the Arab World', in S.E. Ibrahim and N.S. Hopkins (eds), *Arab Society: Social Science Perspectives*, American University in Cairo Press, Cairo

Abun-Nasr, J. (1975) *A History of the Maghreb*, Cambridge University Press, London

Abu Uras, M. (1969) 'The military and the revolution' (in Arabic), *Dirasat Arabiyya*, 5, no. 11, pp. 7–84

Adam, H. (1985) 'South Africa: the search for legitimacy', *Telos*, 59

Ageron, C.R. (1980) 'Les classes moyennes dans l'Algérie coloniale: origine, formation et évaluation quantitative', in CRESM, 51980° pp. 52–74

Ahsan, S.A. (1984) 'Economic policy and class structure in Syria: 1958–80', *International Journal of Middle East Studies*, 16, pp. 301–23

Ajami, F. (1978/9) 'The end of pan-Arabism', *Foreign Affairs*, Winter, 1978/9

—— (1981) *The Arab Predicament: Arab Political Thought and Practice Since 1967*, Cambridge University Press, Cambridge

Aliboni, R. *et al.* (1984) *Egypt's Economic Potential*, Croom Helm, London

421

Allush, N. (1968) 'The people's war is the only way to victory' (in Arabic) *Dirasat Arabiyya, 4*, no. 7, pp. 45–56

'Amarah, M. (1980) *Al-Islam wa as-Sulta ad-Diniyyah*, Beirut

Amin, G.A. (1979) *Al-Mashriq al-'Arabi wa al-Gharb*, Center for Arab Unity Studies, Beirut

Amin, G.A. and 'Awny, E. (1985) *International Migration of Egyptian Labour: A Review of the State of the Art*, Manuscript Report, International Development Research Center, Ottawa

Amin, S. (1980) *The Arab Economy*, Editions de Minuit, Paris

—— (1982a) 'Y a t-il une économie politique du fondamentalisme islamique?', *Peuples Mediterranéens, 21*

—— (1982b) *Irak et Syrie 1960–80: du projet national à la transnationalisation*, Editions de Minuit, Paris

Amirouche, A. (1985) 'Présentation empirique du stock d'équipement en matériel des entreprises industrielles privées en Algérie', *Revue du CENEAP*, (Centre national d'études et d'analyses pour la planification), *2*, Algiers, pp. 63–78

An Na'im (1986) *Constitutionalism and Traditional Islamic Law in the Sudan*, unpublished manuscript

Ansari, H.N. (1984) 'The Islamic militants in Egyptian politics', *International Journal of Middle East Studies, 16*, pp. 123–44

Antonius, G. (1955) *The Arab Awakening*, Khayat, Beirut

Arab Employment Institute (1983) *Promotion of Labor Mobility within the Arab World*, Joint Report, reprinted from *Arab Affairs, no. 23*, Tangier

Arab Institute of Planning in Kuwait (AIPK) and Centre for Arab Unity Studies (1983) *Al-'amala al-ajnabiyya fi aqtar al-khalij al-'arabi*, (foreign employment in countries of the Arabian Gulf), CAUS, Beirut

Arab Times (1985) 31 March, 12 May

Arabian Government and Public Services (1983) *Directory*, Beacon, London

Arendt, H. (1982) *L'impèrialisme*, Fayard, Paris

Arjomand, S.A. (1984) 'Introduction: social movements in the contemporary Near and Middle East' in Arjomand, S.A. (ed.), *From nationalism to revolutionary Islam*, Macmillan, London, pp. 1–27

Arrow, K. (1951) *Social Choice and Individual Values*, Wiley, New York

Arslan, 'A. (1984) *Mudhakkarāt* (Memoirs), Yusif Ibish (ed.), ad-Dar al-Taqadumiyya, Beirut

Ashford, D. (1961) *Political Change in Morocco*, Princeton University Press, Princeton, (New Jersey)

As-Subhi, E.H. (1985) Assistant Secretary General for Political Affairs, Gulf Cooperation Council, interview with author, 8 May, Riyadh

Al Awaji, I.M. (1971) *Bureaucracy and Society in Saudi Arabia*, unpublished PhD thesis, University of Virginia

'Awdah, 'Abd al-Qader (1951) *Al-Islam wa Awda'una as-Siasiyyah*

Ayubi, N. (1980) *Bureaucracy and Politics in Contemporary Egypt*, Ithaca, London

—— (1982a) 'Bureaucratic inflation and administrative inefficiency:

the deadlock in Egyptian administration', *Middle Eastern Studies*, *28*, no. 3

—— (1982b) 'Organisation for development: the politico-administrative framework of economic activity in Egypt under Sadat', *Public Administration and Development*, *2*, no. 4

—— (1982–3) 'The politics of militant Islamic movements in the Middle East', *Journal of International Affairs*, *36*, no. 2, autumn/winter

—— (1983) 'The Egyptian brain drain', *Journal of Middle East Studies*, *15*

Aziz, M. (1979) *Anmat al-infaq w'al-istithmar fi aqtar al-khalij al-arabi* (expenditure and investment patterns in countries of the Arabian Gulf), Institute of Arab Research Studies, Cairo

Al-'Azm, S.J. (1973) *Dirasa Naqdiyya li-Fikr al-Muqāwama al-Filisti-niyya*, Al-Tali'a, Beirut, 148–55

Baker, R. (1979) *King Husain and the Kingdom of Hejaz*, Oleander Press, Cambridge

Al-Banna, H. (1981) *Majmu'at Rasa'il al-Imam ash-Shahid*, Al-Mu'assasah al-Islamiyyah, Beirut

Barakat, H. (1983) 'Ideological determinants of Arab development', in Ibrahim Ibrahim (ed.), *Arab Resources*, Centre for Contemporary Arab Studies, Georgetown University, Croom Helm, London, pp. 169–83

Baram, A. (1981) 'The June 1980 elections to the National Assembly in Iraq: an experiment in controlled democracy', *Orient*, *22*, no. 3, pp. 391–412

Barbour, M. (1965) *Morocco*, Thames and Hudson, London

Barrada, H. (1980) 'La monarchie, la gauche et l'alternance', *Jeune Afrique*, *1043*, pp. 194–9

Basa, N. (1983) 'Turkische Perspektiven zu Integration und Reintegration'. In J.C. Papalekas, (ed.), *Die Auslander Frage: Gastarbeiter im Spannungsfeld von Integration und Reintegration*, Maximilian-Verlag, Herford, pp. 139–45

Batatu, H. (1978) *The Old Social Classes and the Revolutionary Movements of Iraq*, Princeton University Press, Princeton, (New Jersey)

—— (1981a) 'Some observations on the social roots of Syria's ruling military group and the cause for its dominance', *Middle East Journal*, *35*, pp. 331–44

—— (1981b) 'Iraq's underground Shia movements: characteristics, causes and prospects', *Middle East Journal*, pp. 578–94

—— (1984) *The Egyptian, Syrian and Iraqi revolutions: some observations on their underlying causes and social character*, Georgetown University Centre for Contemporary Arab Studies, Washington DC

—— (1985) 'Class analysis and Iraqi society', in Ibrahim and Hopkins, pp. 379–84 (reprinted from *Peuples méditerranéens*, 1979)

Beblawi, H. (1982) 'The predicament of Arab Gulf oil states: individual gains and collective losses', in M. Kerr and E.S. Yassin (eds), *Rich and poor states in the Arab world*, Westview Press, Boulder, p. 167

Beblawi, H. and Fahmi, R. (1984) 'The Kuwaiti stock market', in H.

Beblawi, *The Arab Gulf economy in a turbulent age*, Croom Helm, London, pp. 173

Beblawi, H. and Luciani, G. (1987) 'The Arab rentier state', in *Nation, state and integration in the Arab world* vol. 2, Croom Helm, London

Bedrani, S. (1982) *L'agriculture algérienne depuis 1966*, Economica, Paris

Belaid, A. (1985) 'La necessaire clarification', *La Révolution Africaine, 12*, pp. 25f (September)

Benachenhou, A. (1973) 'Forces sociales et accumulation du capital au Maghreb', *Annuaire de l'Afrique du Nord*, pp. 315–42

—— (1982) *L'expérience algérienne de planification et de développement*, Office des publications universitaires, Algeria

Benhouria, T. (1980) *L'économie de l'Algérie*, Maspero, Paris

Benissad, M.E. (1982) *L'économie du développement de l'Algérie: sous-développement et socialisme*, Economica, Paris

Benkheira, M.H. (1985) 'Etat et mouvement ouvrier dans l'Algérie indépendante', in Sraieb, N. *et al. Le mouvement ouvrier maghrébin*, CNRS, Paris, pp. 197–208

Bennoune, M. (1985) 'The industrialization of Algeria: an overview', in Barakat, H. (ed.), *Contemporary North Africa: issues of development and integration*, Centre for Contemporary Arab Studies, Washington DC, pp. 178–213

Bensaid, Said (1987) 'Al-Watan and Al-Umma in contemporary Arab use' in G. Luciani (ed.) *The Foundations of the Arab State*, Croom Helm, London

Bernard, C. (1984) 'Les economies maghrebines à la redécouverte des vertus de la P.M.I.', *Grand Maghreb*, Nos. 28 and 29

Bernard, C. *et al.* (1982) *La politique de l'emploi-formation au Maghreb 1970-80*, Paris

Bhagwati, J. (ed.) (1972) *Economics and World Order*, Free Press, New York

—— (1984) 'Incentives and disincentives: international migration', *Weltwirtschaftliches Archiv, 120*, 4, pp. 678–700

Bill, J.A. (1972) 'Class analysis and the dialectics of modernisation in the Middle East', *International Journal of Middle East Studies, 3*, pp. 417–34

Birks, J.S. and Sinclair, C.A. (1980a) *International Migrations and Development in the Arab Region*, International Labour Office, Geneva

—— (1980b) *Arab Manpower: The Crisis of Development*, Croom Helm, London

—— (1981) 'Demographic settling amongst migrant workers', in *International Population Conference*, International Union for the Scientific Study of Population, Liège, pp. 733–52

Birks, J.S., Seccombe, I.J. and Sinclair, C.A. (1986) 'Migrant workers in the Arab Gulf: the impact of declining oil revenues', *International Migration Review*, 20, 799–814

Blair, T.L. (1970) *The Land to Those who Work it: Algeria's experiment in worker's management*, Anchor Books, Garden City, (New York)

Blau, P.M. (1964) *Exchange and Power in Social Life*, Wiley, New York

Bohning, W.R. (1972) *The Migration of Workers in the United Kingdom and the European Community*, Oxford University Press, London

Bourgey *et al.* (1982) *Industrialisation et changements sociaux dans l'Orient arabe*, Editions du CERMOC, Beirut

Boutros-Ghali, B. (1963) 'The foreign policy of Egypt', in J.E. Black and K.W. Thompson (eds), *Foreign policy in a world of change*, Harper and Row, New York

Douzidi, A.M. (1984) 'Emploi et chomage en Algérie (1967–83)', *Les Cahiers de CREA* (Centre de recherches en économie appliquée), 2, Algiers, pp. 57–76

Bowen-Jones, H. (1984) 'The philosophy of infrastructure development', in M.S. Azhary (ed.), *The impact of oil revenues on Arab Gulf development*, Croom Helm, London

Brahimi, A. (1978) *Dimensions et perspectives du monde arabe*, Economica, Paris

Brown, L. (1974) *The Tunisia of Ahmed Bey, 1837–1855*, Princeton University Press, Princeton

Burke III, E. (1986) 'Understanding Arab social movements', *The Maghreb Review*

Burke III, E. and Lubeck, P. (1985) *Explaining social movements in two OPEC countries: divergent outcomes in Nigeria and Iran*, (mimeo)

—— (1987) *Comparative studies in society and history*, Rienner, Boulder, Colorado

Cahen, C. (1977) *Tarikh al-'Arab wa ash-Shu'uh al-Islamiyya Mundhu Dhuhūr al-Islam Hatta Bidayat al-Imbaratoriyya al-'Uthmaniyya*. (The History of Arabs and Islamic Peoples since the Rise of Islam and until the Beginning of the Reign of the Ottoman Empirc), Dar al-Haqiqa, Beirut

Callaghy, T. (1984) *The State–Society Struggle: Zaire in comparative perspective*, Columbia University Press, New York

Camau, M. (1984) 'L'etat tunisien: de la tutelle au désengagement', *Maghreb-Machrek, 103*, pp. 8–38

Centre d'etudes et de recherches sur le Moyen-Orient Contemporain (1985) *Mouvements communautaires et espaces urbains au Machreq*, Beirut

Chackerian, R. and Abcarian, G. (1983) *Bureaucratic Power in Society*, Nelson Hall, Chicago

Chackerian, R. and El-Fathaly, O. (1983) 'Administration and the forgotten issue in Arab development', in I. Ibrahim (ed.) *Arab resources: the transformation of a society*, Croom Helm, London

Chackerian, R. and Shadukhi, S.M. (1983) 'Public bureaucracy in Saudi Arabia: an empirical assessment of work behaviour', *International Review of Administrative Sciences, 69*, no. 3

Chatelus, M. (1982) 'Le monde arabe vingt ans aprés: de l'avant pétrole à l'après pétrole — les économies des pays arabes', *Maghreb-Machrek, 101*, pp. 5–45

—— (1984) 'Attitudes toward public sector management and re-assertion of the private sector in the Arab world', paper presented to the annual meeting of the Middle East Studies Associations of America (M.E.S.A.), San Francisco (publication forthcoming)

Chatelus, M. and Schemeil, Y. (1984) 'Towards a new political economy of state industrialisation in the Arab Middle East', *International Journal of Middle East Studies, 16 (2)*, pp. 251–65

Chaulet, C. (1984) *La terre, les frères et l'argent*, Thèse lettres et sciences humaines, Université Paris V, roneo

Chazan, N. (1983) *The Anatomy of Ghanaian politics*, Westview, Boulder, (Colorado)

Choucri, N. *et al.* (1983) *Migration in the Middle East: Transformations, Policies and Processes, vol. I*, Technology Adaptation Program, Massachusetts Institute of Technology, Cambridge, Mass.

—— (1986) 'A new view of migrants and remittances in the Middle East and change', paper presented at the annual meeting of the Population Association of America, San Francisco

Cobban, H. (1984) *The Palestinian Liberation Organization: People, Power and Politics*, Cambridge University Press, Cambridge, p. 197

—— (1985) *The Making of Modern Lebanon*, Hutchinson, London, pp. 213, 226

Cohen, B.J. (1973) *The Question of Imperialism: the Political Economy of Dominance and Dependence*, Basic Books, New York

Cohen, R. and Service, E. (1978) *The Origins of the State*, ISHI, Philadelphia

Colombe, M. (1951) *L'évolution de l'Egypte 1924–50*, Maisonneuve, Paris

Colonna, F. (1980) 'Paysans et encadreurs: á propos des transferts de savoirs et de modéles entre villes et campagnes en Algérie' in Rassam, A. and Zghal, A.K., *Système urbain et développement au Maghreb*, Cerés Productions, Tunis

—— (1983) 'Les spécialistes de la médiation: naissance d'une classe moyenne au Maghreb' in *Histoire sociale de l'Algérie, 8*, Publications du centre de recherches et de documentation en sciences sociales et humaines, Oran

Cote, M. (1985) 'Campagnes algériennes', *Mediterranée*, Revue géographique des pays méditerranéens, *55 (3)*, pp. 41–50

Courlet, C. and Judet, P. (1981) 'La semi-industrialisation', *Cahiers I.R.E.P.-Developpement*, Université des Sciences Sociales, Grenoble

Criscuolo, J. (1975) *Armée et nation dans les discours du Colonel Boumedienne*, Université P. Valéry, Montpellier

Crystal, J. (1985) 'Coalitions in Oil Monarchies: Patterns of State-building in the Gulf', paper delivered at the 1985 Annual Meeting of American Political Science Association, New Orleans

—— (1986) *Patterns of state-building in the Arabian Gulf: Kuwait and Qatar*, unpublished PhD dissertation, Harvard University, Cambridge, Mass.

Ad-Dabbagh, M. (1962) *Qatar*, Khayat, Beirut

Daddab and Mihyuddin (1984) 'Industrialisation in the Arab Gulf', in Azhary (ed.), *The impact of oil revenues on Arab Gulf development*, Croom Helm, London

Dahl, R. (1966) (ed.) *Political Oppositions in Western Democracy,* Yale University Press, New Haven, (Connecticut)

—— (1973) *Regimes and Opposition,* Yale University Press, New Haven, (Connecticut)

Ad-Dajani, A.S. (1978) *Al-Filistiniyyun fi al-Watan al-'Arabi,* (The Palestinians int he Arab World), Cairo

Davis, E. (1984) 'Ideology, social class and Islamic radicalism in modern Egypt', in Arjomand, S.A. (ed.), pp. 134–57

Dawisha, A.I. (1980) *Syria and the Lebanese crisis,* Macmillan, London

Debbasch, C. *et al.* (1970) *Pouvoir et administration au Maghreb,* CNRS, Paris

Deeb, M. (1979) *Party Politics in Egypt: the world and its rivals 1919–39,* Ithaca Press, London

Degenhardt, H.W. (1983) *Political Dissent,* Gale Research, New York

Dessouki, A.E.H. (1982) 'The shift in Egypt's migration policy: 1952–1978', *Middle Eastern Studies, 18,* 1

—— (1984) 'Intikhabat 1984', *Al Ahram,* 15 June

Devlin, J. (1982) 'Syria' in R.E. Harkavy and E.A. Kolodziej (eds), *Security policies of developing countries,* Lexington Books, Lexington, (Kentucky)

Dhaher, A., al-Salem, F. and Al-Salem, M. (1984) 'Expatriate labor in the Arab Gulf States: the citizens and political status', *The Arab Gulf, 16,* 185–92

Dib, G. (1978) 'Migration and naturalisation laws in Egypt, Lebanon, Syria, Jordan, Kuwait, and the United Arab Emirates', *Population Bulletin of the United Nations Economic Commission for Western Asia (ECWA) Part One: Migration Laws,* no. 15

—— (1979) 'Migration and naturalization laws in Egypt, Lebanon, Syria, Jordan, Kuwait and the United Arab Emirates', *Population Bulletin of the United Nations Economic Commission for Western Asia (ECWA) Part Two: Naturalization Laws,* no. 16

El Dib, M.A.M., Ismail, S.M. and Gad, O.A. (1984) 'Ba'd ad-Dawafi' wa al-Athar al Iqtisadiyyah li-hijrat al-'Amala az-Zira 'iyyah ji al-Qarya al Misriyyah', *Dirasat Sukkaniya, 11,* 27–46

El Din, G. (1984) Muhammad al Awad, *Volume, Directions and Characteristics of Sudanese Migrations in the Arab Countries,* n.p.

Downs, A. (1957) *An Economic Theory of Democracy,* Harper and Row, New York

Drysdale, A. (1981) 'The Syrian political elite, 1966–76: a spatial and social analysis', *Middle Eastern Studies*

Duwaidar, Muhammad (1983) *Al-Ittija al-rai'bi al-iqtisad al-misri* (the rentier orientation of the Egyptian economy), Munsha'at al-Ma'arif, Alexandria

Easton, D. (1965) *A Framework for Political Analysis,* Prentice Hall, Englewood Cliffs, (New Jersey)

Al-Ebraheem, H.A. (1975) *Kuwait: A Political Study,* Kuwait University, Kuwait

—— (1984) *Kuwait and the Gulf,* Center for Contemporary Arab Studies, Georgetown University, Washington; Croom Helm, London and Canberra

ECWA (Economic Commission for Western Asia) (1984) *Industrial development and structure in the Arab world, present and future: scenarios for the year 2000*, United Nations, N.Y.

Eickelman, F.D. (1981) *The Middle East — an anthropological approach*, Prentice Hall, Englewood Cliffs, N.J.

Eisenstadt, S. (1964) 'Convergence and divergence of modern and modernising societies: indications from the analysis of the structuring of social hierarchies in Middle Eastern Societies', *International Journal of Middle East Studies*, 8, pp. 1–27

El Kenz, A. (1983) *Monographie d'une expérience industrielle en Algérie: le complexe sidérurgique d'El Hadjar (Annaba)*, thèse de doctorat détat en sciences humaines, Université de Paris VIII

Entelis, J.P. (1982) 'Algeria: technocratic rule, military power', in I.W. Zartman (ed.), *Political elites in Arab North Africa*, Longman, New York, pp. 92–143

Eqbal, A. (1966) 'Trade Unionism' in L.C. Brown (ed.), *State and society in contemporary North Africa*, Middle East Institute, Washington DC

Etienne, B. and Tozy, M. (1979) 'Le glissement des obligations islamiques vers le phénomène associatif à Casablanca', *Annuaire de l'Afrique du Nord*, pp. 235–59

Evans, K. (1985) 'Confidence has been shaken', in *Financial Times*, 11 February

Evans, P. (1979) *Dependent Development*, Princeton University Press, Princeton, (New Jersey)

Evans, P., Rueschemeyer, D. and Skocpol, T. (eds) (1985) *Bringing the State Back In*, Cambridge University Press, Cambridge

Farah, T.E. (1987) 'Attitudes to the Nation and the State in Arab Public Opinion Polls', in G. Luciani and G. Salamé (ed.) *Politics of Arab Integration*, Croom Helm, London

Farah, T.E. Al-Salem, F. and Al-Salem, M.K. (1980) 'Alienation and expatriate labor in Kuwait', *Journal of South Asia and Middle Eastern Studies*, 4, 3–40

Fargues, P. (1980) *Réserves de main d'oeuvre et rente pétrolière: étude démographique des migrations de travail vers les pays Arabes du Golfe*, CERMOC, Beirut

—— (1987) 'La migration obéit-elle à la conjoncture pétrolière dans le Golfe? L'example du Kowéit', mimeo presented at Aix

Al-Fasi, 'A. (n.d.) *Māqasid ash-Shari'ah*

Fergani, N. (1984) *Al-Hijra ila an-Naft*, (The migration to oil), Centre for Arabic Unity Studies, Beirut

—— (1985) 'Migrations inter-Arabes et développement', *Revue Tiers-Monde*, 21, 583–95

—— (1987a) 'Hawla at-Tawajjuhat al-'Arabiyyah li-al Misriyyah ji Muntasaf ath-Thamaninat wa 'Alaqátihabi al-'Amal ji al-Buldan al-'Arabiyyah an-Nafityyah' *al-Mustaqbal al-'Arabi*, 99, 25–37

—— (1987b) 'On labour migration in Egypt (1947–1985)', paper presented at a Roundtable on 'Migration dans de monde Arabe: tendences et perspectives', Aix-en-Provence

Field, M. (1984) *The Merchants*, John Murray, London

—— (1985) 'Businessmen question government optimism', in *Financial Times*, 22 April

Fiori, G. (1970) *Antonio Gramsci, Life of a Revolutionary*, New Left Books, London

Fischer, M. (1982) 'Islam and the revolt of the petit bourgeoisie', *Daedalus, 111*, pp. 101–25

Forst, R. (1976) 'Origins and early development of the Union Marocaine du Travail', *International Journal of Middle East Studies, 7(2)*, pp. 271–87

Franklin, R. (1985) 'Migrant labor and the politics of development in Bahrain', *MERIP Reports, 15*, 7–13, 32

Fromm, E. (1960) *The Fear of Freedom*, Routledge and Kegan Paul, London

Garson, J. (1981) 'Les Algériens', 'Les Marocains' in Garson, J.P. and Tapinos, G. (eds), *L'argent des immigrés*, papers and documents of the INED, PUF, Paris, pp. 31–70 and 133–72

Garzouzi, E. (1963) 'Land reform in Syria', *Middle East Journal*, winter spring

Geertz, C. (ed.) (1963) *Old Societies and New States*, Free Press of Glencoe, New York

Gellner, E. and Micaud, C. (eds) (1974) 'The unknown Apollo of Biskra: the social base of Algerian puritanism', *Government and Opposition*, pp. 277–310

—— (1981) *Muslim society*, Cambridge University Press, London

—— (1983) 'The tribal society and its enemies', R. Tapper (ed.), *The conflict of tribe and state*, Croom Helm, London

Gerth, H.C. and Wright Mills, C. (1970) *From Max Weber*, Routledge and Kegan Paul, London

Al-Ghabra, S. (1986) *Palestinians in Kuwait: The Family and the Politics of Survival*, unpublished PhD dissertation, University of Texas, Austin

Ghoshah, A. (1971) *Ad-Dawla al-Islamiyyah, Dawlah Insaniyyah*, Amman

Gibb, H. (1955) 'Constitutional organisation: the Muslim community and the state', in Majid Khadduri and Hubert J. Liebesny (eds), *Law in the Middle East*, Middle East Institute, Washington DC

Gordon, D. (1986) *Decolonisation and the State in Kenya*, Westview, Boulder, (Colorado)

Gulf Cooperation Council (1985) 'Decisions of the Third Meeting of the Ministers of Labor and Social Affairs of the GCC Member Countries, General Assembly 6th of May, Riyadh', GCC Information Department, Riyadh

Haddad, G. (1971) *Revolutions and Military Rule in the Middle East, t. 2., The Arab states, part 1: Iraq, Syria, Lebanon and Jordan*, R. Speller, New York

Haddad, Y. (1986) 'Muslim revivalist thought in the Arab world: an overview', *The Muslim World, LXXVI*, 3–4, pp. 143–76

Hadjseyd, M. (1985) 'Quelques aspects de l'évolution du secteur privé industriel', *Revue du CENEAP, 2*, Algiers, pp. 49–62

Haim, S. (1962) *Arab Nationalism: An Anthology*, University of California Press, Berkeley

Halbaoui, Y. (1965) 'La population et la population active en Syrie', *Population*, pp. 697–714

Halpern, M. (1962) 'The Middle Eastern armies and the new middle class' in J. Johnson (ed.), *The role of the military in underdeveloped countries*, Princeton University Press, Princeton, (New Jersey)

—— (1963) *The Politics of Social Change in the Middle East and North Africa*, Princeton University Press, Princeton, (New Jersey)

—— (1970) *The Politics of Social Change in the Middle East and North Africa*, Princeton University Press, Princeton, 51–78

Hamada, K. (1979) 'Macroeconomic strategy and coordination under alternative exchange rates', in R. Dornbusch and J.A. Frenkel (eds), *International Economic Policy, Theory and Evidence*, Johns Hopkins University Press, Baltimore

Hamdan, D. (n.d. ca. 1983) 'Aliens Residence Law', 'Nationality Law' and 'Labour Law' texts in *Contractor's Directory*, Kuwaiti Contractors Union, Safat

Hannoyer, J. and Seurat, M. (1979) *Etat et secteur public industriel en Syrie*, Centre d'études et de recherches sur le Moyen-Orient contemporain, Beirut

—— (1980) 'Le monde rural avant les réformes', in Raymond, A. (ed.), *La Syrie d'aujourd'hui*, CNRS, Paris, pp. 273–96

—— (1985) 'Grands projets hydrauliques en Syrie: la tentation orientale', *Maghreb Machrek*, pp. 24–42

Harbi, M. (1975) *Aux origines du FLN: le populisme révolutionnaire en Algérie*, Christian Bourgeois, Paris

—— (1980)*Le FLN, mirage et réalité: dex origines à la prise du pouvoir (1945–62)*, Jeune Afrique, Paris

Harik, I. (1968) *Politics and Change in a Traditional Society: Lebanon, 1711–1845*, Princeton University Press, Princeton

Haseeb, K. and Makdisi, S. (eds) (1982) *Arab Monetary Integration, Issues and Prerequisites*, Croom Helm, London

Hashemite Kingdom of Jordan (1979) *Results of Housing and Population Census, vol. 2, Part One*, Department of Statistics, Amman

—— (1982) *Annual Report*, Ministry of Labour, Amman

—— (1984) *Annual Report*, Ministry of Labour, Amman

Hasib, K. (1985) 'Kalimat al-Mustaqbal al-'Arabi', *al-Mustaqbal al-'Arabi, 73*

Heller, M. and Safran, N. (1984) Saudi Arabia and the new middle class, Harvard Middle East Papers

Helms, C.M. (1981) *The Cohesion of Saudi Arabia*, Croom Helm, London

Helmy, A. (1985) 'Arab fund for economic and social development', interview with author, 17 June, Kuwait

Herfurth, M. and Haart, H.H. (1982) *Social Integration of Migrant Workers and Other Ethnic Minorities: Documentation of Current Research*, Pergamon Press, Oxford

Hermassi, E. (1972) *Leadership and National Development in North Africa: A Comparative Study*, California University Press, Berkeley

—— (1984) 'La société tunisienne au miroir islamiste', *Maghreb-Machrek, 103*, pp. 39–56

—— (1987) 'State-building and regime performance in the Greater Maghreb', in G. Salamé (ed.) *The Foundations of the Arab State*, Croom Helm, London

Hinnebush, R.A. (1984a) 'The re-emergence of the Wafd party', *Sixteenth International Journal of Middle East Studies, 1*, pp. 99 121

—— (1984b) 'The National Progressive Party', *III Arab Studies Quarterly, 4*, pp. 325–51

—— (1985) *Egyptian politics under Sadat: the post-populist development of an authoritarian modernising state*, Cambridge University Press, Cambridge

—— (1987) 'Political parties in the Arab States: Libya, Syria, Egypt', in W. Zartman and A. Dawisha (ed.), *Beyond Coercion: Durability of the Arab State*, Croom Helm, London

Hirschman, A.O. (1968) 'The political economy of import substituting industrialisation in Latin America', *The Quarterly Journal of Economics, 82 (1)*

—— (1970) *Exit, Voice and Loyalty*, Harvard, Cambridge, (Massachusetts)

—— (1973) 'The changing tolerance for income inequality in the course of economic development', *The Quarterly Journal of Economics, 87 (4)*

Hodges, T. (1981) 'Political conflicts sharpen', *New African*, April

Hoffman Nowotny, H.J. and Hondrich, K.O. (eds) (1982), in *Bundesrepublik Deutschland und in der Schweiz: und Integration: eine Vergleichende Untersuchung*, Campus Verlag, Frankfurt/Main

Holt, P. (1966) *Egypt and the Fertile Crescent, 1516–1922*, Longman, London

Hopkins, N.S. (1984) 'Development and Centre Building in the Middle East', in Cantori, L.J. and Harik, I. (eds), *Local politics and developments in the Middle East*, Westview Press, Boulder, (Colorado)

Hopwood, D. (ed.) (1972) *The Arabian Peninsula: Society and Politics*, Allen and Unwin, London

Hourani, A. (1962) *Arabic Thought in the Liberal Age*, Oxford University Press, London

—— (1983) *Arabic Thought in the Liberal Age — 1798–1839*, Cambridge University Press, Cambridge (new edn)

—— (n.d.) *Al-Fikr al-'Arabi fi'Asr an-Nahda*, Dar al-Nahar, Beirut

Howarth, D. (1964) *The Desert King: Ibn Saud and his Arabia*, McGraw Hill, New York

Hudson, M.C. (1980) *Arab Politics: The Search for Legitimacy*, Yale University Press, New Haven

Huntington, S. (1969) *Political Order in Changing Societies*, Yale University Press, New Haven

Hurewitz, J.C. (1969) *Middle East politics: the military dimension*, Praeger, New York

Ibn 'Ashur, M. (1344 A.H.) *Naqd 'Ilmi li-Kitab al-Islam wa Usul al-Hukm*, Cairo

Ibn Khaldun (n.d.) *Al-Muqaddimah*, (in Arabic), Al-Muthanna Library, Baghdad

—— (1967) *The Muqaddimah*, (translated from Arabic by Franz Rosenthal), Princeton University Press, Princeton

Ibrahim, S.E. (1982) *The New Arab Social Order: A Study of the Social Impact of Oil Wealth*, Westview Press, Boulder, (Colorado)

Ibrahim, S.E. and Cole, D.P. (1980) 'Anatomy of Egypt's militant Islamic groups', *International Journal of Middle East Studies, 12*, pp. 423–53

Ibrahim, S.E. and Hopkins, N.S. (eds) (1985) *Arab Society: Social Science Perspectives*, The American University in Cairo Press, Cairo

Ibrahim, S.E. and Sabagh, G. (1982) 'Oil, migration and the new Arab social order', in Kerr, M.H. and Yassin, E. (eds), *Rich and poor states in the Middle East*, Westview Press, Boulder, (Colorado) and American University in Cairo, Cairo, pp. 17–70

IMF (1984a) *Government Finance Statistics Yearbook*, Washington, DC

—— (1984b) World Economic Outlook, Washington, DC

Ionescu, G. and de Madariaga, I. (1968) *Opposition*, Watts, London

Islam, N. and Henault, G. (1979) 'From GNP to basic needs: a critical review of development administration', *International review of administrative sciences, 45*, no. 3

Ismael, J. (1982) *Kuwait: Social Change in Historical Perspective*, Syracuse University Press, Syracuse (New York)

Issawi, C. (1950) *An Arab Philosopher of History*, John Murray, London

—— (1982) *An Economic History of the Middle East and North Africa*, Columbia University Press, New York

—— (1983) 'Why Japan?' in Ib. Ibrahim (ed.) *Arab Resources*, Croom Helm, London

—— (1984) *An Economic History of the Middle East and North Africa*, Columbia University Press, New York

Jabber, F. (1973) 'The Arab regimes and the Palestinian Revolution, 1967–71', *Journal of Palestine Studies, 11*, 2, 101

Jadaane, F. (1981) *Usus at-Taqaddum 'inda Mufakkiri al-Islam fi al-'Alam al-'Arabi al-Hadith*, Al-Mu'assasah al-'Arabiyyah li ad-Dirasat wa an-Nashr, Beirut

Janowitz, M. (1977) *Military Institutions and Coercion in the Developing Nations*, Chicago University Press, Chicago

Jarry, E. (1984) 'La première entreprise de Syrie, Milihouse, n'a de militaire que le nom', *Le Monde*, 6 May

Al-Jasr, A. (1985) Information Department, GCC, interview with author, 8 May, Riyadh

Kadi, L.S. (1966) *Arab Summit Conferences and the Palestinian Problem*, Institute for Palestine Studies, Beirut, 92–3

Karsenty, J. (1975) 'Les investissements dans l'agriculture algérienne', *Annuaire de l'Afrique du Nord*, pp. 115–42

Kazziha, W. (1979) *Revolutionary Transformation int he Arab World*, London, 93

Keeley, C.B. and Saket, B. (1984) 'Jordanian migrant workers in the Arab region: a case study of consequences for labor supplying countries', *The Middle East Journal, 38*, 685–98

Keilany, Z. (1973) 'Socialism and economic change in Syria', *Middle Eastern Studies*

Kelidar, A. (1979) *The Integration of Modern Iraq*, St Martin's Press, New York

Kelman, H.C. (1969) 'Patterns of personal involvement in the national system: a social-psychological analysis of political legitimacy', in J.N. Rosenau (ed.), *International politics and foreign policy: a reader in research and theory*, The Free Press, New York

Kepel, G. (1984) *Le prophéte et le pharaon*, La Découverte, Paris

—— (1985) 'Les oulémas, l'intelligentsia et les islamistes en Egypte: système social, ordre transcendental et ordre traduit', *Revue français de science politique, 35 (3)*, pp. 424–45

Keohane, R.O. (1984) *After Hegemony, Cooperation and Discord in the World Political Economy*, Princeton UniversityPress, Princeton NJ

Kerr, M. and Yassin, E. (1982) *Rich and poor states in the Middle East*, Eastview Press, Boulder

Khaddam al-Halim, A. (1983) Interview in *al-Mostaqbal*, 19 November, p. 15

Khadduri, M. (1955) *War and Peace in the Law of Islam*, Johns Hopkins University Press, Baltimore, (Maryland)

—— (1969) *Republican Iraq*, Oxford University Press, Oxford, 20

Khoury, N. (1981) 'The politics of intra-regional migration', in *International Migration in the Arab World: vol. II*, United Nations Economic Commission for Western Asia (ECWA), pp. 753–76

Khuri, F. and Obermayer, G (1974) 'The social bases for military intervention in the Middle East', in C. MacArdle Kelleher (ed.), *Political-military systems: comparative perspectives*, Sage Publications, London

Khalafallah, M.A. (1973) *The Qur'an ad-Dawla*, n.p., n.d.

—— (1984) 'Text, Interpretation and Government in Islam', *Al-'Arabi (Kuwait), 307*, pp. 41–5

Khalid, K.M. (1950) *Min Huna Nabda'*, Cairo, p. 47

Al-Khatib, A. (1963) *Al-Khilafa wa al-Imama*, n.p.

Kingdom of Saudi Arabia (1983) *Statistical Yearbook*, Central Department of Statistics, Ministry of Finance and National Economy

Koury, E.M. (1980) *The United Arab Emirates: Its Political System and Politics*, Institute of Middle Eastern and North African Affairs, Hyattsville, Maryland

Al-Kubaisi, A. (1982) *Al-Idara al-'amma w'al-tanmiya bi dawlat al-imarat al-muttahida* (public administration and development in the UAE), Dar al-Khalij, Al-Shariqa

Kuwait News Agency (1984) *Special Dossier on the Occasion of the Fifth Gulf Cooperation Council Summit Conference in Kuwait*, November

Laqueuer, W. (1968) *The Road to War*, Penguin Books, Harmondsworth

Laroui, A. (1981) *Mafhum ad-Dawla*, Dar at Tanwir, Beirut

Laski, H.J. (1935) *The State in Theory and Practice*, W.H. Allen, London

Lasswell, H. and Kaplan, A. (1950) *Politics and Society*, Yale University Press, New Haven (Connecticut)

Lawless, R. (1985) 'Algeria: the contradictions of rapid industrialisation', in Lawless, R. and Findlay, A. (eds), *North Africa: contemporary politics and economic development*, Croom Helm, London, pp. 153–90

Leca, J. (1980) 'Ville et système politique: l'image de la ville dans le discours officiel algérien', in Rassam, A. and Zghal, A.K. (eds), *Systéme urbain et développement au Maghreb*, Cerés Productions, Tunis, pp. 290–317

Leca, J. and Schemeil, Y. (1983) 'Clientélisme et néo-patrimonialisme dans le monde arabe', *International Political Science Review, 4*

Leca, J. and Vatin, J.C. (1975) *L'Algérie politique: institutions et régime*, Fondation Nationale des Sciences Politiques, Paris

—— (1979) 'Le système politique algérien', in Centre de Recherches et d'Etudes sur les Sociétés Mediterranéennes, pp. 15–90

Leca, J. *et al.* (1979) *Developpements politiques au Maghreb*, CNRS, Paris

Leila, A. (1983) 'Al-hijra wa qadiyya al-wahda al-Arabiyya', *Al-Siyasa Al-Dawliya*

Leveau, R. (1976) *Le fellah marocain, défenseur du trône*, Colin, Paris

—— (1984) 'Aperçu de l'évolution du système politique marocain depuis vingt ans', *Maghreb-Machrek, 106*, pp. 7–36

—— (1985) *Le fellah marocain, défenseur du trône*, Presses de la Fondation Nationale des Sciences Politiques, second edition

Liabes, D. (1985) 'Une approche strictement économique du secteur privé est-elle possible?', *Revue du CENEAP, 2*, pp. 118–37

Locke, J. (1960) *Two treatises of government*, Cambridge University Press, London

Long, D.E. (1976) 'Saudi Arabia', *The Washington Papers, 39*, Sage Publications, Beverley Hills, (California)

Longrigg, S. (1956) *Iraq: 1900 to 1950*, Oxford University Press, London

Longuenesse, E. (1979) 'The class nature of the state in Syria', *MERIP*

—— (1985) Syrie: secteur public industriel, les enjeux d'une crise', *Maghreb-Machrek, 109*, pp. 5–23

—— (1986) 'Migrations et sociétés dans les pays du Golfe', *Maghreb-Machrek, 112*, pp. 8–21

Luciani, G. (1976) *L'Opec nell'economia internazionale*, Einaudi, Turin, pp. 121–3

Lustick, I. (1980) *Arabs in the Jewish State: A Study in the Control of a Minority Population*, University of Texas Press, Austin

Maaoz, M. (1973) 'Society and state in modern Syria', in Milson, M. (ed.), *Society and Political Structure in the Arab World*, Humanities Press, New York

McDermott, A. (1983) 'Syria', in *Middle East Review*

MacIver, R.M. (1926) *The Modern State*, Oxford University Press, London

McLennan, B. (ed.) (1973) *Political Opposition and Dissent*, Dunellen, New York

Maghrcb-Machrek (1986a) 'Dossiers et documents: l'Algérie face au contre-choc pétrolier', *Maghreb Machrek, 112*, pp. 94–100

—— (1986b) 'Dossiers et documents: le secteur privé en Algérie', *Maghreb-Machrek, 113*

Al-Mahafdha, 'Λ. (1973) *Tarikh al-Urdun al-Mu'asir: 'Ahd al-Imara 1921–1946*, Amman: Jordan University

Mahdavi, H. (1970) 'The pattern and problems of economic development in rentier states: the case of Iran', in M. Cook (ed.), *Studies in the economic history of the Middle East*, Oxford University Press, London

Makdisi, S. (1985) 'Observations on the investment behaviour of the Arab countries, in M. Czinkota and S. Marciel (eds) *US-Arab Economic Relations*, Praeger, New York

El-Mallakh, R. (1982) *Saudi Arabia, Rush to Development*, Johns Hopkins University Press, Baltimore, (Maryland) and London

Al-Marayati, A.A. (1972) *The Middle East: its government and politics*, Duxbury, Belmont, (California)

Marouf, N. (1982) 'Administrative development in Kuwait', *Arab Journal*

Marshall, A. (1920) *Principes of Economics*, 8th edn, Macmillan, London, p. 350

Massey, W. (1986) 'The settlement process among Mexican migrants to the United States', *American Sociological Review, 51*, 670–84

Al-Mawdūdi, (1967) *Nadhariyat al-islam wa Hudiuhu fi as-Siyasah wa al-Qanum wa ad-Dustur*, Dar al-Fikr, Beirut

Metral, F. (1980) 'Le monde rural syrien à l'heure des réformes', in Raymond, A. (ed.), *La Syrie d'aujourd'hui*, CNRS, Paris, pp. 297–326

—— (1985) 'Etat et paysans dans le ghab en Syrie: approche locale d'un projet d'état', *Maghreb-Machrek, 109*, pp. 43–63; English version in Ibrahim, S.E. and Hopkins, N. (eds), *Arab society: social science perspectives*, American University in Cairo, Cairo, pp. 336–54

Michaud, G. (1981) 'Castes, confessions et société en Syrie: Ibn Khaldoun au chevet du progressisme arabe', *Peuples méditerranéens, 16*

Michaud, G. and Carrè, O. (1983) *Les frères musulmans*, Gallimard, Paris

Michel, H. (1972) 'Algérie', in Centre d'Etudes et de Recherches sur les Sociétés Mediterranéennes, *La formation des élites politique maghrébines*, Pichon et Durand-Auzias, Paris

Middle East Times (1985) 'Coming to grips with terrorism: high tech and mass communications', *vol. III*, no. 41, pp. 6–8

Miller, J. (1985) 'The embattled Arab intellectual', *The New York Times*

Mintzberg, H. (1979) *The Structuring of Organisations*, Prentice Hall, Englewood Cliffs, (New Jersey)

Montgomery, J.D., Lasswell, H.D. and Migdal, J.S. (eds) (1979) *Patterns of Policy: Comparative and Longitudinal Studies in Population Events*, Transaction Books, New Brunswick, NJ

Moore, B. (1966) *Social Origins of Dictatorship and Democracy*, Beacon, Boston, (Massachusetts)

Al-Moosa, A.A. and McLachlan, K.S. (1985) *Immigrant Labour in Kuwait*, Croom Helm, London

El-Mossadeq, R. (1981) *Les forces politiques face au problème de la democratisation du Maroc*, University of Paris, Paris

Moubarak, W.E. (1979) *Kuwait's Quest for Security: 1961–1973*, unpublished PhD dissertation, Department of Political Science, Indiana University

Moulier Boutang, Y., Garson, J.P. and Silberman, R. (1986) *Economie polique des migrations clandestines de main d'oeuvres*, Publi-sud, Paris

Al-Mubarak, M. (1981) *Nizam al-Islam fi al-Hukm wa ad-Dawlah*, Dar al-Fikr, Beirut

Al-Mujitama' (1984) *vol. 15*, no. 668, 24 April

Muna, Farid A. (1980) *The Arab Executive*, Macmillan, London

Mundell, R. (1968) *International Economics*, Macmillan, London

Murad, Z. (1966) 'About the revolutionary probabilities for the military in the national revoltuion for liberation' (in Arabic), *al-Talia*, 2, no. 11, pp. 40–8

Musa, M. (1964) *Nizam al-Hukm*

Mutawalli, A. (1977) *Mabadi' Nizam al-Hukm fi al-Islam*

Al-Muti'i, M. (1344 A.H.) *Haqitat al-Islam wa Usul al-Hukm*, Maktabat an-Nahda al-Haditha, Cairo

Mutin, G. (1980) 'Agriculture et dépendence alimentaire en Algérie', *Maghreb-Machrek*, 90, pp. 40–64

An-Nabhani, T. (1952) *Ad-Dawlah al-Islamiyyah*, al-Manar Press, Damascus

National Bank of Kuwait (1986) *Kuwait Economic and Financial Bulletin no. 10*, summer

Nettl, J.P. (1968) 'The State as Conceptual Variable', *World Politics*, 20, no. 4, pp. 559–92

Nyrop, R.F. (1979) *Iraq: a country study*, Washington DC

Okun, A. (1975) *Equality and Efficiency: the big trade-off*, Brookings Institution, Washington DC

Ottoway, D. (1984) 'Malaise is apparent after Egyptian election', *Washington Post*, 3 June

Owen, R. (1983) 'The political environment for development', in Ibrahim (ed.), *Arab Resources*, Centre for Contemporary Arab Studies, Georgetown University, Washington DC; Croom Helm, London, pp. 139–46

—— (1985) *Migrant Workers in the Gulf*, Minority Rights Group, London

Palmer, M., Alghofaily, I. and Alnimir, S. (1984) 'The behavioural correlates of rentier economics: a case study of Saudi Arabia', in Stookey, R. (ed.), *The Arabian Peninsula: zone of ferment*, Hoover Institution, Stanford, (California)

Peneff, J. (1981) *Industriels algériens*, CNRS, Paris

Perlmutter, A. (1974) *Egypt: the praetorian state*, Transaction Books, Brunswick, (New Jersey)

Pfeifer, K. (1985) *Agrarian Reform under State Capitalism in Algeria*, Westview Press, Boulder, (Colorado)

Picard, E. (1978) 'Syria returns to democracy', in G. Hermet, R. Rose and A. Rouguiè (eds), *Elections without choice*, Macmillan, London, pp. 129-44

—— (1979a) 'Clans militaires et pouvoir ba'thiste en Syrie', *Orient*, Hamburg, pp. 49-62

—— (1979b) 'Ouverture économique et renforcement militaire en Syrie', *Oriente Moderno*, 59, nos 7-12, pp. 663-76

—— (1979c) 'Le rapprochement syro-iraquien', *Maghreb-Machrek*, 83, p. 9

—— (1980) 'La Syrie de 1946 à 1979', in Raymond, A. (ed.), *La Syrie aujourd'hui*, CNRS, Paris, pp. 143-84

Piore, M.J. (1979) *Birds of Passage: Migrant Labor and Industrial Societies*, Cambridge University Press, New York

Phillips, W. (1967) *Oman. A History*, Longmans, London

Plender, R. (1972) *International Migration Law*, A.W. Sijthoff, Leiden

Pye, L. (1962) *Politics, Personality and National Building: Burma's Search for Identity*, Yale University Press, New Haven

Al-Qardawi, Y. (1974) *Al-Hall al Islami: Farida wa Daruruh*, Mu'assasat ar-Risalah, Beirut

Quandt, W.B. (1969) *Revolution and Political leadership: Algeria, 1954-68*, MIT Press, Cambridge, (Massachusetts)

—— (1974) *The Politics of Palestinian-Nationalism*, University of California Press, Los Angeles

Qutb, S. (n.d.) *Al-Islam wa Mushkilat al Hadara*

Rafiq, 'A. (1974) *Al-'Arab wa al-'Uthmaniyyun, 1516-1916*, Damascus

Rashid, A. (1975) 'Government and administration in the UAE', *Bulletin of Arab Research and Studies*, 6

Rentz, G. (1977) 'Wahhabism in Saudi Arabia', in Hopwood (ed.), *The Arabian Peninsula*, Allen and Unwin, London

Ricardo, D. (1962) *The Principles of Political Economy and Taxation* (1821), Everyman's Library, London, p. 590

Richards, A. and Martin, P.L. (1983) 'The laissez-faire approach to international labour migration: the case of the Arab Middle East', *Economic Development and Cultural Change*, 31, 3, April

Ar Rihani, A. (n.d.) *Muluk al-'Arab*, Dar ar Rihani, Beirut

Rivier, F. (1982) 'Rente pétrolière et politiques industrielles des états non pétroliers: Egypte, Jordanie, Liban, Syrie', in Bourgey *et al.*, *Industrialisation et changements sociaux dans l'Orient arabe*, Editions du CERMOC, Beirut, pp. 169-47

Roberts, H.J.R. (1980) 'Towards an understanding of the Kabyle question in contemporary Algeria', *The Maghreb Review*, pp. 115-224

—— (1983) 'The economics of Berberism: the material base of the Kabyle question in contemporary Algeria', *Government and Opposition*, pp. 218-35

Rosenthal, E.I.J. (1958) *Political Thought in Medieval Islam: an introductory outline*, Cambridge University Press, Cambridge

Roughton, R.A. (1969) 'Algeria and the June 1967 Arab-Israeli war',

The Middle East Journal, p. 444

Rubin, B. (1981) *The Arab States and the Palestine Conflict*, Syracuse University Press, Syracuse, p. 22

Al-Rumayhi, M. (1982) 'Factors of social and economic development in the Gulf in the eighties', in R. Khalidi and C. Mansour (eds), *Palestine and the Gulf*, Institute for Palestine Studies, Beirut

Russell, S.S. (1986a) 'Remittances from international migration: a review in perspective', *World Development*, *14*, 6, pp. 677–96

Sabagh, G. (1982) 'Migration and social mobility in Egypt', in Kerr and Yassin, *Rich and Poor States in the Middle East: Egypt and the new Arab order*, Westview Press, Boulder, (Colorado), pp. 71–95

Sa'd eddine I. (1979) and Abd al-Fadil, M.I., (1983) Intiqal al-'Amala al'Arabiyya: al-Masnakil, al-'Athār, as-Siyasāt (The movement of Arab manpower: problems, effects and policies), Centre for Arab Unity Studies, Beirut

Sader, M. (1982) 'Le développement industriel de l'Irak', in Bourgey *et al.*, *Industrialisation et changements sociaux dans l'Orient arabe*, Editions du CERMOC, Beirut, pp. 235–81

Al-Sadham, A.R. (1985) Secretary General, Civil Service Board, Saudi Arabia, Interview with author, 7 May, Riyadh

Sadowski, Y. (1984) *Political Power and Economic Organisation in Syria*, PhD dissertation, University of California, Los Angeles

Safir, N. (1985) 'A propos de la constitution du travailleur collectif dans l'industrie mécanique algérienne', and 'Quelques aspects sociaux du développement de l'industrie mécanique', in *Essais d'analyses sociologiques*, 2, OPU-ENA L, 2, Algeria, pp. 191–218 and 219–66

Salamé, G. (1980) *As-Siyassa al-Kharijiyya as-Sa'udiyya Mundhu 1945: Dirasa Fi al-'Alaqāt ad-Duwalyya, Ma'ahad al-Inma' al-'Arabi*, Beirut

—— (1982) *'Institutionalisation du pouvoir et affinités tribales dans les pays arabes du Golfe'*, in *Al-Abhath*, AUB, Beirut, Vol. XXX

—— (1986) 'Lebanon's Injured Identities: Who Represents Whom During a Civil War?', The Centre for Lebanese Studies' Papers, Oxford

—— (1987) (ed.), *The Foundations of the Arab State*, Croom Helm, London

Salibi, K. (1965) *The Modern History of Lebanon*, Weidenfeld and Nicolson, London

Al-Salim, F. (1982) *Al-Khadamat al-hukumiyya fi dawlat al-kuwait* (Government services in the State of Kuwait), University of Kuwait, Kuwait

Sani Bey, A. (1924) *Al-Khilafah wa Sultat al-Ummah*

Sayad, A. (1983) 'Le phénomène migratoire: une relation de domination', *Annuaire de l'Afrique du Nord*, 365–405

Sayigh, R. (n.d.) *Palestinians: from peasants to revolutionaries*, Zed Press, London, 102

Sayigh, Y. (1982) *The Arab Economies*, Croom Helm, London

Schatzberg, M. (1980) *Politics and the State in Zaire*, Westview, Boulder (Colorado)

Schiff, Z. (1984) *Israel's Lebanon War*, Simon and Schuster, New York

Schimi, M. (1979) *Juin 1977: étude des elections legislatives au Maroc*, SOMADED, Casablanca

—— (1985) 'Les elections legislatives au Maroc', *Maghreb-Machrek*, 107, pp. 23–51

Seale, P. (1966) *The Struggle for Syria*, Oxford University Press, Oxford, pp. 192–3

Seccombe, I.J. and Lawless, R.I. (1986) 'Travailleurs migrants et débuts de l'industrie pétrolière dans la Golfe arabe, 1930–1950', *Maghreb-Machreq*, 112, April–June

Seers, D. (ed.) (1981) *Dependency Theory, A Critical Reassessment*, Francis Pinter, London

Semmoud, B. (1982) 'Croissance du secteur industriel privé en Algérie dans ses relations avec le secteur national', *Revue canadienne des études africaines*, 2

Serageldin, I., Socknat, J., Birks, S., Li, B. and Sinclair, C. (1981) *Manpower and International Migration in the Middle East and North Africa*, Technical Assistance and Special Studies Division, World Bank, Washington DC, 30 June

Serageldin, I. *et al.* (1983) *Manpower and International Labour Migration in the Middle East and North Africa*, Oxford University Press, London

—— (1984) 'Some issues related to labor migration in the Middle East and North Africa', *The Middle East Journal*, 38, 615–42

Seurat, M. (1980) 'Les populations, l'état et la société', in Raymond, *La Syrie aujourd'hui*, CNRS, Paris, pp. 87–141

—— (1982) 'Etat et industrialisation dans l'Orient arabe: les fondements socio-historiques' in Bourgey *et al.*, *Industrialisation et changements sociaux dans l'Orient arabe*, Editions du CERMOC, Beirut, pp. 27–67

Shah, N.M. (1987) 'Changing characteristics of migrant workers in Kuwait', paper presented at the annual meeting of the Population Association of America, Boston

Sharabi, H. (1966) *Nationalism and Revolution in the Arab World*, D. Van Nostrand, Princeton

Sherbiny, A.A. and Serageldin, I. (1982) 'Expatriate labor and economic growth: Saudi demand for Egyptian labor', in M.H. Kerr and Y. El-Sayed (eds), *Rich and Poor Countries in the Middle East: Egypt and the New Arab Social Order*, Westview Press, Boulder

Shlaim, A. (1987) 'Israeli interference in international Arab politics: the case of Lebanon', in G. Luciani and G. Salamé (eds) *Politics of Arab Integration*, Croom Helm, London

Skocpol, T. (1982) 'Rentier State and Shi'a Islam in the Iranian Revolution', *Theory and Society*, 11, pp. 265–83

Smith, A. (1960) *The Wealth of Nations* (1776), Everyman's Library, London, p. 412

Spagnolo, J. (1977) *France and Ottoman Lebanon, 1861–1914*, Ithaca Press, London

Springborg, R. (1981) 'Baathism in practice: agriculture, politics and political culture in Syria and Iraq', *Middle Eastern Studies*, 15

—— (1986) 'Iraqi *infitah*: agrarian transformation and growth of the private sector', *Middle East Journal*, 40, no. 1, pp. 33–53
Sraieb, N. *et al.* (1985) *Le mouvement ouvrier maghrébin*, CNRS, Paris
State of Kuwait (1959) *Law No. 15 of 1959* (Nationality Law) as amended up to 1982. Department of Legal Advice and Legislation
—— (1972) *Population Census 1970*, The Planning Board, Central Statistical Office, October
—— (1977a) *Annual Statistical Abstract*, Central Statistical Office, Ministry of Planning
—— (1977b) *Population Census 1975*, Central Statistical Office, Safat
—— (1979) 'Review of employment activity and the basic features of expatriate manpower during the year 1978', Statistical Section, Employment Control Division, Manpower Organization Department, Ministry of Social Affairs and Labour, January
—— (1983) *Annual Statistical Abstract*, Central Statistical Office, Safat
—— (1984a) *Annual Statistical Abstract*, Central Statistical Office, Ministry of Planning
—— (1984b) *Kuwait: Facts and Figures*, Ministry of Information
—— (1985) *Social Statistics 1985*, Central Statistical Office, Safat
—— (1986) *Monthly Digest of Statistics*, vol. 7, October, pp. 1, 10, 21
—— (1986) *At Ta'dad al-'Am: As-Sukkau wa al-Masakin wa al-Munsha'at 1985*, Central Statistical Office, Safat
Stauffer, T. (1981) 'The dynamics of petroleum dependency; growth in an oil rentier state', *Finance and Industry*, 2
Stinchcombe, A. (1968) *Constructing Social Theories*, Harcourt, Brace and World, New York
Stork, J. (1979) 'Oil and capitalism in Iraq', *Peuples Méditerranéens — Mediterranean People*, 9, p. 145
As Subhi, E.H. (1985) Assistant Secretary-General for Political Affairs, GCC, interview with author, 8 May, Riyadh
Suleiman, M. (1987) 'The role of education in domestic and inter-Arab integration in the Arab world', in G. Luciani and G. Salamé (eds) *Politics of Arab Integration*, Croom Helm, London
Swodoba, A. (1983) 'Exchange rate regimes and European–US policy interdependence', in A.V. Hooke (ed.) *Exchange Rate Regimes and Policy Interdependence*, IMF, New York
Syria, Ministry of State for Cabinet Affairs (1984) *The importance of administrative development and the creation of a specialised agency thereof, memorandum* (in Arabic), Damascus
Tabbarah, R. (1982) 'Organizer's Report — Roundtable Discussion', *International Migration in the Arab World*, proceedings of an ECWA Population Conference, UN Economic Commission for Western Asia, Beirut
Talha, L. (1983) 'Maghrébins en France: émigrés ou immigrés? Présentation générale', *Annuaire de l'Afrique du Nord*, 3–10
Thiery, S.P. (1982a) *La crise du système productif algérien*, l'Université des Sciences Sociales de Grenoble, Grenoble

—— (1982b) 'Emploi, formation et productivité dans l'industrie algérienne', in Bernard, C. et al., *La politique de l'emploi — formation au Maghreb 1970–80*, CNRS, Paris

Tilly, C. (ed.) (1975) *The Formation of National States in Western Europe*, Princeton University Press, Princeton, (New Jersey)

Tinbergen, J. (1952) *On the Theory of Economic Policy*, North Holland, Amsterdam

Turner, B.S. (1979) 'The middle classes and entrepreneurship in capitalist development', *Arab Studies*

United Nations (1982) *International Migration Policies and Programmes: A World Survey*, Population Studies, no. 80, Department of International Economic and Social Affairs, New York

United Nations Fund for Population Activities (1983) 'The state of world population', United Nations, NY

Van Dam, N. (1979) *The Struggle for Power in Syria: sectarianism, regionalism and tribalism in politics, 1961–80*, Croom Helm, London

Van Dusen, M. (1971) *Intra and inter-generational conflict in the Syrian army*, unpublished PhD dissertation, Johns Hopkins University Press, Baltimore

—— (1975) 'Syria: downfall of a traditional elite', in Tachau, F. (ed.), *Political elites and political development in the Middle East*, Schenkman/Wiley, Cambridge

Van Nieuwenhuijze, C.A.O. (1965) *Social Stratification and the Middle East*, Brill, Leiden

—— (1971) *Sociology of the Middle East*, Brill, Leiden

Vatikiotis, P. (1961) *The Egyptian Army in Politics*, Indiana University Press, Bloomingdale

—— (1978) *Nasser and His Generation*, St. Martin's Press, New York

—— (1980) *The History of Egypt*, Johns Hopkins University Press, Baltimore

Von Sivers, P. (1984) 'National integration and traditional rural organisation in Algeria 1970–80: background for Islamic traditionalism?', in Arjomand, S.A. (ed.), *From National to Revolutionary Islam*, Macmillan, London, pp. 94–118

Waterbury, J. (1983) *The Egypt of Nasser and Sadat: the political economy of two regimes*, Princeton University Press, Princeton, (New Jersey)

Watkins, M. (1934) *The State as a Concept of Political Science*, Harper and Brothers, New York

Weber, M. (1947) *The Theory of Social and Economic Organisation*, Oxford University Press, New York and London

—— (1958) *The Protestant Ethic and the Spirit of Capitalism*, Charles Scribner's and Sons, New York

—— (1978) Weber: Selections in translation, W.G. Runciman (ed.), Cambridge University Press, Cambridge

Weinbaum, Marvin G. (1979) *Bureaucratic norms, structures and strategies in agricultural policies in the Middle East*, paper submitted at the Middle East Studies Association Annual conference, Salt Lake City, (Utah)

Weiner, M. (1965) 'Political integration and political development',

The Annals of the American Academy of Political Science, 358, pp. 52–64, March

—— (1982) 'International migration and development in the Gulf: Indians in the Persian Gulf', *Migration and Development Review, 8,* 1–36

Weiner, M. and Choucri, N. (1986) 'The internationalization of policies affecting international migration: case studies in the Middle East and South Asia', (mimeo), Massachusetts Institute of Technology, Cambridge, Mass.

Weinstein, John M. (1981) 'A structural analysis of the moderniser's dilemma', *Comparative Development, 16,* nos 3 and 4

Weulersse, J. (1946) *Paysans de Syrie et du Proche-Orient,* Paris

Wickwar, Hardy (1963) *The Modernisation of Administration in the Near East,* Khayat, Beirut

Winder, B. (1965) *Saudi Arabia in the Nineteenth Century,* Macmillan, London

Wittfogel, K. (1957) *Oriental Despotism,* Yale University Press, New Haven, pp. 48–9

World Bank (1980) *Economic Memorandum for Egypt,* Washington, DC

—— (1983) *World Tables: social data,* vol. II, IBRD, Washington DC

—— (1984) *World Development Report,* Washington, DC

—— (1985) *World Development Report,* IBRD, Washington DC

Zahlan, A. (ed.) (1978) *Technology Transfer and Change in the Arab World,* Pergamon Press, Oxford

Zamir, M. (1985) *The Formation of Modern Lebanon,* Croom Helm, London

Zartman, W.I. (1964) *Destiny of a Dynasty,* University of South Carolina, Columbia

—— (1970) 'The Algerian army in politics', in C. Welch (ed.), *Soldier and state in Africa,* Northwestern University Press, Evanston, (Illinois)

—— (1974) 'Algeria: a post revolutionary elite', in Frank (ed.), *Political elites and political development in the Middle East,* Schenkman/Wiley, Cambridge

—— (ed.) (1980) *Elites in the Middle East,* Praeger, New York

—— (ed.) (1982) *Political Elites in Arab North Africa,* Longman, New York

Zeine, Z.N. (1958) *Arab–Turkish Relations and the Emergence of Arab Nationalism,* Khayat, Beirut

Zolberg, A. (1981) 'International migrations in political perspective', in M.M. Kritz, C.B. Keely and S.M. Tomasi (eds) *Global Trends in Migration: Theory and Research on International Population Movements,* Center for Migration Studies, New York

Zolberg, A. and Suhrke, A. (1984) 'Social conflict and refugees in the Third World: the case of Ethiopia and Afghanistan', presented at American Political Science Association Annual Meeting, Washington DC

Zurayk, H. and Ghulmiyah, (1985) 'Emerging issues in international migration', presented at a Conference Bellagio, Italy

Index

Gordon, D. viii
government: authoritarian 191;
    Caliphate as system of 281;
    Islamic 256–60; military
    oligarchy as 6, 15–17; in modern
    era 17–24; opposition see
    opposition; pluralist 14; policy of
    323–4; in rentier state 88, 91–2;
    revolutionary 212; secular
    12–15; typologies of 4–17
Gramsci, A. 32
gross domestic product (GDP): and
    export/import ratios 329; and
    military budgets 209; per capita
    and increases 67; remittances on
    97; Syrian 174
Gulf Cooperation Council (GCC)
    112, 122, 334, 414, 418

Haart, H.H. 354
Haddad, G. 194, 203
Haddad, Y. 385
al-Hafez, General A. 196
Haim, S. 2, 4
Halpern, M.I. 152, 190, 302
Hamada, K. 321
Hamdan, D. 384
Hannover, J. 177–8
Harbi, M. 156–7
Harik, I. xxii, 43; on origins of the
    Arab state system 1–28
Hasib, K. 50
Hassan II (King of Morocco) 10
health, spending on 126
Hegel, G.W.F. 29
Heller, M. 152
Helms, C.M. 38, 45
Helmy, A. 388
Henault, G. 140
Herfurth, M. 354
Hermassi, E. 4, 184, 401
Herzl, T. 63–4
Hinnebush, R.A. 233, 236–7, 403
Hirschman, A.O. 76, 158
Hodges, T. 231
Hoffman Nowotny, H.J. 354
Holt, P. 16, 18, 19
Hondrich, K.O. 354
Hopkins, N.S. 182
Hopwood, D. 10, 13, 18
Hourani, A. 3, 55, 288
Howarth, D. 10
Hudson, M.C. xvii, xviii, 79, 152,
    306
Huntington, S. 194
Hurewitz, J.C. 205

ibn al-Husayn, Y. 8
Hussein, S, 207, 215: as leader of
    Iraq 195, 296–8; and
    Palestinians 308; and war with
    Iran 205
'hydrocarbon' societies 67–70

Ibn 'Ashir, M. 254
Ibn Badis 251–2
Ibn Khaldun xxiii, xxiv, xxvi, 4, 260,
    287; and Muqaddimah 31–4,
    37–8, 47, 52
Ibn Tumart 10
Ibrahim, S.E. 184, 351
identity of individual with state
    46–7, 49
ijtihad 281–2
iltiham 32, 35
imam: office of 261; and system of
    government 5–6, 7–12
immigrants see migration; migrants
immunity of state 38–44
imperialism, economic impact of
    21–4
income: in Algeria 165; industrial
    113; state, origin 71–2
industrialisation 107–8; efficiency
    120; objectives 111–18; output
    118–19
industry: Arab, and development
    118–23; coordination, lack of
    103–4; employment in Iraq 179;
    manufacturing 118, 119–20;
    share, in Algeria 158; state
    support 121
inefficiency in Arab bureaucracies
    137–8, 142
infitah 292; in agriculture 181–2;
    and migration 375; and military
    regimes 215–16
institutional development and
    migrants 387–9
institutional homogeneity 413
integration: definition of 395; and
    disintegration 398, 403;
    economic 334–5, 340, 345, 408;
    ethnic and cultural factors
    396–7; and migration 350–5,
    356–7, 408–9; political see
    political; politics of 394–419;
    and private sector 410; territorial
    see territorial; into world system
    44–6
interdependence: and Arab
    economy 325–41; and economic
    policy 323–5; factors 322–3; and

447

449